RELATIONSHIPS AS DEVELOPMENTAL CONTEXTS

The Minnesota Symposia on Child Psychology

Volume 30

RELATIONSHIPS AS DEVELOPMENTAL CONTEXTS

The Minnesota Symposia on Child Psychology

Volume 30

Edited by

W. Andrew Collins
University of Minnesota

Brett Laursen
Florida Atlantic University

LEA
LAWRENCE ERLBAUM ASSOCIATES, PUBLISHERS
1999   Mahwah, New Jersey   London

Lawrence Erlbaum Associates, Inc., Publishers
10 Industrial Avenue
Mahwah, New Jersey 07430

Library of Congress Cataloging-in-Publication Data

Relationships as developmental contexts / edited by W. Andrew Collins,
  Brett Laursen.
      p.   cm. — (The Minnesota symposia on child psychology ; v.
  30)
    Based on papers presented at the 30th Minnesota Symposium on Child
  Psychology, held October 24–26, 1996, at the University of
  Minnesota.
    A tribute to Willard W. Hartup, Regents' Professor of Child
  Development and director of the Institute of Child Development from
  1971 to 1982, on the occasion of his retirement.
    Includes bibliographical references and indexes.
    ISBN 0-8058-2616-5 (hardcover : alk. paper).
    1. Interpersonal relations in children—Congresses. 2. Child
  development—Congresses. I. Collins, W. Andrew, 1944–   .
  II. Laursen, Brett Paul. III. Hartup, Willard W. IV. Minnesota
  Symposium on Child Psychology (30th : 1996 : University of
  Minnesota). V. Series: Minnesota symposia on child psychology
  (Series) ; v. 30.
  BF723.I646R46 1999
  153.4′18—dc21
                                                          98-45394
                                                            CIP

Books published by Lawrence Erlbaum Associates are printed on acid-free paper,
and their bindings are chosen for strength and durability.

Printed in the United States of America
10 9 8 7 6 5 4 3 2 1

Willard W. Hartup

Contributors

Catherine L. Bagwell
Department of Psychology
Duke University
Durham, NC 27708

Thomas J. Berndt
Department of Psychology
Purdue University
West Lafayette, IN 47907

Ellen Berscheid
Department of Psychology
N309 Elliott Hall
University of Minnesota
75 East River Road
Minneapolis, MN 55455

William M. Bukowski
Department of Psychology
Concordia University
Montreal PQ
Canada H3G 1M8

Elizabeth A. Carlson
Institute of Child Development
University of Minnesota
51 East River Road
Minneapolis, MN 55455

Antonius H. N. Cillessen
Department of Psychology, U-20
University of Connecticut
406 Babbidge Road
Storrs, CT 06269

W. Andrew Collins
Institute of Child Development
University of Minnesota
51 East River Road
Minneapolis, MN 55455

Ganie B. DeHart
Department of Psychology
State University of New York at Geneseo
1 College Circle
Geneseo, NY 14454

Judy Dunn
Institute of Psychiatry
De Crespigny Park
Denmark Hill
London SE5 8AF
England

J. Mark Eddy
Oregon Social Learning Center
207 East 5th Avenue, Suite 202
Eugene, OR 97401

Byron Egeland
Institute of Child Development
University of Minnesota
51 East River Road
Minneapolis, MN 55455

Doran C. French
Department of Psychology
Illinois Wesleyan University
Bloomington, IL 61702

Wyndol Furman
Department of Psychology
University of Denver
Denver, CO 80209

E. Mavis Hetherington
Department of Psychology
Gilmer Hall
University of Virginia
Charlottesville, VA 22903

Willard W. Hartup
Institute of Child Development
University of Minnesota
51 East River Road
Minneapolis, MN 55455

Gerbert J. T. Haselager
Department of Psychology
Catholic University of Nijmegen
P.O. Box 9104
6500 HE Nijmegen
The Netherlands

Robert A. Hinde
Professor Emeritus
St. John's College
Cambridge CB2 1TP
England

Brett Laursen
Department of Psychology
Florida Atlantic University
2912 College Avenue
Ft. Lauderdale, FL 33314

Eleanor E. Maccoby
Professor Emeritus
Department of Psychology, 2130
Stanford University
Stanford, CA 94305

Andrew F. Newcomb
Department of Psychology
University of Richmond
Richmond, VA 23173

Robin O'Neil
Department of Psychology
University of California, Riverside
Riverside, CA 92521

Ross D. Parke
Department of Psychology
University of California, Riverside
Riverside, CA 92521

Kusdwiratri Setiono
Dago Pojok 23
Department of Psychology
University of Padjadjaran
Bandung, Indonesia 40135

Carolyn U. Shantz
Department of Psychology
Wayne State University
71 West Warren Avenue
Detroit, MI 48202

L. Alan Sroufe
Institute of Child Development
University of Minnesota
51 East River Road
Minneapolis, MN 55455

Cornelis F. M. van Lieshout
Department of Psychology
Catholic University of Nijmegen
P.O. Box 9104
6500 HE Nijmegen
The Netherlands

Contents

Preface

This volume contains chapters based on papers presented at the 30th Minnesota Symposium on Child Psychology, held October 24–26, 1996, at the University of Minnesota, Twin Cities. As has been the tradition for this series, the faculty of the Institute of Child Development invited internationally eminent researchers to present their work and to consider problems of mutual concern.

This rich tradition also provided the backdrop for a tribute to Willard W. Hartup, Regents' Professor of Child Development and director of the Institute from 1971 to 1982, on the occasion of his retirement in June 1997. The contributors are former students and former and current colleagues of Willard Hartup, all of whom are active scholars in the study of relationships as developmental contexts. As the first and the final chapters of this volume make clear, Professor Hartup has been both a pioneering scholar in this area and a significant influence on other scholars through his compelling writing, stimulating teaching and mentorship, and distinguished work as editor of the journal, *Child Development*. This volume honors his legacy by advancing the conceptual underpinnings of research on relationships in developmental perspective and presenting new research findings that advance knowledge in the area.

In this volume the chapters on which the symposium presentations were based are arranged into four sections. The first section includes three chapters addressing historical and conceptual perspectives on the study of relationships and development. This section contains a chapter in which Willard Hartup himself, writing with Brett Laursen, distills his view of the origins and pressing issues of research in the area. The second section contains four chapters on the study of close relationships with peers, a topic that owes its current vitality and influence in developmental psychology to Willard Hartup's continuing intellectual leadership. In Part III, scholars provide new perspectives on intrafamilial and extrafamilial dyadic processes and the links among them. The final section contains commentaries on these chapters, delivered at the conference by three distinguished students of relationships: Ellen Berscheid, Robert A. Hinde, and Carolyn U. Shantz. This section culminates in an appreciation of Willard Hartup's career and research, entitled "An Annotated Hartup."

Financial support for the 30th Minnesota Symposium was provided by the Marian Radke-Yarrow & Leon Yarrow Endowment for Research on Social Development and Relationships, the Institute of Child Development, the College of Education and Human Development, the Center for Research on Interpersonal Relationships, and the Graduate School of the University of Minnesota. Florida Atlantic University provided travel funds for Symposium participants. Special thanks are due to Richard Weinberg, Dean Robert Bruininks, and LuJean Huffman-Nordberg of the University of Minnesota, and Deans John Jurewicz and Charles White, Vice-President Mary McBride, and Ms. Patrice Cochran of Florida Atlantic University. Enthusiastic appreciation is due to the faculty and graduate and undergraduate students of the Institute of Child Development who provided thoughtful consultation and many hours of assistance for Symposium activities. Finally, we recognize with gratitude the contributors who prepared the chapters included in this volume. To Willard W. Hartup, whose intellectual and personal example has inspired this volume, we express our admiration and affection.

W. Andrew Collins
Brett Laursen

HISTORICAL AND CONCEPTUAL PERSPECTIVES ON DEVELOPMENT AND RELATIONSHIPS

Chapter 1

Willard W. Hartup and the New Look in Social Development

W. Andrew Collins
University of Minnesota

The 30th Minnesota Symposium on Child Psychology honored the distinguished career and contributions of Willard W. Hartup. Like Hartup, the contributors to this volume are pursuing a new direction in the study of social development. Although social development traditionally has been defined as "changes over time in the child's understanding of, attitudes toward, and actions with others" (Hartup, 1991), the field largely has been the study of the individual child. The "others" in this definition have been shadowy figures, at best, in the data from which widely accepted tenets of social development have been inferred.

The "new look" celebrated in this volume has grown from the conviction that, in Hartup's words, "(c)hildren's relationships . . . serve both as the contexts in which adaptive behavior arises and the contexts in which adaptive success is measured" (Hartup & Laursen, 1991, p. 253). The chapters exemplify scholarship that realizes the "value added" from a focus on individuals-in-relationships. This introductory chapter sets the stage for these chapters by outlining three ways in which the growing emphasis on relationships already has broadened and enriched the study of social development: by encouraging attention to broader units of social experience; by placing additional emphasis on bilateral perspectives in research on development; and by encouraging functional analyses of individual outcomes in development.

EXPANDED UNITS OF SOCIAL EXPERIENCE

Making the child-in-relationships central to the study of development means that measures of the individual alone are no longer sufficient for understanding psychological processes. Robert Sears (1951) first raised this point in a presidential address to the American Psychological Association almost a half century ago. His words have become a historic cornerstone of research on relationships:

> A diadic unit is essential if there is to be any conceptualization of the relationships between people, as in the parent-child, teacher–pupil, husband–wife, or leader–follower instances. To have a science of interactive events, one must have variables and units of action that refer to such events. (p. 479)

This conceptual ground lay fallow for almost 3 decades, despite periodic reminders of the potential value to be gained from studying bidirectional influences in socialization (e.g., Bell, 1968). Nevertheless, the conviction slowly grew that behavior that had been commonly and facilely attributed to individuals alone might reflect unique conditions of their interactions with particular partners (e.g., Hinde, 1979).

Willard W. Hartup has been both a forceful and effective voice within developmental psychology for the meaning and significance of a relationships perspective and an influential practitioner of the approach in his own research. In the early years of his career, from the mid-1950s through the 1960s, Hartup infused his fundamental sympathy with relationship variables into studies that were conceived within the behaviorist paradigms of that era (see Laursen, this volume). By the early 1970s, he clearly placed the nature and implications of relationships at the center of both his research and his integrative writing about the field. One pioneering essay captures the flavor of the ideas that he advanced in times that were relatively innocent of dyadic perspectives. In 1973, Hartup and Lempers proposed a dyadic, interactional perspective on attachment, well before such a concept was the article of faith that it is today. Criticizing the prevailing approaches, they noted:

> In all of these cases, an interactional phenomenon has been reduced to a set of individual differences and attachment characterized as an appendage of the organism rather than as a dimension of the social intercourse in which the organism is engaged. (p. 238)

They further proposed a truly interactional strategy that:

would help to elucidate developmental transitions in attachment occurring at pubescence, at departure from the nuclear household, in courting, during various phases of the marital relationship, and at parental retirement. Certain other attachments (e.g., between siblings in adulthood) should be studied interactionally simply because their functional significance in adult socialization is presently unknown. (p. 251)

From the vantage point of the 1990s, those words, written in the mid-1970s, seem prescient indeed.

During this period other voices also were calling for a systematic approach to studying dyads. Some of the most influential of these voices are heard again in this volume (for a historical account, see Berscheid, 1994; Berscheid & Reis, 1998). Thanks to the collective efforts of many scholars, a science of relationships is now underway, representing a convergence of ideas from different disciplines and from several subfields of psychology. Relationship researchers have achieved more compelling ways of specifying and analyzing relationships. The prevailing standard now is to define relationships in terms of ongoing behavioral interdependencies, rather than in terms of emotional tone or social roles. This interdependency criterion allows variations in relationship properties, such as emotions, categorical status, role-related behaviors and positive rather than negative emotionality, to be regarded as objects of study, rather than as a basis for sampling. Moreover, much of the conceptual groundwork for future work now exists, and far more sophisticated data-analytic methods are available than was the case a decade ago. The relative shift toward concern with dyadic units has not been smooth, however, nor can it yet be regarded as complete. Scholars continue to grapple with questions of methods and statistical strategies and, realistically, must continue to do so as understanding of the phenomena of interest broadens and deepens.

BILATERAL PERSPECTIVES ON DEVELOPMENTAL CHANGE

In relationship approaches developmental change is seen not as the result of unilateral processes *in* the child or *operating on* the child, but as the result of bilateral processes involving children and their closest associates as codeterminants changes and their sequelae. This goes beyond the recognition of bidirectional influences to the implication that each dyad is a unique and potent context for behavioral development.

This point carries several related implications for thinking about social development. One point is that what is apparently a change in the individual often may reflect social processes between the individual and significant others. For example, biological puberty, a change that seemed quintessentially intraindividual, now is known to affect behavioral development indirectly, mediated by the expectations and perceptions of others that are elicited by pubertal changes (Brooks-Gunn & Reiter, 1990). Studies of menarche indicate that negative attitudes are most likely for girls exposed to familial attitudes of secrecy and distaste about biological functions and little information about what to expect and how to respond (Brooks-Gunn & Ruble, 1982; Rierdan, Koff, & Stubbs, 1989). Thus, what seems to be intraindividual change may actually be attributable to interactions with significant partners or on the relationship between child and partner (e.g., Hinde, 1979; Kelley et al., 1983).

For developmentalists, the most compelling and the most challenging implication of bilaterality is that developmental changes in both interactors affect the course of their relationship. This is easiest to grasp in the interactions of children with their siblings or with their peers. That two 30-month-olds sustain cooperation more readily than two 16-month-olds (Eckerman, Davis, & Didow, 1989) reflects the greater maturity of both children, not just one (Hartup & Laursen, 1991). Moreover, young children of different ages clearly vary in their contributions to the interactions between them. Dunn (1993) has reported that, when the younger of a pair of siblings was 24 months old, the primary correlate of joint play between the sibs was the temperamental characteristics of the older sib. By the time the younger sib was 36 months old, however, joint play was correlated with the temperamental characteristics of the younger child as well. To be sure, as both siblings reach middle childhood and adolescence, the points on which they perceive *differences* between them and the degree of differences diminishes somewhat, as the cross-sectional studies of Furman and Buhrmester (Buhrmester & Furman, 1990) have shown us. In the first 2 decades of life, however, developmental differentials are embedded in bilateral patterns that often once were attributed uniquely to developmental changes in only one of the two individuals.

One frequently cited example comes from research on attachment. Sroufe and collaborators (Elicker, Englund, & Sroufe, 1992; Shulman, Elicker, & Sroufe, 1994) reported that, when two toddlers or school-age children interact, the qualities of their interactions are a joint function of their respective early relationships. Two toddlers who both have histories of secure attachments to their mothers tend to interact with each other harmoniously and with high levels of reciprocity, and secure toddlers also tend to interact smoothly with toddlers who have histories of anxious–resistant attachments to caregivers. Secure toddlers and toddlers who are *avoidant* toward their mothers, however, are much more likely than children in either of the other combinations to be highly aggressive toward each other—and both children, not just one, contribute to this tendency

(Pastor, 1981). Thus: "it is not simply that children behave differently depending on the relationship histories of their partners, but that relationships with different partners themselves vary in quality" (Sroufe & Fleeson, 1986, p. 59).

Tracking bilateral processes becomes even more complex when two people of different ages interact, for example, older with younger peers or adults with children. One reason for this is that developmental and power differentials contribute to the unique functioning of the dyad. Another reason, as Hartup and Laursen (1991) pointed out in the essay of which this volume is the namesake, is that different *rates* of change in two partners of different ages make it difficult to determine which partner is contributing more to the ongoing adaptations between them.

This emphasis on bilaterality means that measures of the individual alone are no longer sufficient for understanding the processes of social development. In the words of Robert Hinde and Joan Stevenson-Hinde (1987), "it is necessary to treat the child not as an isolated entity but as a social being, formed by and forming part of a network of relationships which are crucial to its integrity" (p. 2).

A bilateral developmental perspective makes doubly challenging the identification of age-appropriate behavioral indicators of relational phenomena. To take one example, intimacy is typically expressed between parents and children through much physical contact and cuddling in infancy and early childhood; but in later periods, intimacy is more likely to be manifested in sharing of thoughts and feelings. Hartup and Stevens (1997) recently proposed that these different behaviors constitute the surface structure and that intimacy comprises the deep structure of social relationships. Developmental research on relationships thus is complicated significantly by the need to determine the deep structures that are functionally significant across age periods and to identify age-appropriate surface structures for these in each different age period (Collins & Sroufe, in press; Sroufe, Carlson, & Shulman, 1993).

FUNCTIONAL ANALYSES OF DEVELOPMENTAL OUTCOMES

Adopting dyadic units and attending to bilateral processes have stimulated a shift away from viewing developmental outcomes only in terms of individual traits or habit patterns, toward thinking of outcomes in terms of competences for participating in social life. In his essay titled "On Relationships and Development," Hartup (1986) noted that relationships were significant contexts for socialization not only because they provide an opportunity for the inculcation of social norms, but because they constitute

"important templates or models . . ." for "the construction of future relationships" (p. 2). Eleanor Maccoby (1992), in her historical analysis of
research on the role of parents, also noted that a relationship perspective
means viewing outcomes as dynamic capacities for relating effectively to
others. Although parental effectiveness has long been construed as a set
of parental competencies for nurturing and regulating children's behavior,
Maccoby proposed that, from a dyadic perspective, effective parenting also
means creating a relationship with the child in which it is possible "to
induct the child into a system of reciprocity" (p. 1013).

This broadened perspective on developmental outcomes is partly responsible for one of the signal contributions of the "new look" to developmental psychology: namely, the recognition that diverse relationships
are functionally linked in the child's development. Parents and peers, for
example, were viewed for generations as incompatible or contradictory
influences in socialization. Foreshadowing a now widely held view, Hartup's
(1979) paper, "Two Social Worlds of Childhood," proposed that parent–
child and child–child relationships serve distinctive and unique, but clearly
interrelated, functions in socialization. That formulation has now been
realized in some of the most influential recent research on social development. Two lines of research findings exemplify this direction.

The first finding comes from studies documenting functional links among
diverse relationships in children's development. Relationships with parents
and peers, for example, are more highly interrelated than is commonly
recognized in both the development of behavior patterns and their manifestations (e.g., DeBaryshe, Patterson, & Capaldi, 1993; Dishion, Patterson, &
Griesler, 1994; Vuchinich, Bank, & Patterson, 1992). Dishion, Patterson, and
Griesler (1994) have shown how friendships between deviant peers serve to
maintain or increase deviant behaviors in adolescence, over and above the
effects associated with parental influences (Dishion, Patterson, Stoolmiller,
& Skinner, 1991). These authors explain that peer rejection limits the pool
of available peers from which an adolescent can select friends. Given
attraction among similar others (Kandel, 1978), children and adolescents
with antisocial traits tend to befriend others with antisocial traits (Dishion,
Andrews, & Crosby, 1995); and these friendship dyads display higher rates
of conversation about antisocial behavior and substance abuse in an effort
to elicit positive reinforcement and more firmly establish common ground
between the interactants. Thus, friendships sustain antisocial patterns that
were once considered the result of personality traits or the unilateral
operation of rearing influences (Collins, Gleason, & Sesma, 1997).

A second, similar account focuses on peer-group norms and pressures,
rather than friendship processes. Brown and colleagues (Brown, Mounts,
Lamborn, & Steinberg, 1993; Durbin, Darling, Steinberg, & Brown, 1993)
found that particular parenting practices (e.g., emphasis on academic

achievement, parental monitoring, and facilitation of joint parent–child decision making) and parenting styles (e.g., variations along dimensions of demandingness and responsiveness) are associated with certain adolescent behaviors and predispositions. These behaviors then guide adolescents into particular peer groups, such as "brains," "jocks," or "druggies." Like Dishion, Brown assumes that like-minded peers gravitate toward one another. Once adolescents affiliate with a peer group, peer norms reinforce the behavioral styles that were the impetus for the affiliation.

Examples are not limited to negative relationship outcomes, nor to primarily social ones. Hartup (1996) and his collaborators (Daiute, Hartup, Sholl, & Zajac, 1993), among others (e.g., Azmitia & Montgomery, 1993), have documented the beneficial effects on cognitive performance of collaboration with peers and, most particularly, with friends. These findings offer compelling evidence that qualities of exchanges help to explain the nature of the outcomes. Such an insight is less readily apparent when one focuses on the nature of the "end product" alone, without reference to the interpersonal contexts in which outcomes emerge and are sustained.

SOME FINAL WORDS

These three points of change in social development are meant to show how an emphasis on relational phenomena, rather than only on individual indices of experience and manifestations of competence, have broadened and invigorated the field. This volume provides numerous new instances of the vitality that has resulted from taking seriously the idea that relationships are an essential unit of psychological functioning. That the chapters come from collaborators, colleagues, and friends of Willard Hartup shows how, and to what a considerable extent, he and his professional relationships have contributed to this revitalization.

REFERENCES

Azmitia, M., & Montgomery, R. (1993). Friendship, transactive dialogues, and the development of scientific reasoning. *Social Development, 2,* 202–221.

Bell, R. Q. (1968). A reinterpretation of the direction of effect in studies of socialization. *Psychological Review, 75,* 81–95.

Berscheid, E. (1994). Interpersonal relationships. *Annual Review of Psychology, 45,* 79–129.

Berscheid, E., & Reis, H. T. (in press). Attraction and close relationships. In D. Gilbert, S. Fiske, & G. Lindzey (Eds.), *The handbook of social psychology* (4th ed., pp. 193–281). New York: Addison-Wesley.

Brooks-Gunn, J., & Reiter, E. (1990). The role of pubertal processes. In S. S. Feldman, & G. R. Elliott (Eds.), *At the threshold: The developing adolescent* (pp. 16–53). Cambridge, MA: Harvard University Press.

Brooks-Gunn, J., & Ruble, D. (1982). The development of menstrual-related beliefs and behaviors during early adolescence. *Child Development, 53*, 1567–1577.

Brown, B. B., Mounts, N., Lamborn, S. D., & Steinberg, L. (1993). Parenting practices and peer group affiliation in adolescence. *Child Development, 64*, 467–482.

Buhrmester, D., & Furman, W. (1990). Perceptions of sibling relationships during middle childhood and adolescence. *Child Development, 61*, 1387–1398.

Collins, W. A., Gleason, T., & Sesma, A., Jr. (1997). Internalization, autonomy, and relationships: Development during adolescence. In J. E. Grusec & L. Kuczynski (Eds.), *Parenting and children's internalization of values* (pp. 78-102). New York: Wiley.

Collins, W. A., & Sroufe, L. A. (in press). Capacity for intimate relationships: A developmental construction. In W. Furman, C. Feiring, & B. B. Brown (Eds.), *Contemporary perspectives on adolescent romantic relationships*. New York: Cambridge University Press.

Daiute, C., Hartup, W. W., Sholl, W., & Zajac, R. (1993, March). *Peer collaboration and written language development: A study of friends and acquaintances.* Paper presented at the Society for Research in Child Development, New Orleans, LA.

DeBaryshe, B. D., Patterson, G. R., & Capaldi, D. M. (1993). A performance model for academic achievement in early adolescent boys. *Developmental Psychology, 29*, 795–804.

Dishion, T. J., Andrews, D. W., & Crosby, L. (1995). Antisocial boys and their friends in early adolescence: Relationship characteristics, quality, and interactional process. *Child Development, 66*, 139–151.

Dishion, T. J., Patterson, G. R., & Griesler, P. C. (1994). Peer adaptations in the development of antisocial behavior: A confluence model. In L. R. Huesmann (Ed.), *Aggressive behavior: Current perspectives* (pp. 61–95). New York: Plenum Press.

Dishion, T. J., Patterson, G. R., Stoolmiller, M., & Skinner, M. L. (1991). Family, school, and behavioral antecedents to early adolescent involvement with antisocial peers. *Developmental Psychology, 27*(1), 172–180.

Dunn, J. (1993). *Young children's close relationships: Beyond attachment.* Newbury Park, CA: Sage.

Durbin, D. L., Darling, N., Steinberg, L., & Brown, B. B. (1993). Parenting style and peer group membership among European-American adolescents. *Journal of Research on Adolescence, 3*(1), 87–100.

Eckerman, C. O., Davis, C. C., & Didow, S. M. (1989). The growth of social play with peers during the second year of life. *Developmental Psychology, 11*, 42–49.

Elicker, J., Englund, M., & Sroufe, L. A. (1992). Predicting peer competence and peer relationships in childhood from early parent-child relationships. In R. Parke & G. Ladd (Eds.), *Family-peer relationships: Modes of linkage* (pp. 77–106). Hillsdale, NJ: Lawrence Erlbaum Associates.

Hartup, W. W. (1979). Two social worlds of childhood. *American Psychologist, 34*, 944–950.

Hartup, W. W. (1986). On relationships and development. In W. W. Hartup & Z. Rubin (Eds.), *Relationships and development* (pp. 1–26). Hillsdale, NJ: Lawrence Erlbaum Associates.

Hartup, W. W. (1991). Social development and social psychology: Perspectives on interpersonal relationships. In J. H. Cantor, C. C. Spiker, & L. Lipsitt (Eds.), *Child behavior and development: Training for diversity* (pp. 1–33). Norwood, NJ: Ablex.

Hartup, W. W. (1996). Cooperation, close relationships, and cognitive development. In W. M. Bukowski, A. F. Newcomb, & W. W. Hartup (Eds.), *The company they keep: Friendship in childhood and adolescence* (pp. 213–237). New York: Cambridge University Press.

Hartup, W. W., & Laursen, B. (1991). Relationships as developmental contexts. In R. Cohen & A. W. Siegel (Eds.), *Context and development* (pp. 253–279). Hillsdale, NJ: Lawrence Erlbaum Associates.

Hartup, W. W., & Lempers, J. (1973). A problem in life-span development: The interactional analysis of family attachments. In P. Baltes & K. W. Schaie (Eds.), *Life-span developmental psychology: Personality and socialization* (Vol. 3, pp. 235–252). New York: Academic Press.

Hartup, W. W., & Stevens, N. (1997). Friendship and adaptation in the life course. *Psychological Bulletin, 121*, 355–370.

Hinde, R. A. (1979). *Towards understanding relationships*. London: Academic Press.

Hinde, R. A., & Stevenson-Hinde, J. (1987). Interpersonal relationships and child development. *Developmental Review, 7*, 1–21.

Kandel, D. B. (1978). Similarity in real-life adolescent friendship pairs. *Journal of Personality and Social Psychology, 36*, 302–312.

Kelley, H. H., Berscheid, E., Christensen, A., Harvey, J. H., Huston, T. L., Levinger, G., McClintock, E., Peplau, L. A., & Peterson, D. R. (1983). *Close relationships*. New York: Freeman.

Maccoby, E. E. (1992). The role of parents in the socialization of children: An historical overview. *Developmental Psychology, 28*, 1006–1017.

Pastor, D. (1981). The quality of mother-infant attachment and its relationship to toddlers' initial sociability with peers. *Developmental Psychology, 17*, 326–335.

Rierdan, J., Koff, E., & Stubbs, M. L. (1989). Timing of menarche, preparation, and initial menstrual experience: Replication and further analyses in a prospective study. *Journal of Youth and Adolescence, 18*, 413–426.

Sears, R. R. (1951). A theoretical framework for personality and social behavior. *American Psychologist, 6*, 476–483.

Shulman, S., Elicker, J., & Sroufe, L. A. (1994). Stages of friendship growth in preadolescence as related to attachment history. *Journal of Social and Personal Relationships, 11*, 341–361.

Sroufe, L. A., Carlson, E., & Shulman, S. (1993). Individuals in relationships: Development from infancy through adolescence. In D. C. Funder, R. D. Parke, C. Tomlinson-Keasey, & K. Widaman (Eds.), *Studying lives through time: Personality and development*. Washington, DC: American Psychological Association.

Sroufe, L. A., & Fleeson, J. (1986). Attachment and the construction of relationships. In W. Hartup & Z. Rubin (Eds.), *Relationships and development* (pp. 51–71), Hillsdale, NJ: Lawrence Erlbaum Associates.

Vuchinich, S., Bank, L., & Patterson, G. R. (1992). Parenting, peers, and the stability of antisocial behavior in preadolescent boys. *Developmental Psychology, 28*, 247–257.

Chapter 2

Relationships as Developmental Contexts: Retrospective Themes and Contemporary Issues

Willard W. Hartup
University of Minnesota

Brett Laursen
Florida Atlantic University

The importance of relationships to human health and happiness has been recognized for a very long time. Nevertheless, scientific efforts to describe, assess, and establish the significance of these entities have emerged slowly over the last 100 years. Deep-seated and widely held prejudices having to do with the impropriety of studying something so intimate and private as close relationships—including relationships between children and their parents—still constrain progress. Research methods in this area also remain relatively unsophisticated, tempering support for scientific studies both within the behavioral sciences and the natural sciences more generally (Berscheid & Peplau, 1983; Hinde, 1997). Considerable progress, however, has been made since the mid-1960s.

Looking back, one can identify several early developments that established the foundations for that which was to come. Turn-of-the-century works asserting the significance of relationships in human adaptation include Emile Durkheim's (1897/1951) studies showing that protection against suicide accrues to individuals through marital relationships and social integration, Sigmund Freud's (1900/1953) early papers enunciating the centrality of "object relations" in socialization, and James Mark Baldwin's (1897) consideration of relationship networks as the child's "social heredity." Among the hypotheses contained in these early works are the notions that social relationships constitute the origins of the self (ego) and that the self as a psychological construct must be regarded as a "socius," that is, a social entity.

Baldwin's ideas influenced writers in many disciplines in the decades after the *Social and Ethical Interpretations in Mental Development* (Baldwin, 1897) was published. In psychology, extensions of his ideas emerged in Piaget's (1923/1926) accounts of assimilation and accommodation in cognitive development and in Vygotsky's (1978) accounts of the manner in which social exchanges between the child and significant others become "interiorized." In sociology, Baldwin's ideas influenced Charles H. Cooley's (1909) formulations concerning the importance of "primary groups" (of the family, playground, and neighborhood) and social relationships to the construction of human nature. George Herbert Mead's (1934) ideas concerning the manner in which "symbolic interaction" between the child and significant others forms the basis of internalized individuality also derive, in part, from Baldwin's notions. These ideas, in turn, influenced generations of social scientists, including those studying child development and the family.

Freud's ideas were carried forward in many different variants—each containing important assumptions about early relationships, their origins, and their significance in personality development (see Munroe, 1955). Erikson's (1950) notion concerning the significance of mutual regulation in early development was one milestone. Sullivan's (1953) formulation demonstrating the centrality of relationships with significant others in the emergence and functioning of the "self-dynamism" (a process, not an entity) was another milestone—one that bears Baldwin's stamp as well as Freud's. Still another achievement was Bowlby's (1969) re-working of psychoanalytic notions about early relationships and their importance in personality development—this time within an evolutionary framework.

The story of who influenced whom in thinking about relationships and their developmental significance is a complex tale—one that has not yet been told. We assert only the germinal significance of the ideas of James Mark Baldwin and Sigmund Freud as well as the extensive cross-fertilization that has occurred across disciplines over the last century. One cannot claim that these early efforts produced a comprehensive theory of relationships and their developmental significance. Nevertheless, a consensus emerged early concerning the importance of relationships to what might be called "interiorization," that is, the process through which external events give rise to the construction of the individual's competencies for transactions with the environment. Empirical research, however, was rare during the early years.

New data and new models of relationships began to emerge roughly 35 years ago. First, Harry Harlow and his associates (Harlow, 1958) conducted ground-breaking experiments with Rhesus monkeys, showing convincingly that relationship perturbations had lasting effects on members of that species as well as showing that some of the processes thought earlier to be important in the construction of relationships between caretakers and offspring (e.g., feeding) might not be. Second, based on studies of young children reared without opportunities to relate consistently to a caretaker, John Bowlby (1951, 1958) formulated modern attachment theory, and Mary Ainsworth and her colleagues (Ainsworth, Blehar, Waters, & Wall, 1978) developed methods for testing it. Third, based on extensive studies of costs and benefits in social relations, especially the conditions creating "interdependence" between two individuals, Harold Kelley and his colleagues (Kelley, 1979; Kelley & Thibaut, 1978) formulated a generative theory of personal relationships that is especially applicable to so-called "close" relationships. Fourth, deriving from a large body of work dealing with mother–infant relationships among various primate species (including human beings), Robert Hinde (1976) produced a conceptual analysis and a blueprint for conducting badly needed descriptive studies. Other contributors might be cited but the work of these individuals has had an unusually strong impact—especially on scientific efforts to better account for relationships and their significance in child development.

Studies dealing with relationships in developmental perspective are now moving swiftly; the contributors to this volume are leaders in this enterprise. The current volume is actually a progress report showing what a century of effort in social science (with emphasis on the last quarter-century) has and has not achieved by way of understanding relationships and their importance in human development. In the balance of this chapter, we focus on three issues that have both historical and contemporary significance: defining and describing relationships; relationships and developmental process; and relationships as contributors to developmental outcome.

DEFINING AND DESCRIBING RELATIONSHIPS

Definitions

Although turn-of-the-century writers succeeded in convincing the scientific community that child development proceeds through social interaction as well as individual activity, relationships were defined in terms that are difficult to comprehend or tie to observables. Early psychoanalytic writings, for example, identify the "anaclitic relationship" (i.e., "leaning against") as the basis of the infant's dependence on the mother and the foundation for the development of the ego. Although the mother's actions toward the child were believed to determine its nature, this tie was viewed largely from the child's side, especially as it is constrained by psychosexual development. Little attention was given to the mother's tie to the child, although most 19th-century writers attributed greater affection by mothers for their babies than the reverse (Kagan, 1983). Within psychoanalytic theory, the mother was described as the "object" of the child's affections and "cathexis" was the term formulated to describe the affect attached to mental representations of this external object. Charming analogies were employed to describe these cathexes including one that likens them to the pseudopodia—that is, amebic protrusions generated for purposes of moving about or taking in food that can subsequently be withdrawn into the main body of the organism (Freud, 1914/1957).

As useful as these metaphors may have been to the psychoanalysts, difficulties arose when assimilation to the constructs and methods of other theories was attempted (Sears, 1944). Some of the difficulty came because referents in natural language for terms like "object relations" are not immediately apparent, others because specifying behavioral observables for experimental (quantitative) analysis was next to impossible.[1] Still other difficulties arose because relationship constructs are not easy to accommodate within any theory designed to account for individual behavior. Most psychological theories are about processes that underlie behavior change in individuals rather than groups, even though many of these theories address transactions between the person and the environment. Considerable extrapolation is needed nevertheless to show how interpersonal attraction and relationships can be explained in terms of intrapsychic processes, for example, reinforcement (Hinde, 1997).

One noteworthy attempt to account for social interaction and relationships in terms of reinforcement theory was made by Sears (1951). Most of the important elements in the model are shown in Fig. 2.1. This figure, taken from the original paper, recognizes, first, that relationships consist of behavioral interdependencies, that is, situations in which changes in one individual effect changes in the other and vice versa. Second, the model assumes that these interdependencies involve thoughts and other cognitions (S_{cog}), emotions (encompassed by S_D), and actions (S_{ext}). Third, the model attempts to explain how interactions between two individuals are affected by past interactions and may affect other interactions in the future, that is, through reinforcement deriving from drive reduction. Relationship dynamics over the long term are not explained in the figure but are attributed in the manuscript to anticipatory reactions emerging from the interaction between the individuals.

A similar and widely cited model omitting the reinforcement baggage was presented by Harold Kelley and his collaborators (Kelley et al., 1983). This model (Fig. 2.2) also emphasizes the multidimensional nature of relationship interdependencies by encompassing thoughts and emotions as well as actions. The model begs off, however, from any attempt at

---

[1]Sears (1951) suggested, however, that such attempts might be a . . . "ride on the tail of a kite that was never meant to carry such a load" (p. 329).

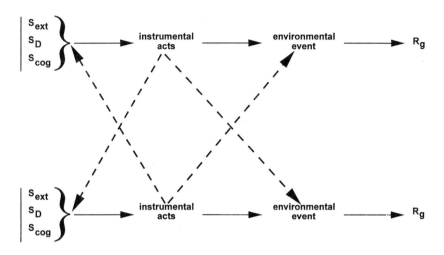

FIG. 2.1. *The dyadic sequence.* Social influence in the interaction between two individuals conceived as connections between stimuli (external, drive, and cognitive) and goal responses. From Sears (1951). Reproduced with the permission of the American Psychological Association.

accounting for why relationships come about or endure. Consequently, the model can be applied to many different kinds of relationships and utilized within many different theoretical frameworks. Other variations on these models have been proposed that emphasize social information processing (Bradbury & Fincham, 1989) and behavioral sequential dependencies (Gottman, 1983).

Still another conceptual advance emerging at about this same time was Hinde's (1976) model showing that relationships need to be viewed within a hierarchy of "levels of social complexity" (Fig. 2.3). This contribution recognizes that relationships are influenced by the group and societal structures in which they are embedded as well as the psychological and social processes on which they are based.

The significance of these formulations lies in their clear recognition that relationships are behavioral aggregates, that these aggregates involve bilateral influence processes, that these interdependencies extend over time, and that relationships are embedded within other individual and social structures. Using these models, one can avoid the need to resort exclusively to natural language in order to define a relationship; behavioral criteria can be used instead. One must, of course, acknowledge the molecularity of these models and the difficulties this creates in conducting empirical work based on them. Nevertheless, these definitional efforts provide a framework within which empirical results concerning almost any relationship phenomenon can be viewed.

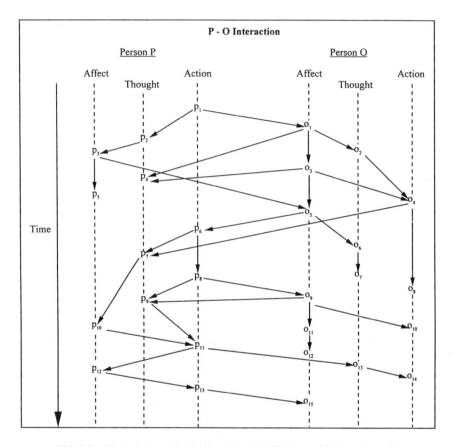

FIG. 2.2. *The basic data of a dyadic relationship.* The lives of both persons in a relationship involve a chain of events, each chain including affect, thought, and action. The events are causally connected within chains (p or o) and the two chains are causally interconnected. Interchain connections constitute the essential feature of interpersonal relationships. From Kelley et al. (1983). Reproduced with the permission of the author and publisher (W. H. Freeman).

Description

Relationships come in different sizes and shapes: One important way that relationships differ from one another has to do with who the child's partner is. Although it is nearly a truism to declare that children's behavior varies according to the partners with whom they interact, empirical studies have been somewhat hit-or-miss. We know that bargaining strategies differ

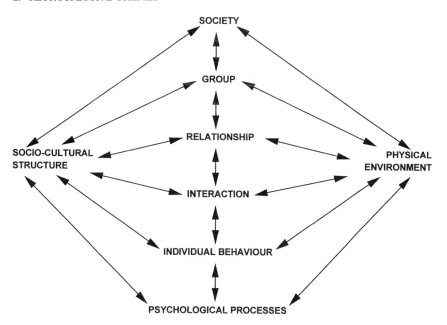

FIG. 2.3. *Simplified view of the levels of social complexity.* Relationships
continually influence, and are influenced by, their component interactions
and thus by the individual participants and by diverse psychological processes
within those individuals; the groups and society in which they are embedded;
the sociocultural structure of beliefs, values, institutions; and the physical
environment. From Hinde (1997). Reproduced with permission of the
author and publisher (Psychology Press).

according to whether the partner is a parent or a friend; stronger strategies,
for example, are used by children with friends than with parents (Cowan,
Drinkard, & MacGavin, 1984). We know that relationships formed between
infants and depressed mothers include a higher proportion of insecure
attachments than relationships involving nondepressed mothers (Radke-
Yarrow, Cummings, Kuczynski, & Chapman, 1985); other variations in the
mother–child relationship are linked to maternal demographics (e.g., her
age) and personality, including the mother's recollections about her own
childhood attachments (Grossman, Fremmer-Bombeck, Rudolph, & Grossman, 1988). We know also that children's relationships with friends vary
according to the aggressiveness of their partners (Dishion, Andrews, &
Crosby, 1995) and whether that aggression is "overt" or "relational"
(Grotpeter & Crick, 1996). On balance, however, characteristics of partners
have not been used to describe or classify relationships involving children
and adolescents as extensively as they might be.

Relationships differ from one another in a great many other ways: Some
relationships are *diverse* in terms of the number of different activities in

which the parties engage; others are less so. Some relationships are *intimate*; other are not. Some relationships are *symmetrical* in the sense that social power is distributed more-or-less equally between the partners; others are asymmetrical. *Security* and *coerciveness* also vary. Some eight or ten major dimensions of relationships have now been specified and these are discussed extensively by Hinde (1997). Others can be identified; there is really no limit but our imaginations in constructing a language suitable for describing the ways that relationships differ from one another.

This century has brought us a long way toward a lexicon for defining and describing relationships. The lexicon changes continually, like natural language does, and future scientists will use vastly different constructs in relationships research from those we use now. Our efforts to describe relationships and their relevance to child development is only beginning to catch up to the descriptive advances made elsewhere in biological and natural science over the last several hundred years (Hinde, 1997).

RELATIONSHIPS AND DEVELOPMENTAL PROCESS

Focusing on a Figure

Human beings, along with other primates, seem to be biologically prepared for relationships through response biases evident at birth and afterward. The attachment system, for example, is constructed on the basis of infant reflexes, including one group that Bowlby (1969) called "signals" (crying, smiling, vocalizing) and another called "executors" (clinging, visual tracking, following). The system cannot emerge, however, in the absence of complementary response biases in the parent (commonly called "caregiving"). Peer relations require different biases—specifically, two children must be able simultaneously to encode the behavior of self and other, integrate these encodings cognitively, and choose responses that will "fit" the situation so that coordinated activity (e.g., play) can occur between them.

Most observers have concluded that the explanation for why a relationship emerges between two individuals lies in the interaction between them, that is, the impact they have upon one another. Caretakers must interact with their children *over time* before attachments are evident and toddlers must interact with one another *over time* before friendships manifest themselves. Through more than 60 years, the prevailing view was that the infant's wanting to be with specific others results from being fed by them or provided with other forms of primary gratification. Social learning theorists referred to this process as *secondary drive*, suggesting that the motivation underlying attachment and other social relationships is secondary, or derived, from gratifying conditions that are more basic or "primary." Freud (1900/1953) referred to the process as cathexis, a construct symbolizing the investment of "psychic energy" in specific objects such as caregivers, siblings, and friends. Notably absent in those formulations was any explanation for why the mother (an object) forms a focused relationship or attachment to the child. Not until Sears' (1951) attempt to shift attention from monadic to dyadic sequences was the theory of secondary drive extended to social interaction.

An attack on the secondary drive construct, however, was already under way: Empirical studies showed that attachment behavior could be elicited in the absence of being fed or receiving any other conventional reward in such species as geese (Lorenz, 1935), Rhesus monkeys (Harlow & Zimmerman, 1959), puppies (Scott, 1963), and sheep (Cairns, 1966). Observers of human infants came to the same conclusion (cf., Ainsworth, 1967; Schaffer & Emerson, 1964). But one question remained: How exactly does social interaction transmutate into enduring relationships? Some social learning theorists (Gewirtz, 1961) shifted paradigms, arguing that the attachment system (and possibly other relationships) emerge on the basis of instrumental rather than classical conditioning. Because the mother's appearance and movements attract the infant's attention without being associated with feeding (Fantz, 1963), one does not have to assume that drive reduction is the key event that transforms mother–child interaction into relationships. But, although these accounts explained why the mother acquires the capacity to elicit smiles and vocalizing from the infant, the theory was not successful in explaining why specific behaviors become integrated into a relationship "system."

Instrumental learning was nevertheless included among four processes that Bowlby believed to be at work in determining the infant's "focusing on a figure" (a phrase he used to refer to the specific attachment to the caretaker that emerges during the third quarter of the first year). The feedback received by the infant through caretaking was thought to be most important, especially the mother's responsiveness to the infant's distress and readiness to initiate interaction (see early studies by Schaffer & Emerson [1964] and Ainsworth [1967] for supporting data). The three other processes recognized as contributing to focusing on a figure were: (a) preferences for "approaching" certain classes of stimuli typical of the behavior of humans toward an infant (especially those which are in some way contingent on the infant's actions (Watson, 1966); (b) mere exposure enabling discrimination between the caregiver and others; and (c) a genetically determined bias favoring approach to familiar objects (a notion somewhat at odds with present-day thinking about the infant's preference for novelty). On the basis of these mechanisms, continued interaction between mother and child was believed to result in an integrated system that functions to protect the child from danger and relieve anxiety and distress.

As for relationships between children and other children, Buhler (1931) noted the interest of 6-month-old babies in one another as revealed by observing them and, later, following them. Not until the 1970s, however, were observations made by Lee (1973) and others that showed some infants are singled out for unusually large amounts of attention by their agemates, and that this focusing is contingent on the sought-after child's "responsiveness." More recent observations confirm and extend these earlier findings by showing that reciprocities in social interaction seem to be the most clearly identified antecedent of this focusing on a figure (Howes, 1983). And yet psychological interpretations of these results have not, generally, been compelling. Reciprocal interaction may undergird early friendships because these contingencies are reinforcing to the individuals in themselves (Watson, 1966). Alternatively, these interactions may be the basis for equity or equivalence expectations within the individuals involved. Or they may indicate similarities between the children in disposition and attitude that, in turn, dispose them toward mutual attraction (Newcomb, 1961). Considering the circumstances repeatedly shown to be involved in friendship formation (common ground, a "climate of agreement"—see Gottman [1983]), it is surprising that investigators have not been more interested in the mechanisms responsible.

Mother–child and child–child relationships do not comprise the child's entire social world. Fathers and children evince focused attachments yet recent studies show that fathers and mothers engage in behavioral exchanges with their children that are different from one another as well as similar. For example, fathers and children engage in more robust interaction than mothers and children do (Lamb, 1977) although both fathers and mothers can successfully care for young children (Parke & Sawin, 1976). One does not know, however, whether the regulatory processes believed to support focusing on the maternal figure also support focusing on the father. Similar statements can be made about sibling relationships. Thus, although contemporary accounts of focusing on a figure are descriptively sophisticated, the mechanisms responsible remain unclearly specified.

By What Processes Do Relationships Affect the Growth and Development of the Individual Child?

The construct most commonly used to describe the processes by which relationships impinge on development is internalization. Depending on the theoretical framework, however, this construct has vastly different meanings. Theoretical consensus extends only to the general notion that social interaction is the channel through which something "external" (e.g., social rules) becomes "internal." The manner in which one construes internalization, however, varies according to one's views concerning the residuals it leaves behind.

How to Think About Relationship "Residuals." Constructivist theorists generally assume that the residuals of social experience consist of some kind of mental "representation." Significant among these representations in psychoanalytic theory are object (other) and ego. One cannot be conceived without the other, so that both self and other representations were central in the work of Anna Freud (1952), Harry Stack Sullivan (1953), Margaret Mahler (1963), Louis Sander (1975), and others. Representations of relationships themselves sometimes find their way into these theories, but usually as mental substrates from which self- and other-representations emerge (see Mahler, 1963; Main, Kaplan, & Cassidy, 1985). The super ego is another set of mental constructions deriving mainly from social relationships, one that consists of an idealized set of social standards and emotional mechanisms allowing these constructions to serve as the basis of conscience.

A substantial portion of modern cognitive psychology is devoted to figuring out how reality is represented mentally, stored, retrieved, and utilized. Mental representations (including social ones) are assumed in cognitive developmental theory (Piaget, 1937/1954), schema theory (Markus, 1977), and script theory (Schank & Abelson, 1977), each being a way of describing the residual that experience (social or otherwise) leaves with the individual. Within these theoretical frameworks, this residual is thought to consist of generalized knowledge structures that can be used to predict and regulate behavior in situations analogous, but not identical, to those from which the structures were derived. Schemas are organized knowledge structures of many different types used to support the generation of new knowledge through inference. Scripts are particular types of schemas that capture causal and temporal relations that typically characterize an "event" but they are generic rather than episodic, that is, they are not tied to experience in a particular time or place. Both constructs are useful in describing the knowledge structures that constitute *self* and *other*.

More recently, these notions have been extended to include mental representations of "the space between self and other" (Mitchell, 1988) and "self-with-other" (Ogilvie & Ashmore, 1991), that is, relationships. Indeed, one of the most promising new developments in relationships research is the articulation of a body of work focused on what Baldwin (1992) called "relational schemas"—a generic term encompassing interpersonal scripts and other schemas. As Hinde (1997) suggested, certain communalities are evident in these ideas: Each assumes that "knowledge structures are derived primarily from experience, and involve both comparison and evaluation. They involve schemata concerned with self, with others, and with relationships. . . . [and those] concerned with relationships influence those concerned with the self, and vice versa: the precise relation between the two [being] unclear" (p. 34).

Within developmental psychology, one other representational construct has become well-known within the last 30 years: the "inner working model." Closely identified with Bowlby's theory of attachment (1969, 1973, 1980), this formulation draws from psychoanalysis and cognitive developmental theory but also from the thinking of an engineer (Craik, 1943) and a biologist (Young, 1964). Inner working models are described as brain structures used to "transmit, store, and manipulate information [about the environment] that helps in making predictions as to how . . . set-goals can be achieved" (Bowlby, 1969, p. 80). These representations are deliberately called "working" models to avoid the implication that the reality being represented is static or that the mental representations themselves are unchanging. Recent writers have stressed that these models consist of generalizations about self, others, and relationships, expectations about them (Sroufe, 1983), or scripts (Bretherton, 1985); the idea that these models consist of thousands of discrete response tendencies is rejected by almost everyone.

Most behaviorist–mechanistic views of social relations avoid elaborate constructions such as relational schemas and inner working models, based on the argument that they are too difficult to tie to observables. Performance theorists (e.g., Patterson, 1982) thus avoid them in favor of directly measured interpersonal events believed to control the frequency with which certain behaviors (e.g., problem behavior) are emitted. Other researchers have generated theories of "generalized imitation" to refer to dispositions to behave similarly to others under conditions of uncertainty or difficulty that build up via social experience (Gewirtz & Stingle, 1968). In other instances, the residuals of social interaction are described differently by behaviorally oriented psychologists—as mediated by "cumulative cognitions and expectations developed by [two individuals] about one another" (Maccoby & Martin, 1983, p. 87). Writings by Bandura (1969), Mischel, (1973), and Kelley and Thibaut, 1978) represent neo-behavioral/neo-cognitive notions about the best way to describe selves, others, and relationships between them.

How Are These Residuals Constructed? Relational schemas originate in social experience. Both psychodynamic and cognitive theories have held steadfastly to this view through the entire century, each struggling mightily with the particulars. It has not been difficult to conclude that knowledge about relationships is socially derived, but it is quite another matter to specify how this knowledge is constructed.

Psychoanalytic theory suggested that the major contributors to relational schemas are two forms of "identification"—anaclitic and aggressive (or defensive) identification, sometimes called primary and secondary identification, respectively. Freud's ideas concerning identification were never finalized (Bronfenbrenner, 1960), but the construct generally refers to the processes by which children come to resemble significant others. *Primary identification* refers to the initial undifferentiated state of fusion between the nascent infant ego and the social objects with whom the infant becomes attached. Attachment to the caregiver rests on "oral incorporation" through which the infant attempts to introject the ego of the attached object and thereby sustain the attachment (or the anaclitic relationship). In other words, the first social schemata derive from need fulfillment. *Secondary identification* is triggered by the sexualization of parent–child relationships that occurs during early childhood and the responses of children and their parents to these developments. These conditions create ambivalence in the child's object relations, and this ambivalence furnishes the motivational base for secondary identification—the desire to become the threatening parent (recognized in fantasy). The theory thus emphasizes the formation of early attachments, increases in attachment ambivalence as a function of libidinal changes and parental threat, and the discovery by the child that identification brings about psychic equilibrium. The model thus suggests that "warmth" and "responsiveness" between the child and the caregiver as well as power assertion are substrates for internalization. Subsequent research has not been unkind to those notions (see Hetherington, 1967) although the sexual underpinnings of this theory have mostly been discredited. Finally, one should note that, although parent–child interaction instigates identification, the child does not identify with the parent–child relationship per se, but with parents (usually the same-gender parent) as individual objects.

Social learning theorists made several serious attempts to account for the acquisition of relational expectations, the earliest attempts referring to these constructs as habits (Miller & Dollard, 1941) or customs (Whiting & Child, 1957) and attributing their acquisition to reinforcement. Close examination, however, revealed that internalization does not depend on a series of reinforced trials (Bandura & Huston, 1961), and more eclectic theories were articulated. Bandura (1969), for example, argued that observational learning (i.e., internalization) involves two representational systems—an imaginal and a verbal one—each involving a transmutation of modeling stimuli into images or words for memory representation after which they function as mediators for response retrieval and reproduction. These mediators are believed to be established by contiguity learning, that is, modeling stimuli are believed to elicit perceptual responses in observers that become sequentially associated and centrally integrated on the basis of temporal contiguity of stimulation. Once again, the theory is not strictly relational; the main objective is to explain the transmission of behavioral patterns from one individual to another, not the construction of relational schemata. Theoretical extensions can be imagined, however, that would accomplish this.

Both Baldwin (1897) and Piaget (1932, 1945/1951) relied on equilibration (the child's efforts to resolve intrapsychic discrepancies between existing schemas and ones emerging from new experience) to account for the emergence of new knowledge structures. Both writers published treatises dealing with imitation, thereby recognizing its centrality in socialization, but neither dealt explicitly with relationship expectations and understanding. Not until Youniss (1975) and Selman (1980) began to work in this area, were attempts made: (a) to describe structural changes occurring over time in the child's understanding and expectations about relationships (friendships as well as parent–child relationships), and (b) to specify processes in social interaction that are coordinated with these conceptual changes. Youniss (1975) focused on the childhood shift in friendship expectations from an emphasis on sharing material goods and common activities to an emphasis on sharing feelings, thoughts, and mutual consideration. The significance of "affirmation" was emphasized in relation to these changes, that is, children are believed to associate the experience of positive affect with affirming social interaction beginning at a relatively early age. Selman (1980) emphasized a different developmental linkage— that between the increasing mutuality evinced in children's friendship expectations and the general decline in childhood egocentrism.

The construction of the child's knowledge about self and others was a major concern in the writings of numerous other individuals although relationships knowledge itself was not strongly emphasized in their writings. Among these, Sullivan (1953) emphasized comparisons and evaluations in which children distinguish between the "good me" and the "bad me" in the acquisition of self-understanding; the child's early interactions with its caregivers is the context in which the most significant comparisons were thought to be made. Vygotsky (1978) also recognized the significance of the child's interactions with social agents, most especially exchanges involving finely tuned coordinations between the child and the agent that occur within the "zone of proximal development." Based on the social agent's mediations during this discourse, the child gradually *interiorizes* knowledge structures, which are generalized or abstract rather than situation specific. Social relationships and the child's history of interactions with significant others are thus important to the process of knowledge acquisition as well as aspects of reality to be internalized. Similarly, theories of symbolic interaction (Mead, 1934) argued that interactive exchanges with others are the bases for interiorized social knowledge through their generation of gestural and linguistic symbols having common meaning for oneself and others. Cooperative exchange or symmetrical interactions are especially important in constructing these interiorizations, not one-way processes like imitation or identification. Once again, comparison and evaluation through sustained social interaction are the events thought to give rise to the relevant knowledge structures.

The construction of inner working models was described synoptically in Bowlby's writings (e.g., Bowlby, 1973) and remains somewhat vague in the writings of others. Clearly, these models are believed to evolve out of "events experienced" (Main et al., 1985) meaning the "history of the infant's actions, infant-parent interactions, and the fate of the infant's 'attempts and outcomes'" (p. 75); everyone, including Bowlby (1973), recognizes the process as transactional. But specifying the mechanisms by means of which the child picks up information, abstracts or generalizes it, and employs the model as a template in subsequent social interactions has not been done clearly. This haziness, however, marks our understanding of how knowledge structures are formed generally (Siegler, 1991). Cognitivists have been more creative in describing these structures themselves than in specifying the stimulus–response chains, perceived similarities, comparisons, evaluations, and equilibrations that give rise to them. Although contemporary writers leave no doubt that inner working models are the cognitive residuals of children's relational experience, it is easier to equate these residuals with scripts, schemas, and similar constructs (Bretherton, 1985) than to specify exactly how they are acquired.

RELATIONSHIPS AND DEVELOPMENTAL OUTCOMES

Relationships have long been believed to be responsible for the kinds of individuals we become. And yet, at the same time, many 20th-century investigators have believed the reverse, namely, that the kinds of individuals we are determine the kinds of relationships we construct. Still other investigators assume that developmental causalities extend in both directions so that relationships are, at one and the same time, both independent and dependent variables in social experience.

The idea that relationships account for significant outcome variance in growth and development figures prominently in psychoanalytic thinking. Freud (1940) believed that it is early somatically related traumas that are mainly responsible for the directions taken in personality development rather than relationship qualities themselves. Modes of feeding, weaning, swallowing, and the frustrations associated with them were, for example, believed to be the developmental substrates of the "oral character" rather than general comfort and discomfort in the child's relationship with the mother. Mother–infant interaction was recognized as the context in which the relevant events occur but the emphasis in most of the germinal essays is on early experience rather than early relationships.

When Erikson (1950) asserted that early experiences result in relationships marked generally by trust or mistrust, and that these social orientations are used by the child in coping with subsequent developmental crises, relationships emerged as major explanatory constructs in theories of personality development. Other theorists, including Mahler (1963), Sander (1975), and Sullivan (1953) were relationship centered rather than trauma centered, and by the time that Bowlby (1969) espoused similar notions, empirical studies convincingly showed that specific feeding and weaning experiences have very little to do with subsequent personality development (Caldwell, 1964).

In contrast, nativist theorists (e.g., Kagan, 1984) argued that the child rather than relationship characteristics determine subsequent developmental directions. Constitutionally determined differences in temperament (e.g., inhibition) are thought by these investigators to be central in this regard, affecting both early social relationships and subsequent behavioral dispositions. Still other writers assert that combinations of child characteristics and relational vicissitudes are responsible for differential outcomes (see Thompson, 1997). Moreover, child characteristics and relationship experience combine in exquisitely complex variety: Kochanska (1991) found, for example, that certain relationship dimensions (e.g., attachment security) predict developmental outcome (e.g., compliance) for children with some temperamental characteristics (e.g., fearlessness) but not for others (e.g., fearfulness).

The general significance of relationships to the child's development is strongly suggested in increasing numbers of longitudinal studies. Earlier efforts to demonstrate this significance through retrospective studies largely failed for various methodological and design reasons (e.g., Radke-Yarrow, Campbell, & Burton, 1970) and correlational studies dealing with both parent–child and peer relationships have not been convincing in demonstrating developmental causation (Hartup & Stevens, 1997). Prospective studies and panel designs, though, make it increasingly difficult to argue that relational experience and personality dispositions are unrelated (Rubin, Bukowski, & Parker, 1997; Thompson, 1997).

Some of the strongest evidence that close relationships affect developmental adaptation comes from research linking characteristics of early caregiver–child attachment with social and emotional competence. Mediating these effects are thought to be attitudes and expectations acquired within these early relationships about self and others as well as modes of emotional regulation (Sroufe, 1995). Secure attachments, especially, have been traced longitudinally to subsequent competence in the social domain: Relative to their insecure counterparts, children who are securely attached to their caregivers during the first year of life cope better with developmental transitions, have superior social skills which makes them popular with peers and preferred by teachers, and have fewer behavior problems (Sroufe, Egeland, & Kreutzer, 1990). Moreover, competence extends from caregivers to other affiliations (e.g., to friends and romantic partners); in each case, the quality of earlier relationships predicts success in later ones—through childhood, into adolescence, and possibly into adulthood (Sroufe, Egeland, & Carlson, this volume; Hazan & Shaver, 1987).

Less well-established is the significance of relationships to cognitive functioning. Current data suggest that both self-esteem and school achievement are associated with relational experience: Securely attached children have higher levels of self-esteem than insecurely attached children (Sroufe, 1983) and positive friendship experience correlates with concurrent and future assessments of self-worth (Bagwell, Newcomb, & Bukowski, in press; Berndt, 1996). Yet the degree to which relationship qualities are correlated with concept development or with children's modes of thinking remain unclear. Close relationships (both with adult caregivers and with friends) have been implicated in cooperation, social understanding, and cognitive applications (Bukowski & Sippola, 1996; Hartup, 1996) but these claims are poorly substantiated. Evidence is stronger in the area of school performance, where diverse assessments indicate that school engagement and grades are a function of relationship quality: Beginning in the nursery school and extending through secondary school, supportive relations with parents and friends predict higher levels of academic interest and abilities than conflict-ridden and contentious relationships do (Berndt & Keefe, 1995; Cairns & Cairns, 1994; Ladd, 1990; Mounts & Steinberg, 1995). Taken together, these results indicate that relationships may shape the internal landscape in domain specific rather than general ways (Laursen & Bukowski, 1997).

Parent–child and peer relationships may themselves shape this landscape differently. Harlow's (1969) work suggested that relationships with caregivers have their impact primarily on the affectional system (i.e., reproduction and subsequent parenting performance) whereas peer relationships have their impact on the affiliative system (i.e., regulation of affective and instrumental behavior with agemates). Subsequent work with children suggests a somewhat different model, namely, that the scaffolding whereby social skills are acquired in parent–child relationships carries over into other relationship domains (siblings and peers), and the shaping that occurs within these relationships then combines with earlier competencies to determine the child's subsequent adaptation. More complex conjunctions may also occur: For example, in addition to the contributions that parents make to the child's engagement with peers, they socialize the regulation of emotion by the child (Parke, Cassidy, Burks, Carson, & Boyum, 1992).

Relationships may compensate for one another under some circumstances. Longitudinal studies indicate, for example, that friendships eventually develop to the point where they compensate, in some degree, for poor family relationships, just as adaptive family relationships assist the individual in overcoming difficulties with friends (Gauze, Bukowski, Aquan-Assee, & Sippola, 1996). In fact, among older individuals who no longer have living relatives, having close friends predicts feelings of social connectedness; but this is not the case among individuals who have families (Lang & Carstensen, 1994). Causal modeling in this area has scarcely begun, however, and has not reached the level of sophistication required to disentangle linkages among relationships and, simultaneously, their contributions to developmental outcomes.

CONCLUSION

Historical endeavor sometimes leads to the conclusion that there is nothing new under the sun. In the case of relationships and their developmental significance, one must admit that certain questions have remained critical over most of the last century: How are relationships formed and maintained? What role is played by relationships in socialization? What processes are involved? What is the significance of early relationships and what is their relation to subsequent ones? These questions were articulated by investigators many years ago and, to this time, one cannot supply complete and noncontroversial answers to most of them.

Nevertheless, immense progress has been made in understanding the manner in which relationships are involved in human development and adaptation. Some relatively good constructs have been devised to use in describing relationships and subjecting them to quantitative analysis. We understand a great deal about the conditions that establish relationships in the life of the child and some of the dynamics involved. We know a considerable amount about the significance of relationships with other children and the manner in which these relationships are built on earlier ones. Beginnings have been made in understanding the manner in which relationships figure in one's understanding of self and others, although much remains to be learned about the child's mental representations of these entities and how they are laid down. We remain uncertain about relationships and their role in individuation but there can be little doubt there is one. Research conducted since the early 1960s has revealed the complexity of these developmental questions, if not always a completely satisfying way to answer them.

And, so, some things about relationships and development are not new under the sun. But others are. Bridging the old and the new in an important field of knowledge is what every scientist hopes to be able to assist with. Our own good fortune—separately and together—has been to assist as best we can in constructing some of these bridges.

ACKNOWLEDGMENT

Brett Laursen received support for the preparation of this manuscript from the National Institute of Child Health and Human Development (R29 HD33006).

REFERENCES

Ainsworth, M. D. S. (1967). *Infancy in Uganda: Infant care and the growth of love.* Baltimore: Johns Hopkins University Press.

Ainsworth, M. D. S., Blehar, M. C., Waters, E., & Wall, S. (1978). *Patterns of attachment: A psychological study of the Strange Situation.* Hillsdale, NJ: Lawrence Erlbaum Associates.

Bagwell, C. L., Newcomb, A. F., & Bukowski, W. M. (1998). Preadolescent friendship and peer rejection as predictors of adult adjustment. *Child Development, 69,* 140–153.

Baldwin, J. M. (1897). *Social and ethical interpretations in mental development.* New York: Macmillan.

Baldwin, M. W. (1992). Relational schemas and cognition in close relationships. *Psychological Bulletin, 112,* 461–484.

Bandura, A. (1969). Social-learning theory of identificatory processes. In D. A. Goslin (Ed.), *Handbook of socialization theory and research* (pp. 213–262). Chicago: Rand McNally.

Bandura, A., & Huston, A. C. (1961). Identification as a process of incidental learning. *Journal of Abnormal and Social Psychology, 63,* 311–318.

Berndt, T. J. (1996). Exploring the effects of friendship quality on social development. In W. M. Bukowski, A. F. Newcomb, & W. W. Hartup (Eds.), *The company they keep* (pp. 346–365). New York: Cambridge University Press.

Berndt, T. J., & Keefe, K. (1995). Friends' influence on adolescents' adjustment to school. *Child Development, 66,* 1312–1329.

Berscheid, E., & Peplau, L. A. (1983). The emerging science of relationships. In H. H. Kelley, E. Berscheid, A. Christensen, J. H. Harvey, T. L. Huston, G. Levinger, E. McClintock, L. A. Peplau, & D. R. Peterson (Eds.), *Close relationships* (pp. 1–19). New York: W. H. Freeman.

Bowlby, J. (1951). *Maternal care and mental health.* New York: Columbia University Press.

Bowlby, J. (1958). The nature of the child's tie to his mother. *International Journal of Psychoanalysis, 39,* 350–373.

Bowlby, J. (1969). *Attachment and loss. Vol. 1: Attachment.* New York: Basic Books.

Bowlby, J. (1973). *Attachment and loss. Vol. 2: Separation.* New York: Basic Books.

Bowlby, J. (1980). *Attachment and loss. Vol. 3: Loss.* New York: Basic Books.

Bradbury, T. N., & Fincham, F. D. (1989). Behavior and satisfaction in marriage: Prospective mediation processes. In C. Hendrick (Ed.), *Close relationships* (pp. 119–143). Newbury Park, CA: Sage.

Bretherton, I. (1985). Attachment theory: Retrospect and prospect. In I. Bretherton & E. Waters (Eds.), Growing points of attachment theory and research. *Monographs of the Society for Research in Child Development, 50*(1–2, Serial No. 209).

Bronfenbrenner, U. (1960). Freudian theories of identification and their derivatives. *Child Development, 31,* 15–40.

Buhler, C. (1931). The social behavior of the child. In C. Murchison (Ed.), *A handbook of child psychology* (pp. 392–431). Worcester, MA: Clark University Press.

Bukowski, W. M., & Sippola, L. K. (1996). Friendship and morality: (How) are they related? In W. M. Bukowski, A. F. Newcomb, & W. W. Hartup (Eds.), *The company they keep* (pp. 238–261). New York: Cambridge University Press.

Cairns, R. B. (1966). Development, maintenance, and extinction of social attachment behavior in sheep. *Journal of Comparative and Physiological Psychology, 62,* 298–306.

Cairns, R. B., & Cairns, B. D. (1994). *Lifelines and risks.* New York: Cambridge University Press.

Caldwell, B. M. (1964). The effects of infant care. In M. L. Hoffman & L. W. Hoffman (Eds.), *Review of child development research* (Vol. 1, pp. 9–87). New York: Russell Sage.

Cooley, C. H. (1909). *Social organization.* New York: Scribners.

Cowan, G., Drinkard, J., & MacGavin, L. (1984). The effects of target age and gender on use of power strategies. *Journal of Personality and Social Psychology, 47,* 1391–1398.

Craik, K. (1943). *The nature of explanation.* Cambridge, England: Cambridge University Press.

Dishion, T. J., Andrews, D. W., & Crosby, L. (1995). Anti-social boys and their friends in early adolescence: Relationship characteristics, quality, and interactional process. *Child Development, 66,* 139–151.

Durkheim, E. (1951). *Suicide.* New York: Free Press. (Original work published 1897)

Erikson, E. H. (1950). *Childhood and society.* New York: Norton.

Fantz, R. L. (1963). Pattern vision in newborn infants. *Science, 140,* 296–297.

Freud, A. (1952). The mutual influences in the development of ego and id. *Psychoanalytic Study of the Child, 7,* 42–50.

Freud, S. (1940). *An outline of psychoanalysis.* New York: Norton.

Freud, S. (1953). *The interpretation of dreams.* In J. Strachey (Ed. and Trans.), *The standard edition of the complete psychological works of Sigmund Freud* (Vol. 4/5). London: Hogarth Press. (Original work published 1900)

Freud, S. (1957). On narcissism. In J. Strachey (Ed.), *The standard edition of the complete psychological works of Sigmund Freud* (Vol. 14, pp. 67–102). London: Hogarth Press. (Original work published 1914)

Gauze, C., Bukowski, W. M., Aquan-Assee, J., & Sippola, L. K. (1996). Interactions between family environment and friendship and associations with self-perceived well-being during early adolescence. *Child Development, 67,* 2201–2216.

Gewirtz, J. L. (1961). A learning analysis of the effects of normal stimulation, privation, and deprivation on the acquisition of social motivation and attachment. In B. M. Foss (Ed.), *Determinants of infant behaviour* (pp. 213–299). London: Methuen.

Gewirtz, J. L., & Stingle, K. G. (1968). The learning of generalized imitation as the basis for identification. *Psychological Review, 75,* 374–397.

Gottman, J. M. (1983). How children become friends. *Monographs of the Society for Research in Child Development, 48*(3, Serial No. 201).

Grossman, K., Fremmer-Bombeck, E., Rudolph, J., & Grossman, K. E. (1988). Maternal attachment and representations as related to patterns of infant-mother attachment and maternal care during the first year. In R. A. Hinde & J. Stevenson-Hinde (Eds.), *Relationships within families: Mutual influences* (pp. 241–260). Oxford, England: Clarendon.

Grotpeter, J. E., & Crick, N. R. (1996). Relational aggression, overt aggression, and friendship. *Child Development, 67,* 2328–2338.

Harlow, H. F. (1958). The nature of love. *American Psychologist, 13,* 673–685.

Harlow, H. F. (1969). Age-mate or peer affectional system. In D. S. Lehrman, R. A. Hinde, & E. Shaw (Eds.), *Advances in the study of behavior, Vol. 2* (pp. 333–383). New York: Academic Press.

Harlow, H. F., & Zimmerman, R. R. (1959). Affectional responses in the infant monkey. *Science, 130,* 421–432.

Hartup, W. W. (1996). Cooperation, close relationships, and cognitive development. In W. M. Bukowski, A. F. Newcomb, & W. W. Hartup (Eds.), *The company they keep* (pp. 213–237). New York: Cambridge University Press.

Hartup, W. W., & Stevens, N. (1997). Friendships and adaptation in the life course. *Psychological Bulletin, 121,* 355–370.

Hazan, C., & Shaver, P. R. (1987). Conceptualizing romantic love as an attachment process. *Journal of Personality and Social Psychology, 52,* 511–524.

Hetherington, E. M. (1967). The effects of familial variables on sex-typing, on parent-child similarity, and on imitation in children. In J. P. Hill (Ed.), *The Minnesota symposia on child psychology, Vol. 1* (pp. 82–107). Minneapolis: University of Minnesota Press.

Hinde, R. A. (1976). Interactions, relationships and social structure. *Man, 11,* 1–17.

Hinde, R. A. (1997). *Relationships: A dialectical perspective.* Hove, England: Psychology Press.

Howes, C. (1983). Patterns of friendship. *Child Development, 54,* 1041–1053.

Kagan, J. (1983). Epilogue: Classifications of the child. In P. H. Mussen (Series Ed.), W. Kessen (Vol. Ed.), *Handbook of child psychology, 3rd ed., Vol. 1: History, theory and methods* (pp. 527–560). New York: Wiley.

Kagan, J. (1984). *The nature of the child.* New York: Basic Books.

Kelley, H. H. (1979). *Personal relationships.* Hillsdale, NJ: Lawrence Erlbaum Associates.

Kelley, H. H., Berscheid, E., Christensen, A., Harvey, J. H., Huston, T. L., Levinger, G., McClintock, E., Peplau, L. A., & Peterson, D. R. (1983). *Close relationships.* New York: W. H. Freeman.

Kelley, H. H., & Thibaut, J. W. (1978). *Interpersonal relations.* New York: Wiley.

Kochanska, G. (1991). Socialization and temperament in the development of guilt and conscience. *Child Development, 62,* 1379–1392.

Ladd, G. W. (1990). Having friends, keeping friends, making friends, and being liked in the classroom: Predictors of children's early school adjustment? *Child Development, 61,* 1081–1100.

Lamb, M. E. (1977). Father-infant and mother-infant interaction in the first year of life. *Child Development, 48,* 167–181.

Lang, F. R., & Carstensen, L. L. (1994). Close emotional relationships in late life: Further support for proactive aging in the social domain. *Psychology and Aging, 9,* 315–324.

Laursen, B., & Bukowski, W. M. (1997). A developmental guide to the organisation of close relationships. *International Journal of Behavioral Development, 21,* 747–770.

Lee, L. C. (1973, August). *Social encounters of infants: The beginnings of popularity.* Paper presented at the biennial meetings of the International Society for the Study of Behavioural Development, Ann Arbor, MI.

Lorenz, K. Z. (1935). Der kumpan in der umwelt des vogels. *Journal für Ornithologie, 83,* 137–213.

Maccoby, E. E., & Martin, J. A. (1983). Socialization in the context of the family: Parent-child interaction. In P. H. Mussen (Series Ed.), E. M. Hetherington (Vol. Ed.), *Handbook of child psychology, 3rd ed., Vol. 4: Socialization, personality, and social development* (pp. 1–101). New York: Wiley.

Mahler, M. S. (1963). Thoughts about development and individuation. *Psychoanalytic Study of the Child, 18,* 307–324.

Main, M., Kaplan, N., & Cassidy, J. (1985). Security in infancy, childhood, and adulthood: A move to the level of representation. In I. Bretherton & E. Waters (Eds.), Growing points of attachment theory and research. *Monographs of the Society for Research in Child Development, 50*(1–2, Serial No. 209).

Markus, H. (1977). Self-schemata and processing information about the self. *Journal of Personality and Social Psychology, 35,* 63–78.

Mead, G. H. (1934). *Mind and society.* Chicago: University of Chicago Press.

Miller, N. E., & Dollard, J. (1941). *Social learning and imitation.* New Haven: Yale University Press.

Mischel, W. (1973). Toward a cognitive social learning theory reconceptualization of personality. *Psychological Review, 80,* 252–283.

Mitchell, S. A. (1988). *Relational concepts in psychoanalysis*. Cambridge, MA: Harvard University Press.

Mounts, N. S., & Steinberg, L. (1995). An ecological analysis of peer influence on adolescent grade point average and drug use. *Developmental Psychology, 31*, 915–922.

Munroe, R. L. (1955). *Schools of psychoanalytic thought*. New York: Dryden.

Newcomb, T. M. (1961). *The acquaintance process*. New York: Holt, Rinehart & Winston.

Ogilvie, D. M., & Ashmore, R. D. (1991). Self-with-other representation as a unit of analysis in self-concept research. In R. C. Curtis (Ed.), *The relational self* (pp. 282–314). New York: Guilford.

Parke, R. D., Cassidy, J., Burks, V. M., Carson, J. L., & Boyum, L. (1992). Familial contribution to peer competence among young children: The role of interactive and affective processes. In R. D. Parke & G. W. Ladd (Eds.), *Family-peer relationships: Modes of linkage* (pp. 107–134). Hillsdale, NJ: Lawrence Erlbaum Associates.

Parke, R. D., & Sawin, D. B. (1976). The father's role in infancy: A re-evaluation. *The Family Coordinator, 25*, 365–371.

Patterson, G. R. (1982). *Coercive family process*. Eugene, OR: Castalia.

Piaget, J. (1926). *The language and thought of the child*. New York: Harcourt, Brace & World. (Original work published 1923)

Piaget, J. (1932). *The moral judgment of the child*. New York: Harcourt, Brace & World.

Piaget, J. (1951). *Play, dreams and imitation in childhood*. New York: W. W. Norton. (Original work published 1945)

Piaget, J. (1954). *The construction of reality in the child*. New York: Basic Books. (Original work published 1937)

Radke-Yarrow, M., Campbell, J. D., & Burton, R. V. (1970). Recollections of childhood: A study of the retrospective method. *Monographs of the Society for Research in Child Development, 35*(5, Serial No. 138).

Radke-Yarrow, M., Cummings, E. M., Kuczynski, L., & Chapman, M. (1985). Patterns of attachment in two- and three-year-olds in normal families and families with parental depression. *Child Development, 56*, 884–893.

Rubin, K. H., Bukowski, W. M., & Parker, J. G. (1997). Peer interactions, relationships, and groups. In W. Damon (Series Ed.), N. Eisenberg (Vol. Ed.), *Handbook of child psychology, 5th ed, Vol. 3: Social, emotional, and personality development* (pp. 619–700). New York: Wiley.

Sander, L. W. (1975). Infant and caretaking environment. In E. J. Anthony (Ed.), *Explorations in child psychiatry* (pp. 129–166). New York: Plenum.

Schaffer, H. R., & Emerson, P. E. (1964). The development of social attachments in infancy. *Monographs of the Society for Research in Child Development, 29*(3, Serial No. 94).

Schank, R. C., & Abelson, R. P. (1977). *Scripts, plans, goals and understanding*. Hillsdale, NJ: Lawrence Erlbaum Associates.

Scott, J. P. (1963). The process of primary socialization in canine and human infants. *Monographs of the Society for Research in Child Development, 28*(1, Serial No. 85).

Sears, R. R. (1944). Experimental analysis of psychoanalytic phenomena. In J. McV. Hunt (Ed.), *Personality and the behavior disorders, Vol. 1* (pp. 306–332). New York: Ronald.

Sears, R. R. (1951). A theoretical framework for personality and social behavior. *American Psychologist, 6*, 476–483.

Siegler, R. S. (1991). *Children's thinking, 2nd ed*. Englewood Cliffs, NJ: Prentice-Hall.

Selman, R. L. (1980). *The growth of interpersonal understanding*. New York: Academic Press.

Sroufe, L. A. (1983). Infant-caregiver attachment and patterns of adaptation in preschool: The roots of maladaptation and competence. In M. Perlmutter (Ed.), *The Minnesota symposia on child psychology, Vol. 16* (pp. 41–81). Hillsdale, NJ: Lawrence Erlbaum Associates.

Sroufe, L. A. (1995). *Emotional development*. Cambridge, England: Cambridge University Press.

Sroufe, L. A., Egeland, B., & Kreutzer, T. (1990). The fate of early experience in developmental change: Longitudinal approaches to individual adaptation in child development. *Child Development, 61,* 1363–1373.

Sullivan, H. S. (1953). *The interpersonal theory of psychiatry.* New York: Norton.

Thompson, R. A. (1997). Early sociopersonality development. In W. Damon (Series Ed.), N. Eisenberg (Vol. Ed.), *Handbook of child psychology, 5th ed., Vol. 3: Social, emotional, and personality development* (pp. 25–104). New York: Wiley.

Vygotsky, L. S. (1978). *Mind in society: The development of higher psychological processes.* Cambridge, MA: Harvard University Press.

Watson, J. S. (1966). The development and generalization of "contingency awareness" in early infancy: Some hypotheses. *Merrill-Palmer Quarterly, 12,* 123–135.

Whiting, J. W. M., & Child, I. M. (1957). *Child training and personality.* New Haven, CT: Yale University Press.

Young, J. Z. (1964). *A model of the brain.* London: Oxford University Press.

Youniss, J. (1975). Another perspective on social cognition. In A. D. Pick (Ed.), *The Minnesota symposia on child psychology, Vol. 9* (pp. 173–193). Minneapolis: University of Minnesota Press.

Chapter 3

Interpersonal Support and Individual Development

Cornelis F. M. van Lieshout
University of Nijmegen, The Netherlands

Antonius H. N. Cillessen
University of Connecticut, Storrs

Gerbert J. T. Haselager
University of Nijmegen, The Netherlands

The conceptual framework presented in this chapter builds a connection between individual development and the social context of such development. We use the metaphor of developmental tasks to describe and understand development (Baltes, Reese, & Lipsitt, 1980; Havighurst, 1973; Smitsman & van Lieshout, 1992). Individuals encounter a developmental task as a thematically coherent series of problems that must be solved in order to adequately adjust to new demands or take advantage of new opportunities. These developmental tasks are encountered in a context, and this context is, to a large degree, socially determined. Social context is defined as the constraints or opportunities elicited from others. Such opportunities and constraints occur within the interactions, relationships, and groups in which individuals participate across the life span. Three hierarchical levels are thus distinguished within the social context: *interactions, relationships,* and *groups* (Hinde, 1976, 1995; Rubin, Bukowski, & Parker, 1997; van Lieshout, 1995; van Lieshout & van Aken, 1995).

The connections between a person's development and his or her social contexts are manifest in four problem-solving modalities: cognition, behavioral execution, experience of affect, and goal orientation. These problem-solving modalities also correspond to the basic elements of social interaction: the exchange of knowledge, behavior regulation, the exchange of affect, and opposition or facilitation of goal achievement. Partners in a dyadic relationship may differ in terms of these four modalities and how they manifest themselves in social interactions. These differences concern expertise, power, trust versus distrust, and convergence versus opposition of goals. The interpersonal support that partners in a relationship offer each other consists of providing quality information versus withholding information or deception, seeking a balance between respect for autonomy and setting limits on behavior, warmth versus hostility, and acceptance versus rejection of each other's goal orientations. Interactions in groups also reflect the aforementioned modalities as interactions can be based on shared meaning systems, dominance, attraction versus rejection, and agreement versus divergence of group goals.

The developmental tasks of individuals and their social context provide both continuity and discontinuity across the life span. There is continuity when the dimensions of the developmental tasks and personality remain the same across long life episodes and can be assessed using similar measures at different ages. The social context is continuous when it remains comparable across the life span and can be similarly measured across different relationships and groups. Continuity of behavioral and personality dimensions and of social contexts is a prerequisite for the assessment of long-term developmental and contextual change and stability. Development may be marked also by discontinuity, as a consequence of changes in developmental tasks and social contexts across the life course. Such discontinuity typically produces qualitative changes in behavior and social interactions.

We introduce our conceptual framework with a consideration of individual development in terms of developmental tasks and the development of personality. The social context is then discussed in terms of interactions, relationships, and groups. General characteristics of individual development and interpersonal support are elaborated for specific relationships and specific groups, and we conclude with some observations about the continuity and discontinuity of developmental tasks and social contexts across the life course.

INDIVIDUAL DEVELOPMENT

Developmental Tasks

Prior to birth and throughout life, development is shaped by biological and maturational opportunities and restrictions, contextual opportunities and limitations, and specific personal choices. The various developmental tasks confronted by the individual require the reorganization of behavior in specific domains. Reorganization is necessary to adjust to the changes occurring in the self and the environment, and people often experience such reorganization as a sequence of problems or challenges spread across a number of years. Reorganization is goal oriented and often reflects an implicit hierarchy of goals. Developmental tasks are unavoidable, and their solution typically produces the competence needed to cope with subsequent developmental tasks. Failure to solve a developmental task can put an individual at risk for failure to resolve later tasks. Some developmental tasks are largely normative and occur for almost every person at about the same point in the life cycle. Other developmental tasks may be normative because they are historically determined for all members of a specific cohort in a given society. Still other developmental tasks may be nonnormative because they involve only some people at different points across the life course (Baltes et al., 1980; Havighurst, 1973; Smitsman & van Lieshout, 1992).

We distinguish four modalities in an individual's solving of developmental tasks (see Table 3.1, col. 5): cognition (perception, thinking, reasoning, and information processing), emotionality and affect, behavioral execution or acting, and goal orientation (intentionality, motivation and will). The goal orientation differs for developmental tasks in the social and nonsocial domains (see Table 3.1, col. 6). Goals in the nonsocial domain typically concern the achievement of standards of excellence; goals in the social domain typically concern the interrelatedness of the actor's interests with the interests of his or her interaction partners. The cognitive modality concerns an individual's flexibility in analyzing problem situations and generating solutions in the nonsocial domain (Sternberg, 1986) and the flexibility of social–cognitive information processing in the social domain (Crick & Dodge, 1994). Behavioral execution concerns regulation of problem-solving behavior in the nonsocial domain and such forms of social behavior as cooperation, competition, aggression, and altruism in the social domain. Affect in the nonsocial domain concerns the anticipation of success or failure and concomitant interest and involvement or fear of failure and aversion. Affect in the social domain concerns a range of emotions including pleasure in relationships and feelings of security or anger, disappointment, distress, guilt or shame.

Personality Development

We assume that an individual's personality codetermines the individual's style of adjusting to developmental tasks and the types of adjustment problems that he or she experiences (Rothbart, Ahadi, & Hershey, 1994). We define personality as genetically influenced behavioral styles that typify individuals across different situations and different points in time, and that manifest themselves in concrete behavioral responses and potential adjustment problems.

Personality development has been described in terms of the Big-Five personality dimensions (Goldberg, 1990), which relate to the four prob-

TABLE 3.1
Modalities of Problem Solving in Developmental Tasks, Personality, and Interpersonal Support in Interactions, Relationships, and Groups

(1) Groups	(2) Dyadic Relationships — Dimensions of Relationships	(3) Interpersonal Support	(4) Interactions	(5) Problem-Solving Modalities	(6) Developmental Tasks — Social Domain	(6) Developmental Tasks — Nonsocial Domain	(7) Personality Dimensions
Shared Meaning Systems	Expertise	Quality Information vs. Deception	Exchange of Knowledge/Information	Cognition (Thinking)	Flexibility of Information Processing		Openness
Dominance Hierarchy, Coalitions, Conformism	Power	Autonomy vs. Limit Setting	Behavior Regulation	Behavioral Execution (Acting)	Active/Passive Behavioral Execution		Extraversion
Cohesion	Trust vs. Distrust	Warmth vs. Hostility	Exchange of Affect	Affect (Feeling)	Pleasure, Interest vs. Aversion, Anxiety		Emotional Stability
Group Goals, Norms, Values	Convergence vs. Opposition of Goals	Acceptance vs. Rejection of Goals	Facilitation vs. Opposition of Goal Achievement	Goal Orientation, Intentionality (Will)	Inter-related Interests	Standards of Excellence	Agreeableness Conscientiousness

Note. Adapted from van Lieshout (1995). Reprinted with permission of van Gorcum & Comp. BV.

lem-solving modalities (see Table 3.1, col. 7). Openness concerns the flexibility of information processing in both the social and nonsocial domains. Extraversion versus introversion concerns activity or passivity in behavioral execution. Emotional Stability concerns the regulation of emotions in both the social and nonsocial domains. Agreeableness concerns the interrelatedness of one's own interests with those of the interaction partner (i.e., the social domain), whereas Conscientiousness concerns the achievement of standards of excellence (i.e., the nonsocial domain). Agreeableness and Conscientiousness are specifically related to goal orientations in the social and nonsocial domains, respectively. The three remaining Big-Five personality dimensions apply to both the social and nonsocial domains.

In several studies (Scholte, van Aken, & van Lieshout, 1997; van Lieshout & Haselager, 1994), we have shown how Big-Five personality dimensions can be used to describe the personalities of children and adolescents as well as adults. In a longitudinal study of middle childhood to early adolescence, a person-centered approach was adopted for the study of personality development (van Lieshout, Haselager, Riksen-Walraven, & van Aken, 1995). The personality patterns of children were found to be related to adjustment to developmental tasks in a number of different domains. Different patterns of personality development across the elementary school years, for example, were differentially related to the children's school achievement, peer acceptance, and peer rejection.

In sum, individual development is conceptualized as adjustment to developmental tasks, and the pattern of personality development that accompanies such adjustment. The individual encounters a number of challenges and problems in both social and nonsocial contexts. In the following sections, individual development in the context of interactions, relationships, and groups is considered.

SOCIAL CONTEXT

Individual development is embedded in a social context. That is, individuals participate in a myriad of interactions across the life span. These interactions take place in the here-and-now but are also part of a network of relationships that often extend across the life span. These relationships are typically embedded in family groups, school classes, sport teams, or professional settings but they also extend across groups and social arenas.

Interactions

An interaction is defined as an action (X) that person A directs at person B, who then responds with an action (Y) (Hinde, 1976). Actions X and Y are described in a neutral manner, as if they are random actions and reactions from an infinite set of possible actions and reactions. This definition suggests that the individuals are meeting for the first time but, in reality, interactions typically include the actions and reactions of individuals with an already established or vested interest in the interaction (Clark & Reis, 1988).

Because of their interdependent nature, interactions are described as *transactions* or sequences of actions and reactions in which partners exchange interests, support, hostilities, care, materials, or information. For this reason, interactions almost always contribute to the strengthening, maintenance, or weakening of relationships and thereby constitute the bidirectional building blocks of interpersonal relationships.

In our model, interactions are characterized by four tendencies related to the four basic problem-solving modalities: knowledge exchange, behavior regulation, emotional exchange, and the facilitation or opposition of goal achievement (Table 3.1, col. 4). In each interaction, participants exchange information, regulate their own and their partner's behavior, mutually express emotions, and provide feedback with regard to goals and achievements (see also Kelley et al., 1983). Partners in an interaction explain why they engage or do not engage in certain behaviors, encourage each other to engage in or refrain from certain behaviors, threaten each other or provide security, and support or oppose each other's goal achievement. Providing information, encouragement, security, and support are the determinants of interactions with a positive valence. Withholding information, discouragement, threats, and goal opposition are the determinants of interactions with a negative valence. The four tendencies are elaborated in the following sections.

Social Information Processing. The processing of social information is an inherent part of any social interaction sequence. According to Crick and Dodge (1994), processing social information in interactions proceeds through a series of steps. An individual enters the interaction with expectations based on previous social experiences. These expectations guide the individual's encoding and interpretation of cues with regard to the intentions and motives of the interaction partner. Children frequently confronted with aggression, for example, are likely to attribute hostile intent to an interaction partner (Dodge, 1986). The child selects a behavioral response for subsequent enactment based on this interpretation. The interaction partner follows a similar sequence of steps, so interactions are influenced by ongoing and parallel sequences of social information processing.

Deficiencies in interactions may be the result of deficiencies in any of the social-information steps. Antisocial behavior, for example, may arise when children misinterpret a partner's intentions, miscalculate the consequences of their own behavior, or simply lack the appropriate behavioral response (Crick & Dodge, 1994).

Persistent Interactive Orientations. Across time, an individual's social interactions reveal what may be labeled persistent interactive orientations or modes of behavior. These refer to the stable behavioral predispositions that individuals display in their interactions with others. Three major interactive orientations are antisocial behavior, behavioral inhibition and withdrawal, and social responsibility. Hartup and van Lieshout (1995) recently described the developmental pathways for these social–behavioral orientations and demonstrated a sizable amount of stability in the characteristic ways that an individual interacts with others. Similarly, a longitudinal study identified clusters of boys with stable prosocial orientations and boys with stable antisocial orientations across the elementary school years (Haselager, Cillessen, Hartup, van Lieshout, & Riksen-Walraven, 1997). The stability of these behavioral orientations did not go unnoticed by peers, moreover, as concomitant patterns of peer acceptance and rejection were also found.

Affect Recognition and Regulation. The recognition of affect and the regulation of emotions play an important role at the level of interactions. Adequate interactions require competence in this domain. The role of affect in interactions has been clearly illustrated in research with infants. Malatesta and Haviland (1982) demonstrated that the facial expressions of infants trigger consistent maternal responses. Mothers of 3-month-old infants reacted positively to their children's positive emotions, and neutrally or negatively to their children's negative emotions. As a consequence of this interactive pattern, infants learned to express positive emotions more frequently than negative emotions by the age of 6 months. Thus, the socialization of positive emotions in interactions starts at an early age and continues to be an important part of social interactive behavior during subsequent stages of development.

Intentions and Goal Orientations. The efficient modulation of goals in response to the goal orientations or intentions of others is essential for competent interactions. Children infer the intentions and goals of others and learn to coordinate their own intentions and goals with those of others, even when they are incompatible. Three levels in the growth of children's understanding and the use of intentionality have been distinguished (Meltzoff, 1995; Searle, 1983).

An early indicator of children's understanding of intent is the ability to synchronize their actions with the perceived intentions of others. The first coordination of intentions occurs when newborns match their body movements to the goals perceived in the simple motor patterns of adults (Meltzoff & Moore, 1977). The early coordination of intentions has been observed also in the interactions of infants with peers. Synchronized social interaction in the form of mutual imitation and turn taking has been observed in unfamiliar dyads of 12-month-old children (van Lieshout, van IJzendoorn, & de Roos, 1993).

A second level in the understanding of intentions occurs when children perceive the behavior of others as intentions in actions or the intentions of actors. This level is reached around the age of 18 months when infants begin to imitate the intended actions of others. For example, Meltzoff (1995) has demonstrated how 18-month-old infants can infer the intention behind the actions that adults attempted but failed to perform.

The third level develops around 3 years of age with the capacity to reflect on intentions as mental states occurring in the mind of the actor prior to the act. This development in the understanding of intentionality has been demonstrated in reasoning about the intentionality of interactions characterized by moral transgressions. Children between 5 and 15 years old are increasingly capable of considering intentionality as a determinant of personal responsibility in situations where harm has been done (Olthof, 1990; Olthof, Ferguson, & Luiten, 1989). In addition, children are increasingly able to weigh intentionality against other information that might influence the attribution of personal responsibility, such as the avoidability of an outcome or the presence of extenuating circumstances.

Relationships

Thus far, we have discussed interactions without considering their role in the formation and maintenance of relationships. Interactions, especially long chains of interactive sequences, clearly contribute to the formation of relationships. Individuals participate in a network of personal relationships, including parent–child, child–sibling, teacher–student, and friend relationships. Relationships are dyadic in nature. Each involves one person and a single other person.

There are many differences in relationships. For example, relationships with parents and siblings have a biological background; other relationships arise from societal roles, such as teacher–student or employer–employee; still other relationships are based on personal engagement, such as friendships. Many relationships have multiple backgrounds, for example, relationships between parents and their adopted children. Some relationships are symmetrical and horizontal, for example, among colleagues and classmates, whereas others are asymmetrical and vertical, for example, a teacher–student relationship (Hartup, 1989). Some are voluntary, such as friendships and partner relationships in Western societies, and others are involuntary, such as relationships in one's family of origin. Some relationships involve a person's full functioning, such as an early child–mother relationship, and others are limited to specific functional domains, such as those among sport teammates. Some are permanent and some are fleeting.

Despite differences in relationships, *each* relationship contains *four common dimensions* (see Table 3.1, col. 2). These underlying dimensions correspond to the four problem-solving modalities of cognition, behavior execution, emotionality, and goal orientation. Two people in a relationship may be similar or different in their level of *expertise*, knowledge and skill within a domain or domains. They may differ also with regard to *power*, the degree to which one person can prompt or urge the other to execute specific behaviors and the degree to which the other accepts such prompting. The degree to which the people in a relationship *trust or distrust* each other may vary, as can the degree to which they share *convergent or opposite goal orientations.*

Each relationship can be characterized according to these four relational dimensions. For example, a parent–child relationship is characterized by inequality of expertise (parent has greater expertise, child has less), inequality of power (parent regulates behavior, child is regulated), complementary emotions (parent provides security, child needs security), and convergent goal orientations (parent raises the child, child seeks to be raised). In contrast, a friendship is marked by equal or similar levels of expertise, nearly equal power, reciprocity in the provision of and search for emotional support, and convergent or mutually attuned goal orientations. In general, friends have the same level of expertise or their expertise oscillates around the same level; they are equally able to regulate each other's behavior; they both provide mutual security or intimacy; and their goal orientations are convergent in a number of functional domains.

The four dimensions of relationships are paralleled by four *dimensions of relational support* (see Table 3.1, col. 3). These dimensions concern acceptance versus rejection of each other's goal orientations; provision of quality information versus no information or misleading information; the balance between respect for autonomy and setting limits (i.e., coregulation of behavior); and warmth versus hostility in emotional exchanges (Maccoby & Martin, 1983).

Acceptance or rejection of goal orientations seems to affect the other dimensions of relational support. Under conditions of mutually accepted goal orientations, interactions are more frequently characterized by warmth than by hostility; partners respect each other's autonomy and do not consider it necessary to set limits on each other's behavior; and partners communicate and exchange information openly. When goal orientations converge and are accepted, even conflict can make a constructive contribution to the realization of common goals (Laursen & Collins, 1994). Conflicts may be manifest as opposition in behavioral interactions, as differences of opinion with regard to how common goals should or can be reached, as disagreement on informational content or on the manner of exchange, as disagreement on the regulation of behavior, and as opposing exchanges of emotion. Such conflicts can lead to specification of goals for subsequent interactions, explanation of information and points of view, coregulation of behavior, and clarification of the feelings of the interaction partners. In such conflict situations, the shared goal orientations of the partners are not at stake.

When the goal orientations of partners are in conflict, the developmental tasks confronting individuals in the relationship are often incompatible. Opposition of goal orientations can break up voluntary relationships and turn involuntary relationships into a problem, such as, when parents prohibit drug use and adolescents move into the drug scene. Long-standing friendships between children can end when one of the partners matures earlier than the other and thereby develops more "adult" goal orientations. Under conditions of opposing goal orientations, interactions can become contradictory. Conflicts involving goal achievement, the exchange of information, the regulation of behavior, and feelings tend to be serious and often do not get resolved.

Personal Relationships in a Network. As already noted, individuals are typically involved in a number of relationships. One's personal network of relationships crosses the boundaries of groups such as the family, the school class, or the professional team. This personal network of relationships can be studied from either a variable-centered perspective or a person-centered perspective.

In several variable-centered studies (Furman & Buhrmester, 1985, 1992; van Aken & Asendorpf, 1997), similarities and differences in the perceptions of conflict, relative power, and emotional support have been identified for different members of a network (i.e., mother, father, sibling, teacher, same-sex friend, romantic friend). The variables examined in these studies correspond to three of the four dimensions of relational support specified here (see Table 3.1, col. 3), and the findings are in keeping with current theories of the development of personal relationships. During middle childhood and adolescence in particular, changes occur in the supportive functions of different relationships. Parents remain frequent providers of support, but same-sex friends in early adolescence and romantic partners in late adolescence gain importance. Adolescents appear to distance themselves from their families and invest more time and energy in peer relationships (primarily same-sex relationships initially, but eventually romantic relationships also). Advances in cognitive abilities facilitate self-exploration and the consensual validation of the adolescent's self-concept. Adolescents may join agemates in discussing matters related to sexual maturation and physical appearance. Interest in and concern for matters outside of the family may also emerge in connection with the adolescent's ongoing search for autonomy and increased emotional independence from his or her parents. Young adults may seek romantic involvement to meet the need for a long-lasting relationship and sexual intimacy. In sum, specific relationships play different roles at different points in time and they differ with regard to information, behavior regulation, emotional support, and goal orientations.

In a person-centered approach to the study of relational networks, the focus is on within-person comparisons across partners. A comprehensive set of characteristics is usually examined instead of single dimensions. For example, van Aken, van Lieshout, and Haselager (1996) examined the degree of agreement between the view that adolescents have of themselves and the view that their significant others (i.e., parents, teachers, and best friends) have of them. Agreement increased with age and was typically higher for girls. Older adolescents appear to know themselves better than younger adolescents and have growing insight into their own functioning. Adolescent girls are ahead of boys in this respect, but this difference disappears in late adolescence or early adulthood (Cohn, 1991). Older adolescents increasingly use the same criteria as others to describe themselves, which also leads to a higher concordance between the views of the adolescents and the views of the significant others. Self-parent and self-peer agreement was also found to be higher than self-teacher agreement, which presumably reflects the differential importance of settings and relationships. Agreement was also related to competence in several domains, including school achievement, peer acceptance, and self-esteem. The findings were interpreted in terms of the supportive functions of personal relationships. The agreement of self-descriptions and descriptions by others reflects not only the accuracy of the self-description but the embeddedness of a person in a network of relationships. Agreement between an adolescent's self-description and the descriptions provided by important others is one of the ways in which relational embeddedness operates on the psychological adjustment of the adolescent. Social-support theories emphasize the importance of feelings of embeddedness for the psychological adjustment of a person, and research findings support this claim (Sarason, Pierce, Bannerman, & Sarason, 1993). Although the model presented in this chapter pertains to any relationship, we limit our discussion in the following sections to parent–child and peer relationships.

Parent–Child Relationships. A number of studies have shown that the quality of parent–child interactions and the security of their attachment have clear developmental implications. Responsiveness of the primary caretaker contributes to the quality of the infant–caretaker attachment (Isabella, 1993; van den Boom, 1994; Vereijken, Riksen-Walraven, & Kondo-

Ikemura, 1997), and securely attached toddlers, as opposed to those who are insecurely attached, tend to be better problem solvers, more cooperative and compliant in interactions with their mothers, and share more positive emotions with their mothers. Securely attached toddlers are also more attractive playmates for their peers in later years. With the exception of a few short-term intervention studies (van den Boom, 1994), however, the foregoing findings are all correlational. A causal relation between sensitive parenting and the security of attachment and later developmental functions has yet to be demonstrated.

In two intervention studies, Riksen-Walraven and her coworkers attempted to enhance the quality of parent-infant interaction in order to prevent educational lags in children from disadvantaged lower-class and minority families. The first intervention study (Riksen-Walraven, 1978), directed at lower-class parents with 9- to 12-month-old infants, was aimed at improving two aspects of parental support: responsiveness to the infant's signals and the amount and variety of perceptual–cognitive stimulation provided. The second study (Riksen-Walraven, Meij, Hubbard, & Zevalkink, 1996), directed at Dutch-Surinam minority parents with 13- to 18-month-old babies, was devised to improve the quality of parental support on dimensions deemed important for development in the second year of life: supportive presence, or the provision of adequate emotional support when needed and the avoidance of hostility; respect for autonomy, or allowing children to experience their own competence; structure and limit setting, or adequate structuring of the situation with clear and consistent limits; and the quality of instruction, or provision of adequate instruction (Erickson, Sroufe, & Egeland, 1985). Parental responsiveness and the provision of perceptual–cognitive stimulation in the first study are conceptually related to the supportive presence and quality of instruction identified in the second study. Respect for autonomy and limit setting are particularly relevant for infants in the second year of life. The dimensions of parental support isolated in these experiments correspond to three of the four dimensions of relational support specified in the present model (see Table 3.1, col. 3). The fourth dimension or a convergence of goal orientation is presupposed when the parents agree to participate in the intervention program. By accepting the goals of the intervention program, the goal orientations of the parents converge with the interests of the child.

Both studies found positive effect for these interventions on several aspects of parental support. As expected, the interventions also positively affected infants competence in several domains. In the first study, increased parental responsiveness predicted ego-resiliency across the elementary school years, although only for girls. Girls whose parents participated in the responsiveness program clearly benefitted between the ages of 1 and 7 years, and the benefits remained throughout the elementary school years

(Riksen-Walraven & van Aken, 1997). These studies show that most dimensions of parental support contribute to the long-term development of competence in children and that it is possible to enhance parental behavior along these dimensions.

Friendships. Most individuals are involved in friendships throughout their lives, and most friendships are long-lasting relationships. A number of studies have tried to specify the developmental significance of friendships (see Bukowski, Newcomb, & Hartup, 1996; Hartup, 1996; Hartup & Stevens, 1997). A recent meta-analysis comparing the behavioral and affective characteristics of friend and nonfriend relationships among children revealed differences in four domains (Newcomb & Bagwell, 1995). Friendships were characterized by (a) more positive engagement, (b) more efficient conflict management, (c) stronger task orientation in joint tasks, and (d) relational properties such as reciprocal and intimate affiliation, similarity, equality, mutual liking, closeness, loyalty, and lower dominance and power assertion.

Hartup (1996, p. 4) relates the observed differences between friends and nonfriends to four "cognitive and motivational conditions" that closely resemble the four problem-solving modalities and concomitant characteristics of relationships specified in this chapter.

1. Friends know one another better than nonfriends and share joint domains of interest. They are able to communicate with one another more effectively, share common expertise, and exchange information with regard to the content of their friendship.

2. Friends have more common expectations than nonfriends, particularly with regard to assistance and support. In regulating each other's behavior, equality and similarity prevail over dominance and power assertion.

3. An affective climate more favorable to exploration and problem solving exists between friends than nonfriends.

4. The content of friendships implies common goals and convergent goal orientations. Friendships are voluntary. A serious opposition of goals can disrupt a friendship. Nevertheless friends more readily seek to resolve disagreements and thereby support continued interaction than nonfriends.

Having friends provides a context for social and emotional growth. Between 80% and 90% of all individuals are involved in a mutual friendship, with some differences depending on age, gender, and living conditions (van der Linden & Dijkman, 1989). Children who have friends are more socially competent and less troubled than children who do not have friends. Troubled children and those referred to a clinic are more frequently found to have no friends than nontroubled or nonreferred children. Although friends provide a supportive context for adjusting to the diversity of developmental tasks and adverse circumstances, Hartup (1996) warns that the quality of friendship is confounded by the simple fact of having friends. Having friends is typically associated with other supportive circumstances that make it hard to disentangle the effects of having friends from these circumstances.

Who are children's friends? Empirical evidence supports the similarity–attraction hypothesis (cf. Hartup, 1996). Individuals generally choose friends who resemble themselves. Common ground, or common sociodemographic characteristics such as chronological age, neighborhood, school grade, and ethnic background, may contribute to the similarity of friends. The similarity of friends also extends to behavior. In school classes, for example, friends are found to be more similar than nonfriends in prosocial and antisocial behavior, shyness/dependency, sociometric status, and depressive symptoms. Friends are also more similar than nonfriends in social perceptions of others. That is, friends evaluations of classmates' behaviors resemble each other more than nonfriends (Haselager, Hartup, van Lieshout, & Riksen-Walraven, 1998). These similarities foster within-friendship support. Friends with similar backgrounds, expertise and skills, affective orientations, and common goals seem most effective in supporting each other. Friends provide mutual socialization within their domains of interests, independent of whether the goals are prosocial or antisocial.

Bully–Victim Relationships. According to Olweus (1993), an individual is being bullied or victimized when he or she is repeatedly exposed to the negative actions of others. These negative actions are essentially aggressive behaviors that take many forms including direct bullying (i.e., relatively open verbal or physical attacks on a victim) and indirect bullying (i.e., intentional exclusion from a group and social isolation). The different forms of bullying often co-occur and are highly interrelated. Bullying is distinct from a single incidental aggressive act as the negative actions involved in bullying are deliberately and repeatedly aimed at the same target over time. Characteristic of bullying is an imbalance in the power and strength of the perpetrator and the victim. Typically victims are unable to defend themselves through actions, words, or forging alliances.

A bully–victim relationship is an asymmetric power relationship, and this asymmetry distinguishes the relationship from all other peer relationships. In a bully–victim relationship, partners have similar expectations about forthcoming interactions ("If we meet, there will be bullying"), show opposite behaviors in an asymmetric power relationship ("I will attack him or her" vs. "I will be attacked/I will not be able to resist"), experience different emotions ("I will have fun" vs. "I will be afraid and distressed"), and have opposite goal orientations ("I will look for him or her" vs. "I want to avoid him or her").

One might claim bullying occurs in a relationship although this is not the complete story. Haselager (1997) recently found support for a three-level model of bullying and victimization, involving the individual, relational, and group levels. Perpetrators and victims have different individual characteristics (Farrington, 1993; Olweus, 1993) and bully–victim relationships usually occur in the context of a group. In a large sample of 2,300 elementary-school children, Haselager (1997) distinguished four categories of involvement in bullying: noninvolved, bully, victim, or bully/victim. Each child was classified according to his or her involvement in bullying at the individual, relational, and group levels. Configurations (so-called Types) that occurred more often than expected by chance were next identified using configurational frequency analysis (von Eye, 1990). One type was children identified as a bully at all three levels; a second type was children identified as victims at all three levels. These types were then qualified according to peer and self-reported adjustment measures. The results indicated that involvement in bullying at each of the three levels contributed independently to the prediction of children's self-reported adjustment (e.g., social isolation, depressive symptoms) and peer-reported adjustment (e.g., peer acceptance, shyness/withdrawal). For a subsample of approximately 200 boys, bullying in the later elementary-school years was predicted by teacher-reported personality measures 4 and 5 years earlier. Agreeableness was the only personality dimension, however, to significantly contribute to the prediction of the later type of involvement in bullying.

In sum, individual involvement in bullying, acknowledgment of involvement in bullying by both partners, and one's reputation with regard to such involvement contribute independently to the prediction of individual adjustment in elementary-school children. The type of bullying involvement is predicted by early Agreeableness.

Groups

Interpersonal relationships are embedded in social groups, which are defined as collections of individuals who develop and maintain relationships in a systemic context. The structure of such groups can be described in terms of the nature, quality, and pattern of the component relationships (Hinde, 1976, 1995). The four modalities that characterize interactions in relationships also characterize interactions in groups (see Table 3.1, col. 1). First, information exchanges in groups are based on shared meaning systems, which are based on a common philosophy of life or common cultural values. Second, the behavior of group members is largely regulated by group structure (e.g., dominance hierarchies, coalitions) and group dynamics (e.g., conformity). Third, the nature of the emotional exchanges within the group can determine the specific patterns of attraction and rejection, and the overall level of group cohesion. Fourth, group members can either share common goals or be opposed, which will strongly influence subsequent group interactions (Hartup, 1983).

Two types of groups have been studied extensively by developmental scholars. First, a large body of research exists on Family interactions and relationships. Second, Peer interactions and relationships have been studied, primarily within the school context. Each of these two types of social groups is considered.

Family Groups. A family is a complex interconnected system of individuals and relationships (Belsky & Isabella, 1988). Each family member plays a unique role with specific role-related behaviors and a separate developmental orientation and trajectory (Hartup, 1989). The developmental trajectories of family members are also interconnected. For example, the parent–child relationship is complementary (the parent raises the child; the child is raised) and asynchronous (the parent develops at a slower pace than the child). Sibling relationships are also complementary and asynchronous (Hartup, 1989).

Consideration of the family as a system implies that each family member's behavior depends, in part, on the behavior of other family members. The relationship between two family members can, in turn, influence a third. Two hypotheses exist with regard to interconnections between marital relationships and parent–child relationships. Erel and Burman (1995) considered the evidence for the *spillover hypothesis,* which predicts a positive correlation between the qualities of marital and parent–child relationships. Strong support for this hypothesis was found to suggest that parents with a satisfying and supportive relationship are more capable of responding sensitively to the needs of their children than parents in conflict. Van Aken and Asendorpf (1997) reported support for the *compensatory hypothesis,* which suggests that a positive relationship with one parent compensates for and buffers against negative family influences. A positive mother–child relationship, for example, compensated for the detrimental effects of a negative father–child relationship in the development of children's self-esteem.

Going beyond correlational findings, increased marital conflict has been shown to predict increased externalizing and internalizing problems and decreased marital conflict has been shown to predict decreased problem behaviors among children (Grych & Fincham, 1990). The negative effects of parental conflict on children were stronger when the conflict was frequent, physical, distressing, and visible; when the conflict concerned the child; and when the conflict remained unresolved.

These findings suggest a one-way influence of parental conflict on children, but children also influence the quality of parental relations. As recently demonstrated by van Lieshout, de Meyer, Curfs, and Fryns (1998), the behavior of children born with a genetic dysfunction impact both the child-rearing behaviors of parents and the parent–child relationship in general. In other words, family influences should be conceptualized as bidirectional. The behaviors of parents influence the behaviors of their children, and the characteristics of children elicit characteristic behaviors from parents and siblings. Such bidirectional family influences produce transactional processes across the course of development and thereby influence long-term developmental outcomes.

Peer Groups in the School Context. Across development, children increasingly spend time in interactions outside the family, in peer groups that have been studied most frequently in the context of schools. At the dyadic level, peer relationships can be friendships, bully–victim relations, or romantic relationships. At the group level, peer relations are usually measured with sociometric methods that classify children according to one of five sociometric status groups: popular, rejected, neglected, controversial, or average.

In numerous studies, children's peer relations, measured in terms of sociometric status, have been found to be associated with other measures of social competence and adjustment. Of particular interest are those children who have the most difficulties in their interactions with peers, that is, children who are rejected or neglected. In a meta-analytic review comparing different sociometric status groups on aggression, sociability, withdrawal, and academic or intellectual ability, Newcomb, Bukowski, and Pattee (1993) found rejected-status children to be more aggressive and withdrawn, and less sociable and cognitively skilled than average-status children. The finding that the rejected group stands out on aggression and withdrawal is somewhat surprising, and it has been suggested on the basis of this finding that the rejected group is heterogeneous, with aggressive-rejected and withdrawn-rejected subgroups. Cillessen, van IJzendoorn, van Lieshout, and Hartup (1992) found about half of the rejected boys in their study to be aggressive, impulsive, and disruptive. Another third of the rejected boys were withdrawn, anxious, prone to depression, and low in self-esteem. Whereas aggressive-rejected children tended to initiate fights with peers, withdrawn-rejected children tended to attract attention because of their overly dependent behaviors and ineffective attention seeking. Aggressive-rejected children are also more likely to become bullies, and withdrawn-rejected children are more likely to become victims (de Poorte, Veling, Haselager, & van Lieshout, 1994).

Children in the neglected group appear to experience few adjustment difficulties. They seem to prefer little involvement with the group, which leads to low social visibility. They are indifferent to the group and the group may not be very prominent for them. Neglected-status children are less aggressive and less sociable than average-status children but no more socially anxious, withdrawn, or depressed than average-status children (Newcomb et al., 1993). Neglected children often have a reciprocal best friend and average friendship skills (de Poorte et al., 1994). The limited number of behavioral problems characteristic of these children suggests that they are not at risk for later problems.

Given differences in social competence associated with differences in children's peer-group status, researchers have questioned the stability of measures of sociometric status. A distinction has been made between continuous measures of children's group relations (e.g., social preference) and categorical measures of group relations (e.g., sociometric status types). The stability of continuous measures has been addressed in a large number of studies that demonstrated modest to high stability coefficients across varying methodologies and samples (Cillessen, Bukowski, & Haselager, 1997). The stability of the categorical status types has been studied less frequently and is more modest. The data suggest that the popular and rejected groups are the most stable status types. At least moderate stability of peer social status exists over time, although this conclusion is qualified by the age group studied and the measures used (Cillessen et al., 1997).

A large number of longitudinal studies have traced the development of peer relations and social competence from infancy through early adulthood. In one such study, de Roos (1995) investigated the antecedents of various aspects of peer competence in kindergarten. The antecedents investigated at 12, 24, and 42 months of age were child characteristics (temperament and signaling behavior), maternal sensitivity (responsiveness and interference), security of mother–child attachment, and antagonism and affiliation in dyadic play sessions. The aspects of peer competence studied were social cognitions, interactive behaviors in class, interactive behaviors in small play groups (triads), and peer evaluations. The results revealed a complex pattern of relations between early antecedents and later aspects of peer competence. The predictive power of the antecedents depended on the age of the subject and the aspect of peer competence being examined. Difficult temperament and maternal interference were the best predictors of lower levels of prosocial cognitions and prosocial behavior in triads, higher levels of antisocial behavior in classes, and higher antagonism and withdrawal in peer evaluations. From the age of 12 months, early antagonism was uniquely and positively related to antisocial behavior in triads; from the age of 24 months, early antagonism was uniquely and negatively related to peer evaluations of withdrawal. Early affiliation did not predict any aspect of peer competence in kindergarten. Early negative signals predicted later prosocial behavior in triads and peer evaluations of affiliation and withdrawal. Gender differences were also observed for the prediction of later peer competence. Early antecedents predicted later peer competence better for kindergarten girls than for boys. In sum, the results indicate that peer competence at 5 years of age is anticipated by child characteristics, mother–child characteristics, and peer competence four years earlier.

Various follow-forward and follow-back studies have examined the implications of children's peer competence in elementary school for later long-term development (Parker & Asher, 1987). Relations between peer difficulties at an early age and subsequent school dropout, juvenile delinquency, and psychopathology have received particular attention. The findings suggest that adequate peer relations are necessary for adequate social development. The direction and degree of causality, however, are still at issue. Further consideration is required to determine whether peer status is an epiphenomenon of other variables.

Recently, researchers have begun to examine the role of personality differences in peer social status. Haselager (1997) assessed the relation between children's personality dimensions and their sociometric status across the elementary-school years. Information on the Big-Five personality factors was obtained from teacher evaluations of children's personality characteristics. Agreeableness and Conscientiousness were moderately but stably related to social preference; that is, the correlations reached the same levels in both early and later elementary-school years. Agreeableness and Conscientiousness both reflect children's basic goal orientations. Agreeableness focuses on interpersonal goals. Agreeableness covers the broad domain of prosocial and antisocial interactions, and concerns the orientation of children toward the interests and goals of their interaction partners while they attempt to achieve their own interpersonal goals. In sociometric measures of peer attraction, classmates apparently consider whether group members pursue prosocial or antisocial goals in group activities. Conscientiousness focuses on standards of excellence and dependability. These standards of excellence are not limited to scholastic achievement but may also concern other interests and athletic abilities. In sociometric measures of peer attraction, classmates seem to consider whether group members pursue standards of excellence in group activities.

One study of the links between personality and peer competence involved 13- and 14-year-old adolescents (Scholte, van Aken, & van Lieshout, 1997). In this study, the Big-Five personality factors were assessed with self-ratings and peer nominations for the same trait characteristics. Factor analysis of the self-ratings yielded the Big-Five personality dimensions, as expected. Factor analysis of the peer nomination data, however, produced five factors that did not clearly match the Big-Five factors: Aggression–Unattentiveness, Achievement–Withdrawal, Self–Confidence in group involvement, Sociability–Enthusiasm, and Emotionality–Nervousness. Three of these seem to match the factors previously found in peer evaluation using the Revised Class Play method of assessment (Masten, Morison, & Pellegrini, 1985). Aggression–Unattentiveness, Sociability–Enthusiasm, and Emotionality–Nervousness are similar to the Aggressive–Disruptive, Sociability–Leadership, and Sensitivity–Isolation factors of the Revised Class Play. The peer-based dimensions found in these studies do not reflect the personality characteristics of the children, but their functioning in the class group. That is, peer evaluations appear to be based not on the personality characteristics of individual children but on their contribution to the group (i.e., support of group goals and norms, group cohesion, and the group hierarchy). Put differently, the Big-Five personality traits may constitute a comprehensive taxonomy of the factors relevant to personality development, whereas the peer-based factors represent a comprehensive map of children's functioning in groups.

Scholte et al. (1997) subsequently used the Big-Five factors derived from the self-ratings and the new factors derived from the peer nominations to predict adolescents' peer acceptance and peer rejection. In one set of analyses, the self-based factors were entered into the regression equation first, followed by the peer-based factors. In this analysis, the self-based factors explained 7% and 3% of the variance in peer acceptance and rejection, respectively. The peer-based factors explained an additional 36% and 28% of acceptance and rejection. In a second set of analyses, the peer-based dimensions were entered into the regressions first, followed by the self-based factors. In this analysis, the peer-based factor explained almost all of the variance in peer acceptance and rejection, with little additional variance explained by the self-based Big-Five factors.

The peer-based factors were differentially related to peer status. Aggression–Unattentiveness predicted high rejection; Sociability and Self-Confidence predicted high acceptance; and Aggression–Unattentiveness, Achievement–Withdrawal, and Emotionality–Nervousness predicted low peer acceptance. These findings indicate that adolescent peer-evaluations are based less on personality traits than on the contributions of peers to the group. Of the personality dimensions related to peer status, Agreeableness was the clearest and most consistent predictor of peer acceptance and rejection. The more adolescents described themselves as agreeable, the more accepted and the less rejected they were by their classroom peers.

CONCLUSION: A LIFE-SPAN PERSPECTIVE

In this chapter we presented dimensions that characterize the social context of interactions, relationships, and groups. These dimensions are continuous across the life span. The equivalence of the instruments used to measure them across the life span is critical for the assessment of stability and change in the individual's social environment. Despite continuity in the basic dimensions of the social context across the life span, there are also many sources of discontinuity. The social context may change as a result of changing situational circumstances, changing relationships, and changing group contexts. Changes also occur in the primacy of relationships across an individual's life span. The prominence of child–parent, sibling, friendship, and partner relationships clearly changes, as do the individuals involved in these relationships and groups. Changes in the social context produce discontinuity and qualitative changes in the individual's social environment.

The dimensions of interpersonal support found in the social context correspond to the problem-solving modalities for developmental tasks, dimensions of competence acquired in subsequent developmental tasks, and dimensions of personality. These dimensions in an individual's development are also continuous across the life span. Across long life episodes, individual stability and change can be assessed. At the same time, an individual's development is marked by discontinuity as a consequence of the different developmental tasks. At different points in the life span, individuals are engaged in different developmental tasks. Put another way, there is clear evidence for both continuity and discontinuity in an individual's development as well as in the social context for this development. Sources of continuity largely complement the sources of discontinuity.

ACKNOWLEDGMENTS

We thank Marcel A. G. van Aken and J. Marianne Riksen-Walraven for their comments on an earlier draft of this chapter. We are grateful to Lee Ann Weeks for upgrading the quality of the English language of this paper.

REFERENCES

Baltes, P. B., Reese, H. W., & Lipsitt, L. P. (1980). Life-span developmental psychology. *Annual Review of Psychology, 31,* 65–110.

Belsky, J. & Isabella, R. A. (1988). Maternal, infant, and social-contextual determinants of attachment security. In J. Belsky & T. Nezworski (Eds.), *Clinical implications of attachment* (pp. 41–94). Hillsdale, NJ: Lawrence Erlbaum Associates.

Bukowski, W. M., Newcomb, A. F., & Hartup, W. W. (1996). *The company they keep: Friendships in childhood and adolescence.* Cambridge, England: Cambridge University Press.

Cillessen, A. H. N., Bukowski, W. M., & Haselager, G. J. T. (1997). *Stability of sociometric measures of children's peer relations.* Unpublished manuscript, University of Connecticut.

Cillessen, A. H. N., van IJzendoorn, H. W., van Lieshout, C. F. M., & Hartup, W. W. (1992). Heterogeneity among peer rejected boys: Subtypes and stabilities. *Child Development 63*, 893–905.

Clark, M. S., & Reis, H. T. (1988). Interpersonal processes in close relationships. *Annual Review of Psychology, 39*, 609–672.

Cohn, L. D. (1991). Sex differences in the course of personality development: A meta-analysis. *Psychological Bulletin, 109*, 252–266.

Crick, N. R., & Dodge, K. A. (1994). A review and reformulation of social information-processing mechanisms in children's social adjustment. *Psychological Bulletin, 115*, 74–101.

de Poorte, I. M., Veling, G. M., Haselager, G. J. T., & van Lieshout, C. F. M. (1994). Gedragstypering van kinderen met een problematische sociometrische status [Behavior of children with an at-risk sociometric status type]. *Tijdschrift voor Orthopedagogiek, 33*, 268–283.

de Roos, S. A. (1995). *Peer competence and its antecedents during the first years of life: A longitudinal study.* Unpublished doctoral disseration, University of Nijmegen.

Dodge, K. A. (1986). A social information processing model of social competence in children. In M. Perlmutter (Ed.), *Minnesota symposia on child psychology* (Vol. 18, pp. 77–125). Hillsdale, NJ: Lawrence Erlbaum Associates.

Erel, O., & Burman, B. (1995). Interrelatedness of marital relations and parent-child relations: A meta-analytic review. *Psychological Bulletin, 118*, 108–132.

Erickson, M., Sroufe, L. A., & Egeland, B. (1985). The relationship between quality of attachment and behavior problems in preschool in a high-risk sample. In I. Bretherton & E. Waters (Eds.), Growing points in attachment theory and research. *Monographs of the Society for Research in Child Development, 50*(1–2, Serial No. 209), 147–186.

Farrington, D. (1993). Understanding and preventing bullying. In M. Tonry & N. Morris (Eds.), *Crime and justice, Vol. 17* (pp. 381–458). Chicago: University of Chicago Press.

Furman, W., & Buhrmester, D. (1985). Children's perceptions of the personal relationships in their social networks. *Developmental Psychology, 21*, 1016–1024.

Furman, W., & Buhrmester, D. (1992). Age and sex differences in perceptions of networks and personal relationships. *Child Development, 63*, 103–115.

Goldberg, L. R. (1990). An alternative "Description of Personality": The Big-Five factor structure. *Journal of Personality and Social Psychology, 59*, 1216–1229.

Grych, J. H., & Fincham, F. D. (1990). Marital conflict and children's adjustment: A cognitive-contextual framework. *Psychological Bulletin, 108*, 267–290.

Hartup, W. W. (1983). Peer relations. In P. H. Mussen (Series Ed.), E. M. Hetherington (Vol. Ed.), *Handbook of child psychology: Vol. 4. Socialization, personality, and social development* (pp. 103–198). New York: Wiley.

Hartup, W. W. (1989). Social relationships and their developmental significance. *American Psychologist, 44*, 120–126.

Hartup, W. W. (1996). The company they keep: Friendships and their developmental significance. *Child Development, 67*, 1–13.

Hartup, W. W., & Stevens, N. (1997). Friendship and adaptation in the life course. *Psychological Bulletin, 121*, 355–370.

Hartup, W. W., & van Lieshout, C. F. M. (1995). Personality development in context. *Annual Review of Psychology, 46*, 655–687.

Haselager, G. J. T. (1997). *Classmates: Studies on the development of their relationships and personality in middle childhood.* Unpublished doctoral dissertation, University of Nijmegen.

Haselager, G. J. T., Cillessen, A. H. N., Hartup, W. W., van Lieshout, C. F. M., & Riksen-Walraven, J. M. (1997). *Developmental patterns of social competence in elementary school and acceptance and rejection by peers.* Unpublished manuscript, University of Nijmegen.

Haselager, G. J. T., Hartup, W. W., van Lieshout, C. F. M., & Riksen-Walraven, J. M. (1998). Similarities between friends and nonfriends in middle childhood. *Child Development, 69*.

Havighurst, R. J. (1973). History of developmental psychology: Socialization and personality development through the life span. In P. B. Baltes & K. W. Schaie (Eds.), *Life-span developmental psychology: Personality and socialization* (pp. 3–24). New York: Academic Press.

Hinde, R. A. (1976). Interactions, relationships and social structure. *Man, 11,* 1–17.

Hinde, R. A. (1995). A suggested structure for a science of reelationships. *Personal Relationships, 2,* 1–15.

Isabella, R. A. (1993). Origins of attachment: Maternal interactive behavior across the first year. *Child Development, 64,* 605–621.

Kelley, H. H., Berscheid, E., Christensen, A., Harvey, J. H., Huston, T. L., Levinger, G., McClintock, C. G., Peplau, L. A., & Peterson, D. (1983). *Close relationships.* New York: Freeman.

Laursen, B., & Collins, W. A. (1994). Interpersonal conflict during adolescence. *Psychological Bulletin, 115,* 197–209.

Maccoby, E. E., & Martin, J. A. (1983). Socialization in the context of the family: Parent-child interaction. In P. H. Mussen (Series Ed.), E. M. Hetherington (Vol. Ed.), *Handbook of child psychology: Vol. 4. Socialization, personality, and social development* (pp. 1–102). New York: Wiley.

Malatesta, C. Z., & Haviland, J. M. (1982). Learning display rules: The socialization of emotion expression in infancy. *Child Development, 53,* 991–1003.

Masten, A. S., Morison, P., & Pellegrini, D. S. (1985). A revised class play method of peer assessment. *Developmental Psychology, 3,* 523–533.

Meltzoff, A. N. (1995). Understanding the intentions of others: Re-enactment of intended acts by 18-month-old children. *Developmental Psychology, 31,* 838–850.

Meltzoff, A. N., & Moore, M. K. (1977). Imitation of facial and manual gestures by human neonates. *Science, 198,* 75–78.

Newcomb, A. F., & Bagwell, C. L. (1995). Children's friendship realtions: A meta-analytic review. *Psychological Bulletin, 117,* 306–347.

Newcomb, A. F., Bukowski, W. M., & Pattee, L. (1993). Children's peer relations: A meta-analytic review of popular, rejected, neglected, controversial, and average sociometric status. *Psychological Bulletin, 113,* 99–128.

Olthof, T. (1990). *Blame, anger, and aggression in children: A social-cognitive approach.* Unpublished doctoral dissertation, University of Nijmegen.

Olthof, T., Ferguson, T. J., & Luiten, A. (1989). Personal responsibility antecedents of anger and blame reactions in children. *Child Development, 60,* 1328–1336.

Olweus, D. (1993). *Bullying at school: What we know and what we can do.* Oxford, England: Blackwell.

Parker, J. G., & Asher, S. R. (1987). Peer relations and later personal adjustment: Are low-accepted children at risk? *Psychological Bulletin, 102,* 357–389.

Riksen-Walraven, J. M. (1978). Effects of caregiver behavior on habituation rate and self-efficacy in infants. *International Journal of Behavioral Development, 1,* 105–130.

Riksen-Walraven, J. M., Meij, J. T., Hubbard, F. O., & Zevalkink, J. (1996). Intervention in lower-class Surinam-Dutch families: Effects on mothers and infants. *International Journal of Behavioral Development, 19,* 739–756.

Riksen-Walraven, J. M., & van Aken, M. A. G. (1997). Effects of two mother-infant intervention programs upon children's development at 7, 10 and 12 years. In W. Koops, J. B. Hoeksma, & D. C. van den Boom (Eds.), *Development of interaction and attachment: Traditional and non-traditional approaches* (pp. 79–91). Amsterdam: North-Holland.

Rothbart, M. K., Ahadi, S., & Hershey, K. L. (1994). Temperament and social behavior in children. *Merrill-Palmer Quarterly, 40,* 21–39.

Rubin, K. H., Bukowski, W., & Parker, J. G. (1997). Peer interactions, relationships, and groups. In N. Eisenberg (Vol. Ed.), *Handbook of child psychology. Vol. 3: Social, emotional, and personality development* (pp. 619–700). New York: Wiley.

Sarason, B. R., Pierce, G. R., Bannerman, A., & Sarason, I. G. (1993). Investigating the antecedents of perceived social support: Parents' views of and behavior toward their children. *Journal of Personality and Social Psychology, 65*, 1071–1085.

Scholte, R. H. J., van Aken, M. A. G., & van Lieshout, C. F. M. (1997). Adolescents' personality factors in self-ratings and peer nominations and their prediction on peer acceptance and peer rejection. *Journal of Personality Assessment, 69*, 534–554.

Searle, J. R. (1983). *Intentionality: An essay in the philosophy of mind.* Cambridge, England: Cambridge University Press.

Smitsman, A. W., & van Lieshout, C. F. M. (1992). Kenmerken van ontwikkelingstaken [Characteristics of developmental tasks]. *Nederlands Tijdschrift voor de Psychologie, 47*, 243–245.

Sternberg, R. J. (1986). A triarchic theory of intellectual giftedness. In R. J. Sternberg & J. E. Davidson (Eds.), *Conceptions of giftedness* (pp. 223–243). Cambridge, England: Cambridge University Press.

van Aken, M. A. G., & Asendorpf, J. B. (1997). Support by parents, classmates, friends, and siblings in preadolescence: Covariation and compensation across relationships. *Journal of Social and Personal Relationships, 14*, 79–93.

van Aken, M. A. G., van Lieshout, C. F. M., & Haselager, G. J. T. (1996). Adolescents' competence and the mutuality of their self-descriptions and descriptions of them provided by others. *Journal of Youth and Adolescence, 25*, 285–306.

van den Boom, D. C. (1994). The influence of temperament and mothering on attachment and exploration: An experimental manipulation of sensitive responsiveness among lower-class mothers with irritable infants. *Child Development, 65*, 1457–1478.

van der Linden, F. J. & Dijkman, T. A. (1989). *Jong zijn en volwassen worden in Nederland [Being young and becoming an adult in The Netherlands].* Nijmegen, The Netherlands: Hoogveld.

van Lieshout, C. F. M. (1995). Development of social giftedness and gifted personality in context. In M. W. Katzko & F. J. Mönks (Eds.), *Nurturing talent: Individual needs and social ability* (pp. 31–42). Assen, The Netherlands: van Gorcum.

van Lieshout, C. F. M., de Meyer, R. E., Curfs, L. M. G., & Fryns, J. P. (1998). Family contexts, parental behaviour, and personality profiles of children and adolescents with Prader-Willi, Fragile X or Williams Syndrome. *Journal of Child Psychology and Psychiatry, 39*, 699–710.

van Lieshout, C. F. M., & Haselager, G. J. T. (1994). The big-five personality factors in Q-sort descriptions of children and adolescents. In C. F. Halverson, G. A. Kohnstamm, & R. P. Martin (Eds.), *The developmental structure of temperament and personality from infancy to adulthood* (pp. 293–318). Hillsdale, NJ: Lawrence Erlbaum Associates.

van Lieshout, C. F. M., Haselager, G. J. T., Riksen-Walraven, J. M., & van Aken, M. A. G. (1995, April). *Personality development in middle childhood.* Paper presented at the meetings of the Society for Research in Child Development, Indianapolis.

van Lieshout, C. F. M., & van Aken, M. A. G. (1995). Ontwikkelingstaken, persoonlijkheidsontwikkeling en relationele ondersteuning [Developmental tasks, personality development, and relational support]. In J. R. M. Gerris (Ed.), *Gezin: Onderzoek en diagnostiek* (pp. 62–74). Assen, The Netherlands: van Gorcum.

van Lieshout, C. F. M., van IJzendoorn, H. W., & de Roos, S. A. (1993). Contributions of actor and partner to dyadic interactions in toddlers: A longitudinal study. In J. Nadel & L. Camaioni (Eds.), *New perspectives in early communication development* (pp. 202–214). London: Routledge.

Vereijken, C. M. J. L., Riksen-Walraven, J. M., & Kondo-Ikemura, K. (1997). Maternal sensitivity and infant attachment security in Japan: A longitudinal study. *International Journal of Behavioral Development, 21*, 35–49.

von Eye, A. (1990). *Introduction to configural frequency analysis: The search for types and antitypes in cross-classifications.* Cambridge, England: Cambridge University Press.

Part II

DEVELOPMENTAL PERSPECTIVES ON CLOSE RELATIONSHIPS WITH PEERS

Chapter 4

Knowing the Sounds: Friendship as a Developmental Context

Andrew F. Newcomb
University of Richmond

William M. Bukowski
Concordia University

Catherine L. Bagwell
Duke University

知 音

An ancient Chinese legend relates the story of a man who was adept at playing the ch'in, a quiet and meditative string instrument. The man played only for a particular friend, for he believed that his friend was the one person who could understand the beauty of his music and the feelings and emotions that emerged from his fingertips onto the strings. When his friend died, the man broke his ch'in; no longer was there anyone who knew the message in his melodious sounds.[1]

CONCEPTUAL FRAMEWORK

In the spirit of this legend, Chinese poets often use the two characters that mean "to know, the sounds" to represent a good friend, someone who understands and appreciates the essence of another. The writers who employ this definition of a friend perpetuate the idea that friendship is a dyadic relationship characterized by a combination of intimacy, mutual understanding, attachment, interpersonal sensitivity, and affection. They acknowledge that friendship is a unique and powerful social context.

---

[1]The story of the Chinese legend of the ch'in comes from a personal communication with Stephen Addiss, Tucker-Boatwright Professor in the Humanities, University of Richmond.

The goal of our chapter is to extend this concept of friendship as a social context by providing an empirical basis for it. Building upon themes derived from Bill Hartup's extensive influence on the study of friendship relations, our empirical presentation focuses on interpersonal influence as a central process within the developmental context afforded by children's friendships. Our consideration of friendship as a developmental context is further predicated on the recognition that the peer system consists of three interdependent levels of complexity: the individual, the dyad, and the group. In keeping with the focus of Hartup's interests, our primary emphasis is on the dyadic level, especially the interactions and relationship properties that are characteristic of friendship.

A recurring theme throughout this volume is that Bill Hartup's contributions to developmental psychology and to our understanding of the sounds of friendship are synonymous. During each of the past four decades, his formative contributions have shaped and redefined how we view and interpret the phenomena represented in the legend of the ch'in. His work marks the field's progression from examining peers as a source of social reinforcement to examining friendship as a fundamental relational context that guides and controls development. Hartup has emphasized the importance of friendship for adaptation within the social, behavioral, and cognitive domains. He views friendship as a multidimensional construct that involves phenomena from the individual and dyadic levels of relationship complexity. This multidimensional perspective provides the cornerstone for our current examination of friendship as a developmental context.

Inherent in our conceptual view is the assumption that human behavior and development occur within a multitude of settings. These settings represent the framework or conditions for development and account for unique variance within any developmental model. As such, context must not be viewed as simply an environment or set of circumstances; instead, context is a frame of reference or structure that governs development and change. Friendship is exactly this sort of structure, and as a critical developmental context, friendship serves a set of specific developmental functions.

Originally, the effects that friends have on each other were demonstrated in laboratory studies, largely relying on paradigms taken from social learning theory. Early studies showed that children not only provide high levels of positive reinforcement for each other but that they provide reinforcement in greater frequencies to friends than to nonfriends (Hartup, Glazer, & Charlesworth, 1967). In this regard, friends shape each other's behavior, influencing each other's personality and social development. Since this propaedeutic work, these effects have been demonstrated with other techniques, and other theoretical positions have been offered to explain this influence. We now know that when friends interact with each other they engage in the mutual regulation of behavior and affect (Newcomb & Brady,

1982), and they strive to find common ground (Gottman, 1983). This capacity to develop a common experience promotes the continuity of the relationship (Hartup, 1992), enhances children's recall of positive aspects of their friendship experience (Newcomb & Brady, 1982), and may account for the positive effects that friendship has on development (Hartup, 1993, 1996).

The argument that individuals are influenced by friends is seen in the well-worn clichés telling us that "No man is an island" and "It is not who you are that matters, it is who you know." Since Darwin (1859/1964), scholars have understood that the functioning of an individual organism is not apart from the environment in which the organism is situated. Indeed, friends create a shared environment based on the common and unique characteristics of the two individuals. This shared environment is distinct from the environments that exist in other friendship pairs in its norms, its activities, and its goals. As such, the developmental context of friendship must be seen as the product of features that both children bring into the friendship. A consequence of this view is that not all friendships are alike; instead, each friendship derives from the attributes of two different children. Specifically, individual differences in friendship relations arise because all children are not alike and because not all children choose the same type of peers as friends.

In this chapter, our central goal is to examine the process of interpersonal influence in the context of the friendship dyad and to consider how the influence process operates at different levels of relationship complexity. First, we examine the linkages between the individual and the dyad. In particular, we explore two issues: (a) how different pathways between individual and dyadic variables serve as affordances for friendship, and (b) how interpersonal similarity emerges in friendship relations and has an impact on development. Second, we move beyond the social context of the dyad to the broader set of circumstances that are created by linkages between the dyad and the friendship network. Again two issues are of import: (a) how dyadic friendship serves as a gateway for children to access other social experiences in the peer world, and (b) how friendship dyads and the friendship network combine to affect development.

We address these issues with data from a short-term longitudinal study that involved a single cohort of 334 preadolescents who were assessed for the first time in the spring of fifth grade. These youngsters then moved from five elementary schools to a single middle school for sixth grade. In middle school, assessments were completed at both the beginning and the end of sixth grade. For all data collections, children nominated their three best friends and their three least-liked peers. They also completed a class play measure that included 14 roles (see Bukowski & Newcomb, 1984, for details). Standardized nomination scores for the 14 roles were used to form the four composite behavioral indices of observable prominence (e.g., liked by everybody, team captain), aggression (e.g., picks on smaller kids, causes trouble), class competence (e.g., smart, tries to help everybody), and immaturity (e.g., afraid and acts like a little kid, sad). Finally, the children completed a 60-item rating scale inventory that tapped the children's values and beliefs. A subset of these items was used to index the degree to which the children were tolerant of antisocial behavior (e.g., it's okay to beat up another kid).

In our analyses of similarity between friends, we computed the absolute difference between the two friends' scores on each of the four composite indices of aggression, class competence, immaturity, and observable prominence. Thus, for these dyadic similarity scores, small values indicate high levels of similarity, and large values reveal low levels of similarity. The behavioral characteristic scores were standardized; thus, the similarity scores are expressed in standard deviation units. Three specific definitions are important for understanding our findings. First, mutual friendships were those in which each child chose the other as either a first or second best friend. Second, a random peer was a randomly selected peer who had not been chosen as either a friend or a disliked peer. Finally, our index of popularity is a child's social preference score, that is, peer acceptance minus peer rejection (Coie, Dodge, & Coppotelli, 1982; Newcomb & Bukowski, 1983).

LINKAGES BETWEEN THE INDIVIDUAL
AND THE DYAD

Popularity as an Affordance for Friendship

Friendship is linked to phenomena that occur at different levels of social complexity. As such, although friendship is a dyadic construct, it is not independent of individual characteristics of children who are members of dyads and are in turn embedded within larger social groups. Considering this interrelatedness, studies of peer relations consisting of simple bivariate associations between constructs underestimate the richness of the structure and processes of the peer system. The aim of this section is to examine the particular pathways that bring together these various individual, dyadic, and group variables.

Our analyses are guided by assumptions that certain individual characteristics are antecedent to popularity and that children with different characteristics are attracted to different types of peers as friends. Together these premises imply that a child's characteristics are associated with the child's popularity as well as with the characteristics of the peers the child chooses as a friend. We examine how the link between popularity and friend characteristics is associated with the individual characteristics of the child in two sets of analyses. First, we address how characteristics of children operate to determine who is most likely to be involved in a mutual friendship. Second, we examine whether characteristics of children's friends are the result of processes at the level of the individual child or whether the influence of the individual child is mediated by associations with popularity.

Figure 4.1 shows our model depicting linkages between individual characteristics, popularity, and friendship in the fall of sixth grade ($N = 276$). The model provided a strong fit to the observed data (Comparative Fit Index = .99) and produced a nonsignificant chi-square value ($\chi^2_{(4)} = 8.41$). The critical aspect of this model is that popularity, or liking, mediates the association between a child's characteristics and whether the child has a friend. The paths on the left side of the model link characteristics of the child with popularity and show that a child's individual characteristics predict the degree to which the child is liked by peers. The existence of these pathways is well-documented in research on the behavioral antecedents of popularity (see Newcomb, Bukowski, & Pattee, 1993, for a review). The path on the right side of the model shows popularity as an antecedent to friendship and is consistent with the view that popularity is an affordance for friendship. Thus, popular children have more opportunities for friendship than do unpopular children and are consequently more likely to have a friend than are less popular children (Moreno, 1934).

In this model, the association between individual characteristics and mutual friendship is completely mediated by popularity. The quality of the

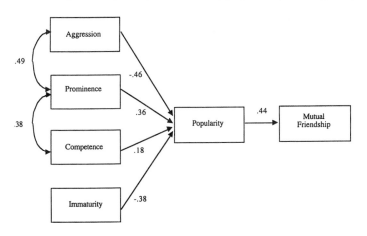

Note. For all paths, $p < .001$.

FIG. 4.1. Path model of linkages among individual child characteristics, popularity, and friendship in the fall of sixth grade.

model was unchanged when we added direct paths linking social behaviors (i.e., individual characteristics) and mutual friendship. These findings indicate that children who vary in their level of aggression, for example, are differentially likely to have a friend because they differ in how popular they are with peers. The model does not invalidate the observation that children with particular characteristics are more or less likely than others to have a friend. Instead, our findings help explain the process that underlies this association.

Figure 4.2 presents our model of the associations among individual child characteristics and characteristics of the child's friends in the fall of sixth grade ($N = 276$). Given the finding that popularity mediates the relation between an individual child's characteristics and whether he or she has a friend, our goal was to determine whether popularity also mediates the relation between what a child is like and what the child's friend is like. This model produced a nonsignificant chi-square value ($\chi^2_{(5)} = 5.13$) and an excellent goodness of fit (Comparative Fit Index = 1.00). Adding a direct path between the child's popularity and any of the friend's characteristics did not change the quality of the model.

Taken together, the models in Figs. 4.1 and 4.2 suggest that a child's characteristics determine how popular they are with peers, and popularity in turn affects whether the child has a mutual friend. The child's popularity, however, has no bearing on what that friend is like. These findings establish the complex interdependent nature of the individual, dyadic, and group

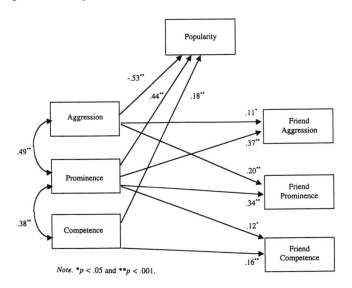

FIG. 4.2. Path model of linkages among individual child characteristics, popularity, and characteristics of the child's friends in the fall of sixth grade.

levels of relationships and demonstrate that the context of a particular friendship is determined by features of the individual child and his or her place in the larger peer structure.

Interpersonal Similarity in Dyadic Friendship Relations

The findings discussed earlier reveal that not all children choose the same type of peers as friends, and thus the context of friendship varies considerably as a function of the child's characteristics as well as the friend's characteristics. The consequence of these variations is that the impact of friendship will also vary across children, and the effect of having one friend rather than another can be substantial. We propose that the differences among friendships differentially affect children's subsequent development via the process of mutual influence.

Research with adolescents and adults has demonstrated that the characteristics of one's friend will influence that person's behaviors. The best known evidence for this phenomenon is Kandel's (1978) investigation of the association between friendship patterns and interpersonal similarity on self-report measures of behavior and attitudes. Kandel reported that interpersonal similarity, especially in self-reported drug use, was not only a feature of adolescent friendship pairs but that similarity existed prior to the formation of the friendship, predicted the continuity of the friendship relation, and increased as the friendship continued. These findings demonstrate that there is a systematic process underlying patterns of affiliation in adolescence and that the friendship dyad provides an important context for interpersonal influence.

Similar claims have been made by Cairns and his colleagues who proposed that within the friendship relation, friends create a shared environment based on their common characteristics (Cairns, Cairns, & Neckerman, 1989; Cairns, Cairns, Neckerman, Gest, & Gariepy, 1988). According to this perspective, interpersonal similarity promotes friendship formation and then enhances the continuity of the relationship. Moreover, due to the process of mutual influence, friends become increasingly similar to each other as the friendship relation continues. Considering the attention that has been devoted to the phenomenon of interpersonal similarity in adult friendship relations and to children's peer relations during the past two decades, it is surprising that these interpersonal processes have been largely ignored with children. In spite of Kandel's (1978) compelling findings regarding the association between patterns of adolescent friendship and drug use, very little is known about the extent of interpersonal similarity in childhood and early adolescent friendship relations. Specifically, it is not known if interpersonal similarity in personality and social behavior is related to the development of friendship and to the stability of children's relationships with friends and, more importantly, if increased levels of interpersonal similarity result from the sustained interaction of friends.

To understand the developmental context friendship provides, there is a clear need to investigate the relation between interpersonal similarity and children's experiences with friends, especially from a longitudinal perspective. As such, we address four related questions regarding interpersonal similarity and friendship relations: (a) Are children more similar to their mutual friends than to nonfriends? (b) Does interpersonal similarity between friends exist prior to the formation of their relationship? (c) Does the degree of similarity between friends predict the stability of their friendship? and (d) Do friends become more similar as their relationship continues?

Similarity Between Mutual Friends. We first focused on similarity between friends by comparing whether early adolescents were more similar to a mutual friend than to a randomly selected classmate. If interpersonal similarity facilitates friendship, then higher levels of similarity would be expected between friends than between nonfriends. Overall, early adolescents were generally more similar to their mutual friend than to a randomly selected peer on the behavioral characteristics of aggression, class competence, and immaturity. As shown in Table 4.1, these findings were replicated at three different assessments indicating that similarity between friends is a robust phenomenon that is evident across different social contexts (i.e., in elementary and middle school and early in the school year as well as at the end of the school year). In contrast, mutual friends were no more similar in their observable prominence than were random peers in fifth and sixth grade.

Similarity Prior to Friendship Formation: Selection Effects. Next we examined whether interpersonal similarity between friends exists prior to the formation of the friendship. Specifically, we considered the degree of similarity in the fifth-grade social reputations of early adolescents and those children who would become their new friends after entering a consolidated middle school for sixth grade. These comparisons were based on data obtained before the two children actually met (i.e., when they were students in separate elementary schools). If interpersonal similarity is an important antecedent to friendship development, one would expect interpersonal similarity to exist prior to the friendship's formation.

In these analyses, 77 sixth-grade friendships comprised of children who were not schoolmates during fifth grade were identified. One child from each dyad was randomly paired with a same-sex peer, and the degree of similarity on fifth-grade characteristics between the child and his or her friend and the child and the randomly chosen peer was assessed. For two of the four social characteristics—observable prominence and class com-

TABLE 4.1

Similarity Between Mutual Friends Versus Between Randomly Paired Classmates on the Behavioral Characteristics of Aggression, Observable Prominence, Class Competence, and Immaturity

Behavioral Characteristic		Mutual Friends		Random Classmates			
Time of Assessment	N	M	SD	M	SD	F	df
Aggression							
Spring of fifth grade	110	.54	.57	.80	.79	9.41****	1, 106
Fall of sixth grade	98	.58	.64	.78	.72	5.28**	1, 94
Spring of sixth grade	105	.63	.67	.93	.76	3.97**	1, 101
Observable Prominence							
Spring of fifth grade	110	.68	.71	.76	.80	< 1.0	1, 106
Fall of sixth grade	98	.92	.76	1.03	.82	< 1.0	1, 94
Spring of sixth grade	105	.88	.82	1.16	.91	< 1.0	1, 101
Class Competence							
Spring of fifth grade	110	.62	.57	.91	.72	11.36****	1, 106
Fall of sixth grade	98	.60	.61	.87	.65	6.25**	1, 94
Spring of fifth grade	105	.62	.59	.80	.65	3.56*	1, 101
Immaturity							
Spring of fifth grade	110	.57	.71	.83	.68	7.21***	1, 106
Fall of sixth grade	98	.56	.63	.86	.81	12.27****	1, 94
Spring of sixth grade	105	.43	.41	.74	1.12	13.90****	1, 101

Note. Similarity was indexed by computing the absolute difference between the subject scores on each measure. Small values indicate high levels of similarity; large values reveal low levels of similarity.

$*p \leq .10.$ $**p \leq .05.$ $***p \leq .01.$ $****p \leq .001.$

petence—children were more similar to a peer who would become a friend 6 months later than to a randomly chosen peer (see Table 4.2). The same pattern emerged for aggression, but this difference was only marginally significant ($p < .07$). There were no differences in prior similarity between new sixth-grade friends and random peers on the immaturity scale.

Similarity as a Predictor of Friendship Stability. We next examined the association between interpersonal similarity and the continuity of friendships over the sixth-grade school year and expected that more similarity would be observed in stable than nonstable relationships. In this analysis, the degree of similarity between mutual friends who would remain friends across the sixth-grade year was compared to the degree of similarity in friendships that were not stable across this interval. Stable friendship pairs

TABLE 4.2
Similarity Prior to Friendship Formation: A Comparison of New Mutual Friends and Randomly
Paired Classmates on the Behavioral Characteristics of Aggression, Observable Prominence,
Class Competence, and Immaturity

Behavioral Characteristic		Mutual Friends		Random Classmates		
Time of Assessment	N	M	SD	M	SD	F(1, 255)
Aggression	77	.60	.66	.75	.70	3.48*
Observable Prominence	77	.68	.67	.93	.93	12.31***
Class Competence	77	.71	.58	.87	.73	4.60**
Immaturity	77	.77	.72	.76	.67	< 1.0

Note. Similarity was indexed by computing the absolute difference between the subject scores on each measure. Small values indicate high levels of similarity; large values reveal low levels of similarity.
$*p \leq .10.$ $**p \leq .05.$ $***p \leq .01.$ $****p \leq .001.$

were defined as dyads in which reciprocal friendship nominations were made in both the fall and spring of sixth grade. Nonstable friendships were those that were reciprocated only in the fall of sixth grade. Comparing the degree of similarity in these two groups in the fall addresses whether similarity is a marker for the stability of the relationship.

Indeed, as shown in Table 4.3, children who remained friends across the school year were more similar than nonstable friendship pairs on aggression and class competence. In contrast, similarity on the reputations for observable prominence and immaturity did not forecast the stability of friendships over time. These findings indicate that, at least for the constructs of aggression and class competence, children are more likely to maintain a friendship if they choose a friend who is similar to them on these dimensions than if they choose a friend who is less similar.

Similarity as an Outcome of Friendship: Socialization Effects. Finally, we examined the notion of socialization within the context of friendship and considered whether friends become more similar to each other as their relationship continues. To address this question, changes in interpersonal similarity were examined for mutual friendship pairs in which there was little similarity in the fall of sixth grade. For each of the four role scores, we identified pairs of mutual friends in which the absolute difference between the friends was more than half of a standard deviation larger than the group mean for pairs of mutual friends. These friendship dyads were

TABLE 4.3
Similarity as a Predictor of Friendship Stability: A Comparison of Stable Mutual Friends on the
Behavioral Characteristics of Aggression, Observable Prominence, Class Competence,
and Immaturity

Behavioral Characteristic	Stable Friendships (N = 60)		Nonstable Friendships (N = 34)			
	M	SD	M	SD	F	df
Aggression	.50	.73	.78	.83	3.84**	1, 92
Observable Prominence	.51	.54	.72	.63	3.05*	1, 92
Class Competence	.64	.59	.99	.96	9.86***	1, 92
Immaturity	.73	.72	1.04	1.23	2.46	1, 92

Note. Similarity was indexed by computing the absolute difference between the subject scores on each measure. Small values indicate high levels of similarity; large values reveal low levels of similarity.
*$p \leq .10$. **$p \leq .05$. ***$p \leq .01$.

further identified as being either stable (i.e., reciprocated friendship nominations in the fall and spring of sixth grade) or nonstable (i.e., reciprocated friendship nominations only in the fall of sixth grade). If friends become more similar to each other as their friendship continues, the friendship pairs that remain stable across the school year were expected to show increasing levels of similarity.

As illustrated in Fig. 4.3, the results revealed an interaction between friendship stability and time for aggression ($F(1, 20) = 5.24$, $p < .05$) and class competence ($F(1, 20) = 6.28$, $p < .05$). These interactions were not significant for observable prominence and immaturity. Specifically, in the spring of sixth grade, initially dissimilar children who maintained their friendship over the school year became more similar to one another on aggression and class competence than they had been 6 months before. In contrast, there was no difference between similarity scores in the fall and spring for initially dissimilar children whose friendships did not continue over the school year. The figure also shows that, in comparison to the baseline degree of similarity for friends at each time period, initially dissimilar stable friends had nearly reached a normative level of similarity on these two characteristics.

Summary of Similarity Effects. Our findings on similarity in friendships show that variations in the context of friendship are not random. Children select their friends in systematic ways, and thus children choose for

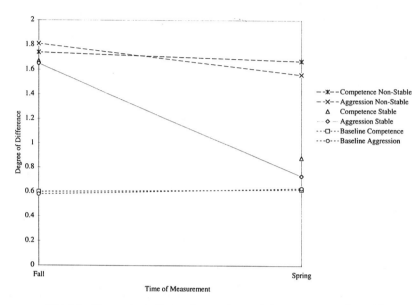

FIG. 4.3.   Change in similarity of aggression and class competence for stable
and nonstable friendships across sixth grade.

themselves a context that affects their development. For example, by
associating with other aggressive children, an aggressive child participates
in a context in which aggression is normative. This selection process
appears to function as a means for children to self-select different
socialization opportunities. Choosing to engage in a particular context may
perpetuate or accentuate the features that led a child to initially select
that context. At the same time, it is important to recognize that not all
children have equal access to the same social situations. Some individuals
may be able to actively select contexts, yet once social niches are filled,
other children may be exposed to social contexts by default. A clear
implication of this process is that the effects of friendship are not uniform.
The sounds of friendship vary, and the nature of these sounds has
important implications for children's development.

LINKAGES BETWEEN THE DYAD AND THE GROUP

Friendship as a Gateway to the Rest of the World

Friendship is, for many children, the social domain where they spend the
largest share of their time, and as a consequence, it is the environment
where they learn about life away from the family setting. Accordingly, the

child's understanding of the social world is based at least in part upon the characteristics of the friendship. For example, by associating with others who are athletic or who are grade-conscious, a child will come to see these values as part of reality and will therefore carry them into other contexts.

Friendships are also an important avenue by which children are linked to other people. When a child has a friend, there is a direct relationship with the friend and also indirect associations with the friend's friends. At the simplest level, two possible sets of circumstances result from a child having a mutual friend, and in each case, a different consequence may accrue from linkages to the friendship network of one's friend. In the first instance, a child has a friend who is not very popular and thus has indirect links to relatively few (or no) peers. Alternatively, a child who has a very popular friend has indirect links to several (or many) other peers. Even with a mutual friend, the first child is, relatively speaking, still isolated. In contrast, the second child is just a step away from a larger friendship network.

The metaphor of friends as a gateway to the rest of the world helps us understand how children are influenced by their friends. This influence may occur via two mechanisms, and we present empirical evidence for each of these processes. First, the number of links that children have with others should be associated with the number of links their friend has with others. As a result, children who have popular friends will, via their indirect links to this large network, become more popular over time. Second, children's norms and values will be influenced by their friend's behavior. Children whose friends display particular behaviors should come to see those behaviors as normative. For example, having a friend who is aggressive may change a child's views about the acceptability of aggressive behavior.

The Influence of a Friend's Friends. Our interest in whether a child's friend provides a gateway to the broader peer network undergirds the question of whether children of average or low popularity become more popular over time if they have a popular friend. To address this question, we conducted a path analysis to examine changes in popularity between the fall and spring of sixth grade as a function of a child's characteristics and the characteristics and popularity of the child's friend. Specifically, we took children who were of average or lower popularity in the fall of sixth grade ($N = 204$) and constructed a model that included measures of the child's and the friend's aggression, observable prominence, and popularity. Two models were tested—an initial model followed by a model that included a direct path between the friend's popularity in the fall and the child's popularity in the spring. We were interested in whether this direct link between the friend's popularity and the child's subsequent popularity would significantly improve the model.

In the initial model, we included four sets of links (see Fig. 4.4). First, paths were drawn between the aggression and observable prominence scores and the corresponding child and friend popularity scores. Second, paths were drawn to represent the association between the behavioral characteristics for the child in the fall and spring and the friend in the fall (e.g., child aggression in fall linked with child prominence in fall). Third, in parallel to the analyses reported in Fig. 4.2, paths were drawn between child characteristics in the fall and friend characteristics in the fall. Fourth, paths were drawn between similar measures in the fall and the spring to reflect the stability of behavioral characteristics (e.g., child aggression in fall linked with child aggression in spring). The Comparative Fit Index obtained for this model was .95, and the chi-square value was 28.56 ($df = 18$, $p < .05$).

This first model was then reevaluated following the inclusion of the direct path between friend popularity in the fall and child popularity in the spring. The Comparative Fit Index of this second model was .99, and the chi-square value was 23.94 ($df = 17$, $p > .10$). The chi-square of the second model differed significantly from the chi-square obtained with the first model (change in chi-square = 4.62, $p < .05$), and the coefficient for the additional path was significant ($p < .01$).

The most striking aspect of these findings is that the popularity of a child's friend is a strong predictor of changes in the child's popularity. This finding demonstrates that if a child has a friend who is popular, the

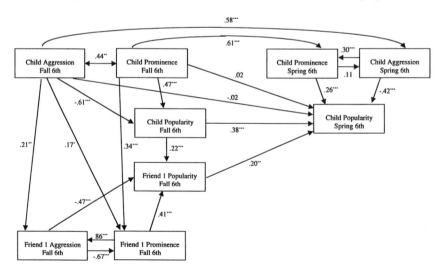

Note. *$p < .05$, **$p < .01$, and ***$p < .001$.

FIG. 4.4. Path model showing changes in a child's popularity as a function of friend characteristics across sixth grade.

child is likely to become more popular over time. Conversely, if a child has a friend who is unpopular, the child is likely to become less popular over time. Our interpretation of these results is that a child's friend serves as an entry point into the peer system. That is, the friend functions as a gateway to a child's subsequent popularity with peers because the friend has access to a a large number of liked peers. In this way, the friend's popularity provides a context for the child to become more strongly linked with other peers.

Although the major focus of our analysis was on the popularity of a child's friend, it should be noted that the characteristics of the friend are indirectly implicated in the gateway process. By choosing a peer with high prominence as one's friend, a child is choosing a popular peer as one's friend. Conversely, by choosing an aggressive peer as a friend, one is choosing an unpopular peer as one's friend. In this way a child's choice of friends indirectly influences one's subsequent popularity. Clearly, the type of peer with whom a child chooses to associate partially determines a child's position within the peer group.

In these analyses, it was not the features that the child brought to the relationship that determined the child's subsequent experiences. Instead, it was characteristics of his or her friend. In one of the most widely cited studies in child psychology, Sameroff and Chandler (1975) showed that an individual's characteristics did not predict the long-term adjustment of at-risk infants; instead, this adjustment was predicted by systemic features. Our findings reveal exactly the same pattern. Consequently, these findings suggest that efforts to study the peer system from the perspective of individual characteristics are unlikely to tell a complete story. By recognizing the impact of the broader context afforded by friendship, a clearer view of children's experiences within the peer group is obtained.

Changes in Attitudes as a Function of Friend Characteristics. Our second hypothesis about how friendship serves as a gateway to the rest of the peer world considers changes in attitudes as a function of characteristics of children's friends. To examine whether children's view about aggression would change as a function of the aggressiveness of their friend, children's tolerance of aggression was examined at two times (Bukowski, Sabongui, & Newcomb, 1996). Stable mutual friends were identified as pairs of children who chose each other as best friends in both the fall and spring of sixth grade. Within each pair, one child was identified as the target child and the other was identified as the friend. Each target child was paired with another target child who had the same score on the aggression tolerance measure in the fall but whose friend's aggression score differed from the aggression score of the first target child's friend by at least a standard deviation. Thus, in the fall, the two target children were equal in their aggression tolerance but differed in whether they had an aggressive or a nonaggressive best friend.

Children with an aggressive friend and children with a nonaggressive friend were compared for changes in tolerance for aggression over the 6-month interval. As shown in Fig. 4.5, there was no change in aggression tolerance from fall to spring for the children who had a nonaggressive friend ($F(1, 9) = 1.17, p > .05$). However, there was an increase in aggression tolerance over time for children whose friend was aggressive ($F(1, 9) = 8.36, p < .01$). Again, these findings show that characteristics of the child's friend determine the trajectory of the child's development. By engaging in a context in which norms for behavior vary (as represented by the friend's aggression), a child's attitude toward aggression changes. These findings illuminate the impact of the friendship context on children's beliefs about the appropriateness of an important social behavior.

The Interface of Friendship Dyads and the Friendship Network

When considering the features, functions, and effects of friendship, investigators typically refer to a child's best friend. However, most children and adolescents name at least several close friends, and many have more than one best friend (Hartup, 1993). These multiple friends often form a child's

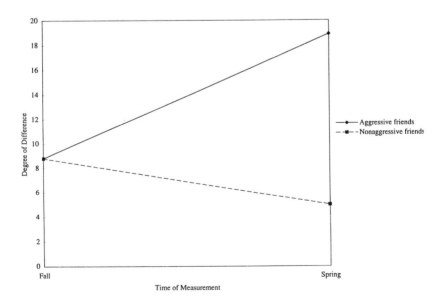

FIG. 4.5.   Change in aggression tolerance as a function of the aggressiveness of a child's friend.

friendship network. Peer cliques or friendship networks are interaction-based groups comprised of children who hang around together and associate with one another both in and out of school. Often these networks include pairs of mutual friends; however, not all ties within the clique represent mutual friendship choices.

The importance of affiliations with peer cliques increases in early adolescence. Interactions with peers and friends claim a larger amount of time for adolescents than for children, and peers comprise a larger proportion of their central social networks (Blyth, Hill, & Thiel, 1982; Brown, 1990). The quest for autonomy and the search for identity contribute to the enhanced importance of friendship networks as adolescents locate their peer group niche. The goal is to establish membership in a clique that is emotionally supportive and is consistent with the adolescent's interests and personal characteristics. Furthermore, the transition from self-contained elementary school classrooms to larger more impersonal middle schools and high schools is challenging, and associations with groups of friends help adolescents maneuver their constantly shifting social environment (Brown, Eicher, & Petrie, 1986). These factors further account for the increasing importance of cliques in adolescence and the potential influence members of friendship cliques have on one another.

The question of how friends affect a child's social development, and specifically, the question of how characteristics of one's friends influence adjustment raises the issue of which friends to assess. Do the features and qualities of a child's single best friendship explain the influence and effects of his or her friendships, or is it necessary to consider the child's entire friendship network? There are at least three possible answers to this question. First, a child's best friendship should be his or her most significant peer relationship and may have the most influence on the child's behavior and attitudes. As highlighted by Sullivan (1953), a close, supportive, collaborative relationship with a best friend provides a degree of intimacy and mutual engagement that is not found in any other relationship.

As noted earlier, many children and adolescents report more than one best friend or several close friends without one best friend, and Sullivan's description of friendship should not be interpreted as suggesting that a child may only have one true friendship. Thus, the second possibility is that the members of a child's peer clique may exert considerable influence on his or her development. To accurately understand the implications of friendship on social and emotional development, the entire friendship network as opposed to a child's single best friendship should be considered. The dynamic nature of friendships in childhood and adolescence and the fluidity and instability in many relationships (Cairns & Cairns, 1994) suggest that the child's friendship network may better explain how relationships with friends influence development. Specifically, best friends may change over time, but a child is likely to at least remain in the same general friendship network.

Finally, the third possible explanation is that it may not matter whether the characteristics of one's best friend or of the broader peer clique are examined. The child's friends all may be similar such that the influence of one's best friend may not differ substantially from that of the peer network as a whole. Berndt (1996) suggests that measures of the quality of multiple friendships are generally more correlated with other measures than they are with the quality of an adolescent's best friendship, yet the correlations are quite similar. It is possible that the identity or characteristics of children's friends follows the same pattern. Alternatively, friendship networks and best friendships may exert unique influences on children's behavior and attitudes that depend upon the variable of interest, such as delinquency and antisocial behavior, positive characteristics, or academic goals and achievement.

Inasmuch as the friendship dyad is embedded within a network structure, the effects of the friendship and the network are difficult to disentangle. Nevertheless, teasing these effects apart is important to determine whether a child's experiences beyond the best friend dyad contribute uniquely to their psychosocial well-being. Our examination of the best friend as a gateway to the broader peer network, specifically whether the popularity of a child's friend predicts changes in the child's popularity, addressed this type of question. The findings presented in Fig. 4.4 demonstrated that a friend's links with other children enhance a child's subsequent involvement in the larger peer group.

We reexamined these analyses to understand better the relative importance of the friendship network vis-à-vis the best friend dyad. In particular, we expanded the focus to include variables representing features of the child's network of friends in addition to features of the peer chosen as the best friend. Our goal was to examine whether information about a child's other friends and their characteristics adds to what we know about the child based on information about the first best friend. This first-friend-versus-the-network comparison may not be what network theorists have in mind when they think about the effects that network experience has on development, but it is one approach to assessing the relative impact of different participants in the peer system.

Path analysis was again used to assess whether changes in a child's popularity over a 6-month interval could be uniquely predicted with measures taken from either a child's second or third friend after accounting for the characteristics of the child and the first friend ($N = 194$). In an extension of the model shown in Fig. 4.4, measures of the child's popularity, aggression, and social prominence in the fall and spring and measures of the first best friend's popularity, aggression, and social prominence in the fall were included in an initial model along with these same measures from the peer chosen as the second friend in the fall (see Fig. 4.6). In our first examination of this model, a direct link between the second friend's popularity score and the child's popularity score in the spring was not included. This first model provided a relatively good fit to the data. The Comparative Fit Index was .97 and $\chi^2_{(33)} = 60.02$. When the model was reexamined after a direct link was included between the second friend's popularity score and the child's spring popularity score, the model was unchanged ($\chi^2_\Delta = .57$, $p > .05$). This finding shows that information about the second friend does not add to our ability to predict changes in a child's popularity in the group. When these analyses were repeated using measures taken from the third friend, or from a composite of the second and third, the same pattern of findings was observed. Clearly, it is the first friend choice that appears to influence a child's subsequent experiences in the peer group.

One aspect of the model shown in Fig. 4.6 should not be overlooked. The coefficients leading to the measures of the second friend from both the child fall measures and the measures from the first friend were typically of at least moderate strength. Most importantly, the child characteristics appeared to be more strongly associated with the characteristics of the second friend than with the characteristics of the first friend. Perhaps,

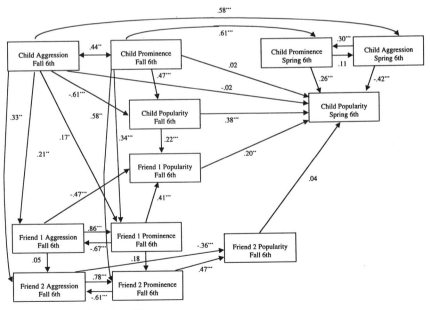

Note. *$p < .05$, **$p < .01$, and ***$p < .001$.

FIG. 4.6. Path model showing changes in a child's popularity as a function of best-friend and other-friend characteristics across sixth grade.

then, the processes that determine children's friendship choices vary for the first and second choices. This variation, especially when considered in conjunction with the differential importance of the first and second friend's popularity for the child's popularity, shows that not all friends in a child's friendship network are the same. A result of this variability is that any attempt to account for the role of friends in a child's experiences has to distinguish between the role played by different friends.

These analyses represent only one means of comparing the context of the friendship network and the dyadic friendship. They should not be considered comprehensive. Nevertheless, these findings highlight the unique context created by a child's best friend. Taking a broader view of the friendship network may provide information about the child's overall experience in the peer group but may obscure the impact of particular relationships. By adopting a perspective that denies this variation across friendships, such as by treating all friendships as alike or by creating measures by summing indices across relationships, we may fail to see the true impact that friendship has on development.

SUMMARY

The goal of our chapter is to build on Hartup's perspectives on friendship as an important developmental context. The crux of our presentation is that the peer system is a developmental context that encompasses interdependencies among individual characteristics, dyadic relations, and the broader social group. Furthermore, this context is essential for, rather than incidental to, development, and friendships are central elements of this system. Friendship processes affect development via several pathways. One of the most salient is the process of mutual influence. When a friendship is formed, children's characteristics combine with those of their friend to form a frame of reference that partially defines the context of the relationship. Accordingly, when children choose their friends, they choose a developmental context for themselves. Friendship choice is linked to children's own characteristics such that children select friends with whom they are similar. Moreover, similarity is an important determinant of the stability of the friendship, and within their shared environment, friends become more similar as their relationship progresses. The friendship context also has implications for children's links to the broader peer world and for the establishment of behavioral norms. The effects of friendship are not constant across all dyads. There is significant variability across relationships, and it seems that the best friendship may have a unique impact on development apart from other relationships in the broader social network. The legend of the ch'in player emphasizes the unique and special sounds that are significant to friends. Friendship is a context that children know and to which they adapt, and such knowledge and adaptation add significance to life.

ACKNOWLEDGMENTS

The authors express their appreciation to Susan W. Parker, Sally Ramsden, and Amir Georges Sabongui for their work in the conceptualization and data analyses for this project. We also thank Andrew Collins and Brett Laursen for their valuable editorial assistance in the revision of this paper. Finally, we individually and collectively wish to acknowledge the profound impact that Bill Hartup has had on our professional development. We are truly indebted to his wisdom and guidance.

REFERENCES

Berndt, T. J. (1996). Exploring the effects of friendship quality on social development. In W. M. Bukowski, A. F. Newcomb, & W. W. Hartup (Eds.), *The company they keep: Friendships in childhood and adolescence* (pp. 346–365). New York: Cambridge University Press.

Blyth, D. A., Hill, J. P., & Thiel, K. S. (1982). Early adolescents' significant others: Grade and gender differences in perceived relationships with familial and nonfamilial adults and young people. *Journal of Youth and Adolescence, 11,* 425–450.

Brown, B. B. (1990). Peer groups and peer cultures. In S. S. Feldman & G. R. Elliott (Eds.), *At the threshold: The developing adolescent* (pp. 171–196). Cambridge, MA: Harvard University Press.

Brown, B. B., Eicher, S. A., & Petrie, S. (1986). The importance of peer group ("crowd") affiliation in adolescence. *Journal of Adolescence, 9,* 73–96.

Bukowski, W. M., & Newcomb, A. F. (1984). Stability and determinants of sociometric status and friendship choice: A longitudinal perspective. *Developmental Psychology, 20,* 941–952.

Bukowski, W. M., Sabongui, A. G., & Newcomb, A. F. (1996, March). *Attitudes toward aggression and friendship patterns during early adolescence.* Paper presented at the meetings of the Society for Research on Adolescence, Boston, MA.

Cairns, R. B., & Cairns, B. D. (1994). *Lifelines and risks: Pathways of youth in our time.* New York: Cambridge University Press.

Cairns, R. B., Cairns, B. D., & Neckerman, H. J. (1989). Early school drop-out: Configurations and determinants. *Child Development, 60,* 1437–1452.

Cairns, R. B., Cairns, B. D., Neckerman, H. J., Gest, S. D., & Gariepy, J. L. (1988). Social networks and aggressive behavior: Peer support or peer rejection? *Developmental Psychology, 24,* 815–823.

Coie, J. C., Dodge, K. A., & Coppotelli, H. (1982). Dimensions and types of social status: A cross-age perspective. *Developmental Psychology, 18,* 557–570.

Darwin, C. (1964). *On the origin of species by means of natural selection.* New York: Modern Library. (Original work published 1859)

Gottman, J. M. (1983). How children become friends. *Monographs of the Society for Research in Child Development, 48,* No. 3 (Serial No. 201).

Hartup, W. W. (1992). *Friendships and their developmental significance.* In H. McGurk (Ed.), *Childhood social development* (pp. 175–205). Hillsdale, NJ: Lawrence Erlbaum Associates.

Hartup, W. W. (1993). Adolescents and their friends. In B. Laursen (Ed.), *Close friendships in adolescence: New directions for child development* (pp. 3–22). San Francisco: Jossey-Bass.

Hartup, W. W. (1996). The company they keep: Friendships and their developmental significance. *Child Development, 67,* 1–13.

Hartup, W. W., Glazer, J. A., & Charlesworth, R. (1967). Peer reinforcement and sociometric status. *Child Development, 38,* 1017–1024.

Kandel, D. B. (1978). Homophily, selection, and socialization in adolescent friendships. *American Journal of Sociology, 84,* 427–436.

Moreno, J. L. (1934). *Who shall survive? A new approach to the problem of human interrelations.* New York: Nervous and Mental Disease Publishing Company.

Newcomb, A. F., & Brady, J. E. (1982). Mutuality in boys' friendships. *Child Development, 53,* 392–395.

Newcomb, A. F., & Bukowski, W. M. (1983). Social impact and social preference as determinants of children's peer group status. *Developmental Psychology, 19,* 856–867.

Newcomb, A. F., Bukowski, W. M., & Pattee, L. A. (1993). Children's peer relations: A meta-analytic review of popular, rejected, neglected, controversial and average sociometric status. *Psychological Bulletin, 113,* 99–128.

Sameroff, A., & Chandler, M. (1975). Reproductive risk and the continuum of caretaking casualty. In F. Horowitz, M. Hetherington, S. Scarr-Salapatek, & G. Siegel (Eds.), *Review of child development research* (Vol. 4, pp. 187–244). Chicago: University of Chicago Press.

Sullivan, H. S. (1953). *The interpersonal theory of psychiatry.* New York: Norton.

Chapter 5

Friends' Influence on Children's Adjustment to School

Thomas J. Berndt
Purdue University

In his presidential address to the Society for Research in Child Development, Hartup (1996) suggested a framework for understanding the developmental significance of children's friendships. Central to his framework is a distinction between three facets of children's experience of friendship. The first is simply having or not having any friends. The second is the identity of children's friends, which Hartup defined more specifically as the friends' personality traits and other characteristics. The third is the quality of children's friendships, for example, their degree of intimacy or their level of conflict.

Hartup (1996) expressed the least confidence about the first facet, saying that "the developmental significance of having friends is far from clear" (p. 5). One problem is that assessments of whether children have friends usually are confounded with assessments of friendship quality. In most studies, children are credited with having friends only if they have at least one friendship that seems high in quality.

Hartup spoke somewhat more confidently about the significance of the third facet, friendship quality. In recent years, many researchers have tried to assess the quality of children's friendships, and then to determine the effects of high-quality friendships (see Bukowski, Newcomb, & Hartup, 1996; Furman, this volume; van Lieshout, Haselager, & Cillessen, this volume). This research is valuable because it directly examines the relationships between children and their friends. Still, Hartup (1996) was tentative in his statements about the significance of this facet. He concluded that recent studies "provide tantalizing tidbits suggesting that friendship quality bears a causal relation to developmental outcome" (p. 9).

Hartup expressed the greatest confidence about the significance of the second facet, the identity of children's friends. In Berndt's (1992, 1996) theoretical model, this facet refers to the friends' beliefs, attitudes, behaviors, and other characteristics. Hartup (1996) concluded that the effects of friends' characteristics have been firmly established. In his words, "the identity of the child's friends is a significant consideration in predicting developmental outcome" (p. 7).

The primary purpose of this chapter is to reexamine the evidence for this conclusion. Emphasis is placed not on a review of research findings, but on an analysis of the methods that researchers have used to evaluate the influence of friends' characteristics. The chapter is not focused on traditional issues such as the reliability of measures and the internal validity of research designs. Instead, attention is given to the conceptual problems that researchers have faced in assessing friends' influence.

The problems that arise when researchers try to assess friends' influence are not unique. These problems overlap greatly with those in the broader domain of peer-relationships research. Hartup (1970) began his chapter on peer relationships in the authoritative *Manual of Child Psychology* with two paragraphs of orienting comments about peer influences on children. In the third paragraph, he struck a cautionary note, saying:

> It is both challenging and difficult to isolate the variance in children's socialization that derives from contact with peers. Peer interactions affect behavior additively or interactively in conjunction with inputs from the inanimate environment and with inputs from parents and other socializing agents. Neither contrived experiments nor experiments of nature provide very good opportunities for studying behavioral changes which derive directly from peer interaction. The investigator must always tease this information from data that also vary as a function of organismic factors, stimulation from the nonsocial environment, and stimulation from adults. (p. 361)

Slightly more than a decade later, Hartup (1983) wrote the chapter on peer relationships in the renamed *Handbook of Child Psychology*. He began with similar orienting comments and a similar cautionary note. However, he added a sentence that offset the rather pessimistic tone of the earlier chapter: "Nevertheless, contemporary methods enable us to speculate about the nature of these conjunctions [of peer interaction with other experiences] and [about] the manner in which child–child relations augment adult–child relations in the course of socialization" (p. 104). In other words, Hartup concluded that methodological advances had increased researchers' ability to assess peer influences on children's development.

Researchers have continued to use several methods that were reviewed by Hartup (1970, 1983) in an effort to isolate the variance in children's behavior that is due to their peers' influence. Researchers have also devised new methods of measuring peer influence. But researchers have rarely examined these methods critically or compared the findings of research using different methods.

This chapter offers the beginnings of such a critical analysis and comparison. A full exploration of methods for assessing peer influence would be an immense undertaking, so limits on the scope of the chapter were necessary. The chapter does not deal with the influence of all peers who interact with a child. As the title suggests, the chapter focuses on the influence of best friends. However, what researchers have learned about friends' influence has implications for understanding not only the influence of other peers, but also the influences of parents, teachers, and other adults.

Rather than trying to consider all aspects of development that might be influenced by friends, emphasis is placed on school adjustment. As defined here, the broad domain of school adjustment includes children's academic achievement, their attitudes toward school, and their behavior in the classroom. The chapter includes occasional comments about other aspects of development, especially when those aspects were assessed in either classic or state-of-the-art research on peer influence. Yet most often, school adjustment is the outcome under consideration.

Greatest attention is given to three strategies for assessing friends' influence. One strategy is to ask children to respond to hypothetical dilemmas in which friends supposedly encourage them to do specific actions. Research with this strategy often is described as assessing children's conformity to peers. Another strategy is to use experimental designs to determine how discussions with friends affect children's attitudes or decisions. The third strategy is to estimate friends' influence from the degree to which children's characteristics and their friends' characteristics become similar over time.

Each strategy can provide some information about friends' influence, but each has weaknesses that have often been ignored. Conversely, some strategies have strengths that are not fully appreciated. One goal of the chapter is to highlight these weaknesses and strengths. An equally important goal is to show how a careful analysis of the three research strategies can change the interpretation of previous findings. In particular, the analysis casts doubt on some commonly accepted ideas about friends' influence. One of these ideas is that friends' influence is far greater in adolescence than in childhood or in early adulthood. The available data suggest that friends' influence does not change very dramatically with age. Another commonly accepted idea is that friends' influence derives from their use of coercive pressure. Many popular and scholarly writings include assertions that "peer pressure is a big problem," especially in adolescence (e.g., Ansley & McCleary, 1992; Bishop, 1989). By contrast, the available data suggest that coercive pressure is not the primary means by which friends influence children and adolescents. When used by friends, pressure may even be counterproductive, reducing rather than increasing their influence. Evidence for these conclusions is given in the following sections on each research strategy.

MEASURING CONFORMITY TO FRIENDS: RESPONSES TO HYPOTHETICAL DILEMMAS

To see how conformity to friends changes between middle childhood and adulthood, Berndt (1979) adapted a method devised by Bronfenbrenner (1967, 1970) and his colleagues (e.g., Devereux, 1970). The method involved hypothetical dilemmas in which children were supposedly faced with pressure from peers to perform illegal or socially undesirable actions. The dilemmas could be included in group-administered questionnaires, so data from large samples could be collected efficiently.

Figure 5.1 shows one dilemma used by Berndt (1979). The figure also shows the 6-point response scale on which students indicated their decision. (The second question shown in the figure is discussed later.) This dilemma falls within the domain of school adjustment, because students are supposedly invited by friends to cheat on a test at school.

Not all the dilemmas given to students involved school-related behaviors, although 10 dilemmas fell into the same broad category as the "lost-test" dilemma because friends supposedly invited students to join them in antisocial behaviors. Some antisocial behaviors mentioned in other dilemmas were stealing candy from a store, trespassing on private property, and soaping windows on Halloween. Students' responses to these dilemmas were viewed as showing their conformity to friends on antisocial behavior.

Two samples of several hundred students in the third, sixth, ninth, and eleventh or twelfth grades responded to the dilemmas. As Fig. 5.2 shows, in both samples conformity to friends increased steadily from third to ninth grade and then decreased slightly but significantly. Other researchers have reported similar age trends (Aitken, 1980; Bixenstine, DeCorte, & Bixenstine, 1976; Brown, Clasen, & Eicher, 1986; Steinberg & Silverberg, 1986).

Figure 5.2 also illustrates another intriguing finding of the study. Students' responses were scored on a scale from 1 to 6, with higher scores suggesting more conformity to friends. Therefore, the midpoint on the scale, or the score that would indicate no bias toward or against agreeing with the friends' suggestions, was 3.5. Figure 5.2 shows that the mean score at every grade in both samples was below 3.5. Most students at all ages

You and a couple of your best friends find a sheet of paper that the teacher lost. On the paper are the answers to a test that you are going to have tomorrow. Your friends all plan to study from it and they want you to go along with them. You don't think you should, but they all say to do it anyway. What would you <u>really</u> do?

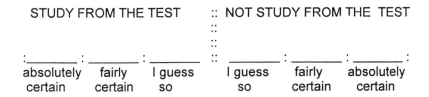

STUDY FROM THE TEST   :: NOT STUDY FROM THE TEST

| absolutely | fairly | I guess | I guess | fairly | absolutely |
| certain | certain | so | so | certain | certain |

How angry would your friends be if you didn't do what they wanted?

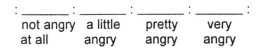

| not angry | a little | pretty | very |
| at all | angry | angry | angry |

FIG. 5.1. A hypothetical dilemma used by Berndt (1979) to measure conformity to friends on antisocial behavior, and the questions students were asked about the dilemma.

said they would not join friends who encouraged them to participate in antisocial activities.

The low level of apparent susceptibility to friends' influence was not mentioned in the original report on these studies. One possible reason for this omission is that the artist who prepared the original figures adopted the usual but misleading practice of truncating the response scale and showing only the range from 1 to 4 that includes all the plotted values. Another, probably more important reason is that tests of statistical significance focus not on the absolute value of a mean score, but on differences in mean scores. Researchers therefore emphasize the findings to which they can attach a test of significance and p-value.

However, attention to the absolute values of these mean scores is important. The students who responded to the dilemmas probably considered their primary decision as either doing or not doing what their friends suggested, and that decision should be taken seriously. In other words, researchers should take seriously that most students say that they would reject their friends' suggestions to engage in antisocial behavior.

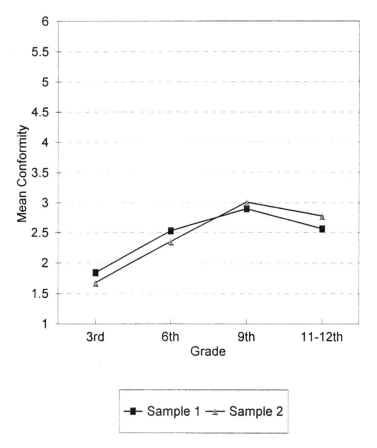

FIG. 5.2. Mean scores for conformity to friends on hypothetical antisocial dilemmas in two samples of 3rd–12th graders. Higher scores indicate greater conformity, and the neutral point is 3.5. Adapted from "Developmental changes in conformity to peers and parents," by T. J. Berndt, 1979, *Developmental Psychology, 15,* pp. 611 and 613. Copyright 1979 by the American Psychological Association. Adapted by the author.

At this point, some readers might question whether such detailed commentary on research published in 1979 is worthwhile. The answer is yes, because hypothetical dilemmas continue to be used to study children's conformity to peers (e.g., Fletcher, Darling, Steinberg, & Dornbusch, 1995). In addition, textbooks on child and adolescent development still cite the findings of Berndt (1979) and other researchers as evidence for age changes in peer conformity (e.g., Santrock, 1996; Shaffer, 1996). Finally, dozens of researchers from many countries have requested copies of the conformity questionnaires used by Berndt (1979). Most of these requests include three elements. First, researchers say that they need a measure of peer conformity for a larger project. Second, researchers ask if the questionnaires can be faxed to them, because they need to include them in a grant application due the next day or they are scheduled to give them to a sample of students during the next week. Third, researchers want to know if short forms of the questionnaires have been validated, or how the questionnaires can be abbreviated. (Recall that the original version had only 10 antisocial dilemmas.)

Requests of this type suggest that researchers typically are too willing to take measures used in previously published research at face value. In particular, researchers too readily assume that a measure labeled *peer conformity* validly assesses the variations in children's conformity to peers. Researchers also readily assume that children's susceptibility to friends' influence can be accurately judged from their responses to a few items on a questionnaire. These researchers do not accept Hartup's (1983) assertion that "isolating the variance in children's socialization that derives from contact with other children is extremely difficult" (p. 104).

Data from additional items on the Berndt (1979) questionnaires suggest that researchers should be more skeptical about the use of hypothetical dilemmas to assess conformity to friends. First, Bronfenbrenner (1967, 1970) viewed children's decisions on his hypothetical dilemmas as measuring their responsiveness to peer pressure. To see if children felt any pressure to conform to friends' suggestions, Berndt (1979) included a question after each dilemma about how angry the friends would be if the children didn't do what the friends wanted (see Fig. 5.1.) Responses to these questions were not significantly related to students' conformity, so they were not discussed in the original report (Berndt, 1979). However, the lack of a relation suggests that students' decisions on the dilemmas did not reflect their responsiveness to perceived pressure. That is, students who agreed with friends' suggestions did *not* do so because they were afraid their friends would be angry if they failed to conform. More surprising, the age changes in judgments about friends' anger were almost the exact inverse of those for conformity itself. Few students at any age expected their friends to be more than "a little angry" at nonconformity. Even so, the level of expected anger decreased significantly between third and ninth grade and then leveled off. These data also suggest that variations in students' conformity should not be attributed to variations in their responsiveness to friends' pressure.

Second, before responding to any dilemmas, children evaluated the antisocial actions in each dilemma. For example, they reported how bad it would be to study from an answer sheet that a teacher lost before a test. Students' evaluations of the antisocial actions were strongly and negatively correlated with their conformity on the dilemmas ($rs = -.55$ to $-.67$, $ps < .001$). In other words, students who thought that an act was less bad were more willing to join friends in doing it.

Students' evaluations of the antisocial actions became more positive between third and ninth grade. Evaluations became slightly less positive between ninth and twelfth grade. Thus, the age trend for evaluations matched that for apparent conformity to friends. The match implies that students agreed to join friends in antisocial actions, when they did, partly because they already had favorable attitudes toward those actions. For example, the ninth graders who agreed to study from the lost test may have said to themselves, "Finding that answer sheet was great. I'm glad my friends let me see it. If I had found it, I would have told them to study from it, too."

Stated more formally, differences in students' apparent conformity to friends were confounded with differences in their standards for behavior. Therefore, the age changes in responses to the dilemmas do not clearly show that friends' influence changes with age. This confounding can be greatly reduced if other kinds of hypothetical dilemmas are used. Students in the first sample described in Berndt (1979) also responded to dilemmas about neutral behaviors. Figure 5.3 presents one example. The two alter-

During gym one day, the teacher gives you free time. You want to jump around on the trampoline. A couple of your best friends are going to go outside to play volleyball and they want you to join them. What would you really do?

USE THE TRAMPOLINE   ::   GO OUT AND PLAY VOLLEYBALL

:___ : ___ : ___   ::   ___ : ___ : ___ :
absolutely fairly I guess   I guess fairly absolutely
certain   certain   so   so   certain   certain

How angry would your friends be if you didn't do what they wanted?

:___ : ___ : ___ : ___ :
not angry a little pretty very
at all   angry   angry   angry

FIG. 5.3. A hypothetical dilemma used by Berndt (1979) to measure conformity to friends on neutral behavior, and the questions students were asked about the dilemma.

natives in the dilemma, using the trampoline and playing volleyball, are neutral rather than antisocial. Because students might have differed in their preferences for one alternative or the other, all dilemmas of this type were written in two versions. In the other version of the example, the friends wanted to use the trampoline and the student wanted to play volleyball. The two versions were used in different forms of the questionnaire. Questionnaire form had some effect on students' responses, but it did not qualify the age differences found.

As Fig. 5.4 shows, the shape of the age trend for neutral conformity was similar to that for antisocial conformity. Conformity increased significantly between third and ninth grade and then decreased. The age changes were smaller for neutral than for antisocial conformity because the changes in neutral conformity were not confounded with changes in individual students' standards.

Even responses to the neutral items may not provide a valid measure of conformity to friends. The term *conformity*, as defined by Hartup (1970), "refers to shifts in attitudes or perceptions in the direction of some socially imposed norms" (p. 405). More specifically, conformity refers to "instances in which the individual experiences conflict between his own norms and the norms he perceives as governing the behavior of others" (p. 405). Students' responses to the hypothetical dilemmas need not have involved any shifts in attitudes or perceptions. These responses may only reflect students' willingness to join friends in various activities. In other words, the responses to such dilemmas may only show how eager students were to do things with friends.

In summary, the use of hypothetical dilemmas to measure children's conformity to friends is problematic. This research strategy may yield more information about individual children's standards for behavior than about their susceptibility to friends' influence. The strategy may still be valuable, however, if data are interpreted carefully. Consider three provocative findings from research using this strategy. First, when responding to hypothetical dilemmas, children and adolescents are more likely to reject friends' suggestions than to go along with them. Susceptibility to friends' influence, even in adolescence, seems much weaker than previous writers have suggested. Second, age changes in responses to the dilemmas are surprisingly modest. The modest age changes cast doubt on the popular belief that friends' influence is dramatically greater in adolescence than in childhood. Third, students rarely say that their friends would be angry if they didn't agree with the friends' suggestions. In other words, children show little awareness of the social pressure that is emphasized in writings about peer influence. Before concluding that friends' influence is not based on coercive pressure, however, evidence obtained using other research strategies should be examined.

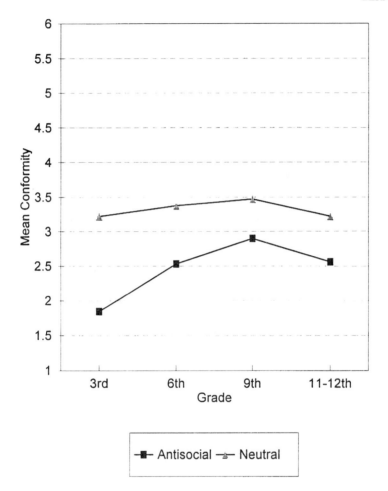

FIG. 5.4. Mean scores at each grade for conformity to friends on hypothetical antisocial and neutral dilemmas. Higher scores indicate greater conformity, and the neutral point is 3.5. Adapted from "Developmental changes in conformity to peers and parents," by T. J. Berndt, 1979, *Developmental Psychology*, *15*, p. 611. Copyright 1979 by the American Psychological Association. Adapted by the author.

OBSERVING FRIENDS' INFLUENCE IN VITRO: EXPERIMENTS ON FRIENDS' DISCUSSIONS

One alternative to the use of hypothetical dilemmas is the direct assessment of friends' influence with an experimental design. More specifically, the alternative strategy is to use an experimental design to show conclusively how discussions with friends change children's attitudes or decisions.

Biological and medical researchers often refer to *in vitro* studies of biological processes or reactions. The Latin words *in vitro* mean, "in glass," and these studies occur in glass beakers or in another artificial environment outside an intact, living organism. Experimental studies of friends' discussion are also *in vitro*, because the discussions occur in a setting controlled by the experimenter that is different from children's usual settings. Discussion topics and other conditions for the discussions are also arranged and controlled by the experimenter.

Hartup (1970, 1983) alluded to the limitations of this research strategy in his references to "contrived experiments." All researchers would prefer to study friends' influence *in vivo*, in the settings when children and their friends normally interact. However, all researchers recognize that experimental control makes it possible to identify the causes of children's behavior. In particular, an experimental design can be used to show that changes in children's attitudes or behavior are the result of discussions with friends.

For example, one experimental study focused on how discussions with a friend affect eighth-graders' academic achievement motivation (Berndt, Laychak, & Park, 1990). The eighth graders first completed a brief questionnaire about their friendships and their liking for their classmates. Based on these responses, each student was paired with a close friend. Each pair of friends was brought to a small room in their school. The two students in the pair then completed a pretest that was intended to assess motivation to achieve in school. The pretest consisted of several dilemmas with alternatives reflecting different levels of achievement motivation. Each child was asked to imagine that he or she was the main character in the dilemma, and then to decide what he or she would do. Figure 5.5 presents one of the dilemmas and the response scale for students' decisions. The two students in a pair responded to the dilemmas independently. They were seated so that they could not see each other's answers.

After completing the pretest dilemmas, the pairs of students were randomly assigned either to an experimental condition or to a control condition. Students in the experimental condition had about 3 minutes to discuss each dilemma with their friend. They were asked to try to agree on one decision (i.e., one point on the response scale) for each dilemma. The discussions were videotaped, with the children's knowledge and consent, but the experimenter was absent from the room. Pairs in the control condition also had a discussion, but they discussed topics such as planning a summer vacation. After the discussions, each student again responded to the dilemmas individually. Before beginning this posttest, the experimenter asked students to think about the dilemmas again and decide for themselves how to answer them, without being concerned with how they had responded earlier. Finally, the students answered a few questions about their relationship with the friend with whom they were paired.

One of the most popular rock groups is coming to town to give one performance. You have eagerly awaited their visit and have already purchased your ticket. Then you learn that the concert is on the night before a big exam. You don't really feel prepared for the exam and you have been having difficulty with the subject. Because of other commitments, this night will be the only time that you can study. If you don't take this time to study, you could get a low grade on the exam, but this may be the only opportunity to see one of your favorite groups in concert.

What would you do?

(check the blank below that shows your decision.)

0	1	2	3	4	5	6	7	8	9	10

0   5   9   10

Definitely   Not   Definitely
stay home   sure   go to the
and study   concert

FIG. 5.5. A hypothetical dilemma used by Berndt et al. (1990) to examine the effects of discussions with a friend on students' achievement-related decisions, and the question students were asked about the dilemma.

Influence during the friends' discussions was expected to be mutual: Students were expected to affect their friends' decisions and to be affected by the friends' decisions. This mutual process was expected to increase the similarity of friends' decisions on the dilemmas. In colloquial language, they would come to a meeting of the minds, or make more similar decisions after the discussions than before. Figure 5.6 shows that this hypothesis was confirmed. The figure shows the mean scores for the discrepancies in the decisions by pairs of friends. Lower scores indicate that the two students in a pair made more similar decisions. On the pretest, the similarity in

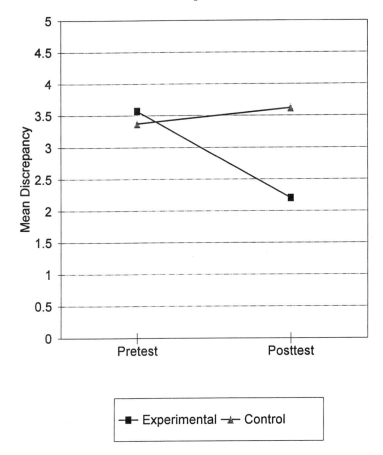

FIG. 5.6. Mean discrepancies in decisions by pairs of friends on achievement-related hypothetical dilemmas. From data reported by Berndt et al.
(1990).

the decisions by pairs of friends was comparable in the two conditions.
On the posttest, pairs who had discussed the dilemmas become more
similar in their decisions; those who had not discussed the dilemmas
showed little change. In short, discussions with a friend influenced students' decisions about these achievement-related dilemmas.

The mean scores on this indicator of friends' influence are worth noting.
On the pretest the decisions by each pair of friends differed by an average
of more than three points (see Fig. 5.6). On the posttest, the decisions by
friends who had discussed the dilemmas (i.e., those in the experimental
condition) still differed by an average of more than two points. Although
the similarity between friends had increased significantly, as already mentioned, why wasn't the posttest discrepancy equal to zero? The discrepancy

was zero *during* the discussions. That is, all pairs had agreed on a single decision.

The posttest discrepancies suggest that not all pairs of friends reached a true meeting of the minds during their discussions. Viewing the videotapes of the discussions confirmed this hypothesis. Friends often had a discussion that led to a fully mutual decision. However, some pairs of friends simply agreed to compromise on a position midway between their original positions, apparently without fully accepting that compromise. In some pairs one student not only dominated the discussion but also grabbed a pencil and checked the decision for the pair without getting the assent of the partner. When friends do not fully agree on a decision, they are not likely to endorse that decision on a posttest completed independently.

Other findings demonstrated the importance of full agreement between friends. The increase in friends' similarity between the pretest and the posttest was greater after discussions rated by adult coders as more cooperative. The increase was smaller when discussions were rated by coders as more aggressive, and when the friends themselves reported more conflict in their relationship. In other words, friends' influence was enhanced in an interpersonal climate of harmony and trust (Hallinan, 1983). Friends had much less influence when they tried to use coercive pressure.

Definite conclusions about friends' influence can be drawn from this study because of its experimental design. Offsetting this advantage of an experimental design is its artificiality. As suggested earlier, the design allowed *in vitro* assessment of friends' influence. But what does this design tell us about friends' influence *in vivo*? Most developmental psychologists would phrase the same question in terms of ecological validity (Bronfenbrenner, 1979). Is what happens in these discussions between friends, under the camera's eye, comparable to what happens in the natural ecology of childhood and adolescence?

A simple yes or no answer to this question would probably be wrong. Friends' discussions in an experimental setting are not completely comparable to those in everyday settings, but neither are they likely to be completely different from those occurring in everyday life. For decades, biological and medical researchers have adopted a similar position. These researchers do not assume that *in vitro* studies of biological processes always yield results matching those from *in vivo* studies. Nevertheless, many of these researchers view *in vitro* studies as valuable, and often an essential preliminary to, *in vivo* studies.

One possible concern about the experiment on friends' discussions can be dismissed fairly easily. Some researchers worry whether children or adolescents act naturally when they are being videotaped. The videotapes of the friends' discussions showed that almost all pairs of friends ignored the video camera once they started talking to each other. A video camera that does not move or make noise is much less interesting to children and adolescents than a close friend.

A more important limitation of experiments on friends' discussions is that they emphasize a single type of influence. These experiments are based on the assumption (one rarely stated explicitly) that friends influence one another primarily as they talk with one another. Other modes of influence are likely. Friends' influence may involve simple imitation of another's behavior. If an elementary-school boy starts throwing paper wads in the classroom, his friends may begin to do the same. Friends' influence may depend on social reinforcement. If a junior-high-school girl gets an A after hours of work on an English paper, and her best friend tells her that's really great, the girl may more often work hard in the future. Still another route of friends' influence is through direct teaching. If a senior-high-school boy does not know how to do a chemistry problem, he may call a friend who is in the same class. The friend then may explain how the problem can be solved, thus increasing the boy's learning and achievement in chemistry. These examples show that attention to only one mode of influence, through discussions with friends, is shortsighted. Experimental studies of friends' discussions are worthwhile because they allow researchers to observe influence processes directly. "Contrived experiments," however, need to be complemented by studies in natural settings.

ASSESSING THE EFFECTS OF FRIENDS' INFLUENCE: LONGITUDINAL STUDIES OF FRIENDS' SIMILARITY

To assess friends' influence in natural settings, researchers have adopted the strategy of measuring friends' similarity. The researchers who first used this strategy often committed two methodological and theoretical errors (see Ide, Parkerson, Haertel, & Walberg, 1981). The first error was asking students to report both on their own behavior and on their friends' behavior, and then defining the correlation between the students' self-reports and their reports on friends as a measure of their friends' influence on them. Correlations of this kind greatly overestimate friends' influence on students (Urberg, Cheng, & Shyu, 1991; Wilcox & Udry, 1986). Students do not always know what their friends think or how their friends behave. When students lack this knowledge, they often guess, and their guesses are biased. Most often students assume that their friends' attitudes and behaviors match their own. This form of projection leads to inflated estimates of friends' similarity, and so to inflated estimates of friends' influence. To avoid this problem, information about friends should come from the friends' self-reports or from other observers of the friends' behavior, not from students who also are reporting about themselves.

The second error made by researchers was assuming that similarity between friends is always the result of their influence on one another. For example, if most students with high grades in school had friends with high grades, researchers inferred that the friends influenced the students' grades (e.g., Ide et al., 1981). The logical flaw in this inference is easy to show with a different example. Most students have friends of the same gender (Berndt, 1996). This similarity is not due to the friends' influence on students' gender. Instead, the similarity is due to students' *selection* of same-gender peers as friends.

Only with a longitudinal design can researchers disentangle the contributions of selection and influence to friends' similarity. Using a longitudinal design, researchers can find out whether friends' similarity on specific characteristics increases over time. Such increases can reasonably be attributed to friends' influence on one another. Longitudinal data have provided support for hypotheses that friends influence important characteristics such as academic achievement, cigarette smoking, and heterosexual behavior (Billy & Udry, 1985; Epstein, 1983; Fisher & Bauman, 1988; Graham, Marks, & Hansen, 1991; Urberg et al., 1991), but the apparent magnitude of friends' influence has often been surprisingly modest. Occasionally, the estimates of friends' influence were not statistically significant.

A recent longitudinal study assessed friends' influence on students' attitudes, behavior, and achievement in junior high school (Berndt & Keefe, 1995). The study included 297 seventh and eighth graders in three public schools. The sample included more than 60% of the students in those grades, more than 95% of whom were White.

During November or December, small groups of students completed questionnaires that included several items about their behavior in school. Six items asked about positive involvement in school (e.g., "How often do you take part in class discussions?") and six asked about disruptive behavior (e.g., "How often do you misbehave in class?"). English and math teachers also rated the students' positive involvement and disruptive behavior, using items corresponding to those for students' self-reports. In addition, these teachers reported the grades that the students received in their subjects on the last report card. These measures of involvement, disruption, and grades were the primary indicators of the students' adjustment to school.

The student questionnaire also included a page on which students could name up to three best friends. More than 90% of the students named three friends. Students often named classmates as best friends, and more than 85% of the students named at least one best friend who was also participating in the study. Scores for these students' adjustment were matched with scores derived from their friends' self-reports and from their teachers' reports on the friends. Students completed the same questionnaires the following April or May, 5 or 6 months after the first assessment.

During the same period, teachers again provided reports on the students' behavior and grades.

One possible way to analyze these longitudinal data would be to see whether students who remained best friends became more similar over time (e.g., Kandel, 1978). This analytic strategy is problematic because it implicitly assumes that friends have no influence on one another if they do not remain close friends for the entire interval between assessments. A plausible alternative assumption is that students are influenced by all their friends, even if some of those friendships do not last more than a few months.

An analytic strategy consistent with the alternative assumption is hierarchical regression analysis. With longitudinal data, hierarchical regression analyses show whether students' characteristics assessed during a second wave of data collection (Time 2) can be predicted from the earlier (Time 1) characteristics of their friends (e.g., Graham et al., 1991). Students who are influenced by their friends' characteristics should, over time, develop characteristics more like those of their friends. If the Time 2 score for students is used as the criterion in a regression analysis, then friends' influence might be indicated by a significant regression coefficient for the Time 1 score for the friends' characteristics.

The analysis is defined as hierarchical because the friends' Time 1 score is not introduced in the first step of the analysis. Students' own characteristics show a combination of continuity and change over time. To ensure that estimates of friends' influence are not confounded with the continuity of students' characteristics, a score for students' Time 1 characteristics must be entered in the regression analysis first. The score for the friends' Time 1 characteristics is entered in a second step. The critical question is whether this second step shows that the score for friends' Time 1 characteristics is a significant predictor of students' Time 2 scores. If it is, the changes during the year in students' characteristics can be attributed partly to the influence of their friends. In short, students became more like their friends.

Berndt and Keefe (1995) did hierarchical regression analyses for all measures of school adjustment. Figure 5.7 shows the results of these analyses in a somewhat unconventional way. For each measure of adjustment in the spring (Time 2), the standardized regression coefficients (or beta weights) are shown for the matching indicators of the students' adjustment and their friends' adjustment in the fall (Time 1). The graph of the coefficients shows their relative magnitudes clearly. An asterisk above a bar indicates that the coefficient was significant at $p < .05$ or better.

Most obvious in the figure are the large coefficients for the Time 1 (fall) measures of the students' adjustment. These coefficients show that there is a high degree of continuity in seventh- and eighth-graders' adjustment to school during a single school year. Students who are high in

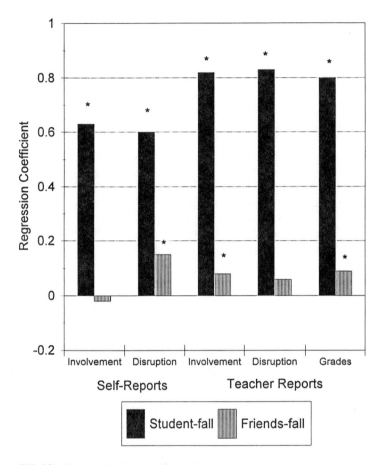

FIG. 5.7. Standardized regression coefficients for the predictors of students'
scores in the spring on measures of school adjustment. In the regression
analyses, students' scores in the fall were entered before the fall scores of
their friends. Asterisks above bars indicate coefficients significant at $p < .05$.
From data reported by Berndt and Keefe (1995).

positive involvement in the fall tend to remain high in positive involvement
in the spring. Students who are disruptive in the fall tend to remain disruptive in the spring. Students' grades tend to be as high or low in the
second semester as in the first.

By comparison, the coefficients for the Time 1 (fall) measures of the
friends' adjustment are small, but significant for three measures of adjustment: self-reported disruption, teacher-rated involvement, and report-card
grades. These coefficients imply that students were influenced by their
friends' disruptive behavior, involvement, and academic achievement. Judging from their self-reports, students became more disruptive during the

year if their friends were more disruptive in the fall. Judging from teachers' reports, students became more involved during the year if their friends were more involved in the fall. Finally, students' report-card grades improved during the year if their friends had higher grades in the fall.

These results must be interpreted carefully. Worth noting explicitly is that the analyses do not imply any overall direction to friends' influence. The data in Fig. 5.7 could be described equally accurately by saying that students' disruption decreased if they had less disruptive friends; their involvement decreased if their friends were less involved; their grades declined if their friends had lower grades. In other words, students became more like their friends, whether those friends had a better or a poorer adjustment to school than the students initially did themselves.

More difficult to answer is whether friends' influence is as weak as the coefficients in Fig. 5.7 suggest. For several reasons, the answer may be no. First, in longitudinal studies the regression coefficients for friends' characteristics only estimate the friends' influence during the period between waves of data collection. That period was 5 or 6 months in Berndt and Keefe (1995). The cumulative influence of friends during childhood and adolescence may be far greater than the results of such short-term longitudinal studies suggest. Second, when talking about the magnitude of any effect, choosing the proper frame of reference is essential. Before concluding that friends' influence on students' adjustment to school is weak, researchers should ask, "compared to what?" Because school adjustment shows high continuity within and across school years (Mounts & Steinberg, 1995), it is difficult to document that other socialization agents such as parents have more influence than friends do (see Melby & Conger, 1996). Conclusions based on comparisons to other sources of social influence are more meaningful than conclusions based on the absolute size of a regression coefficient. Third, not underestimating the influence of friends is just as important as not overestimating it. Very few psychological theories would suggest that friends have little or no influence on adolescents. Most adolescents spend 25% to 30% of their waking hours with friends (Csikszentmihalyi & Larson, 1984). This high frequency of interaction should be accompanied by a high level of mutual influence.

One final question concerns the general strengths and weaknesses of the longitudinal research strategy. For assessing friends' influence in natural settings, this strategy is superior to those described previously, although estimates of the magnitude of friends' influence must be interpreted carefully. By contrast, longitudinal studies rarely provide information about the processes by which friends influence children and adolescents. Consequently, only speculative explanations can be given for differences in friends' influence on different characteristics. For example, in Berndt and Keefe's (1995) study the regression coefficient for friends' self-reported disruption was significant, but that for friends' self-reported involvement was not (see Fig. 5.7). These coefficients imply that friends had a significant influence on the changes during the year in students' self-reported disruption but not in their self-reported involvement. Why does this difference exist? No data that would answer this question were available in the study. Information about influence processes would be necessary to explain the difference, and such information is not often obtained when the longitudinal research strategy is used.

CONCLUSIONS: THE PAST, PRESENT, AND FUTURE

The three research strategies discussed so far do not encompass all those used to explore friends' influence on students. A fourth strategy that was often used during the 1950s and 1960s has almost disappeared from the scientific landscape. During those decades, many researchers tested children and adolescents in some variant of the Asch (1951) procedure for assessing conformity to a group majority. For example, children judged the length of lines, the number of clicks of a metronome, or other perceptual phenomena after hearing several peers give obviously incorrect judgments.

For decades, researchers tried to determine how conformity to the peer majority changed with age. Appraisals of the researchers' success varied over time. In his chapter for the *Manual of Child Psychology*, Hartup (1970) wrote that the available data "present a consistent picture concerning the relation between chronological age and conformity to peer influences" (p. 410). Yet, 13 years later, Hartup (1983) reviewed the literature again and came to a different conclusion: "Although it seemed for a time that laboratory experimentation might document these [age] trends (Hartup, 1970), it has become increasingly evident that conformity is a complex mixture of one's understanding of the origins and nature of social rules, one's motives (e.g., the need to be correct or the need for social approval), and the nature of the social organizations to which one belongs" (p. 161). This conclusion signals a true paradigm shift in developmental psychology. This shift has not been completed, in part because it is neither fully understood nor fully accepted.

The new paradigm can be described by drawing upon Bronfenbrenner's (1989) classification of research models. In Bronfenbrenner's terms, the model underlying many previous studies was a personal-attributes model. Researchers assumed that they could accurately describe how peer influence changes as a function of one personal attribute, chronological age. The same assumption was tested and found false in the many studies with variants of the Asch (1951) procedure.

Researchers have now shifted to what Bronfenbrenner calls the person–context model. The term *context* refers to important features of children's environments. In research on peer influence, greater attention to context is shown in multiple ways. For example, instead of talking generally about peer influence, researchers identify the best friends who are assumed to have the greatest influence on children. Instead of making global assumptions about the direction of peer influence, researchers assess the characteristics of a student's friends and then estimate how those friends influence the student's characteristics. Instead of assuming that friends' influence is comparable for all characteristics, researchers look at specific attitudes and behaviors such as attitudes toward school and academic achievement.

Unfortunately, researchers studying friends' influence have rarely adopted what Bronfenbrenner (1989) called the process–person–context model. This model requires an assessment of the processes, both social and intrapersonal, responsible for the effects of the environmental context on an individual with specified attributes. Psychological theories can serve as guides in identifying processes of socialization, such as discussion, reinforcement, and modeling, by which friends influence specific outcomes, such as children's academic achievement. Psychological theories can also serve as guides in identifying intrapersonal processes, such as identification with friends, by which friends' words and deeds change children's psychological makeup.

Even the process–person–context model may be incomplete. To understand friends' influence fully, researchers may need to use a *relationship*–process–person–context model. That is, researchers may need to consider the features of the relationships between friends when trying to explain how and how much they influence one another. Hartup (1996) suggested the need for this expanded research model in the conclusion to his presidential address. The *relationship* term in the expanded model is similar to the construct of friendship quality in Hartup's framework. Hartup proposed that the effects of friendship quality could be better understood if researchers simultaneously assessed the identity (or characteristics) of children's friends, and vice versa.

A few of the studies discussed in this chapter provided data relevant to Hartup's proposal, but the data are not consistent. As mentioned earlier, Berndt et al. (1990) found that the influence of discussions with a friend was weaker when the friends reported more conflict in their relationship. That is, friends' influence was lower when friendship quality was lower. On the other hand, Berndt and Keefe (1995) assessed friendship quality in their longitudinal study, but they found little evidence that friends' influence on students' adjustment to school differed in strength when these friendships differed in quality.

Still more challenging would be an exploration of the full relationship–process–person–context model. This model has not yet been examined empirically, in part because no theories of friends' influence include hypotheses that refer to all terms in the model. Moreover, an exploration of the full model would require new research strategies. Efforts to generate hypotheses from the full model, and then to devise research strategies for testing them, could greatly enhance understanding of friends' influence. These efforts could also lead to interventions to enhance the positive influences of friends on children's development.

REFERENCES

Aitken, P. P. (1980). Peer group pressures, parental controls, and cigarette smoking among 10 to 14 year olds. *British Journal of Social and Clinical Psychology, 19,* 141–146.

Ansley, L., & McCleary, K. (1992, August 21–23). Do the right thing. *USA Weekend,* pp. 4–7.

Asch, S. (1951). Effects of group pressure upon the modification and distortion of judgment. In M. H. Guetzkow (Ed.), *Groups, leadership and men* (pp. 177–190). Pittsburgh, PA: Carnegie Press.

Berndt, T. J. (1979). Developmental changes in conformity to peers and parents. *Developmental Psychology, 15,* 608–616.

Berndt, T. J. (1992). Friendship and friends' influence in adolescence. *Current Directions in Psychological Science, 1,* 156–159.

Berndt, T. J. (1996). Transitions in friendship and friends' influence. In J. A. Graber, J. Brooks-Gunn, & A. C. Petersen (Eds.), *Transitions through adolescence: Interpersonal domains and contexts* (pp. 57–84). Mahwah, NJ: Lawrence Erlbaum Associates.

Berndt, T. J., & Keefe, K. (1995). Friends' influence on adolescents' adjustment to school. *Child Development, 66,* 1312–1329.

Berndt, T. J., Laychak, A. E., & Park, K. (1990). Friends' influence on adolescents' academic achievement motivation: An experimental study. *Journal of Educational Psychology, 82,* 664–670.

Billy, J. O. G., & Udry, J. R. (1985). Patterns of adolescent friendship and effects on sexual behavior. *Social Psychology Quarterly, 48,* 27–41.

Bishop, J. H. (1989). Why the apathy in American high schools? *Educational Researcher, 18*(1), 6–10.

Bixenstine, V. E., DeCorte, M. S., & Bixenstine, B. A. (1976). Conformity to peer-sponsored misconduct at four age levels. *Developmental Psychology, 12,* 226–236.

Bronfenbrenner, U. (1967). Response to pressure from peers versus adults among Soviet and American school children. *International Journal of Psychology, 2,* 199–207.

Bronfenbrenner, U. (1970). Reaction to social pressure from adults versus peers among Soviet day school and boarding school pupils in the perspective of an American sample. *Journal of Personality and Social Psychology, 15,* 179–189.

Bronfenbrenner, U. (1979). *The ecology of human development.* Cambridge, MA: Harvard University Press.

Bronfenbrenner, U. (1989). Ecological systems theory. In R. Vasta (Ed.), *Annals of child development* (Vol. 6, pp. 187–249). Greenwich, CT: JAI Press.

Brown, B. B., Clasen, D. R., & Eicher, S. A. (1986). Perceptions of peer pressure, peer conformity dispositions, and self-reported behavior among adolescents. *Developmental Psychology, 22,* 521–530.

Bukowski, W. M., Newcomb, A. F., & Hartup W. W. (Eds.). (1996). *The company they keep: Friendship in childhood and adolescence.* Cambridge, England: Cambridge University Press.

Csikszentmihalyi, M., & Larson, R. (1984). *Being adolescent.* New York: Basic Books.

Devereux, E. C. (1970). The role of peer-group experience in moral development. In J. P. Hill (Ed.), *The Minnesota symposia on child psychology* (Vol. 4, pp. 94–140). Minneapolis: University of Minnesota Press.

Epstein, J. L. (1983). The influence of friends on achievement and affective outcomes. In J. L. Epstein & N. Karweit (Eds.) *Friends in school: Patterns of selection and influence in secondary schools* (pp. 177–200). New York: Academic Press.

Fisher, L. A., & Bauman, K. E. (1988). Influence and selection in the friend-adolescent relationship: Findings from studies of adolescent smoking and drinking. *Journal of Applied Social Psychology, 18,* 289–314.

Fletcher, A. C., Darling, N. E., Steinberg, L., & Dornbusch, S. M. (1995). The company they keep: Relation of adolescents' adjustment and behavior to their friends' perceptions of authoritative parenting in the social network. *Developmental Psychology, 31,* 300–310.

Graham, J. W., Marks, G., & Hansen, W. B. (1991). Social influence processes affecting adolescent substance use. *Journal of Applied Psychology, 76,* 291–298.

Hallinan, M. T. (1983). Commentary: New directions for research on peer influence. In J. L. Epstein & N. Karweit (Eds.), *Friends in school: Patterns of selection and influence in secondary schools* (pp. 219–231). New York: Academic Press.

Hartup, W. W. (1970). Peer interaction and social organization. In P. H. Mussen (Ed.), *Carmichael's manual of child psychology* (3rd ed., pp. 361–456). New York: Wiley.

Hartup, W. W. (1983). Peer relations. In P. H. Mussen (Series Ed.), E. M. Hetherington (Vol. Ed.), *Handbook of child psychology. Vol. 4. Socialization, personality, and social development* (pp. 103–196). New York: Wiley.

Hartup, W. W. (1996). The company they keep: Friendships and their developmental significance. *Child Development, 67,* 1–13.

Ide, J. K., Parkerson, J., Haertel, G. D., & Walberg, H. J. (1981). Peer group influence on educational outcomes: A quantitative synthesis. *Journal of Educational Psychology, 73,* 472–484.

Kandel, D. B. (1978). Homophily, selection, and socialization in adolescent friendships. *American Journal of Sociology, 84,* 427–436.

Melby, J. N., & Conger, R. D. (1996). Parental behaviors and adolescent academic performance: A longitudinal analysis. *Journal of Research on Adolescence, 6,* 113–137.

Mounts, N. S., & Steinberg, L. (1995). An ecological analysis of peer influence on adolescent grade point average and drug use. *Developmental Psychology, 31,* 915–922.

Santrock, J. W. (1996). *Adolescence.* Madison, WI: Brown & Benchmark.

Shaffer, D. R. (1996). *Developmental psychology: Childhood and adolescence.* Pacific Grove, CA: Brooks/Cole.

Steinberg, L., & Silverberg, S. B. (1986). The vicissitudes of autonomy in early adolescence. *Child Development, 57,* 841–851.

Urberg, K. A. Cheng, C.-H., & Shyu, S.-J. (1991). Grade changes in peer influence on adolescent cigarette smoking: A comparison of two measures. *Addictive Behaviors, 16,* 21–28.

Wilcox, S., & Udry, J. R. (1986). Autism and accuracy in adolescent perceptions of friends' sexual attitudes and behavior. *Journal of Applied Social Psychology, 16,* 361–374.

Chapter 6

Bootstrapping Through the Cultural Comparison Minefield: Childhood Social Status and Friendship in the United States and Indonesia

Doran C. French
Illinois Wesleyan University

Kusdwiratri Setiono
University of Padjadjaran, Bandung, Indonesia

J. Mark Eddy
Oregon Social Learning Center, Eugene, OR

> *An 11-year-old Malay girl writes that she likes a boy in her class because he is nice, kind, and helps others. She dislikes two other boys in her class. One because he is mean and bullies others, and another, because he is dirty and smells bad.*

It is likely that similar comments could be made by an 11-year-old girl in the United States, thus introducing the question: Is there commonality across cultures in the way children are attracted to and form relationships with their peers? Given the tremendous interest in children's peer acceptance (e.g., Asher & Coie, 1990) and friendship (e.g., Bukowski, Newcomb, & Hartup, 1996), it is surprising that this question has received only limited attention (Krappmann, 1996).

To Compare or Not to Compare Cultures?

Controversy has swirled around the study of cultural differences for the last several decades. Some researchers, such as Whiting and Whiting (1975) and Triandis (1994), have argued that meaningful comparisons are possible between cultures, while others, such as Rogoff, Gauvain, and Ellis (1984), have argued that such comparisons will always be extremely problematic due to the complexity and pervasiveness of culture in all aspects of human life. From our perspective, a comparative approach has utility for assessing cultural differences in attraction and friendships, but only within the context of a comprehensive research strategy that also includes an in-depth study of developmental processes within cultures (Berry, Poortinga, Segall, & Dasen, 1992). Given the limited empirical study of children's social relations in other cultures, tests of the generalizability of findings from the study of North American children are essential. In addition, comparative studies may increase our methodological sophistication by alerting us to the limitations of our measurement procedures as well as by providing a different context for exploring measurement alternatives. Such study may also allow us to discover greater variation in social relationship processes than have been observed in the study of single cultures (Berry et al., 1992).

Following the writings of Berry (1989), we hypothesize that thoughtful, well-designed comparative studies employing both etic (the study of multiple cultures from an external perspective) and emic (the study of a single culture utilizing the perspective of the culture) aspects may provide us with a systematic method of isolating qualities that are likely to be fruitful candidates for more in-depth analysis of culture. Such studies often begin with the use of an imposed etic that involves the transport of measures and paradigms from the culture in which they were developed to a new culture (Berry, 1989). The use of an imposed etic, however, has been widely criticized (e.g., Rogoff et al., 1984) for its failure to adapt measures to the features of the culture.

The Problem: Measurement Bias

Unfortunately, few instruments are truly appropriate for comparative use across different cultural groups, and consequently, measurement difficulties have been ubiquitous in cross-cultural psychological research (Cole, 1992). Ideally, measurement instruments used to compare cultural groups should meet the following requirements (Pumariega, 1996):

1. *conceptual equivalence*: the same theoretical construct is measured by the instrument in each culture;
2. *semantic equivalence*: each item on the instrument has the same relative meaning in each culture;
3. *content equivalence*: the content of each item is relevant to the phenomenon being studied in each culture;
4. *methodological equivalence*: the methods of data collection elicit comparable kinds of responses across cultures.

Meeting these criteria is difficult without a sophisticated understanding of the psychological phenomenon as it occurs within a culture. Because this level of understanding has not yet been achieved within any culture, a requirement that researchers must possess adequate measures prior to launching cross-cultural investigations, creates a proverbial "Catch 22" situation: One cannot measure variables within a culture in the absence of a good understanding of the culture, yet one cannot understand a culture without measuring critical variables. Because there is no reasonable way to enter such a loop, researcher paralysis is the most likely outcome. Notably, measurement difficulties are not confined to cross-cultural investigations. Few, if any, measures of social behavior are free of errors associated with biases of either measurement agent or method. Because measurement biases are assumed to be omnipresent (in both within and between culture comparisons), the search for a single nonbiased measurement procedure is likely to be futile.

In past cross-cultural research, the failure to empirically assess measurement error led to serious difficulties. In some cases, measurement equivalence was accepted without empirical evidence, based only on the appearance of face validity or the persuasability of the investigator. In other cases, empirical demonstration of measurement equivalence was established as a precondition for initiating research, thus essentially foreclosing the exploration of certain topics. Another option, however, is available.

Multiple Agents, Multiple Methods, Multiple Constructs

The multiple-agent, multiple-method, and multiple-construct assessment approach provides an alternative strategy for isolating sources of measurement error and systematically improving measurement precision within the context of cross-cultural investigations. A key assumption of this approach is that measures, regardless of type and source, are biased (Dishion, French, & Patterson, 1995). By examining the multiple trait–multiple method matrix, one can begin to empirically assess the source and magnitude of measurement biases both within and across cultures.

Information from the multiple trait–multiple method matrix can be used to begin the process of "construct validation" (Cronbach & Meehl, 1955). Meehl (1954) described construct validation as a "bootstrapping" process. Patterson and Bank (1986), Capaldi and Patterson (1989), and Patterson, Reid, and Dishion (1992) illustrated the iterative nature of this process in the Oregon Youth Study (OYS). In the OYS, assessment devices were created at the beginning of the study to capture key variables, the reliabilities and validities of these new devices were assessed, and changes were made to improve these variables for the next round of assessment. This process was repeated in each successive round, with a gradual improvement in the psychometric characteristics of the measures. The guiding principle of these successive measurement attempts was that one cannot assume measurement adequacy until it is demonstrated empirically that measures of a construct converge with each other and diverge from other constructs. Unfortunately, this basic convergence requirement is difficult to meet even within a single culture, let alone across cultures. The approach, however, does provide the researcher with an empirical assessment of the adequacy of measurement that is not possible using a single agent and single measure strategy.

Using the multiple-agent, multiple-measure, multiple-construct approach, measurement refinement and exploration of cultural effects can proceed simultaneously. Rather than a precondition for the initiation of cross-cultural research, the refinement of measures can be seen as the outcome of a line of programmatic research that proceeds through numerous iterations over time. Our research provides an example of an early stage of this process, as we assess whether parent, teacher, and peer measures of peer relations, each of which has been used extensively in the United States, can be transported to Indonesia. Simultaneously, we assess the possibility that the correlates of such measures differ between the cultures.

Purpose

In this chapter, we examine differences in the correlates of peer status and friendship between school children in two countries, Indonesia and the United States. The investigations of Chen and his colleagues on peer status in China provide the empirical foundation for the present study. In the first section, we briefly review their work. In the next section, we review the implications of ecological cultural models for understanding the relation between childhood social status within the peer group and individual child characteristics. We focus specifically on the well validated Individualism–Collectivism dimension, a dimension likely to be particularly relevant for understanding cultural differences in the social relationships of children. We then report findings from parallel studies on children's social status and friendships conducted in Indonesia and the United States. We conclude with a discussion of methodology, as well as a discussion of the relevance of cross-cultural work on individual attraction within social groups to a broader understanding of children's relationships.

BACKGROUND

Correlates of Peer Status in China

The most comprehensive study of the correlates of peer status outside of North America has been conducted by Chen and his associates with elementary school-aged Chinese children living in Shanghai (Chen, Rubin,

& Li, 1995; Chen, Rubin, & Sun, 1992). Peer ratings of aggression–class disruption derived from the Revised Class Play (Masten, Morison, & Pelligrini, 1985) were found to be *positively* associated with children's negative sociometric ratings and *negatively* associated with positive sociometric ratings as well as teacher ratings of general social competence and academic adjustment. In contrast, peer ratings of shyness–sensitivity were *positively* associated with positive sociometrics and teacher ratings of competence and academic adjustment and *negatively* associated with negative nominations. In a later study with middle school-aged children, Chen, Rubin, Li, and Li (1996) found that neither positive nor negative sociometric status was associated with parental ratings of child internalizing behavior. In contrast to these findings, within North American samples, internalizing problems such as shyness have been found to be related *negatively* with positive sociometrics and *positively* with negative sociometrics in numerous North American samples (e.g., French & Waas, 1985).

Chen and his colleagues attributed their results to features of Chinese culture (e.g., Confucianism) in which a high value is placed on shyness and self-restraint (Chen et al., 1996). They also emphasized the collectivist, group-oriented nature of Chinese society, which is a ubiquitous feature of children's lives. Disruptive behavior is prohibited and provokes strong sanctions; children are taught to control their individualistic impulses and cooperate with others. To the extent that shy and withdrawn behavior is associated with societal requirements of obedience and submission, such behavior may not be salient to peers and adults, nor is it likely to be seen as pathological.

Individualism–Collectivism

It is not known if these findings apply specifically to Chinese culture or whether similar results would emerge from other cultures in which collectivism is emphasized and children are encouraged to display reticent behavior. Before we discuss our investigations, conducted in the collectivist society of Java, Indonesia, we provide an overview of the Individualistic–Collectivist dimension and the ecocultural models from which it emerged.

Ecocultural models focus on features of social organization that vary across different economic subsistence patterns. For example, in an analysis of 186 preindustrial societies, Schlegel and Barry (1991) found that male adolescent peer groups are larger and assume more importance in permanent and politically integrated societies. Characteristics of economic maintenance, such as parent and child workload, household and community structure and organization, and population density, have been found to significantly impact both the learning environment of children (Whiting & Whiting, 1975) and the extensiveness of their contact with peers (Whiting & Edwards, 1988).

The most important instrumental competencies are tied to subsistence. Child rearing, according to Ogbu's (1981) analysis, is seen as a mechanism to promote these competencies, and social competence is related to other's judgments of the extent to which these are attained. These competencies include desirable personality characteristics as well as the ability to maintain social relationship networks. Barry, Child, and Bacon (1959) argued that in societies with limited food accumulation (e.g., hunter–gatherer societies), individualistic and assertive behavior is esteemed. In contrast, in societies experiencing high food accumulation (e.g., cultures based on agriculture), conscientious, compliant, and conservative behavior is more likely to be valued. These observations evolved into the individualism–collectivism dimension (Triandis, 1995), which has been increasingly employed to understand children's social behavior (Cooper, 1994; Nsamenang, 1992).

Within individualist societies, there is a tendency for individuals to focus on their own needs, interests, and attainments. In contrast, within collectivist societies, individuals tend to be more concerned with the consequences of their actions on other members of their group and to exhibit a greater willingness to engage in self-sacrifice for the common good. Within each type of society, however, there are specific contexts within which individualistic or collectivist orientations are considered most appropriate. For example, it has been suggested that although collectivist societies tend to minimize the exhibition of in-group conflict, they may exhibit considerable conflict with out-group members (Triandis, 1995).

The Impact of Individualism–Collectivism on Peer Relationships

Because independence and self-initiative are stressed in individualistic societies, aggression among peers and family members prompts ambivalent reactions. In certain contexts (e.g., during sports), behavior such as competitiveness, assertiveness, self-reliance, and culturally appropriate violence may be approved. In other contexts, however, aggression may be seen as inappropriate. In contrast, aggression may be more consistently sanctioned in collectivist societies. In the Six Cultures Study, the presence and cohesion of nearby kin was associated with extreme adult reactions to children's aggression (Lambert, 1971). Because child aggression had the potential of disrupting important adult relationships in these cohesive communities, it was swiftly and soundly discouraged.

We might also expect that cooperative behavior would be valued in both types of cultures, but to different degrees and within different contexts. In individualist cultures, cooperation is important to the extent that it assists the individual to fulfill instrumental task demands. Consequently, it may be most prominent within specific, functional relationships that are motivated by shared self-interests of the participants. In contrast, cooperative behavior should be exhibited on a more generalized basis in collectivist cultures. These differences were illustrated by findings (e.g., Kagan & Madsen, 1971; Madsen & Lancy, 1981) that children living in collectivist cultures (i.e., rural Mexican villages, the Ponam of Papua New Guinea, an Israeli kibbutz) were more likely to cooperate in a variety of situations than children raised in more individualistic societies.

Indonesia

Over the past century, the Javanese and Balinese cultures of Indonesia have fascinated such anthropologists and theorists as Margaret Mead, Clifford Geertz, and Gregory Bateson. The Indonesian society of Java was rated by Hofstede (1991) as being on the extreme end of collectivism. Indigenous Javanese society (as well as the Sundanese society of Java), stresses cooperation, conformity to authority, and harmonious integration (i.e., *ruku*) into the group (Koentjaraningrat, 1985). For example, Farver and Wimbarti (1995) note that Javanese children are taught to maintain harmonious social relationships, to screen their emotions from the view of others, and to display obedience, sharing, and empathy.

Many of the numerous ethnic groups in Indonesia have been reported to display extremely low levels of overt interpersonal conflict and aggression. For example, Margaret Mead (1955) observed that Balinese children were not permitted to quarrel or fight. The Javanese adhere to an implicit social rule that face-to-face contact should be harmonious and polite (Keeler, 1987). Showing proper respect to others, keeping opinions to oneself, and being indirect in actions and words are highly valued (Mulder, 1992), so much so that failure to maintain a harmonious relationship leads to feelings of shame (i.e., *malu*) for both parties involved. Besides shame, *malu* implies a culturally approved shyness that children and adolescents are expected to maintain across many social interaction contexts (Koentjaraningrat, 1985).

CHILDREN'S SOCIAL STATUS IN INDIVIDUALISTIC AND COLLECTIVIST SOCIETIES

The present study constitutes an initial exploration of the correlates of children's social status and friendship across two societies, one characterized by collectivism (Indonesia) and one characterized by individualism (the United States). Unfortunately, we know little about children's peer relationships and friendships across cultures: Anthropologists, sociologists, and psychologists alike have given scant attention to this topic. What is known suggests that there are differences in the extent to which friendship relations are voluntary and whether they are prescribed by kinship or other obligation systems (Krappmann, 1996). There also appear to be cultural differences in the type of behaviors expected within friendships. For example, in some cultures, obligation and prohibition systems may set firm parameters on behaviors within friendship relationships (Krappmann, 1996). A variety of other features that differ across and within cultures, such as population density, class distinctions, and school attendance may impact propinquity, with consequent effects on peer networks and friendships (Edwards, 1992).

HYPOTHESES

Based on the earlier discussion, it seems reasonable to expect societal differences in collectivism and individualism to be associated with differences in the correlates of children's peer status and friendship. Although aggression is likely to be uniformly associated with low positive and high negative sociometric status, at least in the context of the classroom, it is likely that this will be particularly pronounced in Indonesia. Predictions regarding anxiety and withdrawal are more difficult to make. We expect such behavior to be associated with social status in the U.S. sample. In the Indonesian sample, in contrast, it is less likely that such behavior will be salient to peers or be seen as pathological.

These general predictions are consistent with the arguments of Stromshak, Bierman, and Brushi (1995), who found that North American classroom norms regarding aggression were associated with differences in the correlates of social status. The display of aggression was more strongly associated with low popularity in classrooms that were low in aggression than in classrooms high in aggression. The converse was true for withdrawal, which was associated more strongly with low status in high aggression than in low aggression classrooms. Given that aggression is tolerated more in the United States than in Javanese culture (Keeler, 1987; Koentjaraningrat, 1985), we expect that aggression will be more strongly associated with rejection in Indonesia than in the United States, whereas the opposite effect should be found for withdrawal.

The power of the multitrait multimethod approach is enhanced with the inclusion of other conceptually related constructs: academic adjustment and reciprocal friendships. There is little reason to expect differences between Indonesia and the United States in the relation between academic adjustment and sociometric status. To the extent that similar patterns of relations between academic adjustment and sociometric scores emerge across the two countries, this will provide us with additional evidence of the validity of Indonesian sociometric measures. On the other hand, because children's friendships are embedded within the larger peer network (Hinde, 1987) and are influenced by its features, there are reasons to expect cultural differences in the correlates of sociometric status to be paralleled by similar differences in the correlates of having or not having friends. Thus, we expect that aggression more powerfully will discriminate between those who have and those who do not have reciprocal friendships in Indonesia than in the United States. In contrast, withdrawal and anxiety should discriminate between those who do and those who do not have reciprocal friendships in the United States, but not in Indonesia.

METHOD

Samples

The Indonesia sample ($n = 960$) was collected in Bandung, a major city located approximately 180 kilometers from Jakarta on the island of Java. Bandung, population approximately 1,000,000, is the third largest city in Indonesia and is a center for university education and technological development.

The U.S. sample ($n = 360$) was collected in Eugene–Springfield, population approximately 200,000, the second largest city in Oregon and a center for university education and agriculture. Participants were part of an ongoing randomized control preventive intervention study, "Linking the Interests of Families and Teachers" (LIFT), conducted by John B. Reid and his colleagues at the Oregon Social Learning Center.

Sample comparability constitutes one of the major difficulties in cross-cultural research (Berry et al., 1992), and this is clearly a problem here. Fifth-grade public school children of approximately the same ages and gender distribution participated in this research. The samples were not matched, however, on several indices, including income, parental education, and religion. The Bandung sample included children from middle- to upper middle-class families of civil servants, college teachers, or similar occupations. Approximately half the participants were Sundanese, with the remainder describing themselves as Javanese or of unspecified ethnic roots; all were Muslim in religion. In contrast, the U.S. sample included lower to middle income White participants with heterogeneous religious backgrounds living in neighborhoods classified as "at risk" for juvenile delinquency problems (see Reid, Eddy, & Fetrow, 1997). Because these samples were far from equivalent on important demographic variables, our comparisons of peer relationships within these two societies must be viewed cautiously.

Procedures

During the baseline phase of LIFT, Reid et al. (1997) obtained measures of social status, peer judgments of aggression, withdrawal, and anxiety, and parent and teacher ratings of problem behavior using the Child Behavior Checklist (CBC-L) and the Teacher Report Form (TRF), respectively. This provided us with a comprehensive multiple-agent and multiple-method assessment of various internalizing and externalizing behaviors. Several years later, we collected similar data in Indonesia.

Indonesia. Permission to conduct the study in Indonesia was obtained as required from the Indonesian government and the five participating schools. A total of 21 classroom groups participated. Of the 100% of parents initially agreeing to participate in the study without reimbursement, 86% returned completed, useable questionnaires. Participating teachers were paid approximately $1.00 for each questionnaire completed on children in their classrooms classified as sociometrically rejected plus a randomly selected group of other pupils. All teachers returned their questionnaires, although data from two teachers (36 students) were omitted because these teachers turned in identical ratings for every child in their classrooms. Complete TRF data were available for 43% of the sample.

United States. Six schools participated in the study, comprising a total of 17 classrooms. Families were recruited via a combination of letters, phone calls, and paid home visits (see Reid et al., 1997, for further details). Of eligible families, 88% agreed to participate. Data from teachers, parents, and peers were available on approximately 99% of participants. Families and teachers were paid $100 U.S. dollars for their participation.

Measures

Sociometrics. Sociometric measures were administered in classroom groups using the same cross-gender, unlimited nomination procedures in each country. Children were presented with lists of their classmates and asked to circle the peers whom they liked and did not like. The correlation between positive and negative sociometric scores was significantly smaller ($z = -5.92$) for the Indonesian sample ($r = -.26$, $p < .01$) than for the U.S. sample ($r = -.56$, $p < .01$).

Children nominated classmates who exhibited aggressive, withdrawn, and anxious behaviors, again using cross-gender unlimited nomination procedures. The revised Peer Evaluation Inventory (Kellam, 1990; Lardon & Jason, 1992) was used. The aggression scale consisted of three items, and the withdrawal and anxiety scales two items each. Reliability values are listed on the diagonal of Table 6.1 and are comparable across countries.

Children also identified classmates who were their "best" friends using an unlimited, cross-gender nomination procedure. We coded the number of reciprocal friendships in the classroom that each child was involved in.

CBC-L and TRF Ratings. The behavior problem sections of the parent Child Behavior Checklist (CBC-L; Achenbach, 1991a) and the Teacher Rating Form (TRF; Achenbach, 1991b) were administered. The use of the CBC-L and the TRF is particularly appropriate in this investigation as these instruments have been translated into a variety of languages and have been used successfully to study behavior problems in countries as diverse as the United States, Thailand, and Kenya (Weisz, Sigman, Weiss, & Mosk 1993). Indonesian versions of these instruments were created through backward and forward translation by native Indonesian speakers. Aggressive, With-drawn, and Anxious–Depressed subscales were scored for each instrument, and comparable internal consistency values for each were obtained across samples (see Table 6.1).

Academic Achievement. Information on academic status was obtained using different procedures in the two countries. We summed Indonesian student grades across five subject areas (mathematics, Indonesian, religion, moral behavior, and science) and standardized these by school to produce a teacher completed academic status score ($\alpha = .94$). The U.S. teachers completed the Teacher Observation of Classroom Adaptation–Revised (TOCA–R; Werthamer-Larsson, Kellam, & Ovesen-McGregor, 1990) and the TRF Social Competence section. Two questions from the TOCA–R and five questions from the TRF were summed to form an academic achievement scale ($\alpha = .90$).

RESULTS

Trait Convergence

Because results were virtually identical for boys and girls within each country, combined gender results are reported. In Table 6.1, the multiple-agent multiple-construct correlations for Aggression, Anxiety, and Withdrawal scores are presented for the Indonesian and the U.S. samples. Validity coefficients (i.e., the correlation between different agents rating the same construct) tended to be significantly higher for the U.S. than for the Indonesian sample (seven out of nine were significant). The U.S. teachers and peers moderately agreed on aggression, anxiety, and withdrawal, with the strongest agreement on aggression. Aggression ratings between parents and peers and between teachers and parents also

TABLE 6.1
Multiple Trait and Multiple Agent Correlation Matrix for Behavioral Ratings Within Indonesia and the United States

Behavior Scales	Aggression			Withdrawal			Anxiety		
	(Pe)	(T)	(Pa)	(Pe)	(T)	(Pa)	(Pe)	(T)	(Pa)
Aggression									
Peer	(.94/.89)	.49*	.15*	.03	0	-.01	.15*	-.10*	-.01
Teacher	.65*	(.95/.96)	.15*	-.12	.19*	-.07	.08	.22*	-.04
Parent	.38*	.44*	(.90/.84)	-.05	-.06	.51*	-.02	0	.57*
Withdrawal									
Peer	-.10	-.02	.04	(.32/.64)	.20*	.05	.49*	.07	0
Teacher	.12	.22*	.17*	.34*	(.75/.87)	.03	.20*	.03	0
Parent	.11	.10	.12	.17*	.17*	(.71/.77)	0	0	.69*
Anxiety									
Peer	.08	.12	.12	.42*	.22*	.09	(.44/.67)	.08	0
Teacher	.12	.36*	.18*	.30*	.61*	.17*	.30*	(.82/.88)	.01
Parent	.21*	.23*	.70*	.16*	.17*	.69*	.09	.23*	(.85/.69)

Note. Correlations above the main diagonal are for Indonesia, below for the United States.
Cronbach's alphas are on the main diagonal.
*p < .01.

correlated moderately with each other. Agreement on withdrawal and anxiety tended to be low, but statistically significant. In contrast, in the Indonesian sample, the only correlation that accounted for a *practically significant* amount of variance (i.e., 25%) was that between teacher and peer ratings of aggression. Only a few of the remaining correlations were statistically significant, and their values were small.

Sociometrics and Behavior, Academic, and Friendship Ratings

Correlations. The correlations between positive and negative sociometric ratings and behavior ratings, academic achievement, and the number of reciprocal friendships are presented in Table 6.2, along with z-tests of the difference between the correlations. The correlations between behavior ratings and sociometrics tended to be stronger for the U.S. sample than for the Indonesian sample. Interestingly, the correlation ($r = .74$, $p < .01$) between peer rated aggression and negative sociometrics was the only correlation that was greater for the Indonesian sample than for the U.S. sample.

TABLE 6.2
Within Country Correlations Between Positive and Negative Sociometric Scores and Behavioral Ratings, Academic Achievement, and Number of Reciprocal Friendships

	Positive Sociometrics			*Negative Sociometrics*		
	Indonesia	*United States*	*z*	*Indonesia*	*United States*	*z*
Aggression						
Peer	-.17*	-.32*	-2.56	.74*	.54*	5.42
Teacher	-.19*	-.29*	n.s.	.39*	.37*	n.s.
Parent	-.10*	-.27*	-2.80	.13*	.33*	-3.35
Withdrawal						
Peer	.03	-.38*	-5.92	.09	.22*	-2.14
Teacher	-.18*	-.35*	-2.51	.04	.24*	-2.81
Parent	-.06	-.23*	-2.75	-.02	.15*	-2.07
Anxiety						
Peer	-.03	-.28*	-4.13	.21*	.27*	n.s.
Teacher	-.05	-.35*	-4.32	.04	.24*	-2.81
Parent	-.03	-.24*	-3.40	-.01	.19*	-2.88
Achievement	.40*	.40*	n.s.	-.34*	-.42*	n.s.
Friendships	.50*	.51*	n.s.	-.24*	-.34*	n.s.

Note. *$p < .01$.

As predicted, consistent results were found across countries in the relation between aggression and sociometric nominations. Across agents and within both countries, aggression was negatively related to positive nominations and positively related to negative nominations. Within each sample, correlations between ratings from different contexts (school and home) tended to be lower than correlations between ratings from the same context (teachers and peers at school).

Finally, and also as predicted, the relation between internalizing ratings and sociometrics differed across samples. Anxiety and withdrawal were each negatively associated with positive sociometrics and positively associated with negative sociometrics in the U.S. sample. In contrast, a pattern of nonsignificant relations between withdrawal and anxiety and sociometric ratings emerged in the Indonesian sample. Finally, virtually identical correlations between achievement and sociometric ratings emerged within each country despite differences in measurement.

Reciprocated Friendships

The final set of analyses focused on differences between those children who had at least one reciprocated classroom friendship and those who did not. Across countries, the mean number of reciprocated friendships was higher in the United States than in Indonesia (mean = 2.46, SD = 1.80 versus mean = 1.77, SD = 1.60; t = 6.69, p < .01). In the U.S. sample, peer and teacher rated withdrawal differentiated children who did and did not have a reciprocated classroom friend (see Table 6.4). In contrast, in the Indonesia sample, peer and teacher rated aggression differentiated the groups. Interestingly, in neither country were parent ratings related to the presence or absence of reciprocated classroom friends.

DISCUSSION

Reliability and Convergence

We found good reliability of measures and low to moderate convergence in the U.S. sample. In contrast, we found little convergence in the Indonesian sample despite the similar reliability of the measures. The exception is the moderate convergence between teacher and peer ratings of aggression. Similarly, there is some evidence that peers and teachers converge in the assessment of withdrawal, although the magnitude of this agreement raises caution. Each of these correlations, derived from the same social context (the school), were relatively similar within each culture.

In contrast, we have little confidence in the parent ratings in general or in the peer and teacher rating of anxiety, particularly in the Indonesian sample. This suggests that further work is necessary to refine these measures

TABLE 6.3
Within Country Means, Standard Deviations and Comparison t-Values of Children With None or
With One or More Reciprocal Classroom Friendships

	Indonesia			United States		
	None	*One or More*	*t*	*None*	*One or More*	*t*
Aggression						
Peer	.34	-.08	5.19*	-.04	0	n.s.
	(1.34)	(.87)		(.95)	(.98)	
Teacher	9.82	4.92	3.96*	3.41	3.89	n.s.
	(ll.35)	(7.26)		(5.59)	(6.87)	
Parent	8.03	7.34	n.s.	7.26	7.27	n.s.
	(5.36)	(4.92)		(4.87)	(6.00)	
Withdrawal						
Peer	.15	-.05	n.s.	.59	-.11	9.05*
	(1.12)	(.93)		(1.05)	(.96)	
Teacher	4.19	3.06	n.s.	2.59	1.52	3.07*
	(4.03)	(3.72)		(2.80)	(2.02)	
Parent	2.92	2.71	n.s.	2.05	2.00	n.s.
	(2.53)	(2.34)		(2.05)		
Anxiety						
Peer	.11	-.03	n.s.	.22	-.05	n.s.
	(1.12)	(.95)		(1.07)	(.98)	
Teacher	8.49	7.52	n.s	3.19	2.13	n.s
	(5.99)	(5.72)		(3.22)	(3.08)	
Parent	5.46	5.49	n.s.	3.77	3.64	n.s.
	(3.57)	(3.82)		(3.96)	(3.81)	
Achievement	-.45	.11	-6.28*	-.33	.04	n.s.
	(1.03)	(.96)		(1.07)	(1.02)	

Note. Peer and achievement scores are standardized within country. All other scores are raw totals.
*$p < .01$.

before we can use them to explore features of Indonesian social behavior or psychopathology. Such a finding was predictable, given the different cultural meaning and function of withdrawn, anxious, and shy behavior in Indonesia relative to the United States.

Cultural differences in measurement may go beyond measurement error, and be of theoretical importance (Dishion et al., 1995). This is illustrated most clearly by the work of Weisz and his colleagues (Weisz, Chaiyasit, Weiss, Eastman, & Jackson, 1995) who found that Thai children obtained higher teacher ratings of aggression than did U.S. children. Observation, however, revealed that Thai children engaged in less negative behavior than U.S. children. Thus, Thai adults may be particularly sensitive to mild forms of aggressive behavior. The apparent measurement problem with adult ratings of child behavior reveals the impact of culture on these judgments. In the present case, it is possible that the divergence of parent ratings from teacher and peer ratings reflects something more than random error and instead may point toward some feature of the way that adults in Indonesian society react to the behavior of their children.

Sociometric Correlates

Our findings imply that sociometric measures tap similar features of peer acceptance and rejection in both the United States and Indonesia. This is most clearly evidenced by the similar cross-method correlations of sociometrics with aggression and achievement. In this case, the use of a multiple-agent multiple-construct investigation strategy allowed us to determine the appropriateness of sociometric measures in Indonesia. In the absence of such a strategy, it may be impossible to resolve debates between those who argue that these measures are or are not appropriate ways to test children's social status in different cultures.

The most consistent finding in the sociometric literature is the relation between aggression and negative sociometric measures (Hartup, Glazer, & Charlesworth, 1967). The present findings, in conjunction with those of Chen and colleagues (Chen et al., 1995; Chen et al., 1996), add support to suggestions that this relation occurs across very different cultural contexts. Why this consistency? First, aggression during the early and middle childhood years appears to be a fundamental disorder of relationships (see Patterson, 1982), rather than a characteristic that solely resides within the individual. Thus, we expect that noxious behaviors will lead to disrupted relationships, negative cognitions, and negative outcomes across cultural contexts. Mulder (1992), for example, points to some members of Javanese society who fail to display the expected patterns of social behavior and consequently exist in marginal societal roles. The presence of aggressive children across cultures may also be partly attributable to the presence of biological factors (e.g., attention deficit and hyperactive tendencies) that underlie the display of oppositional and aggressive behavior (Dishion et al., 1995). This may well lead to cultural similarity of a subgroup of individuals who are aggressive and rejected across cultures, despite the fact that the actual type and severity of rule infraction is highly variable.

The picture with respect to internalizing disorders is less clear. On a broad level, convergence with the findings of Chen et al. (1995; Chen et al., 1996) in China imply that internalizing disorders may not be linked to status differences in Asian collectivist countries to the degree that they are in the United States or Canada. In the present case, however, we cannot be sure that our findings are not a function of the failure to adequately measure anxiety and withdrawal. Refinement of measures of withdrawal and anxiety cannot proceed in the absence of further, emic study of the meaning of these constructs for Indonesians.

Friendship

The moderate correlations typically found between sociometric acceptance and involvement in reciprocal friendships (Asher, Parker, & Walker, 1996) was replicated in the U.S. and Indonesian samples. Children seek out others in part on the basis of their general attractiveness, and are probably influenced by their reputations. In this study, the failure to find that withdrawal was associated with sociometric status in the Indonesian sample was paralleled by the failure to find that withdrawal differentiated between children who did and did not have a mutual friend. Although aggression was strongly associated with group acceptance and rejection in both Indonesia and the United States, only in Indonesia did aggression differentiate between those who did and did not have a reciprocated classroom friend. In the United States aggressive children are involved in social networks and have friends (Cairns, Cairns, Neckerman, Ferguson, & Gariepy, 1989). Because aggressive behavior is less likely to occur and appears to be strongly sanctioned in Indonesian society, it may be that there are few aggressive children and those that exist are less likely to come together to form relationships with each other.

Little is known about the relation between specific friendships and the larger peer networks in which they are embedded (Hartup, 1992b). It has been observed that those in Western cultures are generally more likely than individuals in other cultures to break into dyadic units (Brandt, 1974). By examining variation in patterns of friendship and social networks in other cultures, we may come to more fully understand the relations between nested features of network, clique, and friendship social structures.

We speculate that under some circumstances, the presence of specific friendship pairs may disrupt the solidarity of the larger peer group. Pairing could lead to jealousy and conflict. Further, within small groups, individuals may need to continue to interact with those with whom they have dissolved friendships. There is also the possibility that some children will fail to become involved in a friendship, which may further weaken the cohesion of the larger group.

In Indonesian society, it has been reported that the friendship group or clique is a more common social unit among children than specific dyadic friendships (Koentjaraningrat, 1985). It has also been found that

Indonesians were more likely to subscribe to the notion that it is better to maintain harmonious group relationships than to develop a few close friendships (Noesjirwan, 1978). To the extent that dyadic friendships are less salient, we expect lower consensus among children with respect to the identity of friends. Our finding of fewer reciprocated friendships in the Indonesian than the U.S. population is consistent with this hypothesis. The possibility that methodological differences (including the larger class sizes of Indonesian classrooms) may explain these differences, however, cannot be dismissed.

Cross-cultural study may reveal other features of friendship variation. In some cultures, social relationships are prescribed by kinship ties or formal expectations. For example, Whiting and Edwards (1988) argue that "kinship as well as age and gender relationships affect the choreography of children's interactions" (p. 81). They found dramatic differences in the extent to which 6- to 10-year-old children were in exclusively kin groups (i.e., 3% for the U.S. sample vs. 67% for the Kenya sample). Cohen (1966) also noted that within certain societies, some friendships (i.e., "inalienable friendships") are entered into by ceremony or ritual. Examples of these include "hereditary collectives" or "circumcision mates." To the extent that important functions are served by these quasi-voluntary social relationships, the opportunity to develop voluntary mutual friendships may be limited and their importance diminished (Layton, 1974).

To the extent that friendships are "developmental advantages for children and adolescents rather than developmental necessities" (Hartup, 1992b, p. 176), it is likely that the socialization functions served by friendships can be addressed in other relationships. To the extent that these functions are served by other individuals, such as kin, the importance of peer friendship may be diminished. This question was explored by DeRosier and Kupersmidt (1991), who compared reports of network relationships of U.S. and Costa Rican fourth- and sixth-grade children. The Costa Rican children rated their friendship relationships as less important than family relationships in terms of companionship, relationship satisfaction, intimacy, and instrumental aid.

In short, family or communal relationships simply may be more salient aspects of modern collectivist societies than of modern individualistic societies. Within Western societies, friendships may be more likely to operate within the parameters of exchange relationships that are established and dissolved on the basis of personal costs and benefits.

Cautions

A key assumption of the comparative approach, and in line with our emphasis on multiple agents, measures, methods, and constructs, is the need to study multiple cultures that differ along some well validated dimension

(Triandis, 1994). If such a multiple approach is not possible due to funding or other limitations, one must be content with studies of single cultures or two-culture comparisons. Any two cultures, however, are likely to differ on so many dimensions that one can have little confidence in explanations for whatever differences emerge (Poortinga & Malpas 1986). Furthermore, one cannot rule out the possibility that methodological factors may account for the results no matter how carefully one attempts to develop culturally sensitive instruments.

In this study, we assumed that U.S. children were individualistic whereas Indonesian children were collectivist. This assumption is clearly inaccurate as individual differences in these tendencies are likely to exist among children in both cultures (Triandis, 1995). Further research must "unpackage" these aspects of culture by developing multidimensional models that explain variation within cultures as well as differences between cultures (Weisner, Gallimore, & Jordan, 1988).

Part of this *unpackaging* of culture will involve careful analysis of the contributions of SES. As noted by Anderson (1996), socioeconomic influences on both physical and mental health are quite strong, and these influences may affect the correlates as well as the base rates of health problems. For example, Kohn and Schooler (1983) demonstrated that within high-status U.S. families, where employed members generally work in occupations that foster independence, children are frequently encouraged to behave independently. In contrast, in low-status families, where employed members generally work in restrictive jobs, conformity may be encouraged. It is unclear how such pressures may impact the present findings because similar information is not available on how conformity, collectivism, or other dimensions influence childrearing in Indonesia.

Concluding Comments

The present study represents an attempt to understand cultural differences in social status and friendship. Consistent with our long-term perspective on measurement, the use of the multimethod and multiagent measurement strategy provided an empirical test of the adequacy of our procedures. Studies that lack such checks, or that use data derived from only one source (e.g., Feldman, Rosenthal, Mont-Reynaud, Leung, & Lau, 1991) are intriguing, but may pose fundamental questions of measurement validity. At this point in the evolution of the field, the use of as many "multiples" as possible, whether measure, agent, method, construct, or culture, is vital.

Refinement of measurement procedures will better position us to use sophisticated statistical procedures that elegantly explore the contribution of culture to psychological processes. One set of such procedures are Hierarchical Linear Models (HLM; Bryk & Raudenbush, 1992), which allow for the simultaneous inclusion of multiple levels of analysis. Although researchers often act as if students are independent units, in reality, students are nested within classrooms, classrooms are nested within schools, and schools are nested within cultures. In an HLM model, each level in an analysis is represented formally by its own statistical submodel. These submodels express the relationships among the variables within a given level, and specify how variables at one level influence relations at another level. Ultimately, the use of reliable and valid measures, that are the outcome of the repeated application of a multiple measurement model, in combination with procedures such as HLM, will allow researchers to traverse the cultural minefield with the finesse required to reach the other side.

ACKNOWLEDGMENTS

The Indonesian research was supported by a U.S. Fulbright award to the first author by the American-Indonesian Exchange Foundation. The contributions of L. Wisnubrata, W. Soedradjat, S. Marat, L. Kendhawati, M. Rianasari, and S. Wibowo from the Faculty of Psychology of Padjadjaran University were indispensable. We thank Thomas Achenbach for permission to translate the CBC-L and TRF scales into Indonesian. The U.S. project, the Linking the Interests of Families and Teachers (LIFT) program, was supported by Grant MH-37940 from the National Institute of Mental Health to John B. Reid. We express our appreciation to John Reid, Bev Fagot, Dave Degarmo, Mike Stoolmiller, and Marcia Zumbahlen for their helpful comments on earlier versions of this chapter.

REFERENCES

Achenbach, T. M. (1991a). *Manual for the Child Behavior Checklist/4-18 and 1991 profile.* Burlington, VT: University of Vermont.
Achenbach, T. M. (1991b). *Manual for the Teacher's Report Form and 1991 profile.* Burlington, VT: University of Vermont.
Anderson, N. B. (1996, May). *Socioeconomic influences on health: A challenge to prevention researchers.* Paper presented at the Fifth National Institute of Mental Health National Conference on Prevention Research, Washington, DC.
Asher, S. R. & Coie, J. D. (Eds.). (1990). *Peer rejection in childhood.* New York: Cambridge University Press.
Asher, S. R., Parker, J. G., & Walker, D. L. (1996). Distinguishing friendship from acceptance: Implications for intervention and assessment. In W. M. Bukowski, A. F. Newcomb, & W. W. Hartup, (Eds.), *The company they keep: Friendship in childhood and adolescence* (pp. 366–405). New York: Cambridge University Press.
Barry, H., Child, I. L., & Bacon, M. K. (1959). Relation of child training to subsistence economy. *American Anthropologist, 61,* 51–63.

Berry, J. W. (1989). Imposed etics-emics-derived etics: The operalization of a compelling idea. *International Journal of Psychology, 24*, 721–735.

Berry, J. W., Poortinga, Y. H., Segall, M., & Dasen, P. R. (1992). *Cross-cultural psychology.* New York: Cambridge University Press.

Brandt, V. S. (1974). Skiing cross-culturally. *Current Anthropology, 15*, 64–66.

Bryk, A. S., & Raudenbush, S. W. (1992). *Hierarchical linear models: Applications and data analysis methods.* Newbury Park, CA: Sage.

Bukowski, W. M., Newcomb, A. F., & Hartup, W. W. (1996). *The company they keep: Friendship in childhood and adolescence.* New York: Cambridge University Press.

Cairns, R. B., Cairns, B. D., Neckerman, H. J., Ferguson, L. L., & Gariepy, J. L. (1989). Social networks and aggressive behavior: Peer support or peer rejection? *Developmental Psychology, 24*, 815–823.

Capaldi, D., & Patterson, G. R. (1989). *Psychometric properties of fourteen latent constructs from the Oregon Youth Study.* New York: Springer-Verlag.

Chen, X., Rubin, K. H., & Li, Z. (1995). Social functioning and adjustment in Chinese children: A longitudinal study. *Developmental Psychology, 31*, 531–539.

Chen, X., Rubin, K. H., Li, B., & Li, D. (1996, August). *Adolescent outcomes of social functioning in Chinese children.* Paper presented at the International Congress of Psychology, Montreal.

Chen, X., Rubin, K. H., & Sun, Y. (1992). Social reputation and peer relationships in Chinese and Canadian children: A cross-cultural study. *Child Development, 63*, 1136–1343.

Cohen, Y. A. (1966). Patterns of friendship. In Y. A. Cohen (Ed.), *Social structure and personality* (pp. 351–386). New York: Holt, Rinehart & Winston.

Cole, M. (1992). Culture in development. In M. H. Bornstein & M. E. Lamb (Eds.), *Developmental psychology: An advanced textbook* (3rd ed., pp. 731–790). Hillsdale, NJ: Lawrence Erlbaum Associates.

Cooper, C. R. (1994). Cultural perspectives on continuity and change in adolescent's relationships. In R. Montemayor, G. R. Adams, & T. P. Gullotta (Eds.), *Personal relationships during adolescence* (pp. 78–100). Thousand Oaks, CA: Sage.

Cronbach, L. J., & Meehl, P. E. (1955). Construct validity in psychological tests. In H. Feigl & M. Scriven (Eds.), *Minnesota studies in the philosophy of science: Vol. 1. The foundations of science and concepts of psychology and psychoanalysis.* Minneapolis, MN: University of Minnesota Press.

DeRosier, M. E., & Kupersmidt, J. B. (1991). Costa Rican children's perceptions of their social networks. *Developmental Psychology, 27*, 656–662.

Dishion, T. J., French, D. C., & Patterson, G. R. (1995). The ecology of antisocial behavior. In D. Cicchetti & D. J. Cohen (Eds.), *Developmental psychopathology, Vol. 2: Risk, disorder, and adaptation* (pp. 421–471). New York: Wiley.

Edwards, C. P. (1992). Cross-cultural perspectives on family-peer relations. In R. D. Parke & G. W. Ladd (Eds.), *Family-peer relationships: Modes of linkage* (pp. 285–316). Hillsdale, NJ: Lawrence Erlbaum Associates.

Farver, J., & Wimbarti, S. (1995). Indonesian toddlers' social play with their mothers and older siblings. *Child Development, 66*, 1493–1503.

Feldman, S. S., Rosenthal, D. A., Mont-Reynaud, R., Leung, K., & Lau, S. (1991). 'Ain't misbehaving': Adolescent values and family environments as correlates of misconduct in Australia, Hong Kong, and the United States. *Journal of Research on Adolescence, 1*, 109–134.

French, D. C., & Waas, G. A. (1985). Behavior problems of peer-neglected and peer-rejected elementary-age children: Parent and teacher perspectives. *Child Development, 56*, 246–252.

Hartup, W. W. (1992a). Conflict and friendship relations. In C. U. Shantz & W. W. Hartup (Eds.), *Conflict in child and adolescent development* (pp. 186–215). New York: Cambridge University Press.

Hartup, W. W. (1992b). Friendships and their developmental significance. In H. McGurk (Ed.), *Childhood social development: Contemporary perspectives* (pp. 175–205). Hillsdale, NJ: Lawrence Erlbaum Associates.

Hartup, W. W., Glazer, J. A., & Charlesworth, R. (1967). Peer reinforcement and sociometric status. *Child Development, 38,* 1017–1024.

Hinde, R. A. (1987). *Individuals, relationships, and culture: Links between ethology and the social sciences.* New York: Cambridge University Press.

Hofstede, G. (1991). *Cultures and organizations: Software of the mind.* London: McGraw-Hill.

Kagan, S., & Madsen, M. C. (1971). Cooperation and competition of Mexican, Mexican-American, and Anglo-American children of two ages under four instructional sets. *Developmental Psychology, 5,* 32–39.

Keeler, W. (1987). *Javanese shadow plays, Javanese selves.* Princeton, NJ: Princeton University Press.

Kellam, S. (1990). *The brief Pupil Evaluation Inventory.* Unpublished manuscript, Johns Hopkins University, School of Hygiene and Public Health.

Koentjaraningrat. (1985). *Javanese culture.* New York: Oxford University Press.

Kohn, M. L., & Schooler, C. (1983). *Work and personality: An inquiry into the impact of social stratification.* Norwood, NJ: Ablex.

Krappmann, L. (1996). Amicitia, drujba, shin-yu, phila, Freundschaft, friendship: On the cultural diversity of a human relationship. In W. M. Bukowski, A. F. Newcomb, & W. W. Hartup (Eds.), *The company they keep: Friendship in childhood and adolescence* (pp. 19–40). New York: Cambridge University Press.

Lambert, W. W. (1971). Cross-cultural backgrounds to personality development and the socialization of aggression: Findings from the six cultures study. In W. W. Lambert & R. Weisbrod (Eds.), *Comparative perspectives on social psychology* (pp. 49–61). Boston: Little, Brown.

Lardon, C., & Jason, L. A. (1992). Validating a brief Pupil Evaluation Inventory. *Journal of Abnormal Child Psychology, 20,* 367–376.

Layton, E. (1974). Irish friends and "friends": The nexus of friendship, kinship, and class in Aughnaboy. In E. Layton (Ed.), *The compact: Selected dimensions of friendship* (pp. 93–104). Newfoundland, Canada: Memorial University of Newfoundland.

Madsen, M. C., & Lancy, D. F. (1981). Cooperative and competitive behavior: Experiments related to ethnic identity and urbanization in Papua New Guinea. *Journal of Cross-Cultural Psychology, 12,* 389–408.

Masten, A., Morison, P., & Pelligrini, D. (1985). A revised class play method of peer assessment. *Child Development, 21,* 523–533.

Mead, M. (1955). Children and ritual in Bali. In M. Mead & M. Wolfenstein (Eds.), *Childhood in contemporary cultures* (pp. 40–51). Chicago: University of Chicago Press.

Meehl, P. (1954). *Clinical versus statistical prediction: A theoretical analysis and review of the evidence.* Minneapolis: University of Minnesota Press.

Mulder, N. (1992). *Individual and society in Java: A cultural analysis.* Yogyakarta, Indonesia: Gadjah Mada University Press.

Noesjirwan, J. (1978). A rule-based analysis of cultural differences in social behavior: Indonesia and Australia. *International Journal of Psychology, 13,* 305–316.

Nsamenang, A. B. (1992). *Human development in cultural context: A third world perspective.* Newbury Park, CA: Sage.

Ogbu, J. U. (1981). Origins of human competence: A cultural-ecological perspective. *Child Development, 52,* 413–429.

Patterson, G. R. (1982). *A social learning approach, Vol. 3: Coercive family processes.* Eugene, OR: Castalia.

Patterson, G. R., & Bank, L. (1986). Bootstrapping your way in the nomological thicket. *Behavioral Assessment, 8,* 49–73.

Patterson, G. R., Reid, J. B., & Dishion, T. J. (1992). *Antisocial boys.* Eugene, OR: Castalia.

Poortinga, Y., & Malpass, R. S. (1986). Making inferences from cross-cultural data. In W. J. Lonner & J. W. Berry (Eds.), *Field methods in cross-cultural research* (pp. 17–46). Beverly Hills, CA: Sage.

Pumariega, A. J. (1996). Culturally competent evaluation of outcomes in systems of care for children's mental health. *TABrief, 2*(2), 1–5.

Reid, J. B., Eddy, J. M., & Fetrow, R. A. (1997). *Description and immediate impacts of a preventive intervention for conduct problems.* Unpublished manuscript, Oregon Social Learning Center, Eugene, OR.

Rogoff, B., Gauvain, M., & Ellis, S. (1984). Development viewed in its cultural context. In M. C. Bornstein & M. E. Lamb (Eds), *Developmental psychology: An advanced textbook* (pp. 533–571). Hillsdale, NJ: Lawrence Erlbaum Associates.

Schlegel, A., & Barry, H. (1991). *Adolescence: An anthropological inquiry.* New York: The Free Press.

Stromshak, E. A., Bierman, K. L., & Brushi, C. (1995, April). *The relation between behavior problems and peer rejection in first-grade classrooms characterized by high versus low levels of aggression.* Paper presented at the meeting of the Society for Research in Child Development, Indianapolis.

Triandis, H. C. (1994). *Culture and social behavior.* New York: McGraw-Hill.

Triandis, H. C. (1995). *Individualism and collectivism.* Boulder, CO: Westview Press.

Weisner, T. S., Gallimore, R., & Jordan, C. (1988). Unpackaging cultural effects on classroom learning: Native Hawaiian peer assistance and child-generated activity. *Anthropology and Education Quarterly, 19,* 327–351.

Weisz, J. R., Chaiyasit, W., Weiss, B., Eastman, K. L., & Jackson, E. W. (1995). A multimodal study of problem behavior among Thai and American children in school: Teacher reports versus direct observation. *Child Development, 66,* 402–415.

Weisz, J. R., Sigman, M., Weiss, B., & Mosk, J. (1993). Parent reports of behavior and emotional problems among children in Kenya, Thailand, and the United States. *Child Development, 64,* 98–109.

Werthamer-Larsson, L., Kellam, S. G., & Ovesen-McGregor, K. E. (1990). *Teacher interview: Teacher Observation of Classroom Adaptation–Revised (TOCA–R).* Baltimore: Unpublished manual, The Prevention Center at Johns Hopkins University.

Whiting, B. B., & Edwards, C. P. (1988). *Children of different worlds: The formation of social behavior.* Cambridge, MA: Harvard University Press.

Whiting, B. B., & Whiting, J. W. M. (1975). *Children of six cultures: A psychocultural analysis.* Cambridge, MA: Harvard University Press.

Williams, R. M. (1970). *American society: A sociological interpretation.* New York: Knopf.

Chapter 7

Friends and Lovers: The Role of Peer Relationships in Adolescent Romantic Relationships

Wyndol Furman
University of Denver

Psychologists have long been interested in the influence of parent–child relationships on subsequent relationships. Much less attention has been given to how friendships and peer relationships may also affect other relationships. Certainly, the critical contributions of peer relationships to psychosocial adjustment have been documented (see Hartup, 1983), but we know surprisingly little about their impact on other relationships.

Little has been said about the role peer relationships may play in the development of romantic relationships. Instead, contemporary conceptualizations of romantic relationships have focused principally on the role of parent–child relationships. For example, Shaver and Hazan (1988) proposed that early patterns of attachment with parents would predict patterns of attachment in adult romantic relationships, but they did not discuss the potential contributions of peer relationships.

In the present chapter, I consider how peer relationships may influence romantic relationships. In many respects, romantic relationships are a special type of peer relationship, but for current purposes, the term *peer relationships* refers to those relationships without a sexual or romantic component, whereas the term *romantic relationships* refers to those with sexual or romantic components. I believe most of the ideas presented here apply to both heterosexual and homosexual relationships, but almost no data exist on the latter, and thus this assertion is simply an assertion.

I present two general arguments for the importance of peer relationships in romantic relationships. In the first half of the chapter, I review the evidence for an evolutionary basis for an affiliative behavioral system that plays an important role in peer and romantic relationships. I propose that we are biologically predisposed to affiliate with known peers, and that the affiliative competencies acquired in such interactions carry over into romantic relationships. In the second half of the chapter, I describe a series of empirical studies that provide evidence of three types of links between peer and romantic relationships. First, I show that *representations of friendships* may influence representations of romantic relationships. Second, I discuss how the peer group provides a *context* for establishing such heterosexual relationships. Third, I consider how romantic relationships are influenced by the *identity* of friends and peers.

AFFILIATIVE PROCESSES AND PEER RELATIONSHIPS

In an earlier paper (Furman & Wehner, 1994), we offered a behavioral systems conceptualization of romantic relationships that attempted to integrate the insights of neo-Sullivanian and attachment theories. Specifically, we proposed that romantic partners typically become key figures in the functioning of the attachment, caregiving, sexual, and affiliative behavioral systems. This conceptualization is similar to Shaver and Hazan's (1988) model in which romantic love involves the integration of the attachment, caregiving, and sexual behavioral system. They did not, however, incorporate an affiliative system in their conceptualization. Such a system is particularly important for understanding the contributions peer relationships may play in romantic relationships.

In the sections that follow, I describe the role of the affiliative system and propose the following:

1. Humans are biologically predisposed to affiliate with known others.
2. These interactions with others were adaptive, in part, because they provided protection and cooperative food sharing. Affiliative behavior also provided juveniles opportunities for social play, which may have several functions.
3. Because they are relatively egalitarian in nature, relationships with peers provide particularly rich opportunities for cooperation, mutualism, reciprocal altruism, and social play.
4. Through such interactions, particularly those in friendships, one develops the capacities to cooperate, collaborate with another, and co-construct a relationship.
5. The affiliative competencies that develop in friendships carry over into romantic relationships. Similarly, representations of close friendships influence representations of romantic relationships.

Biological Bases of Affiliation

Human beings are predisposed to affiliate with known others. We are social animals, and have been throughout the course of evolution. Natural groups are characteristic of all humans (Foley, 1987). In fact, the cattarhines from which hominids evolved 35 million years ago were already social in nature (Caporael, Dawes, Orbell, & van de Kragt, 1989). Pliocene hominids gathered in mixed gender and age groups at least 3 million years ago, and about a million years ago *Homo erectus* lived in small groups and hunted cooperatively. Early humans lived in territorial groups of 100 or less (Wilson, 1975). These groups consisted of a number of nuclear families. Different individuals were often related or behaved cooperatively as if they were "bands of brothers" (Wilson, 1975). Since that time, humans have organized into diverse forms of social groups, whose specific nature is influenced by environmental factors, but humans live in groups in almost all instances. Additionally, although humans interact with strangers, they prefer individuals whom they know. In fact, substantial evidence supports the idea that humans need frequent interactions within an ongoing caring relationship (Baumeister & Leary, 1995).

Clearly, some individuals are more extroverted than others, and some of that difference is genetically based. Such genetic variability could occur if there were multiple adaptive peaks for sociability, which seems quite possible given the variability in niches in even the simplest society (Wilson, 1975). The fact that individuals vary in how sociable they are, however, is not inconsistent with the idea that humans are sociable in nature. The current proposition is simply that there is some biological predisposition to affiliate with known others. Individual differences are superimposed on top of that general predisposition.

Ethological Functions of Affiliation. What functions may affiliation have had for hominids on the savanna? One of the most common explanations is that hominid group living would serve a protective function. Isolated nonarboreal individuals on the savanna would be more vulnerable to predation than those in a group (Caporael et al., 1989; Dunbar, 1988; Foley, 1987). Additionally, hominids may have been more successful foraging for food cooperatively and then sharing the resources (Isaac, 1978). On the savanna, food would not be distributed evenly, but instead would be located in batches (e.g., an animal carcass or fruit tree). Accordingly, if a number of individuals were looking, such a batch would be more likely to be found than if only one person were looking, yet the costs of food sharing would not be high because a batch typically contained more food than one individual could eat. A group also would have been able to chase off other carnivores or scavengers who desired the meat that had been located.

Because of these selection pressures, individuals who were social and better able to function in a group would predominate (Caporael et al., 1989).

Some instances of food-seeking strategies, such as fighting off other predators together, are examples of mutualism (Wrangham, 1982); that is, the joint action results in immediate benefits to all parties. Other instances, such as giving away food to another person, fall into the category of reciprocal altruism (Trivers, 1971). There is no immediate benefit, but such behavior can be adaptive if there is an opportunity for subsequent reciprocity.

Trivers (1971) proposed that the chances of selection of such altruism are greatest under three conditions: (a) when individuals live a long lifetime so that there are many opportunities for the reciprocation of altruistic acts, (b) when the altruist interacts with the same small set of individuals, and (c) when the two are mutually dependent such that they gain relatively equivalent benefits from altruistic acts. These considerations may indicate why humans prefer to affiliate with known others. When interacting with someone they know, they have greater opportunities for the reciprocation of altruism; moreover, they have a history of experiences from which to judge whether the person does or does not reciprocate.

Trivers' three conditions are almost uniquely characteristic of hominids. Hominid groups were small and stable, such that individuals would have known the other members; in fact, they were typically related to many of them, which would also increase the adaptiveness of altruistic behavior. In contrast, members of most other species, including most primates, do not have enduring relationships, which may explain why reciprocal altruism is relatively rare except among hominids and a few primates (Wilson, 1975).

Not only does affiliation provide protection and opportunities for mutualism and reciprocal altruism, but it also provides juveniles with opportunities for play. Social play provides opportunities to practice caretaking and sexual behavior and to learn to modulate agonistic impulses appropriately (Konner, 1975). Play may also foster flexibility in the organism and provide opportunities for exploration or discovery (Fagan, 1981).

Attachment and Affiliation. The evolutionary roots of the affiliative and attachment system appear different (MacDonald, 1992). Attachment is characteristic of most primate species and some other mammals (Bowlby, 1969/1982). In contrast, most primates are not very social (Dunbar, 1988). Reciprocal altruism seems to be specific to hominids and perhaps a few other species of higher primates (Wilson, 1975).

Moreover, humans are likely to seek out different individuals depending upon which system is most activated. Infants turn to primary caretakers at times of distress, but at other, less stressful times, they prefer to play with peers, particularly known peers (Lewis, Young, Brooks, & Michalson, 1975;

Nash, 1988). Peers continue to be primary sources of companionship throughout childhood (Buhrmester & Furman, 1987).

A parent–child relationship also provides few opportunities for mutualism or reciprocal altruism because the relationship is asymmetrical; the joint actions of the two are not likely to be much more effective than the parent's actions alone; similarly, the child has few opportunities to perform altruistic acts for the parent (Trivers, 1971). On the other hand, friendships provide ideal opportunities for mutualism and reciprocal altruism. Friends are dependent on one another and often both benefit from joint actions. Additionally, relationships can last, but they can also be readily terminated if the other person does not reciprocate altruistic acts. In fact, Trivers (1971) suggested that the positive emotions entailed in friendships may emerge as a means of regulating a system of reciprocal altruism.

Social scientists have been wary of providing an evolutionary account of peer relationships, because children had few "peers" during much of our evolutionary past (Konner, 1975). For example, Konner (1975) estimated that in a band of 30 hunter–gatherers, the chance of having three or more peers was only 5.5%. By peers, however, Konner meant agemates (i.e., children born within 6 months of one another). If one broadens the definition to being born within 2 years, the probability of a group of at least four peers grows to 88%. Reciprocal altruism and mutualism should still occur among children who are relatively similar in age, even if they are not identical in age. Moreover, it is important to remember that adults have had peers throughout our evolutionary history. These relationships provide rich occasions for reciprocal altruism and mutualism because they would be symmetrical even if the adults were not identical in age. The opportunities for children to interact with agemates may not have existed in the past or in some societies, but this should not lead us to underestimate the general role of peer relations in our evolutionary history.

Although we distinguish between an attachment and affiliative system in our conceptualization, we do not mean to imply that they are unrelated to one another. The functioning of the attachment, affiliative, and other systems are expected to influence each other and to be coordinated with one another. As discussed subsequently, cognitive representations of relationships are thought to reflect an integration of experiences involving the various systems.

Affiliation in Peer Relationships

Prosocial behaviors do not originate in peer relationships alone, but the egalitarian nature of these relationships provide rich opportunities for reciprocity, cooperation, and reciprocal altruism. Through such interactions, individuals develop the capacity to cooperate, support one another, and co-construct a relationship.

Youniss (1980, 1986) provides a rich description of the development of reciprocity in friendships and peer relations. Before the age of 9 years, children engage in direct reciprocity. Positive behavior is responded to with positive behavior; negative behavior is responded to with negative behavior. When positive acts are reciprocated, children are friends; when negative acts are reciprocated, they are not. Relationships are defined in terms of the concrete interchanges and thus, are not very stable. Around the age of nine, children began to recognize that friendships transcend specific acts of positive reciprocity. Cooperation begins to be treated as a principle, and friendship is defined as a relationship that is sustained by cooperation. Children also emphasize the importance of treating their friends as equals. Certainly, they do not always act this way, but when the principle of equality is violated, they recognize remediation must occur if the friendship is to be sustained. In early adolescence, the principle of equality is expanded into a sense that friends have similar personalities and partially share an identity. They not only respond to each others' needs, but also come to one another with problems and concerns.

Children learn to co-construct or mutually develop a relationship through their interactions with peers. Play or conversation may be a means of developing a shared meaning or elaborating a mutual theme (Youniss, 1986). Because they are peers, neither child's ideas are inherently preferred or accepted; instead each must express his or her ideas or feelings and the two must work together to determine how to proceed. As a consequence, they learn interdependence and mutual respect. As they grow older, children become more effective in producing a joint reality through the relationship they mutually developed. A sense of mutuality or "we-ness" emerges.

Early relationships with caretakers play a critical role in the development of trust and the capacity for intimacy (Collins & Sroufe, in press), but such competencies are further developed in children's friendships. Intimacy and disclosure change from being unidirectional to mutual. Children not only learn how to turn to peers, but also how to listen and be supportive. The mutuality and intimacy of preadolescent friendships or chumships provide opportunities for consensual validation of one's worth (Sullivan, 1953).

Similarly, children's initial lessons in learning how to resolve conflicts occur in interactions with parents, but the interactions with peers provide new challenges. If they choose, parents can determine the outcome of a conflict, whereas the successful resolution of a conflict between peers usually requires negotiation on the part of both parties, as the participants are equal in status and power. Moreover, if the resolution is unsatisfactory to either participant, he or she has the option of ending the relationship. Consequently, coercive conflict strategies are minimized in friendships because of the voluntary nature of the relationship (Laursen, Hartup, & Koplas, 1996).

As these ideas concerning intimacy and conflict resolution illustrate, peer relationships and parent–child relationships are expected to have synergistic effects on development. Earlier experiences with parents influence children's peer relationships. At the same time, friendships and other peer relationships provide further opportunities for development, and the course of that development is not fully dictated by past experiences with parents.

Similarly, the cognitive representations children have concerning friendships are expected to be influenced by representations of their experiences with parents, but they may also be influenced by experiences in friendships (Furman & Wehner, 1994).

The Carryover Into Romantic Relationships

Romantic relationships and friendships share many affiliative features. In fact, when asked to describe their romantic relationships, college students describe the friendship aspects of the relationship almost twice as often as any other aspect, including passion (Hendrick & Hendrick, 1993). Almost half said their best friend was their romantic partner. Romantic theorists' concepts of companionate love (Berscheid & Walster, 1974), storge (Lee, 1976), and friendship-based love (Grote & Frieze, 1994) all emphasize companionship, intimacy, and mutuality.

Affiliative features may be particularly salient in adolescence, as romantic partners are not usually expected to be primary attachment figures until late adolescence or adulthood (Furman & Wehner, 1994). In interviews of 15-year-olds, the most frequently reported advantages of having a dating partner were companionship, intimacy, and support (Feiring, 1996).

Because romantic relationships have such affiliative characteristics, the competencies underlying reciprocity, co-construction of a relationship, validation of worth, and intimacy are likely to be important in the development of romantic relationships as well as friendships. Thus, experiences in childhood peer relationships serve as one of the foundations for the development of the affiliative competencies that are central in romantic relationships. By the same line of reasoning, individual differences in such competencies influence one's attractiveness as a romantic partner. In fact, one of the strongest predictors of interpersonal attraction is the general characteristic of agreeableness, which includes attributes such as being cooperative, kind, and sympathetic (Graziano, Jensen-Campbell, Todd, & Finch, in press).

Differences in affiliative competencies are also expected to predict differences in the characteristics of one's romantic relationships. The necessary longitudinal research does not exist to determine causality, but affiliative features distinguish different romantic relationship styles. For example, those with secure romantic styles are higher in mutuality and couple orientation than those with anxious–ambivalent or avoidant styles (Feeney & Noller, 1991). Enjoyment and friendship are higher in secure individuals than anxious–ambivalents. Finally, differences in cognitive representations of peer relationships are expected to lead to differences in representations of romantic relationships, a topic discussed more extensively in the section that follows.

In summary, I have outlined the case for a biological basis for an affiliative system and suggested that affiliative competencies may develop in peer relationships and carry over into romantic relationships. Portions of the evolutionary argument are admittedly speculative and difficult to test empirically. At the same time, developmental theorists need to give greater consideration to the potential role that selection pressures may have played in the emergence of peer and romantic relationships. It is hoped that the presentation of these ideas will stimulate further work on the affiliative system and its potential role in peer relationships.

LINKS BETWEEN THE REPRESENTATIONS
OF FRIENDSHIPS AND ROMANTIC RELATIONSHIPS

Whereas the preceding section principally stemmed from the ethological literature, the next section considers developmental studies that provide another basis for suggesting that peers play an important role in the development of romantic relationships. Three potential roles are considered. In this section, I illustrate how *representations of friendships* may influence representations of romantic relationships. In the sections that follow, I describe how the peer group provides a *context* for establishing heterosexual relationships, and how romantic relationships are influenced by the *identity* of friends and peers.

Perceptions of Support

As part of an earlier study (Furman & Buhrmester, 1992), we examined children and adolescents' perceptions of their social networks. Students completed the Network of Relationships Inventory in which they rated the degree to which they received seven different types of support from their mothers, fathers, closest siblings, grandparents, closest same-sex friends, and romantic partners. The original report of this study focused on age and gender differences, but reanalyses of the data on the 112 tenth graders provide information about the similarities and differences among adolescents' relationships and the links between them.

The first set of new analyses examined the kinds of support that were sought in different relationships. In order to obtain a common metric for comparing different types of support, scores for each type of support were standardized. Figure 7.1 depicts the support obtained from romantic partners, friends, and parents. The kinds of support obtained from friends and romantic partners were similar to each other, and differed from those obtained from either parent. Adolescents commonly turned to friends and romantic partners for intimacy and companionship, whereas affection, instrumental aid, and a sense of reliable alliance were the more salient features in relationships with parents. This pattern of results is consistent with the idea that friendships and romantic relationships serve similar, though not identical, functions; affiliative features are particularly salient in both.

The next analyses examined the links among the four relationships. Overall indices of support were derived by averaging the scores of the seven support provisions for each relationship. Perceptions of support in relationships with best friends, mothers, and fathers were all significantly correlated with perceptions of support in romantic relationships (r's = .36 to .43, p's < .01). To examine the contributions of different relationships in predicting support in romantic relationships, we conducted iterative multiple regression analyses in which the order of entry of predictors was varied. Support in best friendships provided an increment in prediction

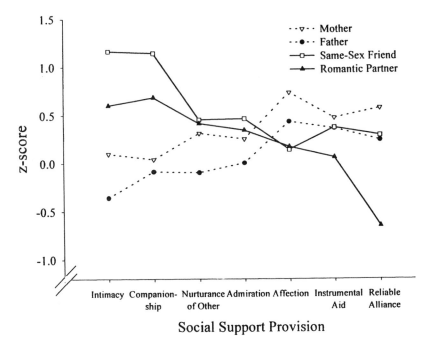

FIG. 7.1. Mean amount of social support provided by romantic partners, friends, and parents.

above that obtained from the two parent–adolescent relationships (parents' $R^2 = .21$, friend increment $R^2 = .04$, each step $p < .05$). Similarly, the two parent–adolescent relationships provided an increment above that obtained from best friendships (friend $R^2 = .15$, parents increment $R^2 = .09$, each step $p < .05$). Thus, both types of relationships provided unique contributions to the prediction of support in romantic relationships, but much of the predicted variance was shared ($R^2 = .11$). Connolly and Johnson (1996) reported a similar pattern of results, although the links were attenuated when the romantic relationships were of a year or longer in duration.

These studies are cross-sectional in nature, but the patterns of relations were also examined in a 3-year longitudinal study of approximately 180 high school students (Connolly, Furman, & Konarski, 1997). Network of Relationships Inventories were completed in Grades 9, 10, and 11. Ratings of support in best friendships were predictive of ratings of support in romantic relationships a year later ($r = .37$, $p < .01$); support in romantic relationships was not predictive of support in best friendships during the subsequent year ($r = .14$, n.s). Unfortunately, this study did not examine the role of relationships with parents.

Relational Styles

These studies were concerned with perceptions of support, but we also have examined perceptions of the different behavioral systems salient in close relationships (i.e., attachment, caretaking, affiliation, and, in the case of romantic relationships, sexuality). Adult attachment researchers commonly characterize conscious attachment styles as secure, dismissing, or preoccupied. We believe that this framework can be applied to the other behavioral systems, and that one can refer to secure, dismissing, or preoccupied *relational styles* (Furman & Simon, in press; Furman & Wehner, 1994). For example, a person with a secure style for romantic relationships may not only think that he or she should be able to turn to a partner at times of distress, but also may value taking care of the other, may desire to invest energy into constructing a mutual relationship, and may value the affectionate and caring elements of sexuality. Someone with a preoccupied style may not only find it difficult to feel comforted by a partner when upset, but may also be too worried about a partner's problems (i.e., compulsive caretaking), may overinvest in relationships in a self-sacrificing manner, and may construe sexual behavior as a way to make oneself feel worthy. Someone with a dismissing style may have little interest in caretaking, little investment in a relationship, and see sex as an opportunity for experimentation or self-gratification, as well as not see a partner as one to turn to at times of distress. Thus, we believe that individuals have cognitive representations or relational styles that refer to all four behavioral systems. In effect, such styles are conscious expectations regarding intimacy and closeness, which may be enacted in terms of attachment, caretaking, sexuality, and affiliation.

Perceptions of different relationship styles were examined in a sample of 165 high school females, who were predominantly Caucasian and middle class (Furman & Wehner, 1994; Wehner, 1992). A Behavioral Systems Questionnaire was developed to assess conscious perceptions of attachment, care received, and affiliation in relationships with mothers, fathers, friends, and romantic partners. Perceptions of sexuality in romantic relationships, and care provided to friends and romantic partners were also assessed. Separate scales assessed secure, dismissing, and preoccupied styles for each of the behavioral systems. The corresponding attachment, care received, and affiliative scales for each of the three styles were found to be substantially correlated with one another in each of the four relationships (mean $r = .51$). This finding is consistent with the idea that representations of different systems are coordinated or integrated, such that they can be conceptualized as relational styles. General relational scores for secure, preoccupied and dismissing styles were calculated by standardizing and averaging the scores for the three different behavioral systems measured in all relationships. The pattern of relations among the styles for different relationships was then examined.

As shown in Table 7.1, high school students' friendship and romantic relational styles were consistently related to one another. Analyses of the specific behavioral system scales revealed consistent links, particularly for the affiliation and care scales (M attachment $r = .18$, caregiving received $r = .33$, care provided $r = .40$, affiliation $r = .45$). In contrast, relational style scores for parents and romantic relationships were less related, as were the specific behavioral system scales (M attachment $r = .00$, caretaking $r = .17$, affiliation $r = .18$) Interestingly, styles for relationships with parents were more related to those for friendships than to those for romantic relationships.

TABLE 7.1
Across Relationship Correlations for General Relationship Styles

Relationships	Secure	Dismissing	Preoccupied
Friends–Romantic	.25**	.35**	.40**
Mother–Romantic	.02	.01	.23**
Father–Romantic	.07	.18*	.08
Mother–Friends	.14	.25**	.28**
Father–Friends	.16*	.25**	.26**
Mother–Father	.29**	.35**	.39**

Note. From Furman and Wehner (1994). Reprinted with permission of Sage Publications.
**$p < .01$. *$p < .05$.

A series of iterative regression analyses were conducted to examine the role of parent and friend styles in predicting romantic styles. The three style scores for friends each provided an increment above that obtained from the corresponding scores for the two parents (secure increment R^2 = .06, dismissing increment R^2 = .10, preoccupied increment R^2 = .13, all p's < .01). Entering the pairs of parent styles after the corresponding friend style did not significantly improve the prediction of any of the three romantic styles (all R^2's < .03, n.s.).

Working Models

The preceding results focused on individual's self-perceptions of relational styles. Although such styles are sometimes equated with working models, these two components of cognitive representations of relationships should be distinguished (Furman & Wehner, 1994). Styles are conscious self-perceptions of approaches to relationships, whereas working models refer to internalized, partially unconscious, representations of relationships, which reflect more automated processing in relationships. Styles can be measured by self-report measures of relationships, such as various romantic attachment questionnaires or the Behavioral Systems Questionnaire described previously. Working models (or states of mind) can be assessed through the Adult Attachment Interview (George, Caplan, & Main, 1985) or derivatives of it designed to assess marriages (Crowell & Owens, 1996; Silver & Cohn, 1992). Styles and working models may differ because some individuals, particularly dismissing ones, may overtly present themselves or their relationships positively as a means of defending against underlying negative models of self and relationships (Cassidy & Kobak, 1988). Consistent with these ideas, working models of parental relationships have been found to be relatively unrelated to self-report ratings of relationships with parents (Crowell et al., 1993).

To examine the links among working models of different relationships, Elizabeth Wehner and I developed interviews for friendships and romantic relationships that were analogous to the Adult Attachment Interview. The three interviews were administered to 54 high school females from the sample previously described. Using Kobak's (1993) Q-sort methodology, multiple coders read transcripts of each interview and sorted 72 to 100 descriptors into nine categories ranging from very characteristic to very uncharacteristic. The descriptors focused on interview discourse and attachment-related features of the relationships. In pilot work, we included affiliation items and found them to be high related to the attachment indices. These Q-sorts of items were correlated with Kobak's prototypic Q-sorts to yield scores for security of attachment (vs. insecurity) and for deactivation or dismissing of attachment (vs. hyperactivation or preoccupied with attachment).

The pattern of correlations among the working model scores for the three relationships resembled that found with our stylistic measures. Ratings of security in friendships and romantic relationships were significantly related ($r = .47$, $p < .01$), as were friendship and romantic ratings of deactivation of attachment ($r = .39$, $p < .01$). Furthermore, 50% of the items in the set of friendship descriptors were significantly related to their corresponding romantic relationship descriptors, including various descriptions of coherence, insight, and availability of partners.

Correlations between parental relationships and romantic relationships were in the right direction, but nonsignificant (security $r = .26$, deactivation $r = .21$, both n.s). Only 5% of the items in the parent Q-sort were related to corresponding items in the romantic relationship Q-sort. Ratings for relationships with parents and friendships, however, were significantly related (security $r = .34$, deactivation $r = .32$, p's $< .05$).

Iterative regression analyses revealed that each of the friendship scores provided a significant increment in the prediction of romantic scores above that obtained from the corresponding scores for relationships with parents (secure increment $R^2 = .20$, deactivating increment $R^2 = .19$, both p's $< .01$). Neither of the two scores for relationships with parents provided a significant prediction increment above that obtained from the corresponding friendship ratings alone (R^2's $< .02$, n.s.).

Accounting for the Links

Taken together, the findings from these studies provide initial evidence that representations of friendships and romantic relationships are related. Both friendships and romantic relationships are egalitarian peer relationships, but the strength of the links in the representations of the two does not simply stem from similarity in the overt characteristics of the relationships. Such an explanation would not account for the findings concerning the correspondence in working models, nor could it explain the correspondence between representations of relationships with parents and friends, which do not share such similar overt features. The significant findings also cannot be attributed to method variance, because the pattern of relations among the scores for the three relationships was not uniform. Instead, the correspondence seems to reflect linkages in the representations of these relationships.

Representations of friendships may mediate a link between views of relationships with parents and those with romantic partners. The observed links between representations of parents and friends and those between representations of friends and romantic partners are consistent with this explanation. At the same time, the mediator explanation is not a sufficient account of the relations as representations of friendships typically accounted for additional variance in the prediction of romantic representations after controlling for representations of relationships with parents. Representations of friendships appear to be important in and of themselves and not just as mediators.

Although the results are encouraging, further work is needed to identify the specific nature of the links. The extent to which the observed links are reflected in or mediated by overt patterns of interaction requires examination. Additionally, some of the findings suggest that affiliative processes may be particularly important, but these results are tentative. In a related vein, the findings are consistent with the ethological arguments presented in the first section of the paper, but the links could be readily accounted for by other explanations that emphasize social learning processes or culture-specific influences.

THE PEER GROUP AS A CONTEXT
FOR ROMANTIC RELATIONSHIPS

The preceding section considered how representations of friendships may be linked to similar representations of romantic relationships. Another way the peer group may influence romantic relationships is by serving as a setting or context for the emergence of heterosexual romantic relationships. Such a role is described in Dunphy's (1963) developmental model of adolescent peer groups. In the first stage, unisexual cliques emerge, consisting of four to six close friends. In the second stage, male cliques and female cliques begin to socialize in a large group context or crowd, marking a step toward heterosexual relationships. In the third stage, the leaders or popular members of each clique begin to date each other, forming a heterosexual clique. In the fourth stage, the peer crowd is fully developed as several heterosexual cliques closely associate with one another. Finally, males and females begin to develop couple relationships; the crowd begins to disintegrate, leaving loosely associated groups of couples.

Dunphy's model was based on case studies, but his ideas have received some empirical support. Adolescents with romantic relationships report larger peer networks and more other-gender friends (Connolly & Johnson, 1996). Rejected and neglected adolescents date less frequently than others (Franzoi, Davis, & Vasquez-Suson, 1994).

The Connolly et al. (1997) longitudinal study described previously provided the opportunity to further test some of Dunphy's ideas. Data were gathered on the number of same and other-gender reciprocated friendships and the number of same- and other-gender peers in an adolescent's general network. Like Dunphy, we hypothesized that cliques of reciprocated friends would precede the emergence of larger networks or "crowds." Furthermore, we thought that participation in same-gender groups would lead to participation in other-gender groups, which in turn would lead to heterosexual romantic relationships. These ideas lead us to propose the model depicted in Fig. 7.2, which was tested using structural equation modeling. Because LISREL is limited in its ability to process dichotomous variables, we did not examine the simple presence or absence of a romantic relationship, but instead measured the amount of companionship with a romantic partner using the Network of Relationships Inventory scores (individuals without such a relationship received scores of 0). The model provided a good fit to the data $(X^2(5) = 9.80$, n.s.). The fit was not satisfactory for alternative models in which the direction of effects from the same- to other-gender variables was reversed, or the temporal sequence of friendship cliques and networks was reordered $(X^2(5)$'s > 12, p's $< .05)$. These findings not only suggest that the peer group serves as context for developing heterosexual romantic relationships, but they also underscore the importance of other-gender relationships. In part, these other-gender relationships may be important because a heterosexual romantic relationship may develop out of other-gender relationships or out of contacts made through such a relationship. These relationships may also provide adolescents with opportunities to learn about the other gender and to learn how to interact with the other gender in a context in which sexuality is constrained. Relationships with other-gender siblings may play a similar role, as young adults with older other-gender siblings have more rewarding interactions with other-gender strangers (Ickes & Turner, 1983).

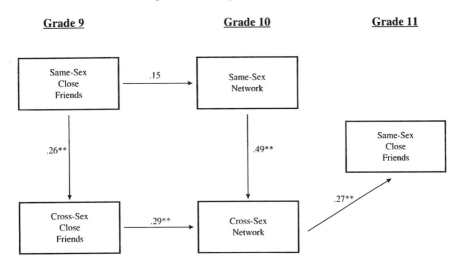

Note. Values shown on arrows are standardized parameter estimates.
**p < .01.

FIG. 7.2. Structural model of peer network variables and romantic companionship.

Finally, it is important to note that the contextual role of the peer group is distinct from the previously discussed role that friendships and other close relationships play in shaping representations of romantic relationships. The structural characteristics of the peer network are associated with whether one has a romantic relationship or not, but other analyses revealed that they are not very related to the supportiveness of that romantic relationship. Similarly, in the studies described in the prior section, relational styles and working models were not very related to the age one began to date or the number of individuals dated. Thus, the nature of one's peer network and one's status in that network seem to play a more important role in determining the *timing* and *extensiveness* of dating than do past relationship experiences (within some limits). Past relationship experiences, however, are expected to have a big impact on the *quality* of the romantic relationships that develop, whenever they do develop (Furman & Wehner, 1994).

THE IDENTITY OF PEERS AND FRIENDS

The identity of one's peers and friends, as well as the quality and number of peer relationships, may affect the nature of one's romantic relationships. Research on sexual behavior illustrates these influences. For example, age at first intercourse is related to perceptions of peers' attitudes about sexual behavior (Daughtery & Burger, 1984) and perceptions of friends' sexual activity (Schulz, Bohrnstedt, Borgatta, & Evans, 1977). Caucasian adolescents, particularly women, tend to have friends whose level of sexual activity is similar to their own (Billy, Rodgers, & Udry, 1984; Billy & Udry, 1985). Concordance between friends could occur as a function of whom one chooses as friends or through the socialization influences of friends. In the one longitudinal study conducted to date (Billy & Udry, 1985), both Caucasian males and females chose friends whose sexual behavior was similar to their own, and females' sexual behavior was influenced by their existing friends' sexual activity.

Not only do peers transmit values, but they are also a major source of information about numerous topics, including sex (Thornburg, 1975). How knowledgeable one's peers are, as well as how much they communicate such information, may affect how accurately informed adolescents are. Aside from this work on sexuality, little empirical work exists on how the identity of one's friends may influence adolescent romantic relationships. Such influences seem likely, however, as the identity of friends influences psychosocial adjustment in general (see Hartup, 1996).

CONCLUDING COMMENTS

The results of these studies provide encouraging support for the general thesis that peer relations may play an important role in the development of romantic relationships. A number of issues, however, require further consideration.

First, this chapter has principally discussed how friendships or other aspects of peer relations may affect romantic relationships, rather than the reverse. The longitudinal data presented here are consistent with this interpretation, but romantic relationships are also likely to affect friendships or parent–adolescent relationships. For example, competencies acquired or honed in the romantic relationships may carry over to other relationships. In particular, the affiliative competencies of reciprocity, mutual intimacy, and co-construction may ultimately be applied in relationships with parents and contribute to the transformation of those relationships into more symmetrical ones (Youniss & Smollar, 1985). The make-up of peer networks is also likely to change as romantic relationships develop. Romantic partners may introduce adolescents to new peers and may remain part of the network themselves even after the romantic relationship has dissolved. In our longitudinal study (Connolly et al., 1997), approximately 20% were part of the adolescents' peer networks a year later.

Finally, one of the major themes of ours' and other attachment theorists' conceptualizations is that romantic partners become central attachment, affiliative, and caretaking figures (Furman & Wehner, 1994; Shaver & Hazan, 1988). As they become central figures, romantic partners may begin to fulfill some of the roles played by other individuals and thus, change the nature of relationships with those individuals. A new romantic partner is a common source of strain in adolescent friendships. Adolescents with romantic relationships interact with their friends less (Laursen & Williams, 1997) and seem less interested in them. Often, in fact, the new romantic partner becomes the best friend, displacing the old friend (Hendrick & Hendrick, 1993). Dating and romantic relationships may also influence the nature of parent–adolescent relationships, as they are indices of the developing autonomy of the adolescent. They can also be a major source of conflict between parents and their adolescents, as many parents will testify.

These descriptions of the potential impact of romantic relationships on other relationships also illustrate the complexity of the links between relationships. In the studies reported here, positive correlations were found between representations of romantic relationships and friendships. Such positive links are consistent with the idea that carryover in competencies or interpersonal approaches occurs. At the same time, some research suggests that adolescents with romantic partners interact less with friends than those without a romantic partner (Laursen & Williams, 1997). Thus, peer relationships may provide adolescents the competencies for interacting with romantic partners and serve as a context for establishing such relationships, but they and romantic relationships may compete for the adolescents' time and attention (Zani, 1993). Romantic partners may even replace or serve as a substitute for friends. The specific type of peer influence also depends on their attitudes toward a particular romantic relationship or toward romantic relationships in general. Thus, communication with and support from the partner's peers can sustain a romantic relationship (Parks & Adelman, 1983), whereas their disapproval may lead to its demise. In some male peer groups, women in general are considered to be objects for sexual conquest, and most ongoing or serious relationships are ridiculed (Alexander, 1990).

Similarly, most adolescent heterosexual peer groups strongly discourage gay or lesbian relationships, and relatively few sexual minority youth have the opportunity to be part of a group of adolescents with the same sexual orientation (Diamond, Savin-Williams, & Dube, in press). Thus, although many of the ideas in this chapter are thought to be applicable to gay or lesbian relationships, one important difference is in the attitudes most adolescents have toward such relationships. Another difference may be in the role played by passionate same-gender friendships—friendships that have the intensity of a romantic relationship, but lack the sexual element (Diamond et al., in press). Such relationships may serve as an important context for clarifying the sexual identity of sexual minority youth, and may fulfill needs traditionally met by romantic relationships without involving undesired sexual behavior with the other sex. Accordingly, experiences in such passionate friendships may be important factors in the development of subsequent gay or lesbian romantic relationships.

Although we have focused on the role of friendships and peer relationships, relationships with parents also play a critical role. An important task for subsequent work is to identify how each relationship contributes to the development of romantic relationships (i.e., what the unique function of each is and what functions are shared). For example, one would expect experiences with both relationships to be related to the general development of trust or mistrust, but peers may play a particularly important role in learning how to trust and be trustworthy in a symmetrical relationship—e.g., how to both disclose and be responsive to disclosures.

This chapter is concerned with the continuities across relationships, but it is important to recognize that the observed links are moderate in size. The correlations could be attenuated by measurement error, but lawful discontinuities should be expected as well. Just as friendships present new challenges and experiences to children, so too do romantic relationships (Furman & Flanagan, 1997). The most obvious is the element of sexuality.

Sheer physical attraction plays an important role in determining whom we are interested in establishing a relationship with and the nature of the interactions that occur in that relationship (Berscheid, 1988). Additionally, romantic relationships also involve the attachment, caretaking, and affiliative systems as well as the sexual system, whereas previous relationships typically have not involved all of these systems. Marriages and other long-term romantic relationships also have the elements of commitment, exclusivity, and usually parenting that pose new developmental challenges. Finally, the other person is different in each relationship and they too shape the nature of the interchanges.

In summary, the specific nature of the links among various relationships will require further empirical work, but the general structure of the answer is already predictable. Each of these relationships will turn out to be important developmental contexts. The influence of friends, parents, and romantic partners will prove to be synergistic—overlapping, but not interchangeable. Each of these themes are ones that Bill Hartup has long emphasized (Hartup, 1980).

ACKNOWLEDGMENTS

Preparation of this manuscript was supported by Grant 50106 from National Institute of Mental Health. Portions of the research presented here were done in collaboration with Duane Buhrmester, Jennifer Connolly, Roman Konarski, and Elizabeth Wehner. Bill Hartup's influence in the development of the ideas in this paper greatly exceeds the specific citations of his work.

REFERENCES

Alexander, E. (1990). *Streetwise: Race, class, and change in an urban community.* Chicago: University of Chicago Press.

Baumeister, R. F., & Leary, M. R. (1995). The need to belong: Desire for interpersonal attachments as a fundamental human motive. *Psychological Bulletin, 117,* 497–529.

Berscheid, E. (1988). Some comments on love's anatomy: Or, whatever happened to old-fashioned lust? In R. J. Sternberg & M. L. Barnes (Eds.), *The psychology of love* (pp. 359–374). New Haven, CT: Yale University Press.

Berscheid, E., & Walster, E. (1974). A little bit about love. In T. L. Huston (Ed.), *Foundations of interpersonal attraction* (pp. 356–381). New York: Academic Press.

Billy, J. O., Rodgers, J. L., & Udry, J. R. (1984). Adolescent sexual behavior and friendship choice. *Social Forces, 62,* 653–678.

Billy, J. O., & Udry, J. R. (1985). Patterns of adolescent friendship and effects on sexual behavior. *Social Psychological Quarterly, 48,* 27–41.

Bowlby, J. (1982). *Attachment and loss: Vol. 1. Attachment.* New York: Basic Books. (Original work published 1969)

Buhrmester, D., & Furman, W. (1987). The development of companionship and intimacy. *Child Development, 58,* 1101–1113.

Caporael, L. R., Dawes, R. M., Orbell, J. M., & van de Kragt, A. J. C. (1989). Selfishness examined: Cooperation in the absence of egoistic incentives. *Behavioral and Brain Sciences, 12,* 683–789.

Cassidy, J., & Kobak, R. (1988). Avoidance and its relation to other defensive processes. In J. Belsky & T. Neworski (Eds.), *Clinical implications of attachment* (pp. 300–323). Hillsdale, NJ: Lawrence Erlbaum Associates.

Collins, W. A., & Sroufe, L. A. (in press). Capacity for intimate relationships: A developmental construction. In W. Furman, B. B. Brown, & C. Feiring (Eds.), *Contemporary perspectives on adolescent romantic relationships.* Cambridge, England: Cambridge University Press.

Connolly, J., Furman, W., & Konarski, R. (1997). *The role of peers in the emergence of romantic relationships in adolescence.* Manuscript submitted for review.

Connolly, J. A., & Johnson, A. M. (1996). Adolescents' romantic relationships and the structure and quality of their close interpersonal ties. *Personal Relationships, 3,* 185–195.

Crowell, J., & Owens, G. (1996). *The Current Relationship Interview and Scoring System, Version 2.* Unpublished document, State University of New York at Stony Brook.

Crowell, J. A., Holtzworth-Munroe, A., Treboux, D., Waters, E., Stuart, G. L., & Hutchinson, G. (1993). *Assessing working models: A comparison of the Adult Attachment Interview with self-report measures of attachment relationships.* Manuscript submitted for review.

Daughtery, L. R., & Burger, J. M. (1984). The influence of parents, church and peers on the sexual attitudes and behaviors of college students. *Archives of Sexual Behavior, 13,* 351–359.

Diamond, L. M., Savin-Williams, R. C., & Dube, E. M. (in press). Intimate peer relations among lesbian, gay, and bisexual adolescents: Sex, dating, passionate friendships, and romance. In W. Furman, B. B. Brown, & C. Feiring (Eds.), *Contemporary perspectives on adolescent romantic relationships.* Cambridge, England: Cambridge University Press.

Dunbar, R. I. M. (1988). *Primate social systems.* Ithaca, NY: Cornell University Press.

Dunphy, D. C. (1963). The social structure of urban adolescent peer groups. *Sociometry, 26,* 230–246.

Fagan, R. (1981). *Animal play behavior.* New York: Oxford University Press.

Feeney, J. A., & Noller, P. (1991). Attachment style and verbal descriptions of romantic partners. *Journal of Social and Personal Relationships, 8,* 187–215.

Feiring, C. (1996). Concepts of romance in 15-year-old adolescents. *Journal of Research on Adolescence, 6,* 181–200.

Foley, R. (1987). *Another unique species: Patterns in human evolutionary ecology.* New York: Longman/John Wiley.

Franzoi, S. L., Davis, M. H., & Vasquez-Suson, K. A. (1994). Two social worlds: Social correlates and stability of adolescent status groups. *Journal of Personality and Social Psychology, 67,* 462–473.

Furman, W., & Buhrmester, D. (1992). Age and sex differences in perceptions of networks of personal relationships. *Child Development, 63,* 103–115.

Furman, W., & Flanagan, A. (1997). The influence of earlier relationships on marriage: An attachment perspective. In W. K. Halford & H. J. Markman (Eds.), *Clinical handbook of marriage and couples interventions* (pp. 179–202). Chicester, England: Wiley.

Furman, W., & Simon, V. A. (in press). Cognitive representations of adolescent romantic relationships. In W. Furman, B. B. Brown, & C. Feiring (Eds.), *Contemporary perspectives on adolescent romantic relationships.* Cambridge, England: Cambridge University Press.

Furman, W., & Wehner, E. A. (1994). Romantic views: Toward a theory of adolescent romantic relationships. In R. Montemayor, G. R. Adams, & G. P. Gullota (Eds.), *Advances in adolescent development: Volume 6, Relationships during adolescence* (pp. 168–195). Thousand Oaks, CA: Sage.

George, C., Kaplan, N., & Main, M. (1985). *An adult attachment interview.* Unpublished manuscript, University of California, Berkeley.

Graziano, W. G., Jensen-Campbell, L. A., Todd, M., & Finch, J. F. (in press). Interpersonal attraction from an evolutionary psychology perspective: Women's reactions to dominant and prosocial men. In J. A. Simpson & D. T. Kendrick (Eds.), *Evolutionary social psychology.* Mahwah, NJ: Lawrence Erlbaum Associates.

Grote, N. K., & Frieze, I. H. (1994). The measurement of friendship-based love in intimate relationships. *Personal Relationships, 1,* 275–300.

Hartup, W. W. (1980). Two social worlds: Family and peer relations. In M. Rutter (Ed.), *Scientific foundations of developmental psychiatry* (pp. 280–292). London: Heinemann.

Hartup, W. W. (1983). Peer relations. In P. H. Mussen (Series Ed.) & E. M. Hetherington (Vol. Ed.), *Handbook of child psychology, Vol. 4. Socialization, personality, and social development* (pp. 103–196). New York: Wiley.

Hartup, W. W. (1996). The company they keep: Friendships and their developmental significance. *Child Development, 67,* 1–13.

Hendrick, S. S., & Hendrick, C. (1993). Lovers as friends. *Journal of Social and Personal Relationships, 10,* 459–466.

Ickes, W., & Turner, M. (1983). On the social advantages of having an older, opposite-sex sibling: Birth order influences in mixed-sex dyads. *Journal of Personality and Social Psychology, 45,* 210–222.

Isaac, G. (1978). The food-sharing behavior of protohuman hominids. *Scientific American, 289,* 90–108.

Kobak, R. R. (1993). *The Attachment Interview Q-Set: Revised.* Unpublished manuscript, University of Delaware, Newark, DE.

Konner, M. (1975). Relations among infants and juveniles in comparative perspective. In M. Lewis & L. A. Rosenblum (Eds.), *Friendship and peer relations* (pp. 99–130). New York: Wiley.

Laursen, B., Hartup, W. W., & Koplas, A. L. (1996). Towards understanding peer conflict. *Merrill-Palmer Quarterly, 42,* 76–102.

Laursen, B., & Williams, V. (1997). Perceptions of interdependence and closeness in family and peer relationships among adolescents with and without romantic partners. In S. Shulman & W. A. Collins (Eds.), *Romantic relationships in adolescence: New directions for child development* (pp. 3–20). San Francisco: Jossey-Bass.

Lee, J. A. (1976). *The colors of love.* Englewood Cliffs, NJ: Prentice-Hall.

Lewis, M., Young, G., Brooks, J., & Michalson, L. (1975). The beginning of friendship. In M. Lewis & L. A. Rosenblum (Eds.), *Friendship and peer relations* (pp. 27–66). New York: Wiley.

MacDonald, K. B. (1992). Warmth as a developmental construct: An evolutionary analysis. *Child Development, 63,* 753–773.

Nash, A. (1988). Ontogeny, phylogeny, and relationships. In S. Duck (Ed.), *Handbook of personal relationships* (pp. 121–141). New York: Wiley.

Parks, M. R., & Adelman, M. B. (1983). Communication networks and the development of romantic relationships: An expansion of uncertainty reduction theory. *Human Communication Research, 10,* 55–79.

Schulz, B., Bohrnstedt, G. W., Borgatta, E. F., & Evans, R. R. (1977). Explaining premarital sexual intercourse among college students: A causal model. *Social Forces, 56,* 148–165.

Shaver, P., & Hazan, C. (1988). A biased overview of the study of love. *Journal of Social and Personal Relationships, 5,* 473–501.

Silver, D. H., & Cohn, D. A. (1992). *Couple attachment interview.* Unpublished instrument, University of California, Berkeley.

Sullivan, H. S. (1953). *The interpersonal theory of psychiatry.* New York: Norton.

Thornburg, H. D. (1975). Adolescent sources of initial sex information. In R. E. Grinder (Ed.), *Studies in adolescence* (3rd ed., pp. 334–340). London: Collier-MacMillan.

Trivers, R. L. (1971). The evolution of reciprocal altruism. *Quarterly Review of Biology, 46,* 35–57.

Wehner, E. A. (1992). *Adolescent romantic relationships: Attachment, caregiving, affiliation, and sex.* Unpublished doctoral dissertation, University of Denver.

Wilson, E. O. (1975). *Sociobiology: The new synthesis.* Cambridge, MA: Harvard University Press.

Wrangham, R. W. (1982). Mutualism, kinship, and social evolution. In Kings College Sociobiology Group (Ed.), *Current problems in sociobiology* (pp. 269–289). Cambridge, England: Cambridge University Press.

Youniss, J. (1980). *Parents and peers in social development: A Sullivan-Piaget perspective.* Chicago: University of Chicago Press.

Youniss, J. (1986). Development in reciprocity through friendship. In C. Zahn-Waxler, E. M. Cummings, & R. Iannotti (Eds.), *Altruism and aggression: Biological and social origins* (pp. 88–106). Cambridge, England: Cambridge University Press.

Youniss, J., & Smollar, J. (1985). *Adolescent relations with mothers, fathers, and friends.* Chicago: University of Chicago Press.

Zani, B. (1993). Dating and interpersonal relationships in adolescence. In S. Jackson & H. Rodriguez-Tom (Eds.), *Adolescence and its social worlds.* Hove, England: Lawrence Erlbaum Associates.

Part III

FAMILIAL RELATIONSHIPS AND LINKS TO OTHER RELATIONSHIPS

Chapter 8

The Uniqueness of the Parent–Child Relationship

Eleanor E. Maccoby
Stanford University

In the last several decades, the study of relationships has become a vigorous scholarly discipline in its own right. Within the field of Psychology, this work represents a shift away from the traditional focus on individuals. Instead, students of relationships examine interactions between individuals, and they take dyads—or sometimes larger configurations of persons—as the unit of study. A particular area of interest has been on *close* relationships—relatively enduring relationships between two or more persons that have especial significance for the individuals involved. Although much of the work on relationships has been done with adult couples, the science of relationships was brought into the mainstream of Developmental Psychology in the 1980s, with the publication of the Hartup–Rubin book on *Relationships and Development* (1986), and the seminal work of Gerald Patterson and his associates on parent–child interaction in families of aggressive (as compared with nonaggressive) children (Patterson, 1982).

Relationships have been described in terms of such attributes as the power gradient between the participants, the nature of emotions predominantly displayed by the individuals toward one another, the amount of conflict, the level of commitment by each toward the partner, and the time-course of close relationships as they are formed, strengthened, maintained, and in some cases dissolved (Berscheid & Peplau, 1983). A taxonomy has grown up in the study of adult pairs, in which relationships are classified on the basis of clusters of these attributes. As we see shortly,

"Exchange" relationships have been distinguished from "communal" or "coercive" ones (Clark & Mills, 1979).

In studies of socialization, in which the childrearing activities of parents and the reactions of children have been assessed, quite a different kind of taxonomy has emerged. Parents' childrearing styles have been classified, for example, as *authoritative, authoritarian,* or *permissive,* but although this classification has grown out of the study of parent–child interaction, it does not describe relationships as such, nor does it take the parent–child dyad as the unit of analysis. Rather, it classifies *parental* behaviors and reactions. Children's interactive characteristics are described separately— for example as compliant or resistive, or attentive or inattentive to the parent. Much work on attachment, although it might be thought of as describing a relationship, focuses mainly on the two individuals involved: on the mother's responsiveness, and the quality of the child's attachment. When some mother–child pairs are described as closely bonded, or mutually indifferent, this represents a focus on the dyad and takes us into the field of relationships.

This chapter explores whether, and how, parent–child relationships can be described and distinguished in the same terms that have been found useful in the study of adult relationships. The adult work, of course, has not been merely taxonomic. The classifications have been based on carefully worked out theories about how relationships function. The interesting questions are: How similar are the interaction processes between parents and children to those that characterize close adult relationships? Do the theoretical analyses of adult relationships help us to understand parent–child relationships? In drawing the comparisons and contrasts, I focus mainly on the relationships between parents and *young* children, but consider too how and whether parent–child relationships become more similar to those between intimately related adults as children grow older.[1]

I will begin by setting out some widely accepted definitions of what a relationship is. Then I will briefly sketch some historical trends in the theorizing concerning different kinds of adult relationships—how they have been classified and contrasted. Then we can consider how parent-child relationships fit, or fail to fit, within the taxonomic system that exists for the analysis of other kinds of relationships.

---

[1]Clearly, although children do form unique relationships with each of their parents—assuming both a father and a mother are present in the household—there are some respects in which the two parents function as a coalition, and children often treat their parents as a joint source of authority. In a similar way, when there are several children in a family, parents sometimes relate to them as a group rather than as individuals. And, siblings can form coalitions vis-à-vis their parents. For the sake of simplicity, this chapter considers the relationships between one or both parents and a given child, without regard to the complexities introduced by siblings.

Relationships Defined

First, the definitions. Relationships can be said to exist between two people when their lives are interdependent. By interdependent we mean that two people's behaviors, emotions, and thoughts are mutually and causally interconnected; that is, that what each does, thinks, and feels depends on what the partner does, thinks, and feels. A relationship is defined as *close* to the extent that it endures, and involves strong, frequent, and diverse causal interconnections (Kelley et al., 1983). When there is an interruption in the chain of mutually linked responses that each partner has come to expect from the other, strong emotions are likely to be aroused (Bercheid, 1986; Mandler, 1975, 1984).

It seems obvious that parent–child relationships qualify as *close,* especially when the child is young. A young child's ability to get food, to dress and undress, to bathe, even to move from place to place, all depend on interactions with a caretaker. And an adult's ability to carry out caretaking functions efficiently depends on the child's producing a set of coordinated responses: for example, lifting a foot to get a pant-leg on, opening the mouth for a spoonful of food. We now know a good deal about the refined, detailed coordination whereby a parent and infant respond and adapt to one another's signals and actions. As children grow older, these moment-to-moment linkages in behavior fade in importance and are replaced by forms of linkage that span greater distance in time and space. But the more distal forms of interaction can continue to create the substance of a close relationship, given that the behavioral streams of the parents and children continue to be mutually dependent, causally linked. Within any parent–child pair, then, both the degree of meshing and the nature of the processes whereby each influences the other will change with the development of the child. But I assume that at every stage, one or both partners in the parent–child relationship must continue to adapt to the behaviors, states, and goals of the other.

Although it must be true that parents and children are biologically prepared to form close relationships with one another, there are cross-cultural and within-cultural variations in how close these relationships typically are, and what form closeness takes. In some cultures and subcultures, fathers seldom interact with young children and cannot be said to have a close relationship with them under the terms of our definition, even though these fathers may be thoroughly committed to their children's welfare in less intimate ways. And, parents differ, within and between cultures, in terms of such things as whether routine caretaking and feeding is done according to the parent's schedule versus adapted to the child's current state, how much playful interaction parents engage in with young children, how emotionally expressive they are, or how much time the two spend in physical proximity to one another. Clearly, from the beginning, the stage is set for qualitatively different kinds of relationships to emerge between different parent–child pairs.

Equity Theory and "Exchange" Relationships[2]

Gouldner (1960) said that the principle of reciprocity is a universal norm. That is, in all social groups, an individual who is benefited by another individual is understood to have an obligation to return a benefit in some form and at some time. *Exchange theory* embodies this principle. It has been meant to explain why some relationships endure and others do not. It assumes, first of all, that each person in a relationship will behave in such a way as to maximize his or her own benefits, and minimize personal costs. But in relationships, each person's costs and benefits are related to those of the partner—often, indeed, controlled by the partner. Exchange theory frames relationships in terms of a social exchange of benefits and services. Some of the concepts are taken from economic theory, but the theory also had strong roots in reinforcement theories in psychology (see Sears, 1951, for an early analysis of social interchange in these terms). Not only must each person derive more benefits than cost from the relationship between them, but the net benefits derived by each from the relationship must be roughly equivalent to those of the partner, when benefits are summed over time. If a cost–benefit balance between the pair does not exist, the relationship will be unstable and is likely to be broken off. When a balance prevails between the parties, an *exchange relationship* can be said to be in place. Kelley and Thibaut (1978) expanded the concept of exchange relationships to include not only people's efforts to maximize personal benefits from a relationship but also their increasing cooperative efforts, as they and their partners became more and more interdependent, to maximize benefits accruing to the pair jointly. Presumably, cooperative efforts would be augmented because the interests and goals of an interdependent pair would become progressively more joint. Still, in exchange relationships, individuals are seen as keeping a running tally of costs and benefits. They expect the effort they make, and their contributions to the partnership, to be proportional to the benefits they receive from it, whether these benefits be to the self only, or in the form of benefits accruing to both members of the pair.

Must the participants in a relationship have equal costs, and equal benefits, for the relationship to endure? Not necessarily. In *equity theory* (a more general form of exchange theory) investments (Homans, 1974) or inputs (Adams, 1965) are part of the cost–benefit equation, so that the person who invests the most has a greater right, understood by both parties,

---

[2]The reader is referred to Roger Brown's lucid exposition of relationships theory (Brown, 1986) as the field stood in the mid-1980s.

to draw resources and benefits from the relationship. Presumably, this balances out the extra benefits the low-investment partner derives by virtue of association with a high-investment partner. "Investment" is a difficult concept to define in human relationships, but it includes a wide range of assets that either partner may bring to the relationship. Assets include anything that is valued, such as physical attractiveness, material goods, social status, good reputation, physical strength, or membership in a prestigious group.

When partners do not bring equal assets to a relationship, a *hierarchical exchange relationship* is likely to develop. It is still true that both parties are free agents, in the sense that each can decide, on the basis of a personal cost–benefit analysis, whether to remain in the relationship. However, a bargain has been struck such that both understand that one partner, by virtue of greater investment, has the greater right to exercise control. In theory, most employer–employee relationships are of this sort. The benefits employees enjoy by virtue of the wages they receive should equal or exceed the costs of the time and energy they devote to furthering the employer's goals.

In *equal-status exchange relationships,* as in hierarchical ones, each partner has independent objectives which each helps the other to realize, but the participants are understood to have equal rights to influence, or make demands upon, the other. Such relationships involve a form of cooperation or reciprocity based on the self-interest of each partner. As noted earlier, each person keeps a reckoning, which may be more or less explicit, more or less detailed, of who owes what to whom. Each person's freedom to make a demand or ask a favor of the other is strictly limited by whether the asker is in a position to repay, and compliance to a partner's request is understood to create an obligation on the part of the partner to do something of equal value for the complier at a future time.

Communal Relationships

In their 1979 paper, Clark and Mills introduced a distinction between exchange relationships and what they called communal relationships. In their view, the difference lies in whether partners feel an obligation to be responsive to one another's needs. Such a sense of obligation is not present in exchange relationships, they claimed, but is present in communal ones, these being most commonly found among kin, but also in certain other relationships as well. In the Clark and Mills account, people in a communal relationship do not keep track of who owes what to whom, and although both partners presumably receive benefits from the relationship, these benefits need not be comparable, since the two persons' needs may not be the same.

In communal relationships, partners are joined in a number of ways. First, they focus more on joint objectives and benefits than individual ones; what they do jointly is seen as being for "us" rather than for "you" and "me." Second, strong emotional ties between members of the pair usually involve a considerable degree of mutual empathy, so that elation, anxiety, or serenity manifested by one partner can be experienced vicariously by the other (Brown, 1986; Wispe, 1978). These elements make it possible for each partner to trust the other—that is, to have confidence that each partner will do what is best for the other and neither will undercut the other out of self-interest. Another element should be noted: Other people perceive a communal pair as having mutual loyalty and joint interests and outcomes. Thus, the pair are treated as a pair and develop a joint reputation. Each becomes vulnerable to public judgments of the partner as well as the self.

Partners in a communal relationship tend to maintain a high state of awareness of each other's emotional states and needs, and are vigilant for information that is relevant to the partner's goals as well as their own. Among older children and adults, there is extensive mutual disclosure between friends concerning personal histories, feelings, tastes, and aspirations, especially in the early stages when a communal relationship is being formed. From then on, partners keep the flow of information going so that each is up to date on the other's enterprises and emotional states. Partners also maintain a state of readiness to be influenced by one another.

Causal Relationships

Coercive relationships are relationships in which the exercise of power is one-sided. Usually this situation develops when the subordinate party is not free to leave. In such relationships as master–slave, or prisoner–guard, power over the subordinate person is achieved through physical restraint and the dominant person's control of rewards and punishments. In the pure case, adaptation as well as power is one-sided. The subordinate person must adapt to the demands of the dominant one, and there are few limits on the dominant person's exercise of arbitrary power. No balance of costs and benefits between the partners in the relationship need be maintained. Adaptation by the subordinate partner can take a variety of forms, including imitation of the powerful other (Bandura, Ross, & Ross, 1963; Bettelheim, 1958) as well as compliance to the demands of the other. To adapt, the subordinate person must have greater, more detailed knowledge about the tastes, motives, and probable reactions of the dominant person than vice versa.

Relationships can be *mutually* coercive when (a) neither party is free to leave, and/or (b) when the dominance issues have not been resolved, so that each person is struggling to impose his or her will upon the other. But even in asymmetrical coercive relationships, where one has achieved control over the other, there are nevertheless forces for redress of balance. Coerced subordinates usually find ways and means of manipulating their manipulators. For example, in military organizations it is well known that low-ranking personnel have ways of sabotaging unwelcome orders, and are often able to train their superior officers with respect to what orders to give. These processes occur within families as well as in more public relationships.

In one sense, coercive relationships can be considered as a special case of exchange relations, in that the subordinate derives benefit of a kind from the relationship. By conforming to the demands of the dominant other, the subordinate can avoid the pain of whatever punishment the other would inflict for noncompliance. However, the fact that control is exercised through force and fear takes the relationship out of the realm of relationships that equity theory is meant to explain—namely, bargains freely entered into by two parties each of whom is in a position to compute, and be guided by, a personal cost–benefit ratio.

Mixed Relationships

Few relationships are pure examples of any one of the relationship types. Among adults, elements of power assertion (coercion) enter at least occasionally into even the most harmonious communal relationship. And even in the absence of coercion, the communal element in a close relationship such as marriage will wax and wane, relative to exchange elements, depending on such things as childbearing, changes in job status or the status of other relationships that each partner independently maintains. When we speak of two persons having a communal relationship, then, we usually mean that this component predominates over the other relationship components.

Relationships as "Natural Categories"

Fiske, in his paper on the "Four elementary forms of sociality" (1992), said that there are distinct forms of social relationships that form natural categories—categories that are recognized in all cultures, each having a set of distinct, widely understood scripts from which participants can enact their roles in the different kinds of relationships. His taxonomy is similar to, but not identical with, the classification of relationships we have been discussing so far. He distinguishes communal relationships, equal-status exchange relationships, and authority-based (hierarchical) relationships, but separates off as a fourth category the market-based relationships in which services are provided in exchange for money. Fiske's work adds a cognitive component to the distinctions among different kinds of relationships, claiming that it matters how relationships are represented cognitively, and that these representations need to be—and are—shared among members of a social community.

A word should be said here about the limits of relationships. Negotiations occur in all relationships concerning how pervasive they shall be. Most participants want to preserve some autonomous regions of activity in which the partner is not involved, and there are often efforts to ward off a partner's intrusion into this private space, as well as efforts to maintain the partner's involvement in the realms where each wants the other to be involved.

PARENT–CHILD RELATIONSHIPS

We now consider the parent-child relationship in light of the kinds of relationships described earlier, focusing mainly on relationships when children are in their early or middle-childhood years. We will ask how helpful these distinctions are as we think about ways of describing the variation in parent–child relationships. I will argue that none of the three relationship types fit the parent–child case very well.

Coercion. First, the case of coercion. Clearly, young children are not free to leave the parent–child relationship. Also, parents have vastly greater knowledge, control of resources, and physical strength. They can and do make demands upon children, monitor their compliance, and administer discipline for infractions. Furthermore, children's strong need for parental affection and approval gives parents another source of power: They can withhold affection and approval, or threaten to do so. All this places in parents' hands a great potential for creating an asymmetrical coercive relationship. And, indeed, if we are to believe some of the historical accounts of childrearing, there were periods when parents typically controlled children through punishment and fear of punishment, creating a relationship that was not too far from that of master and slave.

Still, there have always been limits on parents' exercise of arbitrary power. In most situations, parents are no more free to leave a relationship with a child than the child is to leave the parent. The powerful sense most parents have of an obligation to care for their children probably reflects both genetically "prepared" responses on the part of parents, and conformity to the social requirements for parental performance that is part of the social–moral codes of all societies that we know about. True, under extreme circumstances parents do sometimes abandon children. And there are cultures and situations in which a child may be given away to another family for rearing. But most parents feel and accept as paramount their obligation to care for their children. That being so, children are in a position to develop some coercive power of their own (e.g., see Patterson,

1982); they can take it as a given that their parents will not leave even if coerced. Children's coercive behavior can take a number of forms, depending on age and circumstances, but it includes crying and displays of temper, and the withholding of compliance.

The power of parents to coerce children is limited not only by children's power of countercoercion, but also by constraints on children's ability to obey. Parents cannot demand what children cannot do. I believe this is a primary reason why the exercise of parental coercive power is a minor element in the parent–child relationship during the first year, compared to the role it can play later.

Parents may also be aware that using coercive power with children may stand in the way of some of their longer-term socialization objectives. Bugental and Goodnow (1997), in their chapter on socialization for the new edition of the *Handbook of Child Psychology*, summarized evidence that when parents control children by arousing fear—yelling, threatening, resorting to physical punishment—the children's emotional arousal interferes with their receiving and remembering the message the parent is trying to convey.

Finally, we must not underestimate the importance of parental *counteridentification* with the child. Parents' own egos are invested in their children. They feel pride in their children's accomplishments, and empathic distress over a child's weakness or failures. Insofar as parents see their children as a kind of extension of themselves, they are likely to be restrained from undue harshness. And of course, a parent's deep love for a child can have the same effect.

Hierarchical Exchange Relationships. To what extent can parent–child relationships be described as hierarchical exchange relationships? In one sense, the fit seems good. Parent–child relationships are always hierarchical to some degree. The parent's dominance becomes less in degree, and covers a smaller range of the child's life activities, as the child grows older, but nevertheless the element of parental authority is almost always present, at least until late adolescence. The realities of parental dominance are reinforced by socially prescribed status relationships. Children are enjoined to "Honor thy father and thy mother," and at some point in early childhood they come to understand that parents have the right to direct children's activities and that children are obligated to respect their parents' authority and conform to their demands. One can think of the relationship as a balanced one, in that children are obligated to tender service and obedience to their parents in exchange for the many benefits they receive.

It is doubtful, however, whether what children offer to their parent can ever serve to balance in any quantitative sense what parents provide. There is some evidence that contributions are seen to have more value when made by persons with few resources, but even when the contributions of children are weighted in relation to their abilities, they hardly match the contributions of parents.

The fit of equity theory to parent–child relationships, then, is essentially quite poor. Parents bring a greater "investment" to the relationship in almost every respect. Biologically, a mother has invested 9 months carrying a child and feeding it from her own body before the child is born. Furthermore, the parents' ownership of all the resources a child needs means, in equity theory, that parents are entitled to a great deal of return from the child in the form of service, obedience, flattery, and other forms of one-sided adaptation, if the relationship is to remain in balance. Yet it is obvious that in the early life of the child, adaptation is by no means mainly found in the child.

Mahler and colleagues (Mahler, Pine, & Bergman, 1975) said: "Whatever adaptations the mother may make to the child, and whether she is sensitive and empathic or not, it is our strong conviction that the child's fresh and pliable adaptive capacity, and his need for adaptation (in order to gain satisfaction) is far greater than that of the mother, whose personality, with all its patterns of character and defenses, is firmly and often rigidly set" (p. 5).

We cannot doubt that there is some truth to what these authors say. Yet in our 1983 review of microanalytic studies of mother–infant interaction (Maccoby & Martin, 1983), John Martin and I found much more evidence that mothers were adapting their own moment-to-moment behavior to an infants' prior responses than vice versa. Mothers appear to take the lead through imitating the infant and adjusting the timing of their own behavior, in producing a semblance of reciprocity, and only gradually lead the infant into turn-taking and other forms of genuine reciprocity. The infant's behavioral stream seems to be more self-perpetuating, more resistant to being deflected by the momentary activities of a partner, than that of the mother. (Perhaps this is true, in part, because the infant's behavior is more linked to internal states.) In order to influence the behavior of a very young child, a parent must be extremely sensitive to the child's concurrent state (Shaffer & Crook, 1980). Several studies of children's compliance to their mother (Parpal & Maccoby, 1985; Rocissano, Slade, & Lynch, 1987) found that mothers who had first synchronized their behavior to that of the child and followed the child's lead in a playful interchange had children who were more compliant to the mother's directives.[3] We see then that although parents might be in some sense entitled simply to impose their will on an infant or toddler, because of their enormous investment, there are strict limits on their ability to do so, and we do not see the imbalance

---

[3]See also Westerman, 1990, for further evidence on the importance of a mother's coordinating her inputs with a child's ongoing activities in order to obtain compliance.

in adaptation—with the infant or toddler doing more of the adapting—that equity theory would lead us to expect on the basis of the greater resources parents bring to the exchange.

In a sense, we could see a system of equity in the exchange between parents and children as being biologically built in. Adults are no doubt genetically predisposed to find an infant's cry aversive, and an infant's smiles and other signs of pleasure rewarding. The parent, then, would derive as much gratification from nurturing the infant as the infant does from being cared for, and both could be seen as operating from self-interest. From this standpoint, the child's capacity to smile or to stop crying must be seen as an enormously weighty "investment" that more than balances out the great investment of the parents. To do so, however, would be to stretch the concept of investments beyond any utility. Let us rather simply describe the relationship between parents and young children as one that is unbalanced with respect to the investments and resources contributed by the two parties.

There is probably some shift toward a more equitable exchange as children grow older. Clearly, when the child is very young, parents minister to its needs without any expectation of being repaid. When they make a demand of a 2-year-old, they do not justify it to the child or to themselves by reference to the fact that they have provided the child with food and shelter. And surely young children do not see their parent's overall support as conditional on their own good behavior. In Damon's interviews with children (Damon, 1977), when he asked them for reasons why they should respect their parents' authority, it was not until about age 7 or 8 that children began to talk in exchange terms (e.g., "You ought to do what your mother asks because if you don't she might not do things for you when you want her to.").

We do not know at what age, or to what extent, parents emphasize exchange ideas in their socializing interactions with their children. Certainly a behavior modification regime in which children earn points for compliance with specific parental demands, and can then spend their points for a variety of rewards, fits the exchange principle quite exactly. Indeed, we could argue that in any instance in which a reward is explicitly promised or given for a desired behavior, an exchange mode has been brought into play. Similarly if a child refuses or resists a parental demand and the parent responds with a comment such as "well then don't expect me to do something for you the next time you ask" exchange is the principle of reciprocity being invoked.

In studies of the way parents and children deal with one another with respect to household chores, Goodnow (1996) noted that mothers of school-aged children resist children's demands for unlimited service and stress their own requirements for the children's help, using such comments as, "I am not your servant." These mothers are evidently seeking to establish some principle of equity for the exchange of services within the family, though they are likely to put this in communal rather than exchange terms. That is, in many families parents say that it is not appropriate for family members to pay one another for services exchanged, but that nevertheless all family members should take responsibility for one another's welfare. However, we must suppose that this kind of pressure from parents for reciprocation from children is rare when children are young, and that even in middle childhood no real balance is expected by either party in the value of goods and services exchanged between the two generations.

Communality. Is the parent–child relationship better described as a communal one? Here, once again, the fit is not good. In communal relationships, each takes responsibility for fulfilling the needs of the other, and joins in a partnership in which joint goals are established and each contributes to the joint welfare. For this kind of partnership to be possible, each must accumulate a considerable fund of knowledge about the other's preferences and capacities, and use this knowledge to further the other's interests. First and foremost, children do not take responsibility for their parents' welfare, although parents do for their children's. Young children are able to understand only a very limited segment of a parent's needs, much less do anything effective to fulfill them. Indeed, recent work on children's "theory of mind" indicates that acquiring an understanding that other people have needs and motives distinct form one's own is a slow, cumulative process in childhood.

Of course, *some* communal elements are present: Even in early childhood, strong emotional bonding is present in both parent and child, and empathy is bidirectional too; that is, toddlers respond with distress when a parent is distressed, and reciprocate joyful emotional states as well. But so far as pursuing joint goals is concerned, it is hardly possible for goals to be fully mutual between a parent and young child. The parent's goals are much more complex; the parent is capable of anticipating future events, and can think in terms of long-term welfare as well as in terms of the immediate situation. The goals of an infant or toddler are in the here and now. When mutuality of goals is achieved, it happens primarily because the parent has adopted the child's momentary goals. But for parents, such momentary goal synchrony is embedded within the larger framework of longer-term goals, and for the child it is not. With respect to mutual knowledge, asymmetry also prevails. The parent has extensive knowledge of the child's history, the child's preferences and probable reactions, and the child's mood states. The child develops reciprocal knowledge about the parent only gradually, and never knows as much about the parent's life as the parent knows about the child's.

Another criterion of communality in a relationship is the readiness of partners to respond to one another's influence attempts. Young children are probably biologically prepared to respond to certain signals from parents (witness their inhibition of behavior following an adult's issuing a prohibition in a sharp, peremptory tone of voice; Fernald, 1993). And students of attachment have argued that at least by age 18 months, one must posit a motivation to please others as an already-developed characteristic of children. However, as we have seen, their capacity and willingness to comply is something that is built up only gradually, by virtue of parents' timing their influence attempts sensitively in relation to the child's momentary state. Some parents, at least, are able to lead their young children into a system of reciprocal interaction that involves mutual responsiveness to one another's initiatives.

The recent work by Kochanska (1997) and colleagues (Kochanska, Aksan, & Koenig, 1995) on what they call "committed compliance" is pertinent here: They have shown that certain kinds of parent–child mutuality in early childhood—in particular, the frequent occurrence of shared positive affect—lead to an increased likelihood that a child, at preschool age, will be in a state of readiness to respond willingly to parental influence attempts. In other words, some children by preschool age, by virtue of their earlier socialization, will be able to enter into the kind of communality with a parent that involves mutual responsiveness to a partner's influence attempts—responsiveness that is not based on fear but rather on the desire to please one another and the sense of common interests.

Still, we must be aware of the great asymmetry between parent and child that prevails in even these seemingly communal episodes. In Berscheid's excellent chapter in the Hartup and Rubin book, *Relationships and Development* (1986), she discussed what it is like for an adult to develop a relationship with an infant or a pet, in other words with someone who:

> possesses only a limited repertoire of responses, as well as limited motor and cognitive abilities to develop new responses (e.g., brief attention spans, primitive cognitive structures, poor motor coordination). [Berscheid says that in this situation] the more capable partner (must) carry the burden of developing the relationship, with the less capable partner's limitations dictating the terms. (p. 152)

In order to achieve a meshed sequence of actions or plans with a young child, then, an adult must be capable of tailoring his or her own actions to the child's level, and motivated to expend the effort that is needed to fit an adult's actions into the sequences a young child is capable of.

We see, then, that the relationship between a parent and a young child can hardly be considered communal in the sense that this term is usually applied to relationships between adults. Insofar as communality is involved in a parent–child relationship, it is a one-sided communality that applies primarily to the parent's role, not the child's. One-sided communality is a contradiction in terms. We need a term to characterize a relationship in which a more competent person takes on a commitment to care for, and teach, a less competent one. At the adult level, this would apply to the relationship between mentor and "mentee." Such a relationship prevails much more powerfully, however, between parent and child. Perhaps a term that has an honorable history in developmental psychology can be applied aptly here: a *nurturant* relationship. Or, an *altruistic* relationship. However, both these terms apply more to the characteristics of the more competent partner than to the nature of the relationship between them.

A more truly communal relationship may be the endpoint toward which many parent–child relationships move as children approach adulthood. But basically, we must see the parent–child relationship as unique. In some ways, it does incorporate some of the features that have been noted in adult relationships: It has elements of exchange, elements of communality, elements of coercion. However its overarching characteristic is parental commitment to, and acceptance of, responsibility for, the welfare of the child. In this sense, it is essentially an asymmetrical relationship that cannot be adequately understood in terms of exchange theory.

"Domain Specific" Parent–Child Relationships

In their chapter on socialization, Bugental and Goodnow (1997) imported an idea from cognitive psychology: the idea of domain specificity. They suggested there is probably not a single set of multipurpose socialization processes pertinent to the whole range of social relationships. Rather, they draw on Fiske's (1992) formulation of relationships as natural kinds, and suggest that for each kind, there is a specific set of socialization "rules." Thus socialization may be seen as "domain-specific" in that for different kinds of relationships, interaction will be organized around a distinctive set of socialization tasks and will involve a distinctive set of perceptual sensitivities, social cues, and regulatory processes. In their role as socializing agents, then, parents would have more than one kind of relationship with their children.

What are these relationship kinds or domains? One is the domain of attachment, oriented around processes designed to bring parent and child into proximity especially under conditions of threat. Bugental and Goodnow see this aspect of parent–child interaction as intrinsically communal, because it involves prepared signals and responses in parent and child that support mutual responsiveness, integration of their behavioral streams, and "intersubjectivity." As we noted earlier, however, the idea of one-sided nurturance has to be added to communality to get a full description of what happens between parent and child in this domain. A second domain, the hierarchical or power-based one, they describe as involving "the management of competing interests between individuals with unequal power or resources." Between parents and children, this domain of course is the one involved in episodes of control and discipline. A third domain is that of more equal-status reciprocity; they note, "the relationship between parents and children may at times take on properties more typically found in reciprocal relationships between peers," and is oriented around the reciprocation of positive experiences.[4]

Clearly, Bugental and Goodnow (1997) have identified three kinds of interactive processes very similar to those that students of adult relationships have used to distinguish exchange from communal from coercive relationships. But Bugental and Goodnow are not offering a taxonomy, a typology, of parent–child relationships of the sort that has been derived for adult relationships. Rather than classifying a given parent–child pair as being predominantly of one kind or another, these writers imply that each pair switches from one "domain" to another depending on developmental stages and on the immediate socialization context. They note that the attachment domain predominates during infancy, with the other two domains increasing in importance later on. Though they are not explicit about this, their formulation would be consistent with the view that the power or authority domain predominates during the preschool years, with exchange and reciprocity-based relationship themes growing in importance through the middle-childhood and adolescent years. Nevertheless, what they are suggesting is that a given set of parent–child pairs operate sometimes in one domain, sometimes in another.

It is worth emphasizing how different this idea of domain specificity is from the classical psychometric approach to dimensions of parenting. For many years we have factor analyzed parental attributes to identify major dimensions whereon parents consistently differ from one another. Some analysts of parental characteristics, notably Baumrind (1971), have utilized profiles of parental scores on several dimensions to create typologies of parental styles. But these are meant as general descriptions of the way in which a subgroup of parents function across domains or situations. The idea of a given parent–child pair having a different pattern of interaction in different domains has more kinship with the work of Grusec and her colleagues (Grusec & Goodnow, 1994; Grusec & Kuczynski, 1980; Grusec,

---

[4]Bugental and Goodnow (1997) identify a fourth domain, having to do with membership in, and identification with, groups, but this domain has more to do with socialization within peer groups than within families and is not so pertinent to parent–child relationships as the other three.

Dix, & Mills, 1982), who emphasize the way parenting varies from time to time for a given parent–child dyad, depending, for example, on whether the parent is trying to achieve immediate control of a child's behavior, or control at a later time when the child is out of the parent's sight. These distinctions are largely pragmatic. They presumably grow out of parent's discovery of what works best under different circumstances. Those of us who have been preoccupied with dimensions of parenting whereby parents can be distinguished from one another have surely paid too little attention to the obvious validity of Grusec's claim about the way parents switch styles depending on whether they are ministering to a child's needs or dealing with a transgression, and depending on what their socialization goal is at a given time. Of course, there is nothing in the emphasis on within-parent variability that precludes a parent's having a predominant style which differs from that of other parents, but it is important to recognize that within-parent variation is great enough to modify considerably our ability to label a given parent–child pair with respect to their relationship quality.

Claims about domain specificity and domains as natural kinds go beyond a parent's pragmatic variations in style. In suggesting that the parent–child dyad have distinctive prepared responses for the different domains, Bugental and Goodnow have invoked an evolutionary theme, and in this sense their thinking is more similar to Judith Harris' (1995) suggestion that we as humans have distinctive repertoires for functioning as members of dyads, members of small groups, or as members of large groups.

How does the idea of domain-specific socialization fit in with what the students of adult relationships have had to tell us about the different forms adult relationships can take? We can see parent–child interaction as a multipurpose socializing enterprise which, by switching from one domain to another, plays a role in preparing children for each of the different kinds of relationships—or relationship domains—in which they will participate as adults. Adult communal relationships have been explicitly described as those prevailing mainly among kin, or between mated couples or intimate friends. Presumably children can learn, through being nurtured by their parents and from their own lesser role in striving to please or help their parents, lessons about the reciprocal obligations people have to care for one another. Thus socialization within the family is a training ground for future communal relationships with kin, romantic partners, and intimate friends. The idea that early parent–child relationships provide the basis for internal representations or working models of close relationships, which are then manifested at later points in the life cycle, is a familiar one, and fits in primarily as an exemplar of socialization carryovers within one domain: the communal one.

In-home socialization also prepares children, to a lesser degree, for the equal-status exchange relationships among classmates, coworkers, and short-term friends or acquaintances to whom the rules and processes of intimacy do not apply. Childhood peer groups probably constitute the primary childhood training ground for relationships of this kind, but parents and children do sometimes operate outside a hierarchical mode. They may explicitly exchange goods and services or simply play together; also, by monitoring their children's interactions with peers parents of young children help to support and shape some of the processes of equal-status interchange.

The hierarchical or control domain in parent–child relationships can be seen as a major area of preparation for adult hierarchical relationships, both coercive and noncoercive ones. (Of course, hierarchical relationships within peer groups also constitute an important arena for childhood socialization in this domain, especially for boys.)

In the field of developmental psychology, we have devoted a great deal of research effort in trying to understand the ways in which children's experiences in interaction with their parents help to shape the individual personality traits, competencies, and liabilities that they bring into the various arenas of adult life. It is a somewhat different perspective to think about life-course trajectories as a set of transitions from one set of *relationships* to another. A whole area of expertise has emerged around the enterprise of describing distinctive kinds of adult relationships. As far as childhood relationships are concerned, there has been excellent work done on childhood friendships and peer-group interaction, and excellent work on parent–child interaction, but we are only beginning to try to distinguish and compare them as kinds of relationships in any systematic way. It may be very much worth doing. At least, it will shake up our traditional ways of thinking, and that is always worth a good deal in its own right.

REFERENCES

Adams, J. S. (1965). Inequity in social exchange. In L. Berkowitz (Ed.), *Advances in experimental social psychology* (pp. 262–299). New York: Academic Press.

Bandura, A., Ross, D., & Ross, S. A. (1963). A comparative test of the status envy, social power, and secondary reinforcement theories of identificatory learning. *Journal of Abnormal and Social Psychology, 67,* 527–534.

Baumrind, D. (1971). Current patterns of parental authority. *Developmental Psychology Monograph, 4*(1), Part 2.

Berscheid, E. (1986). Emotional experience in close relationships: Some implications for child development. In W. W. Hartup & Z. Rubin (Eds.), *Relationships and development* (pp. 135–166). Hillsdale, NJ: Lawrence Erlbaum Associates.

Berscheid, E., & Peplau, L. A. (1983). The emerging science of relationships. In H. H. Kelley, E. Berscheid, A. Christensen, J. H. Harvey, T. L. Huston, G. Levinger, E. McClintock,

L. A. Peplau, & D. R. Peterson (Eds.), *Close relationships* (pp. 1–19). New York: W. H. Freeman.

Bettelheim, B. (1958). Individual and mass behavior in extreme situations. In E. E. Maccoby, T. R. Newcomb, & E. Hartley (Eds.), *Readings in social psychology* (3rd ed.). New York: Henry Holt.

Brown, R. W. (1986). *Social psychology* (2nd ed.). New York: The Free Press.

Bugental, D. B., & Goodnow, J. J. (1997). Socialization processes. In W. Damon & N. Eisenberg (Eds.), *Handbook of child psychology: Vol. 4* (5th ed., pp. 389–462). New York: Wiley.

Clark, M. S., & Mills, J. (1979). Interpersonal attraction in exchange and communal relationships. *Journal of Personality and Social Psychology, 37,* 12–24.

Damon, W. (1977). *The social world of the child.* San Francisco: Jossey-Bass.

Fernald, A. (1993). Approval and disapproval: Infant responsiveness to vocal affect in familiar and unfamiliar languages. *Child Development, 64,* 657–674.

Fiske, A. E. (1992). The four elementary forms of sociality: Framework for a unified theory of social relations. *Psychological Review, 99,* 689–723.

Goodnow, J. (1996). From household practices to parents' ideas about work and interpersonal relationships. In S. Harkness, C. Super, & R. Niew (Eds.), *Parents' cultural belief systems* (pp. 313–344). New York: Guilford.

Gouldner, A. W. (1960). The norm of reciprocity: A preliminary statement. *American Sociological Review, 25,* 161–178.

Grusec, J. E., Dix, T., & Mills, R. (1982). The effects of type, severity and victim of children's transgressions on maternal discipline. *Canadian Journal of Behavioural Science, 4,* 276–289.

Grusec, J. E., & Goodnow, J. J. (1994). The impact of parental discipline methods on the child's internalization of values: A reconceptualization of current points of view. *Developmental Psychology, 30,* 4–19.

Grusec, J. E., & Kuczynski, L. (1980). Direction of effect in socialization: A comparison of the parent vs. the child's behavior as determinants of disciplinary techniques. *Developmental Psychology, 16,* 1–9.

Harris, J. R. (1995). Where is the child's environment? A group socialization theory of development. *Psychological Review, 102,* 458–489.

Hartup, W. W., & Rubin, Z. (1986). *Relationships and development.* Hillsdale, NJ: Lawrence Erlbaum Associates.

Homans, G. C. (1974). *Social behavior: Its elementary forms* (rev. ed.). New York: Harcourt Brace Jovanovich.

Kelley, H. H., Berscheid, E., Christensen, A., Harvey, J. H., Huston, T. L., Levinger, G., McClintock, E., Peplau, L. A., & Peterson, D. R. (1983). *Close relationships.* New York: W. H. Freeman.

Kelley, H. H., & Thibaut, J. W. (1978). *Interpersonal relations: A theory of interdependence.* New York: Wiley.

Kochanska, G. (1997). Mutually responsive orientation between mothers and their young children: Implications for early socialization. *Child Development, 68,* 94–112.

Kochanska, G., Aksan, N., & Koenig, A. L. (1995). A longitudinal study of the roots of preschoolers' conscience: Committed compliance and emerging internalization. *Child Development, 66,* 1752–1769.

Maccoby, E. E., & Martin, J. (1983). Socialization in the context of the family: Parent-child interaction. In P. H. Mussen (Ed.), *Handbook of child psychology* (Vol. 4, pp. 1–101). New York: Wiley.

Mahler, M. S., Pine, F., & Bergman, A. (1975). *The psychological birth of the human infant.* New York: Basic Books.

Mandler, G. (1975). *Mind and emotion.* New York: Wiley.

Mandler, G. (1984). *Mind and body.* New York: Norton.

Parpal, M., & Maccoby, E. E. (1985). Maternal responsiveness and subsequent child compliance. *Child Development, 56,* 1326–1334.

Patterson, G. R. (1982). *A social learning approach: Vol. 3. Coercive family processes.* Eugene, OR: Castalia.

Rocissano, L., Slade, A., & Lynch, V. (1987). Dyadic synchrony and toddler compliance. *Developmental Psychology, 23,* 698–704.

Schaffer, H. R. & Crook, C. K. (1980). Child compliance and maternal control techniques. *Developmental Psychology, 16,* 54–61.

Sears, R. R. (1951). A theoretical framework for personality and social behavior. *American Psychologist, 6,* 476–483.

Westerman, M. A. (1990). Coordination of maternal directives with preschoolers' behavior in compliance-problem and healthy dyads. *Developmental Psychology, 26,* 621–630.

Wispe, L. (1978). Toward an integration. In L. Wispe (Ed.), *Altruism, sympathy, and helping* (pp. 303–328). New York: Academic Press.

Chapter 9

Social Capital and the Development of Youth From Nondivorced, Divorced, and Remarried Families

E. Mavis Hetherington
University of Virginia

Coleman (1988, 1990) used the term *social capital* to describe the diverse social resources and mechanisms that advance an individual's well-being and chances of success. Social capital resides in relationships and social organizations that individuals may use to achieve their interests and that promote positive adjustment. It is an asset based on relationships of support, commitment, and trust. Social capital is found both in supportive relationships within the family and in extrafamilial relationships in the community, peer group, church, school, and workplace. Coleman proposes that social capital outside of the family in social relationships with other families and social systems promotes the well-being of parents and children and facilitates salutary family functioning. Social ties and shared values in the church, neighborhood, or with parents of children's friends may enhance parenting, the promotion of positive goals and standards, and the successful adaptation of children, adolescents, and youth.

In Coleman's formulation it is not clear if negative aversive social relationships should be viewed simply as a lack of social capital or if they function as separate factors showing different patterns of influence on children's development and affecting different domains of adjustment than those found with positive supportive relationships. In our own work with children and adolescents, we have found that social capital in the form of positive social relationships is most likely to be associated with positive outcomes such as general well-being, social and academic competence and social responsibility, whereas risk factors in the form of negative, coercive, conflicting, or rejecting relationships are more likely to be associated with externalizing or internalizing problems. However, it is the balance between risk factors and social capital that influences both adaptive and maladaptive behaviors.

Different types of families have access to different types and amounts of social capital. McLanahan and Sandefur (1994) suggested that divorce damages and may destroy social and economic capital that would have been available to children if marital dissolution had not occurred. They propose that this occurs because of the weakening or loss of a bond between the child and the noncustodial parent, who usually is the father. The divorce also may promote uncertainty and a lack of trust not only in parents but also in other social relations. Finally, divorce may disrupt and reduce access to social capital external to the family, in relationships with the noncustodial parents' family and associates, and in loss of friends, neighbors, and teachers associated with residential moves. Remarriage also is a transition that modifies the social capital available to children, as relationships with biological parents change, a stepparent is incorporated into the family, relationships with stepsiblings within or outside of the family and with other step kin such as nonresidential stepparents and stepgrandparents are negotiated, and new children are born into the remarried family. This chapter uses data from the Virginia Longitudinal Study of Divorce and Remarriage (VLSDR) to examine the role of social capital and social risks in the adjustment and attainments of young adults from divorced and remarried families.

Although in our work with children and adolescents, individual characteristics such as temperament, intelligence, ego strength, intraversion–extraversion, locus of control, planfulness, and optimism were found to modify the effects of social risks and social capital on development (Hetherington, 1989, 1991a, 1991b), individual vulnerability and protective factors other than gender are not dealt with systematically here because of length constraints. In addition, although other types of social capital such as relations with grandparents, teachers, neighbors, family of friends, and nonresidential stepparents and stepsiblings were examined in the study, only those dealing with parents, siblings, friends, and romantic partners including spouses are considered in this chapter.

THE VIRGINIA LONGITUDINAL STUDY OF DIVORCE AND REMARRIAGE (VLSDR)

The VLSDR was originally designed to examine adaptation over the course of the first 2 years after divorce in mother-custody families. The initial sample involved 144 families, half nondivorced and half divorced with custodial mothers, and half with a target son and half with a target daughter

4 years of age. The families in the divorced group had been separated between 12 and 18 months at the time of divorce. The parents were White and middle class, and almost all had some education beyond high school. Children and families in the divorced group, as originally planned, were studied at 2 months (Wave 1), 1 year (Wave 2), and 2 years (Wave 3) after divorce. A 6-year postdivorce follow-up when the children were 10 years old (Wave 4), an 11-year (Wave 5) follow-up when they were 15 years old and a Wave 6 follow-up when they were 24 years of age were added. In addition, when the children were an average of 13½ years old, a greatly truncated assessment involving telephone interviews and a mailed packet of questionnaires was interposed between the fourth and fifth full waves of data collection. The nondivorced families were studied at equivalent times. One hundred twenty-one of the original families were present in Wave 6 when the offspring were young adults. However, it rapidly became apparent that our neat balanced design could not be maintained over time. When you are tracking families, you are tracking a moving target. Some nondivorced families had a distressing propensity to divorce, and divorced families a propensity to remarry. By 20 years after divorce in Wave 6, 70% of the divorced women in the original sample had remarried at least once and 43% of the nondivorced couples had divorced at least once. The multiple marital transitions in these families' lives were tracked, and all available families in the original sample were studied in all waves. In addition, in Wave 4 when the child was age 10 the sample was expanded to include 180 families evenly distributed across nondivorced, divorced, nonremarried mother custody, and stepfather families and across boys and girls. In Wave 5 when the children were age 15, the sample was expanded to 300 families and in Wave 6 when the offspring were 24-year-old young adults it was expanded to 450 families similarly balanced across family type and sex of child. The additional subjects were matched with the original subjects on family size, age, education, income, length of marriage and when appropriate, length of time since divorce and time of remarriage. In the cross-sectional analyses of youth in this chapter the sample combines 121 survivors from the original 144 families plus the additional families remaining from the Wave 4, and 5 and the 165 new ones added in Wave 6 samples, a total of 450 families. There was remarkably little attrition between Waves 5 and 6 with only 15 of 300 families dropping out of the study. It should be noted that by Wave 6 there was considerable diversity in the timing of divorce and remarriage in the sample since families from both the original sample and expanded samples in Waves 4 and 5 who had experienced a subsequent marital transition were included in the appropriate family type category in Wave 6.

In some of our discussion, we differentiate between simple and complex stepfamily households. Simple stepfamily households were those where all of the children in the household are full biologically related siblings from the mothers' previous marriage. Complex households contained siblings with diverse degrees of biological relatedness including various combinations of full and half siblings and biologically unrelated stepsiblings. The target youth in stepfamilies was always from the mothers' previous marriage.

The specific instruments used throughout the study are not described because of length constraints; however, the measurement strategy and constructs of interest are discussed. Details of measurement for earlier waves can be found elsewhere (Hetherington, 1987, 1988, 1991a, 1991b; Hetherington, Cox, & Cox, 1982, 1985). Only a subset of measures used in Wave 6 when the offspring were young adults is presented here. In accord with a developmental, contextual perspective, measures were obtained at the individual ontogenic level, at the level of the family microsystem, and at the level of extrafamilial systems. The study used multiple measures, methods, and informants and observations to gain information about the adjustment of parents and children and family relationships, including parent (stepparent), child, marital, and sibling relationships, and relationships with the noncustodial parents and grandparents. In addition, measures were included of behavior, relationships, risks and social capital in other settings— in the peer group, school, workplace, neighborhood, and religious settings. In Wave 6 it was not always possible to obtain observational measures of family interactions because some youth had little contact with their families; however, reports of family and social relationships from multiple informants were obtained for all youths and observations of the target youth interacting with a friend, and with a romantic partner or spouse also were obtained when the youth was involved in an intimate relationship of at least 2 months duration. In addition, observations of parent–child interaction also were obtained when the target youth had a child. Eighty-seven percent were either married or in intimate relations at age 24. Much more detailed measures of extrafamilial relationships, experiences and settings were obtained in Waves 5 and 6 because we had found, as has been reported by other investigators (Miller, Cowan, Cowan, Hetherington, & Clingempeel, 1993; Sim & Vuchinich, 1996), that the contribution to adjustment of family factors declines from childhood through adolescence to young adulthood, although the pattern of decline varies for particular dimensions of family relationships and domains of adjustment.

Although the specific measures used varied with the age of the subjects many similar constructs were measured across age. Throughout the study different aspects of positivity–supportiveness (social capital), negativity–conflict (social risk) and influence–power–control were assessed in all social relationships, as well as stressful life events and social supports. In addition, externalizing, internalizing, social and cognitive competence–achievement, social responsibility and self-esteem were assessed in all waves.

Table 9.1 presents a description of the subset of Wave 6 measures that were used in the analyses described in this chapter.

We turn now to an examination of the life situation, social capital, experiences, and adjustment of 24-year-old men and women from nondivorced, divorced single-parent, and stepfamily households.

THE LIFE SITUATION OF YOUTHS
IN NONDIVORCED, DIVORCED,
AND REMARRIED FAMILIES

The life situation of the expanded sample of 450 24-year-old youths distributed equally across the three family types from the VLSDR is presented first, followed by a description of the developmental course of social relationships, social capital and risks in family and extrafamilial relationships, the adjustment of youths and the associations among social capital, risks and adjustment. Family type × gender MANOVAS followed by univariate tests of significant multivariate effects were run on continuous variables. Chi-square analyses were used for categorical variables. All findings reported in Table 9.2 were significant at least $p < .05$.

As can be seen in Table 9.2, the household income of remarried families (mothers' plus fathers' income) was only slightly lower than that of nondivorced families in contrast to the relatively low household income of the divorced mothers (income plus transfer payments). This was to some extent due to the fact that 85% of our couples were in dual earner families. By the time the offspring were young adults less than 5% of noncustodial parents in divorced and remarried families were contributing financially to the support or education of their children. Furthermore, the improved financial situation of divorced women following a remarriage seemed to confer few economic or educational advantages on stepchildren. Youths from divorced and remarried families were more likely to be high school dropouts and daughters from divorced and remarried families were less likely to complete college than those in nondivorced families. Furthermore, youths from divorced and remarried families had lower incomes than those in nondivorced families. Women were more likely than men to be out of school and out of work and to have lower incomes.

Youths in divorced and remarried families were more likely to have initiated sex at an earlier age and to have had more sexual partners, and young women from these families were more likely to have experienced an out of wedlock pregnancy, birth, or abortion. This early sexual initiation may be associated with the fact that youths in divorced and remarried families left home earlier and were more likely to have cohabitated and to have married earlier, although no differences were found in current

TABLE 9.1
Summary of Instruments Used in This Report

Instrument	Respondent	Construct/Scales
I. Demographics		
Demographic Questionnaire	Y, P, Fr, S, M, F	Sociodemographic, educational, financial, employment, residential, sexual, marital and childbearing history, affiliation with extrafamilial groups such as religious, recreational, school, neighborhood or volunteer groups
II. Adjustment		
Antisocial		Antisocial
Antisocial Problem Solving Observations	Interviewer rating of Y, P, Fr	Antisocial rating
Antisocial Behavioral Events Checklist (developed for this study)	Observer rating of Y, P, Fr	Antisocial behavior in past 24 hours week (e.g., drunkenness, stealing, fighting)
10 Telephone Calls	Y, P, Fr, S	
Antisocial Behavior Trait	Y, P, Fr, S, M, F	
	Y, P, Fr, S, M, F answer for self and target youth	Antisocial behavior in last 12 months, ever (e.g., lying, fighting, substance abuse, trouble with law, traffic violation)
Depressed Mood		
Depression Scale (CESD) (Radloff, 1977) modified for reports of others	Y, P, Fr, S, M, F answer for self and youth	Depressed mood and symptoms
Negative Mood		Negative mood
Problem Solving Observations	Interviewer rating of Y, P, Fr	Negative mood
Negative Mood Rating	Observer ratings of Y, P, Fr	
Behavior Events Checklist	Y, P, Fr, S	Depression/anxiety (e.g., depressed, lonely, helpless, anxious/worried)
Positive Adjustment		
Life Orientation Test (Scheier & Carver, 1985)	Y, P	Positive Scale; Negative Scale; Total optimism
Self-esteem Scale (Rosenberg, 1979)	Y, P, Fr, S answer for self and target youth	Self-esteem

Measure	Respondents	Description
Responsibility Scale (Gough, 1979)	Y, P, Fr, S, M, F answer for self and target youth	Responsible, dependable, conscientious
Socialization Scale (Gough, 1979)	Y, P, Fr, S, M, F answer for self and target youth	Social maturity, integrity, rectitude
Achievement (developed for this study)	Y, P, Fr, S answer for self and target youth	Measure of achievement attainments (e.g., performance at work or school, standards of excellence, ambition)
Well-Being Scale (developed for this study)	Y, P, Fr, S	Well-being in family, social, intimate relations, work, school, economic, residence/neighborhood, leisure, personal
Behavior Events Checklist	Y, P, Fr, S	Prosocial behavior (e.g., helping, sharing, sympathy, support)
Problem Solving Observations Social Maturity Social Competence Scale (developed for this study)	Observer rating of Y, P, Fr Interviewer rating of Y, P, Fr Y, P, Fr, S, M, F answer for self and target youth	Social maturity rating Social maturity rating Popularity, social skills

III. Social Relationships

Measure	Respondents	Description
Dyadic Adjustment Scale (Spanier, 1976)	Y, P	*Scales and Factors* Marital satisfaction Expressiveness Consensus Cohesiveness Overall marital satisfaction
Inventory of Adult Relationships (constructed for this study)	Y, P, Fr, S, M, F	Positivity (affection, support, respect, intimacy, understanding, trust, instrumental aid, involvement, companionship)
Marital Interaction (Johnson et al., 1986) Marital Problems Scale (adapted from Johnson et al., 1986)	Y, P Y, P answers for self and partner	Shared activities Sources of problems in the marriage (e.g., jealousy, explosiveness, drinking, sloppiness, irritability, irresponsibility, sulking)

Measure	Respondents	Description
(Problem solving (constructed for this study). Assesses conflict resolution	Y, P, Fr, S, M, F Answers for self and youth	Positive strategies (compromise, validation, listening, humor, affection). Negative strategies (whine/complain, criticize, contempt, denial, withdrawal, belligerence, irritable/angry, sulk)
Relationship Instability (Johnson et al., 1986)	Y, P	Thinking about breaking up, taking steps toward separation
Who Does What (Cowan & Cowan, 1978)	Y, P	Household tasks & roles, decision making. Child care only for those with children
Marital Oral History Interview (Buehlman & Gottman, 1966; Katz, 1992)	Y, P	Positivity: Y, P fondness, expansiveness, we-ness. Glorifying the struggle, volatile relationships. Negativity: Y, P negativity; disappointment, chaotic relationships, gender stereotyping/traditionality Y, P family of origin
Conflict Tactics Scale (Strauss, 1979) Problem Solving Observations Interactions of youth with partner and youth with friend	Y, P, S, M, F Observer ratings of Y, P, Fr	Reasoning, symbolic, aggression, violence Positivity: affection, validation/respect, communication, humor/delight, pleasure, self-disclosure, problem solving. Negativity: belligerence, disgust/contempt, denial, anger, conflict/disagreement, withdrawal, criticize, sadness, whining, reciprocated negativity. Control/influence: influence, listening/attending, yielding

Note: Y = Youth, P = Partner, Fr = Friend, S = Sibling, M = Mother, F = Father.

TABLE 9.2
The Life Situation of Youths From Nondivorced, Divorced, and Remarried Families

	Nondivorced		Divorced		Remarried		Significant Differences
	Male	Female	Male	Female	Male	Female	
Family of origin household (to the nearest thousand)	63,000	62,000	30,000	31,000	60,000	61,000	ND, R > D
Income of youth	19,000	17,000	15,000	14,000	15,000	13,000	ND > D, R; M > F
Education							
High school dropout	8%	7%	18%	20%	16%	22%	D, R > ND
College enrollment	57%	55%	44%	39%	42%	35%	ND > D, R
College Graduation	33%	37%	27%	23%	28%	21%	F(ND > D, R)
Out of school and out of work	10%	16%	14%	21%	14%	23%	F > M
Sexual history							
Age at first intercourse	15.4	16.0	14.3	14.8	14.5	14.7	ND > D, R
Number of sexual partners	3.9	3.8	5.8	5.9	5.6	5.7	D, R > ND
Teenaged birth	5%	6%	9%	18%	8%	19%	F(D, R > ND)
Teenaged marital birth	3%	4%	4%	7%	4%	8%	F(D, R> ND)
Current status							
Married	34%	45%	34%	49%	32%	50%	F > M
Cohabiting	24%	20%	32%	32%	30%	31%	D, R > ND
Living at home	14%	14%	7%	8%	3%	2%	ND > R
Living alone	8%	6%	10%	7%	9%	7%	
Living with roommates	20%	15%	17%	7%	25%	9%	M > F

Note. ND = Nondivorced, D = Divorced, R = Remarried, M = Male, F = Female.

proportions of those married. Furthermore, youths in remarried families had left home earlier than those in divorced families, with stepdaughters leaving home earlier than any other group. Family conflict was cited as the most common reason for escaping the home by stepchildren. Although relatively few youths had divorced by age 24 (8%), these early divorce rates were more likely to have occurred with youths from divorced and remarried families than for those from nondivorced families.

Although this sample is above national norms in socioeconomic status, the results for the youth in the VLSDR are fairly similar to those for White middle-class families in national samples (McLanahan & Sandefur, 1994) in which effects of being in a single parent or stepfamily household had marked effects on teenaged childbearing, on college graduation for males, and on school dropout rates for both males and females.

THE DEVELOPMENTAL COURSE OF SOCIAL RELATIONSHIPS

Social relationships are not static but change and evolve as the developmental capacities, needs, resources, challenges, and life circumstances of the individual alters. The role of different relationships in satisfying needs also changes across time with the salience and specificity of the relationship between specific relationships and needs shifting.

Buhrmester and Furman (summarized in Buhrmester, 1992) and have drawn on the theorizing of Weiss (1975) and Sullivan (1953) about social provisions and needs to describe the socioemotional structure in children's relationships in terms of companionship, affection, instrumental help, and intimacy–self disclosure. In our general presentation of the developmental course of social relationships, negativity–conflict and influence–control are also included.

In the VLSDR in the first three waves of data when the children were 4 to 6 years of age, residential biological parents provided more companionship, affection, instrumental help, intimacy, and influence than any other relationship. Mothers were higher than fathers in all of these areas except influence where fathers exhibited more effective control. Divorced mothers, in these early years following divorce were less affectionate and controlling and more conflictual and coercive than were nondivorced mothers. There were insufficient stepfamilies to analyze at this time. By the time children were preadolescents at age 10, friends and siblings were assuming increasingly potent roles as companions, sources of affection, and confidants with same-gender friends being more important in these roles than opposite-gender friends. Conflict with friends declined with age and was always lower than in any other relationship from childhood through adolescence. Furthermore, conflict with siblings and friends was greater in divorced and remarried families than in nondivorced families. The relative influence of friends increased in adolescence. This increased influence of peers in adolescence was especially noteable in divorced and remarried families. In early adolescence, as adolescents individuate and become more autonomous, relationships with parents declined in intimacy, influence, companionship, and affection and increased in conflict–negativity, but the decline in influence and increase in conflict was most marked in divorced and remarried families with a notable increase in conflict between divorced mothers and daughters. At all ages, stepfathers were less involved, affectionate, intimate, and controlling in relationships with stepchildren than were biological fathers. Noncustodial fathers played a lesser role than did biological custodial fathers in all six areas of social relations.

Gender differences were found throughout the study with companionship and instrumental help being higher with fathers and sons than fathers and daughters, and intimate self-confiding behavior being higher between mothers and daughters, especially those in divorced families. However, throughout the developmental range in this study even sons were more likely to confide in mothers than in fathers. In adolescence and youth males confided more in female friends than male friends. Females facilitate self-disclosure and intimacy from others. Self-disclosure was significantly greater with friends than with romantic partners in adolescence. When married, women showed as much self-disclosure to friends as to their spouse, but married males disclosed more to their wives than to same or opposite sexed friends.

SOCIAL CAPITAL IN YOUTH

Early adulthood is a period marked by notable life changes. As youths go away to school, obtain jobs, establish social, economic, and intimate relationships and residence outside of the family, family relationships alter. If a firm foundation of supportive, caring family relationships has been established before adulthood, these are likely to continue. The long-term outcomes of conflictual relationships seem more difficult to predict. If the household situation remains relatively stable with the youth residing in the home, negative relations may be sustained, however, if the youth leaves the home and becomes economically independent, although distance may not make the heart grow fonder, less frequent contact and fewer encounters in the hassles of day-to-day living may diminish acrimony among family members. As one mother said, "He's screwing up his life, but it's easier when I don't have to watch it everyday." In addition, as youth become more focused on extrafamilial relationships these relationships affect family relationships. A hostile daughter or son-in-law, the birth of a baby, or notable academic or occupational success may influence relations with the family of origin.

PARENT–YOUTH RELATIONS

Multimethod, multimeasure, multi-informant composites were derived to measure personal attributes of the youth and family members, friends, and partners presented in Tables 9.3, 9.4, and 9.6. Data reduction and factor analytic techniques used parallel those described in Hetherington and Clingempeel (1992; pp. 29–31). Chronbach's alphas for the composites ranged from .67 to .95 ($M = .83$).

Individual family relationships were analyzed with gender and family type MANCOVAS for different measures and informants assessments of various dimensions of the relationship covarying out the effects of parental education and income. Cluster analyses of multimeasure, multimethod composites of relationship dimensions and of youth adjustment were also performed using the K means program of BMDP (Dixon & Brown, 1979). These were followed by a series of chi-square analyses to examine the association between family-type and child gender groups and parent–youth relations (Figs. 9.1 & 9.2), sibling relations (Fig. 9.3), and youth adjustment

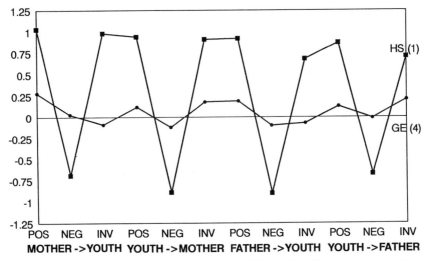

FIG. 9.1. Cluster analysis of parent–youth relations ($N = 403$).

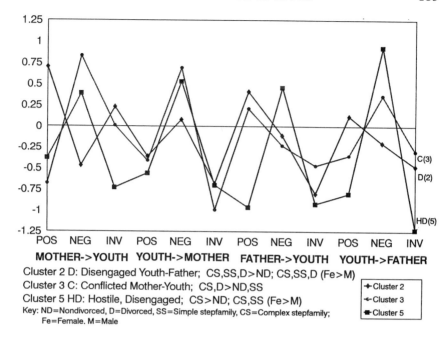

FIG. 9.2. Cluster analysis of parent–youth relations ($N = 403$).

(Fig. 9.4) clusters. The results of the chi-square analyses are summarized at the bottom of each figure.

In the cluster analyses of parent–youth relations presented in Figs. 9.1 and 9.2, stepfathers were included as the fathers in remarried families; noncustodial fathers were included in divorced families only if they had maintained some contact with the youth including contact by phone, letters, or gifts. Thus the sample size is 403 rather than the full 450 families. The clusters presented in the two figures came from a single cluster analysis but the profiles involving positive or good enough family relationships are presented separately from those with more problematic profiles in an attempt for clarity.

Cluster 1 ($N = 93$) was characterized by harmonious, supportive, involved relationships among family members. Nondivorced families were overrepresented in this cluster. Complex stepfamilies (i.e., stepfamilies with half siblings or stepsiblings present) were less likely than any other type of family to be found in this group. Cluster 2 ($N = 82$) was comprised of families with disengaged fathers but positive noncoercive mothers, and with youths who were disengaged from both parents. This was a cluster that had not been present when the offspring were adolescents and was more characteristic of remarried and divorced than of nondivorced families, and of females than of males within those families. Cluster 3 ($N = 65$)

involved conflictual mother–youth and disengaged father–youth relationships and was more characteristic of divorced and complex stepfamilies than nondivorced or simple stepfamilies. Cluster 4 ($N = 109$) was a good enough functioning family where most relationships were about average. There were no gender or family type differences in representation in this group. Cluster 5 ($N = 54$) was characterized by high acrimony and little warmth–support or involvement by family members. Membership in Cluster 5 was more characteristic of complex stepfamilies than of nondivorced families. Within both simple and complex stepfamilies, membership in this cluster was found more often with female than with male offspring.

The first point of note is that half of the families have either mutually supportive harmonious relationships or good enough relationships with their young adult offspring. Although there may be temporary perturbations in parent–child relations in early adolescence, in most families the foundation for positive relations between parents and their youthful offspring is established before adulthood. Parents who have been warm, supportive, authoritative parents with children and adolescents seldom have adversarial or disengaged family relations in youth. The vast majority of families who had been in Cluster 1 the harmonious, supportive engaged cluster in adolescence remained in that cluster or moved to Cluster 4, the "good enough" cluster in youth. About 20% of the families who had been in Cluster 1 or 4 in adolescence migrated to Cluster 2 a cluster characterized by disengagement by youth despite positive behavior by parents. This tended to be associated with geographical distance, a romantic partner or spouse who was hostile to the mother and discouraged contact with the family of origin, occupational preoccupation, or depression in the youth.

Clusters 3 and 5 involving considerable acrimony were smaller in youth than in adolescence. As youth moved out of the home, active negativity became more muted and was replaced by increased disengagement especially between stepchildren and stepfathers. Continued joint residence was associated with continued conflict.

Disengaged parents rarely evolved into warm supportive parents when their offspring were young adults. A notable exception to this involved the birth of a child. When a child was born within wedlock, the biological grandparents and parents drew closer and grandmothers and mothers especially tended to show marked increases in involvement, support, and positivity. To a lesser extent exceptional academic, athletic, or occupational achievement by a son increased the involvement and approval of both nondivorced and noncustodial fathers.

As many of our stepfamily households had increased in complexity with the birth of a child to the remarried couple or a move into the stepfamily household of a child from the fathers' previous marriage, stress, conflict and differential parental treatment of siblings occurred. Biological owness played an important role in parent–child relations, with parents being more involved, affectionate, and feeling closer to their biological child and spending more time in household tasks relating to care of that child than to nonbiologically related stepchildren. In adolescence, parents in complex stepfamilies in comparison to simple stepfamily households reported more childrearing stress and more problems in the marital relationship associated with childrearing. The birth of a child to the remarried couple often was thought of as a means of cementing the new marital relationship. However, when a child from the mother's previous marriage was already present, the birth often was associated with increased conflict between the first child and both the mother and stepfather, as well as with sibling conflict and rivalry and with concomitant decreases in marital satisfaction and increases in psychological distress for mothers.

The difficulty in negotiating relationships in complex stepfamily households was still apparent in these families when the target offspring from the mother's first marriage was a young adult. Both disengagement and hostility were found more frequently in complex stepfamilies with this being more marked in the behavior of stepdaughters toward stepfathers than in any other group. Complex family relations outside of the family involving the marriage and birth of children to the noncustodial parents new family had no effects on parent–child relations within the household or on child adjustment.

The cluster analyses masked some interesting cross-gender relationships found in the MANOVAS and path models. Sons in divorced and remarried families were more likely than daughters to feel close to and maintain contact with noncustodial fathers and stepfathers. Marital conflict was associated with different patterns of parent–child relations with sons and daughters. Conflict between spouses or ex-spouses measured in adolescence was more likely to predict deterioration in contact and affection in father–daughter relationships than father–son relationships when the offspring were young adults. In addition, when the offspring were adolescents or young adults, low marital satisfaction and a measure of marital instability–divorce proneness in parents that included parents thinking about divorce, taking action about divorce (consulting friends, lawyers or clergy, separations, filing a petition) or separation were associated with more irritable, negative, and less positive affectionate behavior and contact between biological fathers and daughters in nondivorced families and stepfathers and stepdaughters in remarried families. They also were associated not only with less affection between mothers and sons in nondivorced and remarried families in adolescence, but also less affection of sons to stepfathers in adulthood.

The links between the parents' marital relationship when offspring were adolescents, and youths' responses to parents in young adulthood were mediated by a decline in supportive affectionate relations by parents toward the opposite-gender adolescent in unhappy conflictual or unstable marriages. This cross-gender effect in response to marital quality was much greater for fathers and daughters than for mothers and sons. Mothers' marital instability had no effects on their parenting of girls, but was associated with a modest decline in positivity in parenting of sons in nondivorced families. The greater deterioration of cross-gender parent–child relations in response to marital problems, plus the finding of fathers' parenting being more sensitive than mother's parenting to marital quality has emerged in a number of other studies (Booth & Amato, 1994; Cowan, Cowan, & Schultz, 1996). It has been proposed that parenthood is a more central role for women than for men and hence is less likely to erode in response to marital problems.

In spite of the focus on conflict and disengagement in this discussion, when looking at youths' ratings of relationships with their parents, most report that they have a close or extremely close relationship with their parents. Eighty percent of youths from nondivorced families report closeness with parents and almost 70% of youths from divorced and remarried families report closeness with custodial mothers. Closeness to noncustodial fathers and stepfathers is considerably lower especially for daughters, but even these relationships in young adulthood are more likely to be characterized by disengagement than confrontations and conflict.

For most families, the period when offspring become young adults is a fulfilling one with more autonomy for both generations, less responsibility for parents, diminished conflict and acrimony, and continued affection and interest in each others well-being. It may not always be the "Whoopie!" experience described by some empty nesters, but it is often a mutually gratifying one for parents and youth.

SIBLING RELATIONSHIPS

Although considerable research has been done on parent–child relationships in divorced and remarried families less is available on the sibling relationship in these families. Little is known about how sibling relationships may exacerbate or protect against adverse consequences of stresses associated with divorce and remarriage. Two hypotheses have been advanced about the role of sibling relationships in coping with stresses such as parents' marital transitions. The first hypothesis is that following a parent's divorce and remarriage siblings may compete for the scarce resources of parental affection and attention, increasing each other's adaptive problems. The second hypothesis is that in the face of such stresses siblings may view relationships with parents as unreliable and painful and turn to each other for support, solace, and alliance. Throughout the adolescent period we found more support for the first hypothesis with negativity, rivalry, and conflict more likely to occur with full siblings in divorced and remarried families than in nondivorced families. When mutual support occurred it was most likely to be found with pairs of female siblings; males received little support from either brothers or sisters. In divorced families older female siblings often played a nurturing, caretaking role that was beneficial to younger female siblings.

In young adulthood as most siblings move out of the home and contact with siblings becomes optional, affective intensity in relations declines and conflict is often replaced by disengagement. Positive relationships are more likely to be sustained than are negative acrimonious relationships. Contact between siblings diminished dramatically between adolescence and young adulthood and was most likely to be maintained by the females in the family. Mothers attempted to draw the family together for shared activities, holidays, and special occasions and to defuse disharmony between siblings. Female siblings also attempted to promote contact, especially with sisters. When one sibling married and the other did not, contact diminished. Geographical distance also decreased both involvement and conflict. Contact was less between young adult male siblings in divorced families than in nondivorced families and was least between male siblings in remarried families. Sibling relationships in remarried families need to be qualified by the biological relatedness of the siblings, that is, by whether they are full siblings from the mother's previous marriage, half siblings with one from the mother's previous marriage and one born to the new remarriage, or nonbiologically related stepsiblings in blended families with one from the mother's previous marriage and one from the father's previous marriage. Because this was a study of stepfather families and inasmuch as fathers rarely get custody of their children the sample of nonrelated stepsiblings having lived in the household was relatively small ($N = 34$) and usually involved sibling coresidence for a shorter period of time than was found in the other sibling groups.

One of the unexpected findings was that not only was involvement and warmth–support higher in young adult biologically related siblings than in nonrelated stepsiblings, but also that conflict and rivalry were higher in biologically related siblings, especially in half siblings than in stepsiblings. There was more of both positive and negative affective engagement in biologically related siblings, and more distancing, disengagement, and affective blandness among unrelated adult siblings. The most troubled, least supportive, and most conflictual and rivalrous relationships were found with half siblings with the sibling born earlier to the mother being most resentful and agonistic toward the sibling born into the new marital relationship. In our observations of sibling interactions in adolescence, more direct statements involving social comparisons and comments about non-shared treatment occurred with these siblings than with any other sibling pairs. The animosity between these pairs was surprising with fantasies or comments about killing the other sibling said in partial jest or sometimes seriously emerging with unexpected frequency. Perhaps this rivalry could be anticipated, because a decline in involvement and affection by the mother—but most notably by the stepfather—to the child born to the mother's first marriage, occurred when a child was born to the new marriage. However, it should be noted that in a study of stabilized long-remarried stepfamilies no differences were found between full and half siblings in stepfamilies (Hetherington, Henderson, & Reiss, submitted).

Figure 9.3 presents the results of a cluster analysis of sibling relations in young adulthood. Only 424 target youths are involved in sibling relationships since 26 are only children without step- or half-siblings. The gender differences in representation in these clusters are due to the greater warmth and involvement of female siblings. Cluster 1 ($N = 112$) is a cluster of warm, harmonious involved siblings. More female than male pairs of siblings promote contact and are warm and supportive in their relationships. More siblings from nondivorced families than any other group of families are found in this cluster and fewest from half siblings in stepfamilies, with more siblings in divorced families and full siblings in stepfamilies falling in between. Cluster 2 ($N = 98$) is a negative-disengaged cluster with low warmth and involvement and high conflict. These siblings avoid contact with each other, but when contact is precipitated through such things as family celebrations or holidays relationships are cold or hostile. Half siblings are overrepresented in this cluster and nonrelated siblings in blended families underrepresented with the other sibling groups differing from the two extremes. That half siblings are underrepresented in Cluster 1 and overrepresented in Cluster 2 is notable and is a reflection of the acrimonious competitive relationship found in these siblings. Siblings in Cluster 2 also come from families in which there have been high levels of conflict, differential treatment, and nonauthoritative parenting.

Cluster 3 ($N = 82$) is an involved, harmonious, but rivalrous group. It differs from Cluster 1 mainly in the elevated rivalry. In observations in adolescence a great deal of playful teasing and social comparison about behavior and attainment was present in these sibling pairs. In young adulthood competition in achievement, in intimate relations, and even about children surfaced although these youths were fond of each other and enjoyed each other's company. Male sibling pairs are overrepresented in this cluster. Parents of offspring in this group tended to be warm and supportive but to have high expectations and demands for their child's performance. Fewer half siblings and blended stepsiblings are in this cluster. Finally, Cluster 4 ($N = 132$) is a disengaged cluster where siblings are not seeing each other or are actively avoiding contact with each other and

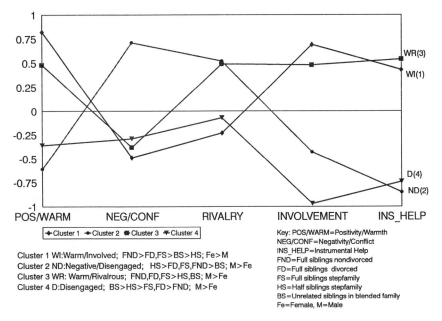

FIG. 9.3. Cluster analysis of sibling relations ($N = 424$).

in which affect is relatively neutral. This was found most often in unrelated stepsiblings and least often in siblings in nondivorced families. In addition, more full siblings both in stepfamilies and in divorced families than half siblings in stepfamilies fell in this cluster.

The proportion of siblings in Cluster 2, the conflictual cluster, declined dramatically from adolescence to adulthood with most migration occurring to Cluster 4 as detachment became a more feasible option in sibling relations and to a lesser amount to Cluster 3. Adolescents who had been in Cluster 1, the warm, involved, supportive cluster seldom moved into an acrimonious or extremely disengaged cluster in young adulthood. They sometimes moved into Cluster 3 with positive but rivalrous relationships as they contemplated and compared their new life situations and successes and failures. However, even positive sibling relations become less influential and friends and romantic partners more influential with the move into young adulthood.

RELATIONSHIPS WITH FRIENDS, ROMANTIC
PARTNERS, AND SPOUSES

In young adulthood time spent with friends and romantic partners increased and these relationships, especially the marital relationship, became more salient to the well-being of youths. At age 24, 390 of our 450 youths were involved in an intimate relationship of at least 2 months duration including 126 who were cohabiting and 184 who were married. We did analyses with intimate relationships treated as a single group and also separate analysis with the marital relationship considered as a distinct group. Although fairly parallel findings for family type differences in the quality of relationships emerged in the various intimate relationships, the impact of the marital relationship on the well-being and adjustment of youth was greater than that of dating or cohabiting relationships.

Children and adolescents from divorced and remarried families had been found to be less socially competent and popular than those from nondivorced families. Some differences in relations with friends in both patterns of interaction and type of friends chosen are still found in adult-hood. In young adulthood in comparison to youths from nondivorced families those in divorced families had smaller social networks and in problem-solving interactions with friends they were observed to be less effective problem solvers. They were less likely to reflect and consider the position of the other person, offer relevant information, explanations, and alternative solutions, or to compromise, and they more often failed to reach an agreed upon decision. In addition, they were more likely to exhibit withdrawal or denial in the face of disagreements. However, there were no differences in youths from the different family groups on negative or positive affect in interactions with friends. Deficits in effective strategies in negotiating disagreements with friends rather than the affective quality of the relationship distinguished between youth who had undergone their parents' marital transitions and those who had not. Furthermore, in a pattern similar to that found in the youths, friends of youths from divorced and remarried families in comparison to those from nondivorced families were more likely to exhibit behavior problems such as alcohol or substance use, out of wedlock pregnancies, trouble with the law, or employment and marital instability.

When cohabitation, but especially marriage and the birth of a child occurred, contact with friends declined. The decline in contact with friends associated with marriage was much greater for men than for women. Males always had been lower than females in self-disclosure but following marriage wives often became the husband's sole confidants, a problem that contributed to their distress in times of marital instability.

In marital interactions the same patterns as were found in relations with friends were observed in less adequate problem solving, and more with-drawal and denying in youths from divorced and remarried families in comparison to those in nondivorced families. However, in the marital relationship greater observed negativity in the form of belligerence, criti-cism, and contempt and more reciprocated, escalating negative exchanges also were found in youths from divorced and remarried families. As has been found in other studies (Gottman, 1994) gender differences were obtained with husbands being more likely than wives to stonewall and deny and women more likely to criticize and express affection and affirmation of their husband's worth. It is interesting to note that no family type differences were observed in positivity in couple interactions, although they emerged in the Marital History Interview. The Marital History Interview, a procedure where ratings are made of couples' discussions of the history of their relationship, has been found to be an outstanding predictor of marital instability and divorce (Gottman, 1994).

On the Marital History Interview more husband and wife negativity and disappointment in the marriage, less talking about the relationship in "we" terms rather than individualist "I" terms, and less fondness and glorifying of the relationship occurred in youths from divorced and remarried families than from nondivorced families. Moreover, in these families husbands were less expansive and detailed in descriptions of their relationships.

Youths from divorced and remarried families in comparison to nondivorced families reported themselves to have less traditional beliefs about marriage and to have more sources of problems in the marriage, such as jealousy, irritating habits, drinking, infidelity, or domineering behavior. Surprisingly, no differences among family groups in marital satisfaction on the Spanier Dyadic Adjustment Scale (Spanier, 1976) were obtained. However, whether measuring all intimate relationships or just marriages, on the Marital Instability Questionnaire, instability in the form of thinking about and acting to break up the relationship was higher in youths from divorced and remarried families. This measure has been found to be a good predictor of separation and divorce (Booth, Amato, Johnson, & Edwards, 1993).

What might be contributing to the differences in reports of marital instability in our young married couples? In order to identify factors that contributed to marital stability or instability as reported by husbands and wives (based on a median split) discriminant function analyses were run separately for husbands and wives and for youths from nondivorced, divorced, and remarried families. Separate analyses were run for different subsets of variables within the larger sets of socioeconomic factors, personal attributes, family and friend factors, and couple factors. Regression analyses predicting marital instability were also run and yielded similar results.

A summary of the significant results for separate discriminant function analyses for husbands and wives from nondivorced, divorced, and remarried families are presented in Table 9.3. The results for wives are based on wives' reports of marital instability and those for husbands on husbands' reports of marital instability on the Instability Questionnaire. The family type notations under the husband and wife columns indicate for which families that variable discriminated between high and low marital instability.

It might have been anticipated that because of differences in family background and their own parents' marital histories different factors would discriminate between marital stability and instability in young married adults from nondivorced, divorced, and remarried families. Few differences, however, are associated with family type. It is gender differences in significant factors discriminating between stable and unstable relationships that are most striking.

The first section of Table 9.3 reveals that husbands who are better educated, attend church, and have lower anxiety about income are more likely to be in stable marriages. Interestingly, only in males from nondivorced families was the wife's earning more than the husband associated with marital instability, perhaps because many youths from divorced and remarried families had been in families with a divorced mother as the sole breadwinner. Wives' concerns about income are also associated with consideration of breaking up the marriage.

Different attributes of the spouse are associated with marital instability in men and women. Depressed wives who have a pessimistic view of life are more likely to have husbands who report higher levels of marital instability, whereas antisocial behavior such as alcoholism and lack of social responsibility in husbands are more likely to be associated with wives' reports of martial instability. However, the more global measure of marital problem behaviors assessed by the Marital Problem Scale, discriminates between stable and unstable marital relationships for both men and women.

A somewhat unexpected finding was that support and conflict in relations with the family of origin and with friends did not affect marital stability but that active interference by the wife's family was associated with husbands' instability. In addition, interference by the husband's family and friends was related to greater marital instability with wives. Perhaps husbands from nondivorced families are less tolerant of economic or employment stresses precipitated by the wife. Paralleling the finding for husband–wife discrepancies in income, only husbands from nondivorced families reported that wives' job interference such as scheduling conflicts, fatigue, and problems in getting time to spend with family members or completing household or childcare tasks erode marital stability.

For couple factors, the composite measures of positivity, negativity, influence, problem solving, reciprocated negativity, and positivity and conflict were based on observations and on both husband and wife reports. Equity, traditionality, participation in housework and childcare, shared interests, time together, and frequency of sex were based on combining husband and wife reports. Satisfaction in household roles, episodes of negative and positive sex, and sexual satisfaction and infidelity were based on individual reports because it was thought that husband's and wife's perceptions, or in the case of infidelity, knowledge, would be critical in these measures.

TABLE 9.3
Factors Discriminating High Versus Low Marital Instability for Husbands and Wives From Different Family Types

	Husbands	Wives
Socioeconomic Factors		
Husband Education	ND, D, R	
Wife Education		
Husband Income		
Wife Income		
Income Discrepancy (H–W)	ND	
Wife Income Anxiety		ND, D, R
Husband Income Anxiety	ND, D, R	
Husband Church Attendance	ND, D, R	
Wife Church Attendance		
Personal Attributes		
Antisocial Behavior	ND, D, R	
Depression		ND, D, R
Social Responsibility	ND, D, R	
Optimism		ND, D, R
Marital Problem Behavior	ND, D, R	ND, D, R
Family and Friends Factors		
Wife's Family		
Support/Positivity		
Conflict/Negativity		
Interference/Influence	ND, D, R	
Husband's Family		
Support		
Conflict		
Interference		ND, D, R
Wife's Friends		
Support		
Conflict		
Interference		
Husband's Friends		
Support		
Conflict		
Interference		ND, D, R
Husband's Job Interference		
Wife's Job Interference	ND	
Couple Factors		
Husband → Wife		
Positivity		
Negativity	ND, D, R	ND, D, R
Positive/Negative Ratio	ND, D, R	ND, D, R
Influence/Power		
Problem Solving		
Positive Reciprocity		
Negative Reciprocity	ND, D, R	

(Continued)

199

TABLE 9.3
(Continued)

Wife → Husband		
Positivity	D, R	
Negativity	ND, D, R	
Positive/Positive + Negative Ratio	ND, D, R	
Influence/Power		
Problem Solving	ND, D, R	ND, D, R
Positive Reciprocity		
Negative Reciprocity	ND, D, R	
Frequency of Conflict	ND, D, R	
Equity		
Husband's Traditionality		
Wife's Traditionality		
Ratio Husband/Wife Participation in Household		
Husband Satisfaction Household Roles	ND, D, R	
Wife Satisfaction Household Roles		ND, D, R
Shared Interests		
Time Together		
Husband Positive Sex		
Husband Negative Sex	ND, D, R	
Husband Sexual Satisfaction	ND, D, R	
Wife Positive Sex		
Husband Negative Sex		
Wife Sexual Satisfaction		
Frequency Intercourse		
Wife Infidelity	ND, D, R	ND, D, R
Husband Infidelity		ND, D, R

Marital Background

Age at Marriage		
Cohabitation	ND, D, R	
Children Before Marriage or Pregnant at Marriage	ND, D, R	ND, D, R

Note. ND = Nondivorced; D = Divorced; R = Remarried.

There was little husband and wife agreement on the reports of negative sexual episodes or infidelity.

Thus, similar factors distinguished between marital stability and instability in youth from nondivorced, divorced, and remarried families. Husbands showed greater marital instability when they were dissatisfied with participation in household roles, when their wives were negative toward them, when they and their wives had poor positivity to negativity ratios, and when wives had poor problem-solving skills. Furthermore, subanalyses indicated that men were especially sensitive to negativity in the form of their wives' criticism and contempt. The most significant discriminator between marital instability and stability in men was wives' reciprocated negativity. Men liked to criticize or be negative toward their spouse without wives reciprocating their attacks. In contrast, negativity in the form of withdrawal, denial, and belligerence by husbands was the most significant discriminator for women's instability. Frequency of conflict was associated with greater marital instability in men but not women. Wives frequently expressed a preference for discussions of marital problems over avoidance of issues. Negativity in husbands also was associated with their own marital instability. In addition, low positivity (affection, affirmation of spouses comments and feelings, respect, intimacy–self-disclosure, communication, support) of wives was associated with marital instability only for men from divorced and remarried families. Perhaps men from such maritally disrupted families need more positive reassurance and support from their wives to sustain their own marriages.

Wives show some parallels to the findings with husbands. The husband's ratio of positive to negative behavior, both spouses' poor problem solving, and the wife's dissatisfaction with household roles are associated with the wives' marital instability in all family types.

It is interesting that it is satisfaction in household roles rather than participation in household roles and positive to negative ratios rather than positivity that show the most consistent discrimination between marital stability and instability. Many other studies have found that positivity in relationships may fail to discriminate between distressed and nondistressed marriages whereas negativity or ratios of positivity to negativity more frequently do (see Gottman, 1994, for a review).

Frequency of negative sexual experiences and lack of sexual satisfaction are associated with marital instability for men but not women. Men in all groups also respond adversely to known infidelities of their wives but their own infidelity is not related to their marital instability. In contrast wives' instability is associated with both their husbands' infidelity and her own infidelity. In this and in other studies we have found that women who engage in extramarital affairs are more likely than men to do so in response to an unsatisfying marriage and when they have an affair it is more likely to be serious and be a threat to the continued stability of the marriage.

Finally, couples who were expecting a child or had a child at the time of the marriage were more likely to be in an unstable relationship, and cohabitation increased men's instability in marriage. Because other investigators have found younger marriages are at greater risk for divorce, the lack of an association between age at marriage and instability might seem unexpected. However, this is a relatively young group of marrieds. Over half of our sample were not yet married and the average duration of marriage in the sample was 14 months. As might have been anticipated, very early marriage was associated with those who had already divorced and hence were not in this sample of currently married couples.

In summary, although there is evidence of more troubled and dysfunctional marital relationships with youth from divorced and remarried females than those from nondivorced families, the socioeconomic, individual, and family process variables that distinguish between marital stability and instability in youths from different family types are similar. It is the differences between men and women in factors that lead them to think about or act to separate and divorce that is most notable.

THE ADJUSTMENT OF YOUTH
FROM NONDIVORCED, DIVORCED,
AND REMARRIED FAMILIES

This chapter focuses on six aspects of adjustment: externalizing, internalizing, social responsibility, social competence, self-worth, and achievement. Although the target youth in our stepfamilies was always from the mother's previous marriage, when appropriate we broke our stepfamilies into simple and complex stepfamilies. Thus in MANCOVAS (covarying out income and education of parents) we had a four-way breakdown for family type (nondivorced, divorced, simple step, and complex step) and two-way for gender. Males scored higher than females on antisocial behavior and achievement and lower on social competence and social responsibility. No gender or family type differences were found in self-worth. Youth in divorced and simple stepfamilies showed greater externalizing antisocial behavior, less social responsibility, and less achievement than those in nondivorced families, however, those in complex stepfamilies showed poorer adjustment in these domains than did any other group. These effects are largest for antisocial behavior and the significant effects are modest, averaging one third to about half a standard deviation difference across domains. There was a marginal ($p<.10$) effect for youth in divorced and stepfamilies to show more internalizing; however, unexpectedly no gender differences in internalizing were found.

Looking at individual variables gives a fragmented picture of adjustment, therefore again we used cluster analysis to obtain profiles of adjustment. The best cluster solution yielded five clusters. Clusters 1 ($N = 80$) and 2 ($N = 84$) are multiproblem clusters characterized by low scores on the desirable attributes and substantially above average scores on internalizing and behavior problems, however, Cluster 1 has a peak more than one standard deviation above the mean on depression, whereas Cluster 2 has a peak almost one standard deviation above the mean on antisocial behavior. Because of the co-occurrence of internalizing and externalizing a cluster in which only one of these forms of deviant adjustment emerged was not obtained. Cluster 3 ($N = 140$) the largest cluster, represents good enough adjustment where most scores hover around the mean, and Cluster 4 ($N = 92$) contains the well adjusted youth with behavior problems and internalizing below the mean and positive attributes averaging about three

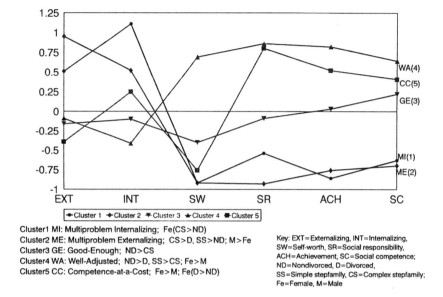

Cluster1 MI: Multiproblem Internalizing; Fe(CS>ND)
Cluster2 ME: Multiproblem Externalizing; CS>D, SS>ND; M>Fe
Cluster3 GE: Good-Enough; ND>CS
Cluster4 WA: Well-Adjusted; ND>D, SS>CS; Fe>M
Cluster5 CC: Competence-at-a-Cost; Fe>M; Fe(D>ND)

Key: EXT=Externalizing, INT=Internalizing,
SW=Self-worth, SR=Social responsibility,
ACH=Achievement, SC=Social competence;
ND=Nondivorced, D=Divorced,
SS=Simple stepfamily, CS=Complex stepfamily;
Fe=Female, M=Male

FIG. 9.4. Cluster analysis of youth adjustment ($N = 450$).

fourths of a standard deviation above the mean. Finally, Cluster 5 ($N = 54$) is an interesting cluster that first emerged in cluster analyses of adjustment in adolescence. It is a Competence at a Cost Cluster characterized by high social responsibility, achievement, and social competence and low antisocial behavior but also by low self-worth and slightly elevated internalizing. Youth who have experienced high life stress and high maturity demands are overrepresented in this sample. These are resilient youth who have paid a cost of self-doubt and low self-esteem in coping with the challenges of their life situation.

More than half of the youth are in Clusters 3, 4, or 5, clusters that are characterized by adequate to extremely good adjustment. However, youth from complex stepfamilies compared to those from nondivorced families are overrepresented in the two multiproblem clusters and underrepresented in the adaptive clusters of Cluster 3 (good enough adjustment) and Cluster 4 (well adjusted). The differences between complex step and nondivorced in Cluster 1, the multiproblem internalizing cluster, occurs only for girls. On Clusters 2 and 3, the divorced and simple stepfamily groups fall between the youth from the nondivorced and complex stepfamilies and are significantly different from them both. There are more females from divorced families than from nondivorced families in the competence at a cost group, which perhaps reflects the greater responsibilities heaped on these girls often at an early age. Females are found more often than males in the competence at a cost and well adjusted clusters and less often in the multiproblem externalizing clusters.

The differences between youths in nondivorced families and in divorced and remarried families in adjustment in the domains of externalizing, social responsibility, and achievement in addition to the more problematic family and social relationships reported earlier suggest that problems in adjustment associated with parental marital transitions although modest may be more long lasting than was previously recognized. This is supported by a meta-analysis by Amato and Keith (1991). It is recognized that children whose parents are later going to divorce, in comparison to those who do not, exhibit behavior problems and difficulties in family relationships before the divorce occurs. Even when the level of problem behavior or conflict preceding a marital transition is partialled out, however, divorce and remarriage and their concomitant stressors increase problem behavior in children. In addition to cross-sectional analyses of concurrent factors that promote or attenuate psychopathology or positive adjustment in children and adolescents, and longitudinal analyses of antecedent conditions that serve as risk or protective factors in children's adjustment. We turn now to a cross-sectional analysis of the contribution of social capital in adolescence and in youth to the adjustment of youths from nondivorced, divorced, and remarried families.

SOCIAL CAPITAL AND SOCIAL RISK FACTORS: CONTRIBUTING TO THE ADJUSTMENT OF YOUTH FROM DIVORCED AND REMARRIED FAMILIES

Discriminant function analyses were performed for males and females on social relationship variables in childhood, adolescence, and adulthood identifying the contribution of social capital or social risk factors to resiliency or vulnerability in youth who had gone through their parents' divorces or remarriages. Only the adolescent and adulthood analyses are presented here. The adolescent analyses involved only youth who were present in both the adolescent and young adulthood waves. The adolescent analyses ($N = 190$) assess relationships in adolescence that predict later resiliency or nonresiliency in youth, whereas the analyses for youth are cross-sectional analyses of concurrent relationships predicting youthful adjustment ($N = 300$). Offspring from nondivorced families are not included in these analyses. The classification of resiliency was made on the basis of cluster membership on the adjustment cluster analysis in youth with those falling in Clusters 1 and 2 being nonresilient and those in Clusters 3, 4, and 5 being resilient. The samples from divorced and remarried families were combined because correlation matrices had indicated that the functional associations between social relationships and youth adjustment in divorced and in stepfamilies were similar with the exception, of course, for relations with the stepfather. A separate analysis for stepchildren was done on this variable. Separate analyses were performed for males and females that included positivity, negativity, total behavior problems, and social responsibility of the partners in each relationship. Table 9.4 presents a summary of the factors within adolescent and young adult relationships that discriminated between youth who were resilient or nonresilient in young adulthood.

The most striking findings in these analyses were the decline in the influence of family factors especially in negativity in parenting, the greater salience of stepfathers and noncustodial fathers for the resiliency of males than females, and the notable impact of the quality of the marital relationship in adulthood on the adjustment of both males and females but especially of males. Dating and cohabiting relationships were less powerful in discriminating resilient from nonresilient youth than were spousal relationships and characteristics.

Relationships with family members in adolescence served as a foundation for later resiliency or problem behaviors in youth. Many fewer family factors in youth than in adolescence discriminate between youthful resiliency or problem behaviors. It was not just the affective quality of relationships with parents in adolescence that was important in later resiliency but parents as role models. However, it is interesting to note that behavior problems or mature responsible behavior in mothers of adolescents discriminated between later resiliency or vulnerability in females but not males, whereas fathers' deviant or adaptive behaviors when the offspring were adolescents discriminated for males but not females. Furthermore, as has been found in other studies (Brook, Whiteman, Gordon, & Brook, 1990; Needle, McCubbin, Wilson, Reineck, & Lazar, 1986), in adolescence, behavior problems in older siblings, such as tobacco, alcohol, drug use, and sexual behavior, did promote these problems in younger siblings, and siblings' social maturity in adolescence was associated with more resilient behavior in youth. However, the lack of a significant discrimination for parent and sibling behavior problems in adulthood suggests that although behavior problems in parents and older siblings may have contributed to the earlier initiation of adolescent behavior problems, these problems in youth maybe sustained or precipitated by antisocial behavior in friends and other intimate relationships.

Behavior problems in friends, spouses, and other intimate relationships as measured both in adolescence and adulthood were associated with more adaptive problems in youths. We had earlier found that adolescents in divorced and remarried families are especially vulnerable to peer influence. The direction of effects in such findings is open to question since longitudinal analyses indicated that individuals who were antisocial in adolescence were more likely to select antisocial friends or partners in adulthood.

TABLE 9.4
Social Capital and Risk Discriminating Between Resilient and Nonresilient Youth From Divorced and Remarried Families

	Adolescence		Young Adulthood	
	Males	*Females*	*Males*	*Females*
Relationship Factors				
Mothers				
Positivity	*			*
Negativity	*	*		
Antisocial	*			
Social Maturity		*		
Noncustodial Fathers				
Positivity	*		*	
Negativity				
Antisocial	*		*	
Social Maturity	*		*	
Stepfathers				
Positivity	*		*	
Negativity	*	*		
Antisocial				
Social Maturity	*		*	
Siblings				
Positivity		*		*
Negativity				
Antisocial	*	*		
Social Maturity	*	*		
Friends				
Positivity				**
Negativity				
Antisocial	**	*	**	*
Social Maturity	*			
Dating and Cohabiting Partners				
Positivity			*	
Negativity			*	*
Antisocial	*	*	*	
Social Maturity				
Spouse				
Positivity			***	**
Negativity			***	**
Antisocial		*	*	
Social Maturity			*	*

*Note. p < .05. **p < .01. ***p < .001.*

Positivity in adult friends played a significant protective role for females but not males.

The marital relationship plays an especially important role in protecting youths or making them more vulnerable to adversity. Negative conflictual marital relationships make youth more vulnerable to developing problems, loving supportive relationships are associated with fewer adaptive difficulties. Longitudinal analyses indicated although a close supportive marital relationship was associated with a decrease in behavior problems from adolescence to adulthood in both men and women and increased social responsibility in men, the attributes of the person you are close to does matter. A close relationship with an antisocial spouse increased behavior problems. This was most notable in problems of alcohol and drug abuse.

CONCLUSIONS

The offspring of divorced and remarried families in comparison to those in nondivorced families have less supportive social capital available to them and encounter more social risks in the form of changing family structure, roles, and relationship and an increase in stressful life events. In spite of these changes, most youth from divorced and remarried families are resilient in coping with the changes and stresses associated with their parents' marital transitions and emerge as reasonably competent individuals.

Although the experiences, risks, and social capital of youths from divorced, nondivorced, and remarried families differ, the processes that help them be resilient in the face of stress are remarkably similar. However, gender differences in the experiences, changes, and salience of social capital associated with adjusting to the challenges in a divorced or remarried family are notable.

The contributions to adjustment of social capital in different relationships change over time with the relationship, with parents being predominant in childhood and a more diverse array of relationships, especially the marital relationship, becoming influential as individual's age. As has been found in other studies, social capital in the form of a supportive marital relationship plays an especially salient role in promoting the well-being of adults and in protecting the individual against sustained adverse effects of stressful experiences such as parental marital transitions.

REFERENCES

Achenbach, T., & Edelbrock, C. S. (1983). *Manual for the child behavior checklist and revised child behavior profile.* New York: Queen City Printers.

Amato, P. R., & Keith, B. (1991). Parental divorce and adult well-being: A meta-analysis. *Journal of Marriage and the Family, 53,* 43–58.

Bank, S. P., & Kahn, M. D. (1982). *The sibling bond.* New York: Basic Books.

Booth, A., & Amato, P. R. (1994). Parental marital quality, parental divorce and relations with parents. *Journal of Marriage and the Family, 56,* 21–34.

Booth, A., Amato, P. R., Johnson, D. R., & Edwards, J. (1993). *Marital instability over the life course: Methodology report for fourth wave.* Lincoln: University of Nebraska Bureau of Sociological Research.

Brook, J. S., Whiteman, M., Gordon, S., & Brooke, D. W. (1990). The role of older brothers in younger brothers' drug use viewed in the context of parent and peer influences. *Journal of Genetic Psychology, 151,* 59–75.

Buehlman, K., Gottman, J. M., & Katz, L. (1992). How a couple views their past predicts their future: Predicting divorce from an oral history interview. *Journal of Family Psychology, 5,* 295–318.

Buhrmester, D. (1992). The developmental courses of sibling and peer relationships. In F. Boer & J. Dunn (Eds.), *Children's sibling relationships* (pp. 19–40). Hillsdale, NJ: Lawrence Erlbaum Associates.

Coleman, J. (1988). Social capital and the creation of human capital. *American Journal of Sociology, 94,* 95–120.

Coleman, J. (1990). *Foundations of social theory.* Cambridge, MA: Harvard University Press.

Cowan, C. P., & Cowan, P. A. (1978). *Test battery for becoming a family project.* Unpublished document, University of California, Berkeley.

Cowan, P. A., Cowan, C. P., & Schulz, M. S. (1996). Thinking about risk and resilience in families. In E. M. Hetherington & E. A. Blechman (Eds.), *Stress, coping and resiliency in children and families* (pp. 1–38). Mahwah, NJ: Lawrence Erlbaum Associates.

Dixon, W. T., & Brown, M. B. (Eds.). (1979). *Biomedical computer programs: P-series.* Berkeley and Los Angeles: University of California Press.

Gottman, J. M. (1994). *What predicts divorce?* Hillsdale, NJ: Lawrence Erlbaum Associates.

Gough, H. G. (1975). *California Psychological Inventory.* Palo Alto, CA: Consulting Psychologists Press.

Hetherington, E. M. (1987). Family relations six years after divorce. In K. Pasley & M. Ihinger-Tollman (Eds.), *Remarriage and stepparenting today* (pp. 125–156). New York: Guilford Press.

Hetherington, E. M. (1988). Parents, children and siblings six years after divorce. In R. Hinde & J. Stevenson (Eds.), *Relationships within families* (pp. 311–331). Cambridge, England: Cambridge University Press.

Hetherington, E. M. (1989). Coping with family transitions: Winners, losers and survivors. *Child Development, 60,* 1–14.

Hetherington, E. M. (1991a). Presidential address: Families, lies and videotapes. *Journal of Research on Adolescence, 1*(4), 323–348.

Hetherington, E. M. (1991b). The role of individual differences in family relations in coping with divorce and remarriage. In P. Cowan & E. Hetherington (Eds.), *Advances in family research: Vol. 1. Family transitions* (pp. 165–194). Hillsdale, NJ: Lawrence Erlbaum Associates.

Hetherington, E. M. (1993). An overview of the Virginia longitudinal study of divorce and remarriage with a focus on early adolescence. *Journal of Family Psychology, 7,* 39–56.

Hetherington, E. M., & Clingempeel, W. G. (1992). Coping with marital transitions. *Monograph of the Society for Research in Child Development,* Vol. 57, Nos. 2–3.

Hetherington, E. M., Cox, M., & Cox, R. (1982). Effects of divorce on parents and children. In M. Lamb (Ed.), *Nontraditional families.* Hillsdale, NJ: Lawrence Erlbaum Associates.

Hetherington, E. M., Cox, M., & Cox, R. (1985). Long-term effects of divorce and remarriage on the adjustment of children. *Journal of the American Academy of Child Psychiatry, 24*(5), 518–530.

Lye, D. N. (1996). Adult child-parent relationships. In J. Hagan & K. S. Cook (Eds.), *Annual Review of Sociology, 22,* 79–102.

McLanahan, S., & Sandefur, G. (1994). *Growing up with a single parent.* Cambridge, MA: Harvard University Press.

Miller, N. B., Cowan, P. A., Cowan, C. P., Hetherington, E. M., & Clingempeel, G. (1993). Externalizing in preschoolers and early adolescents: A cross-study replication of a family model. *Developmental Psychology, 29,* 3–18.

Needle, R., McCubbin, H., Wilson, M., Reineck, R., & Lazar, A. (1986). Interpersonal influence in adolescent drug use: The role of older siblings, parents and peers. *International Journal of the Addictions, 31,* 739–766.

Radloff, L. S. (1977). The CES-D Scale: A self-report depression scale for research in the general population. *Applied Psychological Measurement, 1,* 385–401.

Rosenberg, M. (1979). *Conceiving the self.* New York: Basic Books.

Scheier, M. F., & Carver, C. S. (1985). Optimism, coping and health: Assessment and implications of generalized outcome expectancies. *Health Psychology, 4,* 219–247.

Sim, H., & Vuchinich, S. (1996). The declining effects of family stressors on antisocial behavior from childhood to adolescence and early adulthood. *Journal of Family Issues, 17,* 408–427.

Spanier, K. (1976). Dyadic Adjustment Scale. *Journal of Marriage and the Family, 38,* 27–37.

Straus, M. A. (1979). Measuring intrafamily conflict and violence: The Conflict Tactics (CT) Scales. *Journal of Marriage and the Family, 41,* 75–85.

Sullivan, H. S. (1953). *The interpersonal theory of psychiatry.* New York: W.W. Norton.

Weiss, R. S. (1975). *Marital separation.* New York: Basic Books.

Chapter 10

Social Relationships Across Contexts: Family–Peer Linkages

Ross D. Parke
Robin O'Neil
University of California, Riverside

The study of social relationships has undergone profound shifts in the last two decades. One of the major changes is the recognition of the interdependence of social systems. To illustrate this issue, we focus here on the mutual influence between family and peer socialization systems. To fully appreciate this shift, it is critical to recognize that our changing view of the interrelations between socialization systems is part of a more general change in our conceptualization of the field of developmental psychology. One of the most characteristic shifts in the field is the increasing search for connections across boundaries and the increasing porousness of boundaries. Several types of boundaries can be identified: First, explanatory systems are no longer isolated, but are assumed to mutually influence each other. The era of the grand theories of Freud and Piaget gave way to a variety of mini theories aimed at limited and specific aspects of development—cognitive, affective, social. Each of these theoretical developments is highly restricted in its scope and explanatory area.

However, general strands of evidence imply that this isolation of mini theories may not be appropriate. There is a recognition that the *domains of childhood*—social, emotional, physical, and cognitive aspects are interdependent and that they overlap and mutually influence each other. Consider four examples. First there is a rise in interest in the interplay between social and cognitive development, especially in how social input (e.g., scaffolding) on the part of the parent can increase the level of cognitive performance of children. The reemergence of interest in Vygotskian theory is one form of this interest (Rogoff, 1990). Second, and closely related, is the increased interest in the role of cognitive factors on the explanation of social processes. For example, the recent work on "working models" within the attachment paradigm is a search for an explanation of how the expectations and social rules acquired in the context of the parent–child relationship become *guides* or maps that the child imposes on other social relationships (Thompson, 1997). Third, the ways in which temperament— an index of biological predispositions, interacts with social contextual variables in affecting child outcomes (e.g., Rothbart & Bates, 1997) is a further example of the interplay across domains. Fourth, in recent work, language, communication and perceptual development are often studied in the context of social development (Nelson, 1986).

Barriers are falling not only across content domains within our own discipline, but between disciplines as well. There is a marked increase in interdisciplinary cooperation among disciplines who study children and families, including pediatrics (Tinsley, 1992). Because of the mounting interest in developmental psychopathology, collaboration between child psychiatry and developmental researchers has increased (Cicchetti & Toth, 1997). Increased links with sociology and psychology are indexed by collaborative work on day care, divorce, and timing of parenthood (Cherlin, Furstenberg, Chase-Lansdale, Kiernan, & others, 1991; Furstenberg, Brooks-Gunn, & Morgan, 1987; Hofferth & Phillips, 1991). Geneticists, neurologists, and psychophysiologists are all prominent collaborators with developmental researchers in the 1990s (Gunnar, 1994; Plomin, 1995). Finally, developmentalists and historians are increasingly and actively aware of each other (Elder, Modell, & Parke, 1993). The 1990s represent a rich context for interdisciplinary research on development. Our chapter reflects these trends in our field by focusing on the interplay across social systems in children's socialization.

Socialization is multifaceted with both the peer group and the family each making distinctive and important contributions to children's social development. The independent contributions of both of these socialization systems have been well documented but the links between these systems are less well understood. One consequence of this increased recognition of the porousness of boundaries between domains and disciplines has been the endorsement of the interdependence of socialization systems as well. As Hartup (1979a) prophetically saw, children are embedded in a variety of social systems that function not independently, but rather mutually influence each other in the course of shaping children's development.

In this chapter we first briefly overview support for a tripartite model of linkages between family and peer systems with emphasis on recent work from a longitudinal study of familial influences on children's social development currently being conducted in our lab. We also review recent research on the processes that *mediate* relations between family and peer systems and examine ecological factors such as children's neighborhoods that may *moderate* the links between these two social systems. Finally, we present some exploratory analyses that examine the combined role of these three modes of familial influence on children's peer relationships.

The University of California, Riverside, Social Development project is a longitudinal study that was initiated in 1990 with the goal of understanding the links between children's experiences in their families during early and middle childhood and their developing social competence with peers, based on the tripartite model described by Parke and colleagues (Parke, Cassidy, Burks, Carson, & Boyum, 1992; Parke, Burks, Carson, Neville, & Boyum, 1994). The sample in this study was generated using a two-stage procedure. In the first stage, approximately 800 kindergarten children from nine elementary schools in two Southern California communities were interviewed in order to determine children's level of social acceptance by peers. In the second phase of sampling, this sociometric information was used to select children of varying degrees of social acceptance and the parents of these children were invited to participate in the laboratory assessment phase of the project. The ethnic distribution of the resulting sample of 116 families was approximately 55% Euro-American, 35% Latino, and 10% other ethnicities including Asian and African American. Since 1991, children and their parents have participated in yearly assessments. The assessments in kindergarten through second grade included questionnaires and interviews as well as dyadic interaction tasks between children and their mothers and children and their fathers. In third through fifth grade, the interaction tasks were augmented to include triadic tasks that involved children, mothers, and fathers as well as a set of interaction tasks between children and a self-selected friend and an unacquainted peer.

A TRIPARTITE MODEL OF FAMILY–PEER RELATIONSHIPS

Our work has been guided by a three-tiered model that represents the modes by which parents may influence their children's peer relationships (see Fig. 10.1; Parke, Cassidy, Burks, Carson, & Boyum, 1992; Parke, Burks, Carson, Neville, & Boyum, 1994). First, parents are viewed as influencing their children's peer relationships through their childrearing practices and interactive styles. This first mode of influence on children's relationships with peers is often indirect because the parent's goal is not explicitly to modify or enhance children's relationships beyond the family. Second, this model suggests that parents may directly influence children's peer relationships in their role as instructor or educator. Through such strategies

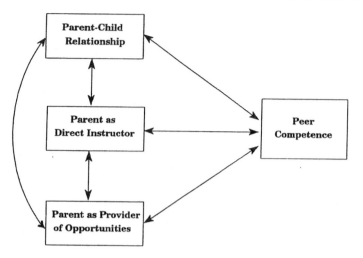

FIG. 10.1. A tripartite model of family–peer relationships.

as providing advice about managing peer relationships, supervising and assisting in early child–peer interactions, parents may explicitly set out to educate their children concerning appropriate behavioral strategies for interacting with peers. A third mode of familial influence is the management of children's social lives (Hartup, 1979b; Parke, 1978). In this role, parents serve as the gatekeepers or providers of opportunities for children to interact with peers and other extrafamilial social partners (Ladd, Profilet, & Hart, 1992; Parke & Bhavnagri, 1989). Social access to peers is thought to provide essential opportunities to practice and refine the skills that develop in the context of the family.

Whereas the three modes of linkage provide a broad brush overview of the role of parents as socializing agents, the model also suggests two critical sets of processes that may account for the development and transmission of skills from the family context to extrafamilial social contexts: (a) the development of skills for understanding and regulating emotions, and (b) the development of cognitive models or representations of the meaning of social relationships to the individual.

Considerable evidence now has emerged in support of this model, particularly at the level of "modes of influence." Recent studies also are detailing the processes that underlie these influences. In addition, the model has undergone refinement along a number of lines (Parke & O'Neil, 1996). For example, the model has been extended to incorporate a systems approach to acknowledge that children are exposed to multiple family subsystems (e.g., parent–child subsystem, the parent–parent subsystem, and sib–sib subsystems). Moreover, the model has been expanded to incorporate a more ecological framework to recognize that families are embedded in external social systems (e.g., neighborhoods, communities) which, in turn, influence the functioning of the family unit (Bronfenbrenner, 1989).

PARENT–CHILD RELATIONSHIP

Parents play a primary role in the development of children's competence with peers through their childrearing practices and interactive styles. Baumrind's (1973) early classic studies found that authoritative parenting was related to positive peer outcomes, and more recent studies have confirmed that parents who are responsive, warm, and synchronous are more likely to have children who are more accepted by their peers (Harrist, Pettit, Dodge, & Bates, 1994; Putallez, 1987). In contrast, parents who are hostile, overcontrolling (Harrist et al., 1994), and high in negative synchrony have children who experience more difficulty with agemates (MacDonald & Parke, 1984). Family interaction patterns relate not only to concurrent peer relationships, but predict children's competence with peers over time as well. Barth and Parke (1993) found that parents who were better able to sustain their children in play predicted better subsequent adaptation to kindergarten.

Not only are differences in interactive style associated with children's social competence, but the affective quality of parent–child interactions also is important. Consistently higher levels of positive affect have been found in both parents and children in popular dyads than in the rejected dyads (Parke, MacDonald, Beitel, & Bhavnagri, 1988). Moreover, data from the kindergarten assessments of our longitudinal study suggested that expressions of positive and negative affect by both mothers and fathers during physical play were linked to children's social competence in both kindergarten and 1 year later (Isley, O'Neil, & Parke, 1996). In same-gender dyads, the strongest predictor of peer- and teacher-rated social competence in first grade was parental expression of negative affect, beta = $-.31$, $p <$ .05, for father–son dyads and beta = $-.35$, $p < .10$ for mother–daughter dyads, when peer-rated social acceptance was the focus of analysis and beta = $-.28$, $p < .05$, for father–son dyads and beta = $-.33$, $p < .05$ for mother–daughter dyads, when teacher-rated social acceptance was the focus of analysis. Boyum and Parke (1995) found similar links between the expression of negative affect and children's social competence. Specifically, children whose fathers directed more anger during a family dinner toward them were less well accepted by their peers. Carson and Parke (1996) extended this finding by showing that reciprocal negative affect exchanges on the part of fathers and preschool-aged children were associated with lower levels of social competence as rated by teachers. It is particularly interesting that the links between reciprocation of negative affect and children's social competence were not evident among mother–child dyads. These findings suggest that social interaction such as rough-and-tumble play with fathers may be an important means through which children learn to manage negative emotions in the context of social interactions with other partners.

PARENT AS DIRECT ADVISOR

Learning about relationships through interaction with parents can be viewed as an indirect pathway, because the goal often is not explicitly to influence children's social relationships with extrafamilial partners such as peers. In contrast, parents may influence children's relationships directly in their role as a direct instructor, educator, or advisor. In this role, parents may explicitly set out to educate their children concerning the appropriate manner of initiating and maintaining social relationships. Research findings suggest that young children gain competence with peers when parents supervise and facilitate their experiences (Bhavnagri & Parke, 1991; Russell & Finnie, 1990); whereas, among older children, greater supervision and guidance on the part of parents of children's peer relationships may function more as a remediatory effort (Cohen, 1989).

Direct parental influence in the form of supervision and advice giving can significantly increase the interactive competence of young children and illustrates the utility of examining direct parental strategies as a way of teaching children about social relationships. As work continues to emerge in this area, however, the findings suggest not only that advice content and style of expressing advice or offering guidance are important components, but that the role supervision of peer relationships and advice-giving play may vary over the course of children's development.

In one phase of our study (O'Neil, Garcia, Zavala, & Wang, 1995), parents were asked to read to their third-grade child short stories describing common social themes (e.g., group entry, ambiguous provocation, relational aggression) and to advise the child about the best way to handle each situation. High quality advice was considered to be advice that promoted a positive, outgoing, social orientation on the part of the child rather than avoidance or aggressive responses. The findings varied as a function of parent–child gender. Among father–son dyads and mother–daughter dyads, parental advice that was more appropriate and more structured was associated with less loneliness and greater social competence among children. For example, more appropriate advice from fathers to sons about how to handle conflict with a peer was associated with less self-reported loneliness ($r = -.40$, $p < .05$). Similarly, more appropriate advice from mothers to daughters was associated with lower levels of depressed mood ($r = -.47$, $p < .05$). Interestingly, when father–daughter dyads and mother–son dyads were the focus of analysis, higher quality advice about how to handle social conflict was associated with poorer teacher-rated social competence (e.g., $r = .46$, $p < .05$ and $r = .48$, $p < .05$ between parental advice content and verbal aggression, for each dyad respectively.) However, in contrast to the gender-specific findings for the content of parental advice, the quality of parent–child interactions during the advice-giving session were positively related to a number of indicators of children's social competence (e.g., less loneliness in mother–son and mother–daughter dyads, $r = -.46$, $p < .01$ and $r = -.30$, $p < .10$, and lower levels of depressed mood in father–son dyads, $r = -.50$, $p < .05$.) Interestingly, other results from our study based on a triadic advice-giving session in which mothers, fathers, and their third grader discussed how to handle problems their child had when interacting with peers, indicated that parental style of interaction appeared to be a better predictor of children's social competence than the actual solution quality generated in the advice-giving session (Wang & McDowell, 1996). Specifically, the controlling nature of fathers' style and the warmth and support expressed by mothers during the advice-giving task were significant predictors of both teacher and peer ratings of children's social competence. When fathers were more controlling during the advice-giving sessions, children were described by teachers and peers as more disliked ($r = -.50$, $p < .01$ and $r = -.50$, $p < .01$, respectively). Maternal warmth and support was associated with less peer-rated dislike ($r = -.34$, $p < .05$). These findings are consistent with earlier work by Pettit and Mize (1993) who found the content of maternal advice as well as maternal style of interaction during the advice-giving session each made a unique contribution to preschoolers' competence with peers. These findings also are consistent with the recent theoretical position of Grusec and Goodnow (1994) that acceptance of social influence is, in part, mediated by the quality of the relationship between the socializing agent and recipient.

COGNITIVE AND EMOTIONAL MEDIATORS
OF RELATIONS BETWEEN FAMILY
AND PEER SOCIAL CONTEXTS

In a general sense, both face-to-face interaction between parents and children and parental supervision and guidance of children's relationships with peers may provide children with the opportunity to learn, rehearse, and refine social skills that are common to successful social interaction with peers. Specific processes have been hypothesized as mediators between parent–child interaction and peer outcomes, including emotion encoding and decoding skills, emotional regulatory skills, cognitive representations, attributions and beliefs, and problem-solving skills (Ladd, 1992; Parke,

Burks, Carson, Neville, & Boyum, 1994). These abilities or beliefs are acquired in the course of parent–child interchanges over the course of development and, in turn, guide the nature of the child's behavior with their peers. These styles of interacting with peers may, in turn, determine the child's level of acceptance by peers.

Affect Management Skills

Children learn more than specific affective expressions, such as anger or sadness or joy in the family. They learn a cluster of processes associated with the understanding and regulation of affective displays, which we term "affect management skills" (Parke et al., 1992). It is assumed that these skills are acquired during the course of parent–child interaction which, in turn, are available to the child for use in other relationships. Moreover, it is assumed that these skills play a mediating role between family and peer relationships. Three aspects of this issue are examined: (a) encoding and decoding of emotion, (b) cognitive understanding of causes and consequences of emotion, and (c) emotional regulation.

Emotional Encoding and Decoding Abilities, Parent–Child Interaction and Peer Acceptance. One set of skills relevant to successful peer interaction and may, in part, be acquired in the context of parent–child play, especially arousing physical play, is the ability to encode emotional signals clearly and to decode others' emotional states. Through physically playful interaction with their parents, especially fathers, children may learn how to use emotional signals to regulate the social behavior of others. They may also learn to accurately decode the social and emotional signals of other social partners. Several studies (see Hubbard & Coie, 1994, for a review) have found positive relations between both emotional decoding and encoding abilities and various measures of children's peer status. This evidence suggests that one component of peer acceptance may be a child's ability to correctly identify the emotional states of other children, and produce clear emotional expression skills. These skills permit presumably more adequate regulation of social interactions with other children; in turn, these abilities may contribute to greater acceptance by peers (Buck, 1975). Moreover, children's decoding and encoding abilities are linked to parent–child interaction (Parke et al., 1989). Parents who are able to sustain parent–child play bouts for longer periods (an index of parental competence as a play partner) had children who were better at recognizing and producing emotional expressions than less competent parents.

The Relation of Emotional Understanding to Peer Competence. Successful peer interaction requires both the ability to recognize and produce emotions and an understanding of other aspects of emotion. Based on interviews with 5- to 6-year-old children about their understanding of emotions, Cassidy, Parke, Butkovsky, and Braungart (1992) found that higher levels of peer acceptance was associated with greater: (a) ability to identify emotions, (b) acknowledgment of experiencing emotion, (c) ability to describe appropriate causes of emotions, and (d) expectations that they and their parents would respond appropriately to the display of emotions. These findings confirm other research suggesting connections between other components of social understanding and peer relations (Dodge, Pettit, McClaskey, & Brown, 1986). The next step, of course, is to determine how variations in family interaction may contribute to individual differences in children's cognitive understanding of emotions (see Cassidy et al., 1992).

Emotional Regulation. Parental support and acceptance of children's emotions is related to children's ability to manage emotions in a constructive fashion. Several recent theorists have suggested that emotional regulatory skills are linked to social competence with peers (Denham, 1993; Eisenberg & Fabes, 1992; Parke, 1994). Parental comforting of children when they experience negative emotion has been linked with constructive anger reactions (Eisenberg & Fabes, 1994). Similarly, parental willingness to discuss emotions with their children is related to children's awareness and understanding of others' emotions (Dunn & Brown, 1994). Finally, Gottman, Katz, and Hooven (1996) found that fathers' acceptance and assistance with children's sadness and anger at 5 years of age was related to their children's social competence with peers at age 8. These data are consistent with earlier theoretical views suggesting that learning to manage moderate levels of negative affect is an important skill for management of social relationships (Sroufe, 1979). Moreover, this work highlights the importance of fathers in learning about relationships, especially in learning the emotional regulatory aspects of relationships. Fathers provide a unique opportunity to teach children about emotion in the context of relationships due to the wide range of intensity of affect that fathers display and the unpredictable character of their playful exchanges with their children (Parke, 1996).

Links Between Children's Emotion Regulatory Abilities, Parental Management of Emotion, and Children's Social Competence. Children's skill in regulating emotions may be important to successful development of peer relationships (O'Neil & Parke, 1996a). In our project, we collected fourth graders' responses to a series of vignettes representing situations that might generate anger, frustration, or excitement. Based on these data, the ability to control the level of emotional arousal and the strategies selected for coping with high levels of emotional arousal appear related to children's social competence with peers. Specifically, children who report better control over their levels of emotional arousal are described by peers as more prosocial ($r = .21$, $p < .05$) and less aggressive ($r = -.20$, $p < .05$). Children's strategies for handling emotional arousal also are linked to their social competence. Children who report using temper tantrums or other displays of anger to cope with their emotional upset are less well accepted by peers ($r = -.26$, $p < .05$) and described as less prosocial ($r = -.26$, $p < .05$) and more disruptive ($r = .37$, $p < .001$) by teachers. In contrast, children who indicate they would use reasoning to cope with emotional upset are described by peers as more prosocial ($r = .20$, $p < .05$). Parental attitudes regarding the expression of negative emotion by their children also are related to children's ability to regulate emotion and level of social competence. Parents who report being more distressed by children's expressions of negative emotion have sons who report being more likely to become sad ($r = .31$, $p < .05$ in father–son dyads) or angry ($r = .25$, $p < .10$ in mother–son dyads) when dealing with a distressing event. In contrast, parents who responded to the display of negative emotion with strategies designed to resolve the problem had children who were less likely to report sadness ($r = -.25$, $p < .10$ for father–son dyads) and more likely to use reasoning ($r = .27$, $p < .05$ for mother–daughter dyads) as a method of coping with upset. In addition, when fathers report that they respond to the expression of negative emotion with problem-solving strategies, daughters are rated by teachers as less disliked by their classmates ($r = -.37$, $p < .05$) and less verbally aggressive ($r = -.31$, $p < .05$), and sons are described by teachers as less physically aggressive ($r = -.31$, $p < .05$).

Preliminary findings of observational data from a subset of our sample also suggest that the strategies parents employ to manage children's negative emotion are linked to children's emotional reactivity, coping, and social competence. For example, maternal sensitivity to children's emotional reactivity is associated with sons' reports of being more likely to use anger to cope with an upsetting event ($r = .39$, $p < .10$) and teachers' perceptions of more aggression ($r = .63$, $p < .01$). The findings from both self-report and observational data suggest that mothers appear to be particularly sensitized to boys' emotion levels when they are underregulated. In contrast, our observational data imply that fathers behave more sensitively in response to the emotional states of children who are better regulators of emotion ($r = -.36$, $p < .10$, for boys anger responses) and who are described by teachers as more socially competent ($r = .48$, $p < .05$, for prosocial behaviors).

Other work from the project examines relations between children's use of socially appropriate rules for displaying negative emotions and social competence with peers. We used the "disappointing gift paradigm" (Saarni, 1992) to assess the ability of children to mask their negative emotions in the face of disappointment. Although Saarni's work suggests this ability improves with age and may be a critical component of successful emotion regulation, to date, researchers have not examined the links between individual differences in the ability to mask or control negative emotions and children's competence with peers. Our data indicate that among fourth graders, children who display negative affect/behavior following the presentation of a disappointing gift (thus, not using display rules) are rated by peers as more withdrawn ($r = .31$, $p < .01$). Girls who are able to maintain levels of positive affect after receiving a disappointing gift are viewed as more socially competent by teachers and their peers ($r = .30$, $p < .05$ and $r = .31$, $p < .05$, respectively). Similarly, children who express more tension and anxiety in response to a disappointing gift are described by peers as more socially avoidant ($r = -.36$, $p < .01$; McDowell, O'Neil, & Parke, 1997).

Together, these studies suggest that various aspects of emotional development—encoding, decoding, cognitive understanding, and emotional regulation—are important in accounting for variations in peer competence. Previous studies have examined the contributions of each of these emotional processes to children's social competence separately, and in turn, have found modest contributions of any single process to children's social outcomes. These predictors are best viewed, however, as a family of emotional processes that operate in concert in real-life contexts. Progress in this area is likely to come from this multivariate view of emotional processes and the incorporation of multiple emotional indices into single-study designs.

Cognitive Representational Models: Another Possible Mediator Between Parents and Peers

One of the major challenges in the investigation of links between family and peer relationships is understanding how children transfer the social strategies they acquire in the family context to their peer relationships. A variety of theories assume individuals process internal mental representations that guide their social behavior. Attachment theorists offer working model notions (Bowlby, 1980; Bretherton & Waters, 1985), whereas social and cognitive psychologists have provided accounts involving scripts or cognitive maps that serve as guides for social action (Baldwin, 1992; Bugental, 1991; Nelson, 1986). Cognitive models of relationships may be transmitted across generations (Burks & Parke, 1996) and these models, in turn, may serve as mediators between family contexts and children's relationships with others outside of the family.

Recent evidence supports the general hypothesis that children of varying sociometric statuses differ in their cognitive models of social relationships. Similarly parents' cognitive models of social relationships also tend to be predictive of variations in children's sociometric status and social competence. Several aspects of cognitive models including attributions, perceptions, values, goals and strategies have been explored (see Grusec, Hastings

& Mammone, 1994; Mills & Rubin, 1993; Parke, Cupp, Spitzer, Isley, & Welsh, 1994; Spitzer & Parke, 1994 for recent reviews). Based on parents' and children's open-end responses to social dilemmas, we have found links between parents' and children's cognitive models of relationships (Burks & Parke, 1996). Moreover, the quality of both mothers' and fathers' goals and strategies for handling social conflict are linked to children's social acceptance (Spitzer & Parke, 1994). Mothers who are high in their use of confrontational strategies have children with high levels of teacher-nominated physical and verbal aggression ($r = -.20$, $p < .05$, $r = -.24$, $p < .05$, respectively). Similarly, mothers who provide specific and socially skilled advice have more popular children ($r = .26$, $p < .01$ and $r = .23$, $p < .05$, respectively). Fathers' strategies that are rated high on confrontation and instrumental qualities are associated with low teacher ratings of children's prosocial behavior ($r = .22$, $p < .05$ with instrumental strategies) and high teacher ratings of physical aggression ($r = .25$, $p < .05$ with instrumental strategies and $r = .23$, $p < .05$ for confrontational strategies), avoidance ($r = .22$, $p < .05$ with instrumental strategies) and being disliked ($r = .23$, $p < .05$ with instrumental strategies). Fathers with relational goals have children who are less often nominated as aggressive by their peers ($r = -.34$, $p < .01$) and rated by teachers as more liked and less disliked ($r = .32$, $p < .01$ and $r = -.33$, $p < .01$, respectively). These studies support the role of cognitive representations of social relationships as a possible mediator between parent–child interaction and peer competence.

BEYOND PARENT–CHILD INTERACTION: PARENTS AS PROVIDERS OF SOCIAL OPPORTUNITIES

Parents influence their children's social relationships not only through direct interactions with their children, but function as managers of their children's social lives (Hartup, 1979; Parke, 1978) and regulate opportunities for social contact with extrafamilial social partners. This management can assume several forms, including parenting monitoring (Dishion, 1990), parental initiation of contact between their own children and play partners (Bhavnagri & Parke, 1991; Ladd & Golter, 1988), and parental facilitation of children's participation in unstructured or organized peer activities (Bryant, 1985; Ladd & Price, 1987).

    In addition to these roles played by parents in arranging children's access to other children, parents' own social networks of other adults, as well as the child members of parental social networks, provide a source of possible play partners for children. Cochran and Brassard (1979) suggested several ways these two sets of relationships may be related. First, the child is exposed to a wider or narrower band of possible social interactive partners by exposure to the members of the parent's social network. Second, the extent to which the child has access to the social interactions of his or her parents and members of their social network may determine how well the child may acquire particular styles of social interaction. Third, parents in supportive social networks may be more likely to have positive relationships with their children which, in turn, may positively affect the child's social adjustment.

Cochran and Davila (1992) provided support for the first issue, namely that there is overlap between parental and child social networks. They found that 30%–44% of 6-year-old children's social networks were also included in the mothers' networks. In other words, children often listed other children as play partners who were children of their mothers' friends.

Other studies suggest that the quality of adult social networks do, in fact, relate to children's social behavior. In an Australian study, Homel, Burns, and Goodnow (1987) found positive relationships between the number of "dependable" friends that parents report and 11-year-old children's self-rated happiness, the number of regular playmates, and maternal ratings of children's social skills. Unfortunately, the reliance on self-reports limits the value of these findings, but does support the importance of parental, or at least maternal, social networks as a factor in potentially affecting children's social relationships.

Recently, work on our project (Lee & Welsh, 1995; Lee, Parke, O'Neil, & Wang, 1997) has extended these findings by showing a relation between the quality as well as the structure of parents' network relationships and independent ratings of children's social competence. In addition, we found maternal and paternal social networks appear to have distinctive links to children's social relationships. For example, when mothers described their relationships with friends and relatives as closer and more enjoyable, teachers rated kindergarteners as more accepted by their classmates ($r = .27$, $p < .05$) and less aggressive ($r = -.31$, $p < .05$). In addition, when mothers' social networks afforded children access to more children close to their own age, children were described as better accepted by peers ($r = .31$, $p < .05$). In contrast, the structural aspects of fathers' networks were linked to children's social acceptance. Fathers with more extensive networks of friends and with more contact with friends had children who were described by peers as more socially accepted ($r = .31$, $p < .05$).

EXAMINATION OF ECOLOGICAL FACTORS THAT MODERATE THE LINKS BETWEEN FAMILY AND PEER SYSTEMS

Ecological factors outside the immediate context of the family such as family structure, the socioeconomic circumstances of the family, the quality of children's neighborhoods, and cultural variations in children's experiences may directly influence or *moderate* the links between family and peer social systems (see Patterson, Vaden, & Kupersmidt, 1991). The neighborhood environment has increasingly come to be viewed as an important context for children's development, and the management of children's activities in the neighborhood an important avenue of influence on the development of children's social competence.

The majority of recent work in this area, however, has focused on poor, urban neighborhoods (Klebanov, Brooks-Gunn, & Duncan, 1994). Our project has extended the examination of neighborhood environments to more heterogenous sites and indicates links between objective and subjective characteristics of the neighborhood, parents' management of children's activities, and children's social competence. The communities selected for our study (O'Neil & Parke, 1996b) comprised neighborhoods reflecting a range of rural, suburban, and urban features and we derived both objective assessments of area quality as well as parental perceptions of the local neighborhoods in which our sample families reside. Additionally, parents' supervisory strategies and rules regarding access to the neighborhood were based on a series of telephone interviews and questionnaires. Our findings suggested that parents', particularly mothers', perceptions of poorer neighborhood quality were related to children's social competence. As indicated in Fig. 10.2, these relations appeared to be mediated by greater use of regulatory strategies such as adult supervision and limitation of children's activities within the neighborhood. For mothers, the impact

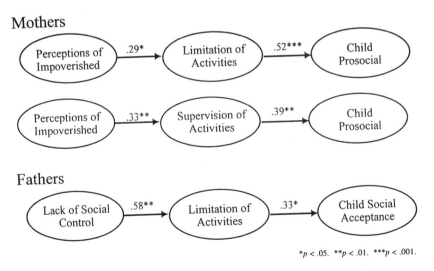

*p < .05. **p < .01. ***p < .001.

FIG. 10.2. Parental regulatory strategies as mediators of the links between parental perceptions of neighborhood quality and children's social competence.

of perceptions of their neighborhoods as impoverished on children's outcomes was mediated by increases in limitation of activities and supervision of activities which, in turn, was associated with higher levels of peer-rated prosocial behavior. A similar mediation effect was evident for fathers. When fathers viewed their neighborhoods as lacking in social control, they limited their children's activities which, in turn, was positively correlated with children's social acceptance. Interestingly, relatively few relations were found between objective ratings of the neighborhood and children's peer relationships. Instead, perceptions appear to be a more potent determinant of parental strategies that, in turn, alter children's social outcomes.

PUTTING THE PIECES OF THE TRIPARTITE MODEL TOGETHER

An Examination of Multiple Domains of Influence

Each of the avenues of familial influence described earlier—parent–child interaction, direct management, and provision of opportunities—is linked to the development of social competence in early and middle childhood. In most cases, each of these domains of influence has been considered in isolation. A major goal of our project has been to consider the *relative* influence of parent–child interaction patterns, management and supervision of children's social relationships, and the provision of social opportunities on the development of children's social competence. To this end, we have begun using regression analyses that include predictors from each of the three domains of familial influence being considered on our project in order to develop models of multiple influence. Initial analyses have been completed for data collected when children were in kindergarten. We next describe analyses that focus on four social development outcome variables: peer-based and teacher-based ratings of social acceptance and peer-based and teacher-based rating of aggressive tendencies. In view of the tendency across studies for links between familial antecedents and child outcomes to vary as a function of parent and child gender, all analyses were conducted separately for mother–daughter, mother–son, father–daughter, and father–son dyads. Because the scope of data collection in each wave is broad, we have reduced the set of independent variables being considered within each domain in order to preserve an appropriate "n to k ratio." Thus, the following strategy was employed: Within each domain of influence, backward stepwise regression was used to eliminate independent variables that did not contribute to the explained variance of each outcome measure. A second hierarchical regression analysis was conducted that included each of the significant predictors from the backward stepwise analyses. Table 10.1 lists the three domains of familial influence that were examined in these models and the variables that were entered into the domain-level regression analyses.

Mother–Daughter Dyads. When the outcome variable of interest was peer-rated social acceptance, five predictors from the domain-level stepwise analyses were entered into the final model: maternal negative affect during physical play; avoidant advice in response to a peer dilemma; specific advice; the number of friends in mothers' social networks; and the number of agemates available through the mothers' network of friends. This model explained a marginally significant 12% of the variance. When mothers gave more specific advice and recommended avoiding confronting a peer during a dispute, daughters were better accepted by classmates. In addition, when girls had more agemates available through their mothers' network of friends, they were more accepted by peers. When the dependent measure being considered was teacher-rated social acceptance, four variables from the domain-level analyses qualified for inclusion in the final model: maternal negative affect during physical play; avoidant advice in response to a peer dilemma; specific advice; and the quality of mothers' relationship

TABLE 10.1
Variables Used in Domain-Level Models to Represent Three Modes of Parental Influence on
Children's Kindergarten Social Competence

A. *Parent–Child Relationship*

      Instrument: parental behavioral style during physical play
      Variables: negative affect
                    positive affect
                    level of arousal and stimulation
                    control behaviors

B. *Parent as Direct Instructor*

      Instrument: open-ended responses to vignettes describing social dilemmas
      Variables: specificity of advice
                    social skill level of advice
                    relational nature of advice
                    confrontational nature of advice
                    avoidant nature of advice

C. *Parent as Provider of Social Opportunities*

      Instrument: social network inventory
      Variabales: number of friends in network
                    number of relatives in network
                    quality of relationship with friends
                    quality of relationship with relatives
                    number of agemates available through friend network
                    number of agemates available through relative network

with relatives. This model explained a significant 28% of the variance in teacher-rated social acceptance. Paralleling the findings for peer-rated social acceptance, girls were better accepted when mothers gave specific advice and recommended avoiding confronting a peer. In addition, daughters were described by teachers as better accepted by classmates when mothers displayed less negative affect in a physical play task. When the outcome measure being considered was peer-rated aggression, four variables qualified for inclusion in the final model: maternal negative affect during physical play; socially skilled advice; confrontational advice; and the number of agemates available through the mothers' network of relatives. This model explained a significant 24% of the variance in peer-rated aggression. Mothers who gave more socially skilled advice had daughters who were described by peers as less aggressive. In contrast, girls were described as more aggressive when their mothers' network of relatives afforded them more same-aged peers. When teacher-rated aggression was considered, three predictors from the domain-level analyses qualified to be included in the model: maternal negative affect during physical play; number of friends in mothers' networks; and number of agemates available through the mother's friendship network. This model explained a significant 19% of the variance. When mothers interacted more negatively during physical play with their daughters, when mothers reported having more friends, and when mothers' network of friends included fewer agemates, daughters were described by teachers as more aggressive.

Mother–Son Dyads. When the outcome variable of interest was peer-rated social acceptance, five predictors from the stepwise analyses were entered into the final model: maternal positive affect during physical play; avoidant advice in response to a peer dilemma; specific advice; the number of agemates available through the mothers' network of friends; and the quality of mothers' relationship with relatives in their networks. This model explained a significant 34% of the variance. When mothers gave more specific advice to their child regarding a dispute with a peer and when mothers' networks included more same-aged peers, sons were better accepted by classmates. When the dependent measure under consideration was teacher-rated social acceptance, two variables from the domain-level analyses qualified for inclusion in the model: socially skilled advice and the quality of mothers' relationship with relatives in their networks. This model explained a significant 13% of the variance in teacher-rated social acceptance. Mothers who gave more socially skilled advice had sons who were described by teachers as better accepted by their classmates. When the social outcome variable was peer-rated aggression, one variable, socially skilled advice, qualified for inclusion in the final model. This model explained a significant 35% of the variance in peer-rated aggression. Mothers who gave more socially skilled advice had sons who were described by peers as less aggressive. When teacher-rated aggression was considered, two predictors qualified to be included in the model: socially skilled advice and the quality of mothers' relationship with relatives in their networks. This model explained a significant 13% of the variance in teacher-rated aggression. When mothers gave less socially skilled advice to their sons, these boys were described by teachers as more aggressive.

Father–Daughter Dyads. When the dependent measure being considered was peer-rated social acceptance, three predictors from the domain-level analyses were entered into the model: paternal negative affect; level of arousal during physical play; and the quality of fathers' relationship with the friends in their networks. This model explained a significant 17% of the variance. When fathers expressed less negative affect and played in a less arousing or stimulating manner with their daughters these girls were better accepted by classmates. In addition, when fathers reported more enjoyment of their friends, daughters were described as less well-accepted. When the sociometric outcome variable of interest was teacher-rated social acceptance, three variables from the domain-level analyses qualified for inclusion in the tripartite model: the expression of positive affect; the extent to which fathers controlled daughters' behavior during physical play; and the extent to which the advice fathers offered daughters was confrontational. This model explained a significant 20% of the variance in teacher-rated social acceptance. Daughters were described by teachers as better accepted by classmates when fathers exercised more control over girls' in the physical play task and when they did not give confrontational advice. No variables qualified for inclusion in models predicting peer-rated and teacher-rated aggression.

Father–Son Dyads. When the dependent measure under consideration was peer-rated social acceptance, three variables qualified for inclusion in the final model: fathers' expression of negative affect during physical play; number of relatives in fathers' networks; and number agemates available through fathers' networks of friends. This model explained a significant 22% of the variance in peer-rated social acceptance. Fathers whose networks included more relatives had sons who were better accepted by their classmates. When the outcome variables of interest was teacher-rated social acceptance, four predictors from the domain-level stepwise analyses were entered into the model: fathers' negative affect during physical play; number of friends and number of relatives in fathers' social networks; and quality of fathers' relationships with relatives. This model explained a significant 21% of the variance in social acceptance. When fathers interacted in a less negative fashion with boys and reported better relationships with their relatives, sons were rated as better accepted. In addition, sons were described as more accepted by peers when fathers' social networks included fewer friends. When the social outcome variable was peer-rated aggression, only one variable qualified for inclusion in the model: the quality of fathers' relationship with relatives. This model explained 7% of the variance in peer-rated aggression. Boys were described as less aggressive when fathers reported deriving greater enjoyment from their network of relatives. When teacher-rated aggression was considered, five predictors qualified to be included in the model: paternal positive affect and level of arousal during physical play; extent to which fathers offered relational advice regarding peer dilemmas to sons; how much fathers reported enjoying friends in their networks; the number of relatives in fathers' networks; the amount of contact with relatives; the enjoyment of contact with relatives; and the number of older and younger children available through fathers' network of relatives. This model explained a significant 35% of the variance in teacher-rated aggression. Similar to mother–son dyads, when fathers had fewer relatives in their social networks, but reported more contact with relatives, sons were described by teachers as more aggressive.

Relative Influence of Mothers and Fathers.　In a final set of regressions, significant variables from mother–child tripartite models and father–child tripartite models were combined in regressions in order to assess the relative contributions of each parent to boys and girls social acceptance and social competence outcomes. When peer-rated social acceptance of daughters was the outcome variable being considered, the model that included mother and father variables explained a significant 47% of the variance. Two mother variables emerged as unique predictors. Girls were better accepted by peers when mothers reported more friends in their social networks and more agemates were available to girls from mothers' social network. In addition, girls were better accepted when fathers expressed less negative affect during play with daughters, when they were less arousing and stimulating during play, and when they reported less enjoyment of their friend network. In contrast, when considering our sample of boys, the model that included mother and father variables explained a significant 36% of the variance, however, father variables did not make unique contributions to the model. Three mother variables emerged as significant predictors; when mothers gave more specific advice about a peer dilemma to sons, when mothers' friendship networks included more same-aged peers, and when mothers reported more enjoyment and closeness to relatives, sons were better accepted by classmates.

When teacher-rated social acceptance of daughters was the outcome variable being considered, the model that included mother and father variables explained a nonsignificant 6% of the variance. No father variables emerged as unique predictors; however, when mothers exercised more control of their daughters' behavior during play, daughters were described by teachers as better accepted by their classmates. When boys were the focus of analysis, the model that included mother and father variables explained a significant 16% of the variance, with only father variables making unique contributions to the model. When fathers expressed less negative affect during play with their sons, and when they reported better quality relationships with relatives in their social networks, sons were described by teachers as more socially accepted by their peers.

When peer-rated aggression of daughters was the outcome variable being considered, only mother variables qualified for inclusion in the model. When considering our sample of boys, one mother and one father variable made unique contributions to explained variance: When mothers gave boys more socially skilled advice and when fathers reported better relationships with their network of relatives, sons were described by peers as less aggressive. The model that included mother and father variables explained a significant 33% of the variance.

When teacher-rated aggression of daughters was the outcome variable being considered, only mother variables qualified for inclusion in the model. When boys were the focus of analysis, the model that included mother and father variables explained a significant 28% of the variance, with two father variables and one mother variable making unique contributions to the model. When fathers played in a less arousing and stimulating manner with sons, when fathers reported that they enjoyed their relative networks more, and when mothers gave more socially skilled advice regarding conflict with a peer, sons were described by teachers as less aggressive.

A Word of Caution. The results from these analyses provide some support for our tripartite model of family-peer linkage. However, a word of caution is in order. Specifically, the relative importance of any one dimension of our model must be viewed as tentative, since the power of any single predictor is likely to vary with the particular operationalization of any variable. The fairness of the test of our three-part model is premised on the assumption that the adequacy of the measurement of each of the three components is equal. However, these are a variety of choices that can be made in terms of the variables that represent each of the constructs in our model. For example, the quality of the attachment relationship or parental disciplinary practices could have been chosen instead of the affective and control dimensions utilized in our study. Similarly, instead of social networks, a more direct index of provision of opportunities could entail the extent to which the parent facilitated contact with other children, which we have utilized in later phases of data collection. Therefore, the relative importance of the three components in our model must be viewed cautiously until a range of variables from each of the three aspects of our model are more fully sampled in subsequent studies. The problem is analogous to the classic problem in psychophysics that Stevens (1951) addressed, namely, how to equate the intensity of stimuli in different sensory modalities (e.g., visual, auditory, or olfactory). The challenge is even more daunting in the social domain. The findings, however, do suggest the value of recognizing the multiply determined nature of the family's contribution to children's social competence.

REMAINING ISSUES

Several issues need to be addressed in future research. First, it is important to underscore that these parental strategies outlined above operate together rather than independently in naturalistic socialization. Two forms of interdependence among the three components of the model should be distinguished. In this chapter, we provide evidence that the three parental strategies make distinctive contributions to children's peer competence, and together provide a more complete account than considering these strategies separately. The analytical approach we have used in our work to date has been based on the assumption that each component of the model is equally weighted and important in determining children's social outcomes. An alternative analytic strategy shifts the focus to parental typologies in which categories of parents differentially invest in one or another strategy. As Parke (1992) noted earlier:

> this array of socialization strategies that is available to parents can be viewed as a "cafeteria model" in which various combinations of items can be chosen or ignored in various sized portions. (p. 426)

Some parents may be less sensitive or spend relatively little time in interaction, but provide multiple opportunities for contact with peers. In contrast, other parents may be highly involved with their children in family settings, but limit their children's peer contacts. Some parents may invest heavily in teaching their children social skills and other parents may regard peer social skills as best acquired in interaction with other children. In recognition of the view that there are multiple pathways toward social competence, different combinations of parental strategies may produce different but equally well-adapted children. Some evidence for a "cafeteria" or "compensatory" model comes from Howes' (1990) finding that a high quality relationship with a day-care provider can, in part, compensate for an insecure attachment with a child's primary caregiver. Exploration of this issue is an important next step in our research program.

Second, a lingering problem in this area of research concerns the issue of direct effects. Two forms of this issue merit distinction. We need to assess the impact of the child on the parent as well as vice versa in our studies of parent–child interaction. For example, child temperament may play a role in both altering parental strategies and in accounting, in part, for the quality of the child's peer relationships. Child characteristics could have a direct impact on children's relationships with peers or an indirect effect through changes in the parent–child relationship, which, in turn, alters children's peer relationships. Second, it is important to assess the impact of peer-based experience on changes in family-centered relationships. To take an extreme example, joining a gang would presumably have a profound impact on the child's relationship with his or her family. Repetti (1996) provides empirical evidence of this type of direction of effect issue. In her work, she found that children who experience difficulties with peers at school (e.g., excluded from an activity) subsequently had more negative interchanges with their parents later that same day. More attention to both of these direction of effect issues is clearly needed.

Third, the distinction between short-term and long-term models of family–peer linkage is important. Most studies have focused on long-term models in which the effects of stable family influences (e.g., interaction style, management strategy, advice-giving style) are assessed and their link to some relatively enduring aspect of the child's relationship with peers is examined. In contrast, a minority of studies have focused on short-term effects of fluctuations in either family functioning or peer experiences on the child's behavior in either the family or peer settings. The recent work of Repetti (1996) is an illustration of the impact of short-term shifts in the quality of peer interaction on later family interaction. Less is known about how short-term problems in the family, such as an argument with a parent or sibling prior to an encounter with peers can alter the child's peer interactions. Moreover, a major puzzle remains, namely the ways in which short-term fluctuations are transformed into long-term stable patterns of either family or peer relationships. Longitudinal studies that track the ways in which short-term change is transformed into stable patterns would clearly be worthwhile. Patterson's (1993) work on the emergence of aggression provided a model for examination of this issue.

Fourth, the issue of intracultural variation needs more attention. Our research program is beginning to address this issue, but our understanding of this complex issue, to date, is relatively meager. Not only are there issues of ethnic identity, per se, that need to be addressed but issues of the relation between ethnicity and the larger social context of the classroom and neighborhood need to be examined. The impact on social relationships of being a member of an ethnic minority group will vary with the ethnic mix of these other contexts. A Latino child in a neighborhood or classroom of largely other Latino children will have different social challenges than a Latino child who is one of only a few Latino children in a predominantly Anglo setting.

The need to understand better developmental issues remains paramount, because the ways in which these three pathways change across time are not well articulated. Two aspects of this issue can be distinguished. First, do the three pathways differ in importance across age? Second, do the forms that these three pathways assume differ as a function of developmental status of the child? Regarding the first issue, it is likely that parent–child interaction is more important in the early years of development, whereas the managerial aspects of the model assume more importance as the child matures. In regard to the second issue, it is likely that the form of enactment of these strategies will shift across development. Advice giving, for example may become less direct and assume the form of consultation as the child develops. Similarly, arranging activities on behalf of the child probably gives way to indirect monitoring of children's social activities.

Finally, as Hartup (1986, 1996) has consistently reminded us, the common strategy in developmental psychology of focusing on the individual as the unit of analysis fails to capture the critical relational aspects of social behavior. From a family systems perspective, it is clear that multiple units of analysis need to be considered including dyads, triads, and familial or group level of analyses as well as individual levels of analyses (Parke, 1988). Parent–child dyads, including mother–child and father–child dyads, each may follow separate developmental courses that merit examination. Similarly, the husband–wife dyad is important to consider both in terms of its impact directly and indirectly on children's own development and their peer relationships (Parke & O'Neil, 1996). In terms of peer relationships, dyadic units need to be considered as well. Friendship, a close dyadic relationship between two individuals is distinct from other forms of peer interaction (Hartup, 1996). Triads can serve as developmental units of analysis as well. Within the family, mother–father–child relationships have been examined and suggest that relationship dynamics shift as one moves from dyadic to triadic units of analysis (Parke, Power, & Gottman, 1979). Children's play groups differ across triadic versus dyadic composition with more possibility of coalitions, conflict, and the need for more coordination of goals in triadic contexts. Finally, family and group-level analysis need to be considered. Families as units change across development and respond to changing circumstances as units. Reiss' notion of family paradigms (Reiss, 1981) or Boss' concept of family boundaries (Boss, 1983) are examples of family-level analysis. Turning to the peer group, the concept of sociometric status is a group-level variable and reflects the degree of acceptance by the peer group (Rubin, Bukowski, & Parker, 1997). The notion of group structure with its resulting hierarchy of power is a further example of this level of analysis. Most importantly, these units of analysis do not operate independently. The interplay among these separate developmental trajectories within the family and peer group can produce a diverse set of effects on the functioning of the units themselves. In addition, the interlocking developmental curves across these units of analysis can produce very different effects both for families and peers, and the relation between these two systems will be determined by the points at which particular individuals, dyads, triads, families, or peer groups fall along their respective developmental life courses.

This movement toward the study of relationships in both family and peer systems is not only likely to provide a richer understanding of the nature of these cross-system linkages but provide a better set of guidelines for intervention and prevention efforts as well. The finest tribute to our colleague and friend, Willard Hartup, would be to move vigorously in the direction he has so wisely laid out for us.

ACKNOWLEDGMENTS

Preparation of this chapter was supported by NSF Grant BNS 8919391 to Ross D. Parke and NICHD Grant 32391 to Ross D. Parke and Robin O'Neil. We are especially grateful to Sue Spitzer, Robert Cupp, Susan Isley, Mara Welsh, Jeanette Lee, Shirley Wang, Lisa Harris, Sandi Simpkins, David McDowell, Mary Flyr, and Christine Strand for their devotion to every aspect of this project. We also thank participating teachers, staff, and students at elementary schools in the Fontana Unified School District and Jurupa Unified School District. We are particularly appreciative of the ongoing support of the superintendents of both school districts, Dr. Karen Harshman and Mrs. Bonita Roberts. Finally, we are grateful to the children and parents in our study for their continued involvement in our project.

REFERENCES

Baldwin, M. J. (1992). Relational schema and the processing of information. *Psychological Review, 112,* 461–484.
Barth, J. M., & Parke, R. D. (1993). Parent-child relationship influences on children's transition to school. *Merrill-Palmer Quarterly, 39,* 173–195.
Baumrind, D. (1973). The development of instrumental competence through socialization. In A. D. Pick (Ed.), *Minnesota symposium on child psychology* (Vol. 7, pp. 3–46). Minneapolis: University of Minnesota Press.
Bhavnagri, N., & Parke, R. D. (1991). Parents as direct facilitators of children's peer relationships: Effects of age of child and sex of parent. *Journal of Personal and Social Relationships, 8,* 423–440.

Boss, P. G. (1983). The marital relationship: Boundaries and ambiguities. In H. I. McCubbin & C. R. Figley (Eds.), *Stress and the family* (Vol. I, pp. 26–40). New York: Bruner/Mazel.

Bowlby, J. (1980). *Attachment and loss: Vol. 3. Loss.* New York: Basic Books.

Boyum, L., & Parke, R. D. (1995). Family emotional expressiveness and children's social competence. *Journal of Marriage and Family, 57,* 593–608.

Bretherton, I., & Waters, E. (1985). Growing points of attachment: Theory and research. *Monographs of the Society for Research in Child Development, 50*(1–2).

Bronfenbrenner, U. (1989). Ecological systems theory. In R. Vasta (Ed.), *Annals of child development* (Vol. 6, pp. 187–250). Greenwich, CT: JAI Press.

Bryant, B. (1985). The neighborhood walk: Sources of support in middle childhood. *Monographs of the Society for Research in Child Development, 50*(3, Serial No. 210).

Buck, R. (1975). Nonverbal communication of affect in children. *Journal of Personality and Social Psychology, 31,* 644–653.

Bugental, D. (1991). Affective and cognitive processes within threat-oriented family systems. In I. E. Sigel, A. V. McGillicuddy-Delisi, & J. J. Goodnow (Eds.), *Parental belief systems: The psychological consequences for children* (2nd ed., pp. 219–248). Hillsdale, NJ: Lawrence Erlbaum Associates.

Burks, J. S., & Parke, R. D. (1996). Parental and child representations of social relationships: Linkages between families and peers. *Merrill-Palmer Quarterly, 42,* 358–378.

Carson, J. L., & Parke, R. D. (1996). Reciprocal negative affect in parent-child interactions and children's peer competency. *Child Development, 67,* 2217–2226.

Cassidy, J., Parke, R. D., Butkovsky, L., & Braungart, J. (1992). Family-peer connections: The roles of emotional expressiveness within the family and children's understanding of emotions. *Child Development, 63,* 603–618.

Cherlin, A. J., Furstenberg, F. F., Chase-Lansdale, P. J., Kiernan, K. E., & others (1991). Longitudinal studies of effects of divorce on children in Great Britain and the United States. *Science, 252,* 1386–1389.

Cicchetti, D., & Toth, S. L. (1997). Perspectives on research and practice in developmental psychology. In W. Damon (Ed.), *Handbook of child psychology* (Vol. 4, pp. 479–584). New York: Wiley.

Cochran, M., & Brassard, J. A. (1979). Child development and personal social networks. *Child Development, 50,* 601–616.

Cochran, M., & Davila, V. (1992). Societal influences on children's peer relationships. In R. D. Parke & G. W. Ladd (Eds.), *Family-peer relationships: Modes of linkage* (pp. 191–212). Hillsdale, NJ: Lawrence Erlbaum Associates.

Cohen, J. S. (1989). *Maternal involvement in children's peer relationships during middle childhood.* Unpublished doctoral dissertation, University of Waterloo, Waterloo, Canada.

Denham, S. A. (1993). Maternal emotional responsiveness to toddlers social-emotional functioning. *Journal of Child Psychology and Psychiatry, 34,* 715–728.

Dishion, T. J. (1990). The peer context of troublesome child and adolescent behavior. In P. E. Leone (Ed.), *Understanding troubled and troubling youth: A multidisciplinary perspective* (pp. 128–153). Newbury Park, CA: Sage.

Dodge, K. A., Pettit, G. S., McClaskey, C. L., & Brown, M. (1986). Social competence in children. *Monographs of the Society for Research in Child Development, 51*(2, Serial No. 213).

Dunn, J., & Brown, J. (1994). Affect expression in the family, children's understanding of emotions and their interactions with others. *Merrill-Palmer Quarterly, 40,* 120–137.

Eisenberg, N., & Fabes, R. A. (1992). Young children's coping with interpersonal anger. *Child Development, 63,* 116–128.

Eisenberg, N., & Fabes, R. A. (1994). Emotion, regulation and the development of social competence. In M. Clark (Ed.), *Review of personality and social psychology, Vol. 14: Emotion and social behavior* (pp. 119–150). Newbury Park, CA: Sage.

Elder, G. H., Modell, J., & Parke, R. D. (Eds.). (1993). *Children in time and place.* New York: Cambridge University Press.

Furstenberg, F., Brooks-Gunn, J., & Morgan, P. (1987). *Adolescent mothers in later life.* New York: Cambridge University Press.

Gottman, J. M., Katz, L. F., & Hooven, C. (1996). Parental meta-emotion philosophy and the emotional life of families: Theoretical models and preliminary data. *Journal of Family Psychology, 10,* 243–268.

Grusec, J. E., & Goodnow, J. J. (1994). Impact of parental discipline methods on the child's internalization of values: A reconceptualization of current points of view. *Developmental Psychology, 30,* 1–19.

Grusec, J. E., Hastings, P., & Mammone, N. (1994). Parenting cognitions and relationship schemas. In J. G. Smetana (Ed.), *Beliefs about parenting: Origins and developmental implications* (pp. 5–19). San Francisco: Jossey-Bass.

Gunnar, M. (1994). Psychoendocrine studies of temperament and stress in early childhood: Expanding current models. In J. E. Bates & T. D. Wachs (Eds.), *Temperament: Individual differences at the interface of biology and behavior* (pp. 175–198). Washington, DC: American Psychological Association.

Harrist, A. W., Pettit, G. S., Dodge, K. A., & Bates, J. E. (1994). Dyadic synchrony in mother-child interaction: Relation with children's subsequent kindergarten adjustment. *Family Relations, 43,* 417–424.

Hartup, W. W. (1979a). The social worlds of childhood. *American Psychologist, 34,* 944–950.

Hartup, W. W. (1979b). Peer relations and the growth of social competence. In M. W. Kent & J. E. Rolf (Eds.), *Primary prevention of psychopathology: Vol 3. Social competence in children* (pp. 150–170). Hanover, NH: University Press of New England.

Hartup, W. W. (1983). Peer relations. In P. Mussen (Series Ed.) & E. M. Hetherington (Vol. Ed.), *Handbook of child psychology, Vol. 4: Socialization, personality, and social development* (pp. 103–196). New York: Wiley.

Hartup, W. W. (1986). On relationships and development. In W. W. Hartup & Z. Rubin (Eds.), *Relationships and development* (pp. 1–26). Hillsdale, NJ: Lawrence Erlbaum Associates.

Hartup, W. W. (1996). Cooperation, close relationships, and cognitive development. In W. M. Bukowski, A. F. Newcomb, & W. W. Hartup (Eds.), *The company they keep: Friendship in childhood and adolescence* (pp. 213–237). New York: Cambridge University Press.

Hofferth, S. L., & Phillips, D. A. (1991). Child care policy research. *Journal of Social Issues, 47,* 1–13.

Homel, R., Burns, A., & Goodnow, J. (1987). Parental social networks and child development. *Journal of Social and Personal Relationships, 4,* 159–177.

Howes, C. (1990). Can the age of entry into child care and the quality of child care predict adjustment in kindergarten? *Developmental Psychology, 26,* 292–303.

Hubbard, J. A., & Coie, J. D. (1994). Emotional correlates of social competence in children's peer relationships. *Merrill-Palmer Quarterly, 40,* 1–20.

Isley, S., O'Neil, R., & Parke, R. D. (1996). The relation of parental affect and control behaviors to children's classroom acceptance: A concurrent and predictive analysis. *Early Education and Development, 7,* 7–23.

Klebanov, P. K., Brooks-Gunn, J., & Duncan, G. (1994). Does neighborhood and family poverty affect mothers' parenting, mental health, and social support? *Journal of Marriage and the Family, 56,* 441–455.

Ladd, G. W. (1992). Themes and theories: Perspective on processes in family-peer relationships. In R. Parke & G. Ladd (Eds.), *Family-peer relationships: Modes of linkage* (pp. 3–34). Hillsdale, NJ: Lawrence Erlbaum Associates.

Ladd, G. W., & Golter, B. S. (1988). Parents' management of preschoolers' peer relations: Is it related to children's social competence? *Developmental Psychology, 24,* 109–117.

Ladd, G. W., & Price, J. M. (1987). Predicting children's social and school adjustment following the transition from preschool to kindergarten. *Child Development, 58,* 1168–1189.

Ladd, G. W., Profilet, S. M., & Hart, C. H. (1992). Parents' management of children's peer relations: Facilitating and supervising children's activities in the peer culture. In R. D. Parke & G. Ladd (Eds.), *Family-peer relationships: Modes of linkage* (pp. 215–253). Hillsdale, NJ: Lawrence Erlbaum Associates.

Lee, J., Parke, R. D., O'Neil, R., & Wang, S. (1997). *The relation between parent and child social networks and children's peer acceptance.* Unpublished manuscript, University of California, Riverside.

Lee, J., & Welsh, M. (1995, March). *The relation of parents' and children's social networks to children's social acceptance and behavior.* Paper presented at the biennial meetings of the Society for Research in Child Development, Indianapolis, IN.

MacDonald, K., & Parke, R. D. (1984). Bridging the gap: Parent-child play interaction and peer interactive competence. *Child Development, 55,* 1265–1277.

McDowell, D. J., O'Neil, R., & Parke, R. D. (1997). *Display rule knowledge and application in a disappointing situation: Relations with social competence.* Unpublished manuscript, University of California, Riverside.

Mills, R. S. L., & Rubin, K. H. (1993). Parental ideas as influences on children's social competence. In S. Duck (Ed.), *Learning about relationships* (pp. 98–117). Newbury Park, CA: Sage.

Nelson, K. (1986). Event knowledge and cognitive development. In K. Nelson (Ed.), *Event knowledge: Structure and function in development* (pp. 1–20). Hillsdale, NJ: Lawrence Erlbaum Associates.

O'Neil, R., Garcia, J., Zavala, A., & Wang, S. (1995, March). *Parental advice giving and children's competence with peers: A content and stylistic analysis.* Paper presented at the biennial meetings of the Society for Research in Child Development, Indianapolis, IN.

O'Neil, R., & Parke, R. D. (1996a). *Parental antecedents of emotion regulation in middle childhood: Links to children's social competence.* Poster presented at the third annual Family Research Consortium Summer Institute, San Diego, CA.

O'Neil, R. & Parke, R. D. (1996). *Objective and subjective features of children's neighborhoods: Relations to parental regulatory strategies and children's social competence.* Unpublished manuscript, University of California, Riverside.

Parke, R. D. (1978). Parent-infant interaction: Progress, paradigms, and problems. In G. P. Sackett (Ed.), *Observing behavior (Vol. 1): Theory and applications in mental retardation* (pp. 69–95). Baltimore, MD: University Park Press.

Parke, R. D. (1988). Families in life-span perspective: A multilevel developmental approach. In E. M. Hetherington, R. M. Lerner, & M. Perlmutter (Eds.), *Child development in life-span perspective* (pp. 159–190). Hillsdale, NJ: Lawrence Erlbaum Associates.

Parke, R. D. (1992). Epilogue: Remaining issues and future trends in the study of family-peer relationships. In R. D. Parke & G. Ladd (Eds.), *Family-peer relationships: Modes of linkage* (pp. 425–438). Hillsdale, NJ: Lawrence Erlbaum Associates.

Parke, R. D. (1994). Epilogue: Unresolved issues and future trends in family relationships with other contexts. In R. D. Parke & S. G. Kellam (Eds.), *Exploring family relationships with other social contexts* (pp. 215–229). Hillsdale, NJ: Lawrence Erlbaum Associates.

Parke, R. D. (1996). *Fatherhood.* Cambridge, MA: Harvard University Press.

Parke, R. D., & Bhavnagri, N. (1989). Parents as managers of children's peer relationships. In D. Belle (Ed.), *Children's social networks and social supports* (pp. 241–259). New York: Wiley.

Parke, R. D., Burks, V., Carson, J., Neville, B., & Boyum, L. (1994). Family-peer relationships: A tripartite model. In R. D. Parke & S. Kellam (Eds.), *Advances in family research (Vol. 4): Family relationships with other social systems* (pp. 115–145). Hillsdale, NJ: Lawrence Erlbaum Associates.

238   PARKE AND O'NEIL

Parke, R. D., Cassidy, J., Burks, V. M., Carson, J. L., & Boyum, L. (1992). Familial contributions to peer competence among young children: The role of interactive and affective processes. In R. D. Parke & G. W. Ladd (Eds.), *Family-peer relationships: Modes of linkage* (pp. 107–134). Hillsdale, NJ: Lawrence Erlbaum Associates.

Parke, R. D., Cupp, R., Spitzer, S., Isley, S., & Welsh, M. (1994, August). *Family-peer relationships: Cognitive mediators.* Paper presented at the biennial meeting of the International Society for the Study of Social Behavior, Amsterdam.

Parke, R. D., MacDonald, K., Beitel, A., & Bhavnagri, N. (1988). The role of the family in the development of peer relationships. In R. Peters & R. J. McMahon (Eds.), *Social learning and systems approaches to marriage and the family* (pp. 17–44). New York: Bruner/Mazel.

Parke, R. D., MacDonald, K. B., Burks, V. M., Carson, J., Bhavnagri, N., Barth, J., & Beitel, A. (1989). Family and peer systems: In search of the linkages. In K. Kreppner & R. M. Lerner (Eds.), *Family systems and life span development* (pp. 65–92). Hillsdale, NJ: Lawrence Erlbaum Associates.

Parke, R. D., & O'Neil, R. (1996). The influence of significant others on learning about relationships. In S. W. Duck (Ed.), *Handbook of personal relationships* (2nd ed., pp. 29–60). New York: Wiley.

Parke, R. D., Power, T. G., & Gottman, J. M. (1979). Conceptualization and quantifying influence patterns in the family triad. In M. E. Lamb, S. J. Suomi, & G. R. Stephenson (Eds.), *Social interaction analysis: Methodological issues* (pp. 231–253). Madison: University of Wisconsin Press.

Patterson, G. R. (1993). Orderly change in a stable world: The antisocial trait as chimera. *Journal of Consulting and Clinical Psychology, 61,* 911–919.

Patterson, C. J., Vaden, N. A., & Kupersmidt, J. B. (1991). Family background, recent life events, and peer rejection during childhood. *Journal of Personal and Social Relationships, 8,* 347–361.

Pettit, G. S., & Mize, J. (1993). Substance and style: Understanding the ways in which parents teach children about social relationships. In S. Duck (Ed.), *Learning about relationships* (Vol. 2, pp. 118–151). London: Sage.

Plomin, R. (1995). Genetics and children's experiences in the family. *Journal of Child Psychology and Psychiatry and Allied Disciplines, 36,* 33–68.

Putallez, M. (1987). Maternal behavior and sociometric status. *Child Development, 58,* 324–340.

Repetti, R. (1996). The effects of perceived social and academic failure experiences on school-age children's subsequent interactions with parents. *Child Development, 67,* 1467–1482.

Reiss, D. (1981). *The family's construction of reality.* Cambridge, MA: Harvard University Press.

Rogoff, B. (1990). *Apprenticeship in thinking.* New York: Oxford University Press.

Rothbart, M. K., & Bates, J. E. (1997). Temperament. In W. Damon (Ed.), *Handbook of child psychology* (Vol. 3, pp. 105–176). New York: Wiley.

Rubin, K. H., Bukowski, W., & Parker, J. G. (1997). Peer interactions, relationships, and groups. In W. Damon (Ed.), *Handbook of child psychology* (Vol. 3, pp. 619–700). New York: Wiley.

Russell, A., & Finnie, V. (1990). Preschool children's social status and maternal instructions to assist group entry. *Developmental Psychology, 26*(4), 603–611.

Saarni, C. (1992). Children's emotional-expressive behavior as regulators of others' happy and sad states. *New Directions for Child Development, 55,* 91–106.

Spitzer, S., & Parke, R. D. (1994, August). *Family cognitive representations of social behavior and children's social competence.* Paper presented at the meeting of the American Psychological Society, Washington, DC.

Sroufe, L. A. (1979). The coherence of individual development. *American Psychologist, 34,* 834–841.

Stevens, S. S. (1951). *Handbook of experimental psychology.* New York: Wiley.

Thompson, R. (1997). Early sociopersonality development. In W. Damon (Ed.), *Handbook of child psychology* (Vol. 3, pp. 25–104). New York: Wiley.

Tinsley, B. J. (1992). Multiple influences on the acquisition and socialization of children's health attitudes and behavior: An integrative review. *Child Development, 63,* 1043–1069.

Wang, S. J., & McDowell, D. J. (1996, March). *Parental advice-giving: Relations to child social competence and psychosocial functioning.* Poster presented at the annual meetings of the Western Psychological Association, San Jose, CA.

Chapter 11

One Social World: The Integrated Development of Parent–Child and Peer Relationships

L. Alan Sroufe
Byron Egeland
Elizabeth A. Carlson
University of Minnesota

For several decades researchers have been concerned with the place of peer relationships in the broader arena of social development. Numerous investigators have suggested that peer relationships may serve unique developmental functions and must be investigated in their own right (Hartup, 1980). For example, Harlow (Harlow & Harlow, 1965) distinguished a "peer affectional system," centered on play, from an "infant–mother affectional system," centered on nurturance. More recently, Furman and Wehner (1994) argued that distinctive basic needs were best met within peer relationships. They argued that an initial core need for "tenderness" was best met within parent–child relationships, whereas needs such as "companionship" may be best met within the peer world. Meeting these needs, as well as needs for acceptance, intimacy, and sexuality, which also are part of peer experience, is critical in human adaptation.

One focus of much developmental writing has been the role of peer experiences as preparation for effective adult functioning, especially successful intimate relationships. Peer relationships are a critical arena for developing notions of equity and reciprocity, for practicing conflict resolution, and for learning to control aggression (e.g., Hartup, 1980; Hartup & Laursen, 1994). Moreover, because adult intimate relationships are symmetrical (occurring between those who are roughly agemates and where neither can call upon the authority of greater chronological maturity), a special role for close childhood friendships has been underscored. Over the course of childhood and adolescence, beginning with same-gender friendships, issues of trust, loyalty, and, ultimately, self-disclosure and sharing of confidences are worked out with agemates. Such capabilities, along with the capacity to sustain closeness in the face of conflict, are deemed to be critical features of adult intimate relationships.

In a classic paper, subtitled "Two Social Worlds," Hartup (1980) anticipated much of the aforementioned discussion on the unique contributions of peer relationships to development. At the same time, he discussed the integration of peer experiences and parent–child relationships. He described how early parent–child relationships might "set the stage" for peer relationships, perhaps leaving an imprint that could be discerned in an individual's interaction with peers. He pointed to an "instrumental base," wherein interactive patterns first evolved in relationships with parents are practiced and elaborated in the world of peers. In addition, he suggested that relations with parents provide a critical emotional base, such that some children bring a positive orientation to their initial encounters with peers. In these ways family relationships "maximize the probability that successful peer experiences will ensue" (p. 288). Moreover, he argued, the peer system does not replace or duplicate the parent–child system, but rather supports it. "The two social worlds of the child seem actually to interact as a complementary synergism" (p. 287).

The major goal of this chapter is to examine the complementarity between family and peer experiences in guiding the course of development, and to do so in light of the extensive empirical base of a longitudinal study from birth through adulthood (e.g., Egeland, Carlson, & Sroufe, 1993; Sroufe, Carlson, & Shulman, 1993). In the developmental view presented, the importance of peer experiences is supported, while at the same time their integration with family experiences is underscored. Peer experiences make unique contributions to social development, but the quality of peer experiences is dependent on foundations laid down in the parent–child caregiving system. Successful peer relationships at any age promote social competence at subsequent ages, but at the same time are conditional upon prior peer experiences, the history of relationships within the family, and current support. In short, parent–child and peer relationships are part of one social world.

Supporting such a viewpoint involves three empirical demonstrations: (a) that peer relationships assessments at any given age do, in fact, predict later social competence; (b) that such predictive peer competencies are themselves predicted by qualities of parent–child relationships that precede them; and (c) that peer and parent–child assessments together predict later social functioning better than does either domain alone. All of this is predicated on an effective, age-sensitive conceptualization of peer competence itself.

THE DEVELOPMENT OF PEER COMPETENCE

Peer relationships represent a developmental system, and this fact is central for the integration proposed. Peer competence develops both in the sense that different tasks are pivotal to peer relationships at each advancing phase of development, and in the sense that peer experiences at each age provide a foundation for negotiating subsequent issues with peers. Demonstrating linkages between parent–child and peer relationships requires first an understanding of this developmental system.

The major issue for the preschool child is to engage the world of peers (e.g., Sroufe, Carlson, & Shulman, 1993). This includes evolving the capacity for sustaining and coordinating interaction with individual peers, as well as participating successfully in group activities. At this age, peer partners also are just evolving interactive capacities. Therefore, initiating and responding to others and sustaining interaction, especially in highly stimulating group situations, calls upon not only interactive and play skills but a considerable capacity for emotional regulation. In fact, those who are successful at this phase (as determined by sociometrics, teacher ratings, or observed participation and centrality in the peer group) are noted to be more affectively positive in bids and responses to peers, to modulate arousal effectively, and to maintain behavioral organization in prolonged interactive bouts (e.g., Sroufe, Schork, Motti, Lawroski, & LaFreniere, 1984).

The issues to be negotiated in the world of peers during middle childhood become much more elaborated and complex (see Table 11.1). First, the capacity for friendships is evolving. A major developmental task is to form durable specific friendships, characterized by loyalty, mutual support, and closeness. Numerous writers have underscored the importance of these special relationships for developing the capacity for intimacy. At the same time, peer groups become much more stable and organized, taxing the child to find an effective place within a more well-defined network. Hartup (1980) described the groups of preschoolers as "aggregates of individuals," whereas those of older children are more tightly organized and are characterized by "reciprocity and synchrony." Peer groups in middle childhood also are strongly rule governed, and to be effective children must master and adhere to the group norms. One of the most notable of these rule systems concerns behavior with respect to the opposite gender in public settings (Thorne, 1986). Rules governing interaction with opposite-gender peer group members must be closely followed, in a manner such that a distinct boundary is maintained between genders (Sroufe, Bennett, Englund, Urban, & Shulman, 1993). Finally, in middle childhood, there is the additional complexity of coordinating loyalty to friends with the demands of group functioning. For competent children the two are mutually supporting: friendships enhance acceptance by and participation in

TABLE 11.1
Changing Issues in Childhood Peer Relationships

Preschool: "Positive Engagement of Peers"

A. Selecting Specific Partners
B. Sustaining Interactive Bouts
    1. negotiating conflicts in interaction
    2. maintaining organization in the face of arousal
    3. finding pleasure in the interactive process
C. Participation in Groups

Middle Childhood: "Investment in the Peer World"

A. Forming Loyal Friendships
B. Sustaining Relationships
    1. negotiating relationship conflicts
    2. tolerating a range of emotional experiences
    3. enhancement of self in relationships
C. Functioning in Stable, Organized Groups
    1. adhering to group norms
    2. maintaining gender boundaries
D. Coordinating Friendships and Group Functioning

Adolescence: "Integrating Self and Peer Relationships"

A. Forming Intimate Relationships
    1. self-disclosing same-gender relationships
    2. cross-gender relationships
    3. sexual relationships
B. Commitment in Relationships
    1. negotiating self-relevant conflicts
    2. emotional vulnerability
    3. self-disclosure and self-identity
C. Functioning in a Relationship Network
    1. mastering multiple rule systems
    2. establishing flexible boundaries
D. Coordinating Multiple Relationships
    1. same-gender and cross-gender
    2. intimate relationships and group functioning

---

the group, and group settings provide an important context for enhancing friendship relationships (Shulman, Elicker, & Sroufe, 1994). Less competent children may be unable to achieve this coordination.

Thus, peer relationships, including friendships and group functioning, are qualitatively different in middle childhood and the preschool period, in terms of durability, coherence of organization, degree of emotional sharing, and extent of mutual coordination and reciprocity. At the same time, such advances build upon foundations laid out in the preschool period. Sustained give and take, practice with affect regulation, investment, and sheer enjoyment of earlier peer experiences support the greater emotional involvement and complexity of relationships in middle childhood. Strong empirical connections most likely will be demonstrated when researchers attend to developmental changes in manifestation of competence across these two periods.

Further complexities challenge the adolescent (Table 11.1). Friendships and group functioning cross gender lines. More intimate relationships emerge, with friends and with sexual partners, based on deeper exploration of self and other. Friendships with same-gender and opposite-gender partners, intimate sexual relationships, same-gender group activities and mixed-gender group functioning all must be coordinated, each to the enhancement of every other. The level of coordination and reciprocity and the level of intimacy are greatly increased, with consequent challenges for emotional regulation. The degree of emotional vulnerability and self-identity relevance of relationships is qualitatively beyond that of the middle childhood period. Again, however, the way to these advances has been prepared by experiences in the preceding periods. Sustaining emotional closeness in the face of misunderstandings and conflict has been practiced in middle childhood, as has dealing with the complexities of competing demands within a network of relationships, albeit one that is not nearly as complex as that faced by teenagers.

CONTINUITY OF INDIVIDUAL FUNCTIONING
IN PEER RELATIONSHIPS

This developmental view of peer relationships, with each phase providing the foundation for subsequent competent functioning, is supported amply by empirical data. In the Minnesota longitudinal study data have been obtained on peer competence across the years of childhood and adolescence. These data include broad characterizations of competence with the total sample ($N = 175$), which are summarized in Table 11.2, but not discussed in detail here. (Generally, teacher rankings of peer competence across ages tend to correlate about .40 or better, depending on the age gap covered.)

Detailed data are also available on all aspects of peer functioning across ages for an intensively studied subsample. The latter children were seen in a laboratory preschool, a 4-week summer camp at age 10, and a series of weekend retreats at age 15. This small sample study ($N = 35$–41 across ages) is unique in that multiple types of peer assessments were available at each developmental period. Assessments included ratings made by teachers or counselors at the end of the term or camp, ratings made by coders based on videotaped records, detailed behavior observation data, ratings based on interviews of the participants, and sociometric measures. These measures showed strong convergence at each age (e.g., ratings of depend-

TABLE 11.2
Social Competence Stability for the Total Sample

| | Preschool | Elementary | | Adolescence | |
		Early	Late	Total	
Preschool teacher ratings	—	.29**	.39***	.42***	.42***
(4 years)		(n = 81)	(n = 82)	(n = 82)	(n = 78)
Elementary teacher rankings					
Early (Grades K-1)		—	.56***	.74***	.40***
			(n = 188)	(n = 189)	(n = 178)
Late (Grades 3-6)			—	.89***	.43***
				(n = 191)	(n = 181)
Total (Grades 1, 2, 3, 6)				—	.45***
					(n = 181)
Adolescent parent/teacher					—
composite score (16 years)					

Note. Pearson product-moment correlations are two-tailed.
$*p < .05.$ $**p > .01.$ $***p < .001.$

ency correlated most highly with observed frequency of adult–child contact; ratings of peer competence with observed social isolation). Moreover, by sampling from them to tap key constructs at different ages, method variance may be minimized. The following results are based primarily on the following kinds of data: (a) in preschool, competence ratings by teachers; (b) in middle childhood, behavior observation of friendship (association scores) and isolation, and ratings of gender boundary maintenance based on video records of encounters across genders; and (c) in adolescence, ratings by counselors of competence and "capacity for relationship vulnerability," and a rating of friendship intimacy based on a friendship interview. (Occasionally other measures are utilized to illustrate certain points.) Definitions of these and other measures may be found in Table 11.3. Different sets of coders were responsible for each variable, and all were blind to previous data.

Results were powerful. Peer competence at any given age, keyed to the salient issues outlined earlier, was found to predict peer competence at every later period (see Tables 11.4 and 11.5). For example, the correlations between teacher-based preschool social competence ratings and various

TABLE 11.3
Definitions of Key Measures

INFANCY

Attachment
Number of times securely attached in the Ainsworth Strange situation at 12 to 18 months (0, 1, or 2)

Early Care
Composite (standardized) of four variables: number of times securely attached, rating of support in 24-month tool problem situation, 30-month Caldwell HOME scale (total), and rating of parental support in 42-month teaching task

PRESCHOOL

Teacher rating of peer competence based on a paragraph description of the competent preschooler (composited across three teachers)

MIDDLE CHILDHOOD

Friendship
Observed proportion of times child was with the most common partner (based on a child sampling procedure)

Isolation
Observed proportion of times child was isolated (based on a child sampling procedure)

Gender Boundary Maintenance
Rating made by coders following repeated review of videotaped record of child's encounters with members of the opposite gender. Based on frequency of active efforts to disown interest in contact with opposite gender (insults, physical distance, etc.) and to maintain closeness with same gender (e.g., seeking partners when other gender members were nearby)

Popularity
A composite score based on nominations as liked (spontaneous and elicited under direct questioning) and disliked

EARLY ADOLESCENCE

Family Balance I: Security
Rating based on videotaped parent–child interaction of the degree of security or emotional safety experienced (manifest in spontaneous expression of views, taking positions and maintaining them even when not held by the other)

General Family Support
A composite of ratings of security, support for autonomy, and overall effective functioning of the parent–child dyad in the taped sessions

ADOLESCENCE

Peer Competence
Composited rating of four counselors, based on a paragraph description of the socially competent adolescent

Capacity for Relationship Vulnerability
Composited rating of four counselors, based on a paragraph description, emphasizing the ability to capitalize on the range of opportunities available at the camp, including those that called for engaging members of the other gender in emotionally involving situations (e.g., an evening party or one-on-one conversations)

Friendship Intimacy
A composite of ratings of closeness and coherence regarding their relationship with a best friend as revealed in an interview transcript

TABLE 11.4
Social Competence Stability for the Subsample

	1	2	3	4	5	6	7
Preschool rating (4 years)							
1 Social competence	—	.57*** (n = 41)	.30 (n = 41)	.47** (n = 35)	.57** (n = 35)	.50*** (n = 39)	.39* (n = 38)
Camp indices (10 years)							
2 Friendship score		—	.55*** (n = 47)	.40** (n = 41)	.38* (n = 41)	.48*** (n = 45)	.64*** (n = 44)
3 Boundary maintenance rating			—	.58*** (n = 41)	.48** (n = 41)	.31* (n = 45)	.31* (n = 44)
Camp reunion indices (15 years)							
4 Social competence ranking				—	.88*** (n = 41)	.47** (n = 40)	.36* (n = 40)
5 Capacity for vulnerability rating					—	.49*** (n = 40)	.38* (n = 44)
Adolescent indices (16 years)							
6 Parent teacher composite score						—	.38** (n = 40)
7 Friendship interview							—

Note. Pearson product-moment correlations are two-tailed.
*p < .05. **p > .01. ***p < .001.

Table 11.5

Correlations Between Measures of Social Competence in Middle Childhood and Adolescence for the Subsample (*n* = 41)

Social Competence Measures	Adolescence (Camp Reunion)					
	Counselor Rankings		Counselor Ratings		Observation	Nomination
	Emotional Health	Social Competence	Social Skills	Capacity for Vulnerability	Isolation	Sociometric
Middle Childhood						
Counselor rankings						
Emotional health	.49***	.53***	.52***	.52***	-.34**	.41**
Social competence	.45**	.57***	.56***	.52***	-.55****	.50***
Counselor ratings						
Social skills	.29	.41**	.40**	.38**	-.57***	.34*
Observations						
Friendship score	.31*	.40**	.41**	.38**	-.04	.42**
Isolation score	-.32*	-.40**	-.37*	-.37*	.45**	-.32*
Child nominations						
Sociometric	.11	.24	.26	.12	-.40*	.39**

Note. Pearson product-moment correlations are two-tailed.
*p < .05. **p > .01. ***p < .001.

249

measures of social competence in the middle childhood summer camp (age 10) ranged from .46 to .57. The correlation between nursery school teacher and adolescent camp counselor ratings of competence was .47. Moreover, many specific relationships were theoretically compelling. For example, the capacity for friendship intimacy in adolescence, as rated from an interview about a specific relationship, correlated .64 with the observation-based measure of intensity of friendship in middle childhood (the amount of time spent with a particular partner during summer camp). This is stronger than the relationship of adolescent friendship intimacy with any other early measure of competence, and it is much stronger than the correlation of the middle childhood friendship competence score with general competence in adolescence ($r = 48$; Ostoja-Starzewska, 1996). An even more striking finding, paradoxical on the surface but demanded by the developmental theory under investigation, is the relationship between gender boundary maintenance in middle childhood and cross-gender intimacy in adolescence (Sroufe, Carlson, & Shulman, 1993). For example, the correlation between gender boundary maintenance in middle childhood and the capacity for relationship vulnerability scale in adolescence (again, see Table 11.3 for definition) was .48 ($p < .005$). It was those who followed the norm of maintaining gender boundaries in middle childhood who were most effectively involved with members of the opposite gender in our adolescent retreats, not those who had been "precociously" involved with the other gender in middle childhood. (Additional correlations between a broad range of middle childhood and adolescent peer competence measures are shown in Table 11.5.)

Finally, we carried out a hierarchical multiple regression analysis, using both preschool competence (composited teacher ratings) and middle childhood competence (a composite of the friendship score and the gender boundary maintenance score) to predict counselor ratings of adolescent social competence. The results showed that both preschool ($F[1, 33] = 9.15$, $R^2 = .22$, $p < .01$) and middle childhood (F change $[2, 32] = 7.51$, R^2 change $= .15$, $p < .01$) measures contributed to the adolescent outcome and that a total of 37% ($R = .61$) of the variance was accounted for. Thus, the first aspect of our thesis is confirmed. Using developmental assessment, early peer experience strongly predicts later peer competence.

ATTACHMENT HISTORY AND PEER COMPETENCE

A second tenet of our developmental position is that peer competence has roots in patterns of dyadic regulation in the preceding parent–child relationship. Although various family relationships (those with fathers, siblings, etc.) have clear relevance for peer competence (e.g., Sroufe, Cooper,

& DeHart, 1996), a primary focus has been early attachment relationships with the primary caregivers and other aspects of early care. Individual differences in the quality of these relationship experiences are predicted to be linked to peer relationships in all phases of development.

There are a number of bases for this prediction, many of which have been summarized previously (e.g., Elicker, Englund, & Sroufe, 1992; Kerns, 1996; Sroufe, 1983, 1988). First, a history of emotional availability and responsiveness, which defines a secure attachment relationship, is a foundation for positive expectations concerning relationships with others, a basic sense of connectedness, and a belief that relating to others will be rewarding. This is the *motivational* base for peer relationships. Second, parental responsiveness leads to a complementary sense of effectance; that is, that the child can have an impact on the caregiver and, ultimately, the broader world. Herein lie the roots of a sense of self-worth and self-esteem, as has now been amply demonstrated by research (e.g., Sroufe, 1983). The child believes not only that others will respond positively but that he or she can master the challenges the social world brings. This is the *attitudinal* base for positive peer relationships. Third, secure attachment provides a literal foundation for mastery of the environment, through its support of exploration. Those with secure histories come to the peer world with exploratory and mastery capacities that make them attractive to others. This includes both a range of object manipulation skills that promote successful play and, of great significance, a capacity to have fun. This is the behavioral or *instrumental* base of positive peer relationships. Fourth, the pattern of smooth, modulated affect regulation achieved within the secure infant–caregiver dyad becomes the prototype for the self-regulation of emotion required in the peer world; that is, the *emotional* base for peer relationships. Indeed, attachment may be defined as the dyadic regulation of emotion. The development of the attachment relationship itself is characterized by a progressively greater role for the child over the first 2 years of life, from emotional regulation orchestrated by the caregiver to joint regulation to guided self-regulation by the child (Sroufe, 1996). Thus, the child has been prepared for the emotional regulation required in peer encounters by the history of regulation within the attachment relationship.

Finally, there is the *relational* base. Certain expectations and understandings regarding reciprocity are laid down even in infancy, when it is the caregiver who must follow the infant's lead, creating a semblance of reciprocity that will only truly be a capability of the child in later years (Hayes, 1984). As discussed by Sroufe and Fleeson (1986), in participating in this vital, responsive relationship infants learn more than the role of the nurtured one; rather, they learn something basic about the nature of relationships. For infants with secure histories, reciprocity in peer relationships will make sense, both in terms of expected patterns of affective exchange and in terms of knowledge about how relationships work. When one signals, the other replies. When one offers, the other receives. When one is in need, the other responds. A bold prediction from attachment theory is that those with secure histories later will be more empathic with peers. Having experienced empathic care, the child will be oriented toward empathic response to the needs of others, once the necessary cognitive development has taken place.

As was the case regarding the stability of individual differences in peer competence, these predictions of a relation between attachment history and later peer relationships have been repeatedly confirmed, age by age (Table 11.6). A host of peer competence indices across ages were significantly related to differences in infant attachment security and to early care more generally (see Table 11.3 for a definition of this variable).

In preschool, the children ranked most highly in social competence by teachers were almost uniformly those with secure histories and those ranked lowest were those with histories of anxious attachment. These judgments were confirmed by detailed behavioral observations of time spent in the group, amount of isolation, frequency of agonistic encounters, expression of positive and negative affect, and involvement or emotional distance in play pairs (Pancake, 1988; Sroufe, 1983; Sroufe et al., 1984; Troy & Sroufe, 1987). Both teacher ratings (Sroufe, 1983) and analysis of videotaped episodes involving children's reactions to distressed classmates (Kestenbaum, Farber, & Sroufe, 1989) strongly confirmed the prediction concerning secure attachment and empathy. In addition, responses of those with histories of avoidant attachment (rooted in histories of chronic rebuff when the infant expresses tender needs) either involved ignoring and simply walking away or were precisely "anti-empathic"; that is, the child's reaction maximized the other's distress (e.g., hitting a child in the stomach who complained of a stomach ache). (Measures of infant temperament were not related to these peer competence measures, and IQ was controlled by group matching in subject selection for the preschool.)

Caregiving history also was powerfully related to targeted aspects of peer competence in middle childhood (see Table 11.6). Thus, those with secure histories, compared to those with anxious attachment histories, were almost twice as likely (83% vs. 47%) to form friendships in the camps (usually with others having secure histories). Moreover, their friendships had greater saliency (they spent more time with their particular friend). Those with secure histories were also observed to spend more time in groups of three or more children, commonly engaged in organized activities (building a fort, setting up a shop; Hiester, Carlson, & Sroufe, 1993). Further, they were better able to coordinate friendships with group participation, and were rated higher on maintaining gender boundaries (and lower on violating

TABLE 11.6
Correlations Between Family Support and Social Competence Outcome Measures for the
Subsample and Total Sample

	Attachment Security (n)	Early History Composite (n)	Family Support (n)
	12 - 18 Months	12 - 42 Months	13 Years
Subsample			
Preschool teacher ratings	.31 (41)	.47** (41)	.37* (38)
Camp indices (10 years)			
Friendship score	.30[a] (47)	.55** (47)	.31* (44)
Boundary maintenance rating	.43[a] (47)	.42** (47)	.24 (44)
Camp reunion indices (15 years)			
Social competence	.46[a] (41)	.44** (41)	.34* (40)
Capacity for vulnerability	.41[a] (41)	.38* (41)	.37* (40)
Adolescent parent/teacher composite score (16 years)	.37[a] (45)	.42** (45)	.25 (42)
Adolescent friendship interview (16 years)	.21 (44)	.41** (44)	.30* (42)
Total sample			
Preschool teacher ratings	.21 (84)	.36** (84)	.23* (75)
Elementary teacher rankings			
Early (K-1)	.09 (187)	.31** (190)	.17* (172)
Late (3-6)	.12 (188)	.38** (191)	.32** (173)
Total (1, 2, 3, 6)	.13 (189)	.35** (192)	.26** (173)
Adolescent parent/teacher composite score (16 years)	.20[a] (178)	.27** (181)	.16* (167)
Adolescent friendship interview (16 years)	.10 (170)	.25** (173)	.19* (156)

Note. Pearson product-moment correlations are two-tailed.
*$p < .05$. **$p > .01$. ***$p < .001$.

gender boundaries) than those with insecure histories (e.g., Elicker et al.,
1992; Shulman et al., 1994; Sroufe, Bennett, et al., 1993).

Attachment history, and early care more generally, also proved to be
strongly related to diverse measures of peer competence in adolescence,
up to 15 years after the infant assessments. These findings held for the
total sample, and even more strongly for the more adequately assessed
subsample (see Table 11.6). For the subsample, counselor ratings of global
competence and ratings targeted at features of competence specific to
adolescence all were significant. One key rating, "capacity for vulnerability,"

tapped the teen's ability to capitalize on the range of relationship opportunities available at the weekend retreat. It was clearly related to attachment history ($r = .41$).

These counselor rating findings were corroborated by interview-based assessments of the adolescent's knowledge of the social network (Weinfield, Ogawa, & Sroufe, 1997) and by detailed behavioral data. For example, all eight teenagers who formed couple relationships during the retreats had been securely attached, and a significantly greater percentage of those who became part of established mixed-gender "crowds" also had secure attachment histories (Sroufe, Carlson, & Shulman, 1993).

In a recent dissertation based on the camp reunion (Englund, 1997), assessments were made of functioning in small and larger group problem-solving situations. This was a "revealed differences" format, in which the group had to decide how to spend $150 in the ensuing segments of the retreat, then carry forward their plan to the larger group, working out a shared solution. Blind ratings of videotaped behavior revealed that those with secure histories were more competent overall and were rated higher in self-confidence and leadership. They were also significantly more likely to be elected spokesperson for their group.

THE ROLE OF FAMILY RELATIONSHIPS AND PEER EXPERIENCES IN SOCIAL COMPETENCE

The final empirical issue concerns whether family experiences and peer experiences are complementary in promoting later social competence. Do peer experiences add to the prediction of middle childhood and adolescent peer competence over and above that predicted by attachment history and other family experience? Is there support for a developmental model in which attachment history promotes successful entry into the peer group, with peer experiences then supporting the developmental trajectory toward later social competence? We examine specifically whether there is a cumulative impact of ongoing experience and whether pathways to competence vary depending on the particular aspect of competence outcome assessed. We conducted a series of multiple regressions, using different combinations of variables, to address these questions.

Early Parent–Child and Preschool Peer Experiences as Predictors of Middle Childhood Peer Competence

The major hypothesis here was supported in that both attachment (or early parenting history more generally) and preschool peer competence independently predicted broad aspects of competence in middle childhood

TABLE 11.7
Hierarchical Regression Predicting Social Competence in Middle Childhood and Adolescence

	R^2				Overall		
Independent Variables	Change	Beta	B	T	R^2	F	df

I. Prediction of friendship score in middle childhood for subsample.

		Change	Beta	B	T	R^2	F	df
A.	1. Infant attachment (12–18 month attachment)	.13	.35	.06	2.35*	.13	5.54*	1, 39
	2. Infant attachment		.20	.03	1.44			
	Preschool ratings (4 years)	.24	.51	.05	3.75***	.36	10.71***	2, 38
B.	1. Early parental care (12–18 month attachment, 24-, 30-, 42-month parental care)	.27	.52	.11	3.76***	.27	14.14***	1, 39
	2. Early parental carae		.32	.07	2.24*			
	Preschool ratings	.14	.42	.04	2.97**	.40	12.89***	2, 38

II. Prediction of counselor rankings of adolescent social competence for the subsample.

		Change	Beta	B	T	R^2	F	df
A.	1. Infant attachment	.21	.46	7.73	3.22**	.21	10.37**	1, 39
	2. Infant attachment		.38	2.39	2.66*			
	Camp friendship score	.08	.30	27.70	2.08*	.25	7.80***	2, 38
B.	1. Early parental care	.19	.44	9.84	3.04**	.19	9.25**	1, 39
	2. Early parental care		.31	7.00	1.78			
	Cano friendship score	.03	.22	20.43	1.24	.22	5.46**	2, 38

*$p < .05$. **$p < .01$. ***$p < .001$.

(friendship scores at camp, camp ratings, and teacher rankings in elementary school), with multiple correlations ranging from the high .40s to .60 (Table 11.7). Multiple regression analyses showed that attachment continued to predict middle childhood competence even after the effects of preschool competence were taken into account. Attachment security supports the emergence of preschool peer competence and yet continues to make a unique contribution to the more personal relationships of middle childhood and to competence with peers in the school setting. At the same time, preschool peer competence made a unique contribution to later social competence. Peer competence in middle childhood reflected the convergence of family and peer experiences.

Follow-up regression analyses of these data yielded somewhat different results using attachment and the broader early history variable as measures of early parental care (parenting from 12–42 months; see Table 11.3 for definition). With the early history variable all three predictions were significant (early history to preschool, preschool to middle childhood, and early history to middle childhood). Using the attachment variable, the attachment to preschool prediction no longer attains significance, but attachment to middle childhood does, and preschool also still predicts middle childhood.

It is important to note that for one aspect of peer competence in middle childhood—gender boundary maintenance—only attachment history (or the broader measure of early care) accounted for significant variance in the regression analyses. Thus, preschool competence, at least as assessed, was not relevant to this emergent aspect of competence. Individual differences in gender boundary maintenance seem to be more a product of parent–child relationships (though, of course, the normative developmental issue is strongly defined by peers).

Early Competence and Middle Childhood Peer Competence as Predictors of Adolescent Peer Competence

The developmental picture here is complex. Middle childhood competence measures consistently do predict adolescent assessments in simple correlations (see Table 11.5). They do add to predictions of adolescent competence after taking into account attachment history (Table 11.7). However, when they are combined in regression analyses with attachment *and* preschool variables they are in many cases no longer significant. Thus, none of our middle childhood *camp* measures added to predictions of our camp reunion outcomes at age 15. However, teacher-based ratings at *elementary school*, especially for Grades 3 to 6, did make a significant contribution to both ratings of general social competence (F change $[3, 31] = 7.08$, R^2 change $= .12$, $p < .05$) and capacity for vulnerability (F change $[3, 31] = 4.51$, R^2 change $= .08$, $p < .05$) in the reunion, raising the multiple correlation from the mid .60s to .70. This, of course, suggests greater overlap of our assessments in the social settings of preschool and summer camp, rather than weakness of the camp measures. Again, the latter show substantial correlations with adolescent outcomes in simple correlations.

Still, the power of early experience with peers *and* caregivers is noteworthy. By age 5, much of the variance in adolescent social competence can be accounted for. Even though numerous capacities are only nascent or not at all apparent in the preschool period (e.g., coordinated group activities, intimacy), the motivational and emotional qualities that are present early predict well to competence with peers throughout the juvenile period. Moreover, much that remains to develop in the peer domain is forecast by infant attachment security and other aspects of early parent–child support.

Middle Childhood Peer Competence and Early Adolescent Parent–Child Relationships as Predictors of Adolescent Peer Competence

Results here are parallel to those in the preceding section. Thus, whereas assessments of parent–child relationships in early adolescence (age 13) modestly predict competence with peers 2 or 3 years later, they generally do not add to variance already accounted for by middle childhood peer competence assessments (multiple correlations in the .40s to .60s). There was one interesting exception. When social competence at summer camp (e.g., the composite friendship and gender boundary maintenance variable at age 10) was entered first in predicting ratings of capacity for relationship vulnerability in adolescence, the Family Balance I/Security score at age 13 (see Table 11.3 for definition) did add significant variance (F change [2, 37] = 4.43, R^2 change = .08, $p < .05$). This variable also predicted friendship intimacy at age 16, based on an interview (Ostoja-Starzewska, 1996). Thus, it seems that family experience continues to influence aspects of peer competence centered on trust, vulnerability, or freedom to experience emotion and emotional closeness.

DISCUSSION

Hartup (1980) anticipated these data two decades ago when he theorized that the parent–child and peer relationship systems are complementary. Attachment history, early care, and early peer experiences converge to predict later social competence, with peer experience making an independent contribution by the preschool period. Taken together, such predictions can be quite strong using highly reliable assessments, with multiple correlations in the .60s to .70. Later parenting experience also supports peer experience in predicting certain aspects of later competence.

Moreover, Hartup was correct in suggesting that early parent–child relationships "set the stage" for successful entry into the peer group and for negotiating specific age-related competence issues. This is the conclusion from the strong correlations between attachment security (and early caregiving history) and preschool peer competence and from the regression analysis results showing that attachment predicts specific age-related issues (e.g., friendship and gender boundary maintenance in middle childhood; capacity for relationship vulnerability in adolescence), even after preschool peer competence (or middle childhood competence) is taken into account; that is, there is a direct as well as an indirect effect of attachment on peer competence in middle childhood and adolescence.

When peer competence is viewed as a developmental system, integrated with family experiences, a particular perspective on peer relationships emerges. Our perspective differs somewhat from that of others (e.g., Furman & Wehner, 1994) in stressing a dynamic, epigenetic view of peer relationships. Peer experiences are not simply added on to parenting experiences but develop within the context they provide. Those with secure histories are better able to embrace the opportunities provided by the peer world. They eagerly, and in an emotionally flexible manner, join the preschool playgroup; they seek the closeness of special friendships in middle childhood and maintain age-appropriate gender boundaries; and they are capable of the emotional vulnerability inherent in self-disclosing adolescent relationships. They have experienced reciprocal and mutual relating previously and can therefore readily master the challenge of maintaining autonomy within the connectedness of the group setting, as well as maintain boundaries between and coordinate various relationships.

Those with histories of anxious attachment often find such challenges daunting or beyond understanding. They do not expect others to be positively engaging (e.g., Suess, Grossmann, & Sroufe, 1992), they do not understand emotional closeness, or they are overwhelmed by the emotional arousal that is inevitably attendant upon relating to peers (Pancake, 1988; Sroufe et al., 1984). This may take the form of self-isolation (Elicker et al., 1992; Sroufe, 1983), antipathy to others (Kestenbaum et al., 1989), exclusivity in friendships or oscillation between allegiance to friends or group loyalty (Shulman et al., 1994), and preoccupation with teachers or counselors (Sroufe, Fox, & Pancake, 1983; Urban, Carlson, Egeland, & Sroufe, 1991).

Thus, peer experiences cannot easily compensate for attachment or other parenting experiences, because the very children most in need of positive peer experiences are those least likely to have them. Expecting others to be rejecting or interpreting their actions as rejecting and turning away prevents children from learning that peers will reciprocate. When associated with aggressive behavior, such expectations actually lead to rejection (Crick & Dodge, 1994; Suess et al., 1992). Being preoccupied with bringing needs for tenderness to teachers likewise precludes rehabilitative peer experiences. Eschewing the closeness of friendships removes the base for self-disclosure, and a jealous, clinging friendship can separate children from the group experiences where much is learned about norm-governed behavior, problem solving, and coordinated behavior. Being unable to modulate emotion makes all aspects of peer relationships unduly challenging, especially sustaining closeness in the face of conflict and tolerating the stimulation of group activities.

For most children there is a cascading effect, wherein early family relationships provide the necessary support for effectively engaging the world of peers, which, in turn, provides the foundation for deeper and more extensive and complex peer relationships. Each phase supports the unfolding of subsequent capacities.

CONCLUSION: A DEVELOPMENTAL PERSPECTIVE
ON SOCIAL RELATIONSHIPS

An elaborated developmental view is supported by these findings. Each phase of peer competence builds on earlier peer experience and, yet, continues to be dependent on attachment history and other aspects of early parent–child support. Moreover, although it was generally the case that social competence drew on both experiences with peers and experiences with parents, certain aspects of competence draw more heavily upon one domain or the other. For example, friendship competence in middle childhood was more strongly related to earlier peer experiences ($r = .57$) than to attachment history ($r = .30$), although each relationship was significant. In contrast, gender boundary maintenance was less strongly related to earlier peer competence ($r = .30$) than it was to attachment history ($r = .43$).

Both family support and peer experiences underlie developing aspects of social competence, but in differing ways and to various degrees. Certain aspects, while relying on the emotional base of early parenting experience, apparently require more practicing and elaboration in interaction with peers. Thus, special friendships and group leadership are features of emerging competence that are strongly related to earlier assessments of peer behavior. Other features, such as gender boundary maintenance, while necessitated by peer group encounters, seem to be more strongly related to attachment history. Gender boundary maintenance itself strongly predicted capacity for relationship vulnerability in adolescence, which was not as strongly related to other aspects of prior peer competence (but was related to attachment history and ongoing security in the family).

Masten and her colleagues (Masten et al., 1995) argue that certain features of adolescent peer competence are emergents; that is, they are not predicated on earlier aspects of peer competence. They point in particular to "romantic competence," arguing that it is not related to earlier peer competence. Some of our findings are similar. However, issues here are complicated and caution is in order. Our own work suggests that even emergent capacities are not without support. Some of this may be discerned only with a broad net of earlier peer competence measures, and some support for emerging capacities may come from earlier experiences outside of the peer domain. In particular, peer issues regarding interpersonal boundaries and trust or intimacy (crucial to romantic competence) may have their foundations in the history of trusting, emotionally supportive relationships with parents.

A strong test of this notion is forthcoming as our ongoing longitudinal study is now focused on young adult romantic relationships, assessed both through interview and behavioral observation. We suspect that again both earlier peer experiences (especially those concerned with boundary maintenance, capacity for vulnerability, and intimacy) and parental emotional support, including attachment history, will prove to be important foundations for effective adult relationships. With regard to intimacy aspects of these relationships, attachment security and subsequent experiences of family closeness may play an especially important role, as has been suggested by others (e.g., Kerns, 1996; Owens, Crowell, Pan, Treboux, O'Connor, & Waters, 1996). It may be that attachment history may be more strongly related to qualitative assessments of adult intimacy than it was to our assessments of individual friendships in middle childhood and adolescence.

REFERENCES

Crick, N., & Dodge, K. (1994). A review and reformulation of social information-processing mechanisms in children's social adjustment. *Psychological Bulletin, 115,* 74–101.

Edwards, C., & Whiting, B. (1977). *Patterns of dyadic interaction.* Paper presented at the biennial meetings of the Society for Research in Child Development, April, New Orleans.

Egeland, B., Carlson, E., & Sroufe, L. A. (1993). Resilience as process. *Development and Psychopathology, 5,* 517–528.

Elicker, J., Englund, M., & Sroufe, L. A. (1992). Predicting peer competence and peer relationships in middle childhood from early parent-child relationships. In R. Parke & G. Ladd (Eds.), *Family-peer relationships: Modes of linkage* (pp. 77–106). Hillsdale, NJ: Lawrence Erlbaum Associates.

Englund, M. (1997). *The contribution of family and peer relationships to the development of social competence in adolescence.* Unpublished doctoral dissertation, University of Minnesota.

Furman, W., & Wehner, E. (1994). Romantic views: Toward a theory of adolescent romantic relationships. In R. Montemayor (Ed.), *Advances in adolescent development, Vol. 3: Relationships in adolescence* (pp. 168–195). Newbury Park, CA: Sage.

Harlow, H., & Harlow, M. (1965). The affectional systems. In A. Schrier, H. Harlow, & F. Stollnitz (Eds.), *Behavior of non-human primates* (pp. 57–74). New York: Academic Press.

Hartup, W. (1980). Peer relations and family relations: Two social worlds. In M. Rutter (Ed.), *Scientific foundations of developmental psychiatry* (pp. 280–292). London: Heinemann.

Hartup, W., & Laursen, B. (1994). Conflict and context in peer relations. In C. Hart (Ed.), *Children on playgrounds: Research perspectives and applications* (pp. 44–84). Ithaca: State University of New York Press.

Hayes, A. (1984). Interaction, engagement, and the origins of communication: Some constructive concerns. In L. Feagans, C. Garvey, & R. Golinkoff (Eds.), *The origins and growth of communication* (pp. 136–161). Norwood, NJ: Ablex.

Hiester, M., Carlson, E., & Sroufe, L. A. (1993). *The evolution of friendships in preschool, middle childhood, and adolescence: Origins in attachment history.* Paper presented at the biennial meeting of the Society for Research in Child Development, April, New Orleans.

Kestenbaum, R., Farber, E., & Sroufe, L. A. (1989). Individual differences in empathy among preschoolers: Concurrent and predictive validity. In N. Eisenberg (Ed.), *Empathy and related emotional responses: New directions for child development* (pp. 51–56). San Francisco: Jossey-Bass.

Kerns, K. (1996). Individual differences in friendship quality: Links to child-mother attachment. In W. Bukowski, A. Newcomb, & W. Hartup (Eds.), *The company they keep* (pp. 137–157). New York: Cambridge University Press.

Masten, A., Coatsworth, J. D., Neeman, J., Gest, S., Tellegen, A., & Garmezy, N. (1995). The structure and coherence of competence from childhood through adolescence. *Child Development, 66,* 1635–1659.

Ostoja-Starzewska, E. (1996). *Developmental antecedents of friendship competence in adolescence: The roles of early adaptational history and middle childhood peer competence.* Unpublished doctoral dissertation, University of Minnesota.

Owens, G., Crowell, J., Pan, H., Treboux, D., O'Connor, E., & Waters, E. (1996). The prototype hypothesis and the origins of attachment working models: Adult relationships with parents and romantic partners. In E. Waters, B. Vaughn, G. Posada, & K. Kondo-Ikemura (Eds.), *New growing points of attachment. Monographs of the Society for Research in Child Development. Serial No. 244, Vol. 60,* pp. 216–233.

Pancake, V. (1988). *Quality of attachment in infancy as a predictor of hostility and emotional distance in preschool peer relationships.* Unpublished doctoral dissertation, University of Minnesota.

Shulman, S., Elicker, J., & Sroufe, L. A. (1994). Stages of friendship growth in preadolescence as related to attachment history. *Journal of Social and Personal Relationships, 11,* 341–361.

Sroufe, L. A. (1983). Infant-caregiver attachment and patterns of adaptation in the preschool. In M. Perlmutter (Ed.), *The Minnesota symposia on child psychology* (Vol. 16, pp. 41–83).

Sroufe, L. A. (1988). The role of infant-caregiver attachment in development. In J. Belsky & T. Nezworski (Eds.), *Clinical implications of attachment* (pp. 18–38). Hillsdale, NJ: Lawrence Erlbaum Associates.

Sroufe, L. A. (1996). *Emotional development.* New York: Cambridge University Press.

Sroufe, L. A., Bennett, C., Englund, M., Urban, J., & Shulman, S. (1993). The significance of gender boundaries in preadolescence: Contemporary correlates and antecedents of boundary violation and maintenance. *Child Development, 64,* 455–466.

Sroufe, L. A., Carlson, E., & Shulman, S. (1993). Individuals in relationships: Development from infancy through adolescence. In D. Funder, R. Parke, C. Tomlinson-Keasey, & K. Widman (Eds.), *Studying lives through time: Personality and development* (pp. 315–342). Washington, DC: American Psychological Association.

Sroufe, L. A., Cooper, R., & DeHart, G. (1996). *Child development: Its nature and course* (3rd ed.). New York: McGraw-Hill.

Sroufe, L. A., & Fleeson, J. (1986). Attachment and the construction of relationships. In W. Hartup & Z. Rubin (Eds.), *Relationships and development* (pp. 51–71). Hillsdale, NJ: Lawrence Erlbaum Associates.

Sroufe, L. A., Fox, N., & Pancake, V. (1983). Attachment and dependency in developmental perspective. *Child Development, 54,* 1615–1627.

Sroufe, L. A., Schork, E., Motti, F., Lawroski, N., & LaFreniere, P. (1984). The role of affect in social competence. In C. Izard, J. Kagan, & R. Zajonc (Eds.), *Emotions, cognition, and behavior* (pp. 289–319). Oxford, England: Oxford University Press.

Suess, G., Grossmann, K., & Sroufe, L. A. (1992). Effects of infant attachment to mother and father on quality of adaptation in preschool: From dyadic to individual organization of the self. *International Journal of Behavioral Development, 15,* 43–66.

Thorne, B. (1986). Boys and girls together . . . but mostly apart: Gender arrangements in elementary schools. In W. Hartup & Z. Rubin (Eds.), *Relationships and development* (pp. 167–184). Hillsdale, NJ: Lawrence Erlbaum Associates.

Troy, M., & Sroufe, L. A. (1987). Victimization among preschoolers: Role of attachment relationship history. *Journal of the American Academy of Child and Adolescent Psychiatry, 26,* 166–172.

Urban, J., Carlson, E., Egeland, B., & Sroufe, L. A. (1991). Patterns of individual adaptation across childhood. *Development and Psychopathology, 3,* 445–460.

Weinfield, N., Ogawa, J., & Sroufe, L. A. (1997). Early attachment as a pathway to adolescent peer competence. *Journal of Research in Adolescence, 7,* 241–265.

Chapter **12**

Siblings, Friends, and the Development of Social Understanding

Judy Dunn
Institute of Psychiatry, London, England

Two themes in Hartup's research and writing stand out for me as especially generative and important for developmental psychologists. The first theme is at a very general, theoretical level. His writing on the conceptual issues involved in thinking about the links between relationships and children's development has a key and distinctive place in the field (e.g., Hartup, 1983, 1992, 1996). For much too long there has been a real separation between those who study the nature of relationships and those who are interested in children's developing cognitive and social capacities. Hartup has consistently presented a coherent framework within which the connections between relationships, cognitive and socioemotional development, and children's well-being can be thought about and studied, and has given us the key questions that need to be asked. The second theme of major importance for developmentalists is his focus on child–child interaction and relationships—most recently his work on friendships (e.g., Hartup, 1996). His emphasis on individual differences in friendship quality, for instance, is surely timely. The demonstration that it is not so much whether you have a friend, but the *kind* of friendship you have that matters, in terms of developmental influence, is just one of a series of important insights that deserve our attention.

In this chapter I take up these two themes in his work—the links between relationships and development, and the significance of child–child relationships—with particular focus on children's developing understanding of others and the social world. There has been over the past decade a remarkable burst of interest among cognitive psychologists in children's understanding of mental life and its relation to people's behavior; this new work has special significance for those interested in young children's social relationships (Astington, 1995; Perner, 1991; Wellman, 1990). The research has documented major changes between the ages of 2 and 5 years in children's comprehension of emotions and mental states and of the significance of feelings, desires, and beliefs to action.

The goal of this chapter is to examine and summarize findings from our own research concerning links between these aspects of children's developing social understanding in early childhood and their sibling and friend relationships. We focus on social understanding as reflected both in formal assessments of children's "mindreading" abilities and emotion understanding, and in aspects of real-life interaction with others that reflect their understanding of those others' intentions, desires, and feelings, ideas or plans. (The term *mindreading* is used here, as it is in the cognitive developmental literature, to refer to children's capacity to understand another's beliefs, thoughts, intentions, desires, and so forth.) Specifically, children's explicit discussion of mental states, their engagement in a shared imaginative world, their ability to take account of others' perspective in conflict, and their connected communication with others are discussed as illustrative examples.

The chapter is organized around three general questions: First, is there evidence for associations between child–child relationships and the development of social understanding? Both normative development and individual differences are discussed. Second, what social processes are implicated in such associations? Third, can we come to conclusions about the direction of effects in these connections between relationships and developing understanding?

The Pennsylvania Study of Social Understanding

In what follows the focus is chiefly on findings from a longitudinal research program in Pennsylvania (Dunn, Brown, Slomkowski, Tesla, & Youngblade, 1991; Dunn, 1995; Slomkowski & Dunn, 1996). Children's social understanding, and relationships with parents, siblings, and friends were examined in a group of 50 children followed from the preschool period through the early school years. Reference is also made to studies in Cambridge, England, in which families were followed for 7 years, from early childhood to adolescence (Dunn, Slomkowski, & Beardsall, 1995). The design of the Pennsylvanian study is outlined in Table 12.1. A combination of naturalistic observations of family interaction in the home, standardized assessments of language and sociocognitive development, and interviews with parents and children concerning close relationships and school experiences was used.

TABLE 12.1
Outline of Procedures

	Time 1	Time 2	Time 3	Time 4	Time 5
Child Age	*33m*	*40m*	*47m*	*67m*	*72m*
Observations					
Child, Mother, Sibling	X		X		
Child, Friend			X		X
Sociocognitive Measures					
Emotion Understanding[a]		X		X	
Mindreading[b]		X	X		
Moral Orientation[c]				X	

[a]*Emotion Understanding:* At 40 months, Denham's (1986) procedures were used. At 67 months, those of Gordis et al. (1989) were used. See Brown and Dunn (1996) for details.
[b]*Mindreading:* Bartsch and Wellman's (1989) procedures for assessing children's understanding of the connection between belief and action (false belief tests) were used. See Dunn, Brown, and Maguire (1995).
[c]*Moral Orientation:* Kochanska's (1991) procedures were adapted for 5 to 6 years olds, see Dunn, Brown, and Maguire (1995).

Sample and Procedures. The families were recruited from sequential birth announcements in a local newspaper. They were predominantly Caucasion and included a wide range of socioeconomic backgrounds. During the family observations (at 33 and 47 months), family conversation was audiotaped, and paper and pencil narrative notes were made. All family members were free to move about the home and carry on their usual routines. The observer targeted her observations on the secondborn child and recorded details of the social context, pretend play, and conflict incidents. Shortly after the observation, she prepared a detailed transcript of the observation, including all family talk and the nonverbal record. The child–friend observations (at 47 and 72 months) were also unstructured. Child and friend were asked to play alone in the child's bedroom or family room; they were provided with a variety of "dress up" clothes and other toys, and an audiotape recorder was left in the room to record their conversation (see Gottman, 1983). Standarized assessments of social understanding were made at 40, 47, and 67 months, as shown in Table 12.1. The children's language development was assessed. (For further details of the sample, methods, and procedures, see Dunn, Brown, Slomkowski, Tesla, & Youngblade, 1991.)

The transcripts at 47 months were coded for the following: *Conflict* incidents (see later, and Slomkowski & Dunn, 1992); *discourse about mental states* (see later, and Brown, Donelan-McCall, & Dunn, 1996). At 72 months, the transcripts were coded for *connectedness* of communication (see later, and Slomkowski & Dunn, 1996), and *conflict strategies* and *resolution* (see later, and Appendix).

ASSOCIATIONS BETWEEN CHILD–CHILD RELATIONSHIPS AND THE DEVELOPMENT OF SOCIAL UNDERSTANDING

The first issue concerns the possible association between children's close relationships with other children, and their understanding of mind and emotion.

In the rapidly growing field of research into these aspects of social cognition, studies of children's peer interactions have a place of special significance. The idea that particular social partners may play distinctive roles in the development of social understanding was originally considered by Piaget (1965), who argued that interaction with peers was of special importance in the growth of moral understanding. We consider here first, findings that describe *normative developmental changes* in children's sophistication concerning inner states as reflected in their interaction with different social partners—adults and children. Second, we consider research describing *individual differences* in children's social experiences with other children and their links with differences in mindreading and emotion understanding.

Normative Patterns of Change and Partner Differences

Children's growing interest in and understanding of why people behave as they do, and their curiosity about mental states and emotions is reflected in marked developmental changes in their discourse about inner states (Bartsch & Wellman, 1995; Brown & Dunn, 1992; Dunn, 1988). In the research conducted in Pennsylvania we examined the conversations about feelings and mental states in which the children engaged with family members and alone with their close friends, as 33-, 40- and 47-month olds. Some striking differences in the pattern of developments in this discourse with different social partners were found. Children referred to mental states markedly more frequently in conversation with their siblings and their friends than they did with their mothers (Brown, Donelan-McCall, & Dunn, 1996). Moreover the children were more likely to refer to *shared* thoughts and ideas when they were with siblings or friends than when they were with their mothers (with whom they chiefly discussed their own mental states). It appeared that the context of establishing and maintaining play with a close friend was one that was especially likely to foster the discussion of feelings, thoughts, beliefs, and memories.

Our examination of how children argued during conflict with different social partners established a parallel point. During conflict with *friends,* children were more likely to take account of the other person's goals, perspectives to offer compromise, or negotiation to resolve the conflict with reason and justification than they were when in conflict with mothers or siblings. Sophisticated reasoning can, of course, be used either to resolve conflict with an antagonist, or to gain one's own ends. The children's argumentative moves in conflict at 47 months were categorized in a three-way fashion that distinguished speaker turns in which the children (a) provided no justification or reasoning for their position ("no argument"), (b) provided justification or reasoning that the children used to gain their own ends ("self-oriented" moves), (c) provided justification or reasoning that through compromise or conciliation took account of the other's perspective toward resolution of the disagreement ("other-oriented" moves). At 47 months, the children were twice as likely to make other-oriented moves in disputes with their friends as they were to do so in conflict with their siblings or mothers.

As Table 12.2 shows, the mean proportion of speaker turns in conflict with friends that were other-oriented was 21% (*SD* 13%), as compared with 8% (*SD* 14%) and 9% (*SD* 9%) of turns with mother and sibling respectively, a highly significant difference (Dunn, Slomkowski, Donelan-McCall, & Herrera, 1995).

Such mean differences in children's talk about inner states and in their management of conflict suggest that close relationships with other children may provide a particularly useful forum in which understanding others' inner states is encouraged. This view is strongly supported by the analyses of individual differences in these domains, which are briefly summarized next.

TABLE 12.2
Mean Proportion of Total Conflict Talk for Different Conflict Management Strategies at 47 Months

Other-Oriented	
Child to mother	.08 (.14)
Child to sibling	.09 (.09)
Child to friend	.21 (.13)
Self-Oriented	
Child to mother	.24 (.32)
Child to sibling	.17 (.14)
Child to friend	.31 (.18)[a]
No Argument	
Child to mother	.70 (.35)
Child to sibling	.70 (.21)
Child to friend	.48 (.18)[b]

[a]Child to friend significantly different from child to sibling at $p < .05$.
[b]Child to friend significantly different from child to mother and child to sibling at $p < .05$.

Individual Differences

A variety of different lines of research now have shown links between individual differences in social understanding and children's experience with other children. Children with siblings are reported to perform more successfully on mindreading tasks than children without siblings (Perner, Ruffman, & Leekham, 1994). Moreover, the number of siblings with whom children interact daily was found in another study to be positively correlated with success on mindreading tasks (Lewis, Freeman, Kyriakidou, & Maridaki-Kossotaki, 1995). Our own data show that it is not simply a matter of having other children around that is important, but that the quality of the child–child relationship is important. For instance, a key predictor of success on the assessments of mindreading and emotion understanding in the Pennsylvania study was the children's previous experience of cooperative play with their older siblings (Dunn et al., 1991), and engagement in joint pretend with an older sibling in particular appears to be important (Youngblade & Dunn, 1995). The analyses of the child–friend conversations about inner states (described earlier) showed, first, that both the length of their friendship and the frequency of their interaction were positively related to explicit reference to mental processes. The detailed examination of the conversational material showed that it was during playful cooperative interactions with their friends that children discussed mental processes especially frequently. Importantly, individual differences in the discussion of mental processes were correlated with differences in concurrent performance on the standard assessment of mindreading, the false belief tasks (Brown et al., 1996).Results from our ongoing study in London replicate these associations in a very different sample of inner-city families, of diverse ethnic groups, living in an extremely deprived area (Hughes & Dunn, 1997). The evidence on associations between conflict behavior and social understanding is also relevant here. The children whose siblings had engaged in frequent other-oriented reasoning in disputes during the 33-month observations, for instance, were more successful on the mindreading tasks than those whose sibling had not done so.

Such findings indicate that it is not simply *having a sibling around* that is key, but the kind of relationship and interaction in which the children engage that matters, in terms of developmental influence in this particular domain; the question of what social processes are implicated becomes then of particular interest.

Social Processes Implicated in These Associations

The examination of antecedents to these individual differences in the assessment of both mindreading and emotion understanding tasks in the Pennsylvania study supports the idea that certain experiences with other children are associated with increased understanding of inner states. Three general points concerning these social processes merit attention.

The first point is that a variety of different social processes appear to be implicated. The Pennsylvania study highlights a number of these. The links between social understanding and the sharing of a pretend world with another child, for instance, are not suprising: The important cognitive features of pretend, and their relation to children's theories of mind have been well characterized and studied by several authors (Harris & Kavanaugh, 1993; Leslie, 1987; Lillard, 1993). What the Pennsylvania results highlight is the *social* nature of pretend play. As Brown notes, "Children 'decouple' reality from fantasy (Leslie, 1987), and entertain multiple hypothetical realities (Perner, 1991) not as solitary cognitive exercises, but while negotiating the social interactions in which these cognitive states are shared" (Brown et al., 1996). And here it is important to note how different joint pretend play with a sibling or friend is from joint pretend with a mother: Our Cambridge studies showed that while mothers chiefly remained in a "spectator" role during joint pretend (offering advice and comment, but not sharing roles), siblings engaged in joint pretend as partners, both participating equally in the narrative and imaginary world (Dunn & Dale, 1984).

Somewhat different processes are implicated in the connections between the confrontation with another child over antagonistic goals, and with the discourse over inner states—each associated with children's understanding of other minds, and emotions. The study also showed that an independent contribution to the variance in success on these tasks was made by a quite different kind of variable: the frequency of interactions between mother and sibling that involved control (Dunn et al., 1991). This suggests that, as well as their more direct participation in interactions that involved sharing ideas or feelings, children's experiences of *observing interactions* between others with whom they share close relationships are linked to the differences in social understanding. Given that understanding other people is such a central feature of human development, we should not be surprised, perhaps, at the variety of experiences that appear to be related to its growth.

The second general point is that although it seems likely that child–child (as opposed to child–adult) interaction is especially formative, it is not clear which features of child–child interaction are of key importance. The claim that child–child interaction may be important in cognitive development contrasts, of course, with the two themes that have until now dominated the study of cognitive development: the Piagetian tradition, in which the child is primarily seen as a socially isolated thinker (but see Dunn, 1996), and more recently the Vygotskian perspective (Vygotsky, 1978). Although the Vygotskian view does take into account the part played by social and cultural influences on cognitive development, the focus has been limited chiefly to adult–child interactions and to relatively didactic, emotionally neutral encounters (see Feldman, 1992; Goodnow, 1990). Yet the evidence we have described here highlights the role of social interaction between friends (equals) and siblings (relative equals) in the growth of communication about and understanding of mental experience. At present we do not know whether what gives the child–child interaction its special significance is the equality of status between the children, the commonality of interests that they share which must lend particular salience to their interactions, the familiarity of the children with one another, or the affective quality of their interactions. Each or all of these may be important.

The third general point concerns the affective quality of the relationship—and of the particular interactions associated with sophisticated understanding. Our findings indicate what may be important in these interactions is not simply an emotionally neutral "meeting of minds," in which children are faced with another child's point of view, or to a new argument or idea. Rather, the results of our research highlight the point that the emotional and pragmatic nature of the interaction is also key to children's understanding of their partner's inner states, or at least to their *use* of such understanding. For instance, we find that the same child can show quite different powers of understanding-in-action depending on the pragmatics and emotional setting of the interaction. Thus children's sophistication of pretend play, their discourse about mental states, and their management of conflict all *differ* in their different close relationships—they are not correlated (Brown et al., 1996; Slomkowski & Dunn, 1992; Youngblade & Dunn, 1995). Although such data remind us that the emotional context is key to the use children make of their understanding and may well be key to the fostering of this understanding, many questions remain unanswered about this link. The data on child–child pretend play, for instance, suggests that the positive emotional setting, in which children are able to *play* with new ideas in a relaxed atmosphere, may be particularly conducive to fostering understanding. In contrast, the data on conflict management suggests that the emotional setting of disputes when children's own goals are frustrated (inevitably very different from the happy setting of joint pretend play) also can be one in which children's understanding and powers of argument are fostered (see Stein & Miller, 1993 for similar arguments). The general point that different social processes are implicated in the development of the broad capacities of mindreading and emotion understanding is underlined. What is in common across so many child–child interactions—and especially those between friends—is that they *matter* to the children; their emotional salience is unquestionable.

In summary, the evidence on children's experiences in joint pretend play, and in talking and arguing with friends and siblings contributes to a plausible argument that close relationships between children can provide a key context for fostering the development of understanding others' emotions and reading others' minds, and for developing key skills of negotiation and conflict resolution. But it is important to note that there is also growing evidence for links between early social understanding and the quality of later relationships between children. This evidence, summarized in the next section, raises the issue of whether or not we can make inferences about the direction of effects in the links between understanding and relationships.

Differences in Social Understanding and Later Relationships

We have so far considered the evidence for concurrent associations between children's social understanding and their interactions with siblings and friends, and the links between early social experiences with these others, and later understanding. The findings of our Pennsylvania study have also shown that the marked individual differences in children's early ability to read other minds, and to understand others' emotions are associated with a number of aspects of their *later* relationships with their friends and siblings. Three examples illustrate this pattern, namely the findings on the connectedness and coordination of communication between friends, on reconciliation and management of conflict between friends, and on the elaboration and sophistication of the shared pretend play in which they engage.

Connectedness of Communication With Friends. In his seminal work on young children's friendships, Gottman emphasized the key importance of children's ability to communicate in a connected way with their friends (1983; Gottman & Parker, 1986). Such connectedness is seen as reflecting both understanding of the perspective of the other, and an ability to coordinate one's own perspective with that of the other. Children who are able to communicate in a connected way with their friends are, it is assumed, tuned in to the other child's thoughts and desires. Gottman showed, indeed, that connectedness of communication was one of the strongest markers of whether initially unacquainted children became friends over time (Gottman & Parker, 1986). In our longitudinal study, then, we examined the possibility that individual differences in the mind-reading and emotion understanding tasks at 40 months were associated with differences in the children's connected communication with their friends as 4-year-olds (Slomkowski & Dunn, 1996). The taperecorded conversations between each child playing at home with his or her friend were analysed in terms of three indices: *connected turns* (episodes in the conversation coded as being logically related), *play turns* (connected turns in which children were playing a game together or engaged in joint activity), and *pretend turns* (turns in which children were engaged in shared pretend play). These three measures reflect a hierarchy in peer interaction in terms of the "demandingness" of the response required (Gottman, 1983) with connected conversation being the basic requirement for interaction, and coordinated play and pretend reflecting increasingly more sophisticated modes of interaction.

The conversations between the friend dyads showed a wide range of individual differences in the extent of each of these aspects of connected communication. And as Table 12.3 shows, differences in the social understanding measures at 40 months were correlated with each of the communication measures from the child–friend observations.

Conflict Resolution at 6 Years. The importance of differences in children's propensity to resolve conflicts amicably with their friends is frequently emphasised as key to the quality of their relationships (see for instance Gottman, 1983; Hartup, 1992). We were interested in whether children who had been relatively mature and sophisticated in their early understanding of another's perspective or feelings would, as 6- and 7-year-olds, be more able to play a constructive role in resolving conflicts with their friends than the children who had been less able to mind read, as 3-year-olds. There is evidence that sociocognitive skills are indeed implicated in the difficulties in social relations experienced by aggressive and rejected children (Asher & Coie, 1990), and problems in managing conflict play a key role here. Yet it is far from clear that such a pattern would apply within the normal range of individual differences in social relations, and indeed as we saw from the Cambridge research on young siblings (Dunn, 1988), skills of conflict management are by no means always used to resolve conflict, but may well be employed by children to gain their own goals at the expense of others.

The conflict incidents that took place during the observations of the children's interactions with their close friends as 6-year-olds, in their first-

TABLE 12.3
Correlations Between Social Understanding at 40 Months and Connected Communication
at 47 Months

	Social Understanding	
Connected Communication	*False Belief*	*Affective Aggregate*
Average length connected episode	.39*	.32
Average length coordinated play episode	.42**	.35*
Average length joint pretend play episode	.33*	.29

Note. Adapted from Slowkowski and Dunn (1996).
*p < .05. **p < .01.

grade year, were analyzed in terms of the strategies and resolution moves made by the children (see Appendix). The associations over time showed that the children who had been especially successful at the social understanding tasks made more attempt to negotiate and resolve conflicts in ways that took account of their friends' views and needs than the children who had not been so mature as 3-year-olds in the social cognition tasks (Table 12.4). It is interesting to note that the *frequency* of conflict between friends was unrelated to the assessments of early understanding. It was not how often children disagreed and quarrelled with their friends that was associated with their early mindreading and emotion understanding, but how they worked toward resolution (see also Katz, Kramer, & Gottman, 1992; Perry, Perry, & Kennedy, 1992). In fact, different aspects of early understanding predicted different features of how children handled their conflicts with their friends as 6-year-olds. Thus use of distraction as a move of conflict mitigation was linked to early mindreading, while submission to the friend at age six was associated with early concern with feelings and moral reparation, and not with early mindreading skills.

Links Between Early Social Understanding and Other People's Later Behavior to the Child. Finally, it was notable that early differences in the children's sociocognitive abilities were associated not only with differences in their own social behavior later, but with differences in the patterns of change over time in others' behavior toward them. So, for example, in families in which the children showed greater understanding of emotions and of other minds as 40-month-olds, their older siblings showed especially marked increases in reflective discussion and interaction with them (Dunn, Creps, & Brown, 1996). These differences in early social understanding, however, were not related to the patterns of change in emotional aspects of the siblings' or children's behavior. That is, a more sophisticated understanding of another family member's feelings and thoughts does not guarantee a more rapid decrease in the hostility or conflict expressed over

TABLE 12.4
Correlations Between Conflict Behavior at Time 5, and Earlier Social Understanding Measures

Conflict Measures	Emotion Understanding	False Belief
Compromise	-.10	.20
Request clarification	.05	.34*
Threats	-.36*	-.12
Distraction	.40*	.37*
Submission	.30	.40*
Frequency of conflict	-.03	.05

*p < .05.

the next few years. Between siblings, we are reminded, greater under-standing does not mean more harmony in the relationship.

CONCLUSIONS ABOUT DIRECTION OF EFFECTS

The data we have considered show first, that the quality of interaction between young siblings is linked to later social understanding, and second, that early differences in social understanding are linked to differences in the quality of children's relationships with their friends and siblings later. What conclusions about *causal* links, and the direction of effects can be drawn?

First, it is possible that a key contribution to the patterns of association over time is made by continuity in child characteristics. The measures of interaction between the 33-month-old children and their siblings (such as those of pretend, and of conflict management) could, for instance, be tapping individual differences in the children's early ability to understand others, well before they could succeed on the standard theory of mind tasks. Thus the association between the experience of joint pretend play with an older sibling and later mindreading task success could be explained by the continuity in mindreading abilities of the younger child. According to this account, the 33-month-old who can join successfully in joint pretend with an older sibling will later be the child who can cope successfully with a false belief task—and we are not in a position to conclude that the experiences of joint pretend per se contribute to the later mindreading skills, though this is of course a very plausible idea.

Other evidence, however, suggests that the story is likely to be much more complicated than simply a tale of continuities in child differences over time. Thus the evidence (described earlier) that differences in children's early mindreading abilities are associated with later differences *in how their siblings engage them in reflective commentary* is provocative and takes us beyond a simple child-continuity account. On both theoretical and common sense grounds it is reasonable to presume that conflict experiences, for instance, are likely to be associated with differences in social understanding both as causes and as sequelae, as are the experiences of joint pretend with friend or sibling. As Hartup (1996) reminds us, child differences may well interact with friend-ship experiences or sibling experiences in relation to developmental out-come, rather than either being main effects.

IMPLICATIONS AND CHALLENGES

Research on the links between children's close relationships with other children and their understanding is at an exciting stage. The following questions and challenges seem especially important for us to address:

1. How far should different aspects of early social understanding be differentiated? For instance, is it important to distinguish understanding feelings from the ability to appreciate others' perspectives and thoughts? If so, which aspects of early understanding are significant for which aspects of later relationships? Some provocative findings from our Pennsylvania study indicate that there are indeed different sequelae of these different aspects of understanding, but these findings should be replicated (Dunn, 1995).

2. How and why do siblings and friends differ in their developmental influence? The work of Azmitia and her colleagues (e.g., Azmitia & Hesser, 1993) is particularly relevant here. Our own results also highlight differences, and the lack of correlation between the *same child's* understanding-in-action as expressed with friend and sibling.

3. What role do different emotional experiences play in the associations between understanding and close relationships? How should we conceptualize the connections between early understanding of others; on the one hand the negative arousal of conflict and disputes, and on the other, the positive affective context of cooperative play? Are there developmental changes in the significance of the affective quality of child–child interactions for the growth of understanding? Evidence from our studies of conflict suggests that there may well be such changes, but that they may differ for children's relationships with siblings and friends. Two contrasting arguments have been put forward concerning understanding and emotion in conflict. The first is that children are more likely to marshall their powers of reasoned argument when they are angry or distressed (Eisenberg, 1992; Stein & Miller, 1993). The second is that when young children are upset and frustrated they are less likely to behave in a relatively mature way (Roberts & Strayer, 1987). The evidence from the Pennsylvania study supports the latter view, at least as far as the 33-month-old children's conflicts with their siblings are concerned.

Children were less likely to use other-oriented reasoning in conflict with their siblings when they were upset (Tesla & Dunn, 1992). However at 47 months in conflict with their siblings the children used reasoned argument (both other oriented and self-oriented) equally often when they were upset or not upset. It appears that there are developmental changes over the third and fourth years in the significance of children's emotional state for the way they act in disputes with their siblings. One conclusion from these data might be that at age 33 months the children were less able to draw on their skills of understanding and reasoning when they were upset, whereas at 47 months they were more able to marshall their powers of argument even when upset—that they were less at the mercy of the emotions than they had been as 2-year-olds.

But the evidence from the investigation of their conflict with friends tells a more complicated story. We examined the correlations between the

TABLE 12.5
Correlations Between Argument Type and Affect Expressed in Child–Friend Observation
(47 Months)

	Argument Type		
	Other Oriented	Self-Oriented	No Argument
Positive affect	.16	-.03	-.10
Negative affect	-.47*	.02	.33*

*p < .05.

different conflict management strategies and the emotions the children expressed throughout the observations of play with their friends (that is, in pretend play, conversations as well as in disputes). Here we found that the use of other-oriented argument was negatively correlated with the frequency of negative affect expressed within the friendship observations, and the incidence of conflict interactions in which the children gave no reasoned argument for their position was positively correlated with the negative affect in the observation (Table 12.5). That is, the children in those friendships in which a high level of negative affect was expressed were less likely to take the partner's perspective in disputes.

The general point that emerges from the evidence so far is that the significance of affective state differs for different relationships and different developmental stages, and for different arenas of social understanding (for further discussion see Dunn et al., 1996).

4. The issue of developmental change brings us to the final question: How longterm are the associations between social understanding differences and the quality of children's close friendships? It is striking that such major and dramatic developmental changes in children's understanding of others take place over the very age period in which their relationships with other children become so prominent. However, Hartup (1996) reminds us of the complexity of patterns of influence here, and of the need for caution in assuming developmental influences linked to children's relationships with their friends. His admonition that we should be sensitive to the variety and interactive nature of the developmental pathways in which close child–child relationships are implicated is surely one we should take seriously.

ACKNOWLEDGMENTS

The Pennsylvania Study of Social Understanding is supported by National Institute of Health Grant HD 23158; the Cambridge, England, research is supported by the Medical Research Council.

APPENDIX

Conflict Coding at 72 Months

Coding scheme developed by Herrera (1996).

Compromise/Bargaining: Child suggests a solution to the dispute that falls between the wishes of both children, or suggests an alternative solution that considers the partner's needs but does not necessarily require a compromise of the child's own wishes.

Request Clarification: Child requests clarification or justification on the partner's needs or views.

Threats: Serious or playful teasing used as a strategy, including rudeness, insults or bavado, and sarcasm.

Distraction: Child makes off-topic, neutral statement (found by Hartup, Laursen, Stewart, & Eastenson, 1988) to distinguish between friends and nonfriends; a strategy for diffusing conflicts without having to "give in").

Submission: Child yields to wishes of the other.

REFERENCES

Asher, S. R., & Coie, J. D. (1990). *Peer rejection in childhood.* Cambridge, England: Cambridge University Press.

Astington, J. (1995). *The child's discovery of the mind.* Cambridge, MA: Harvard University Press.

Azmitia, M., & Hesser, J. (1993). Why siblings are important agents of cognitive development: A comparison of siblings and peers. *Child Development, 64*, 430–444.

Bartsch, K., & Wellman, H. (1989). Young children's attribution of action to beliefs and desires. *Child Development, 60*, 946–964.

Bartsch, K., & Wellman, H. M. (1995). *Children talk about the mind.* Oxford, England: Oxford University Press.

Brown, J. R., & Dunn, J. (1996). Continuities in emotion understanding from 3 to 6 years. *Child Development, 67*, 789–802.

Brown, J. R., & Dunn, J. (1992). Talk with your mother or your sibling? Developmental changes in early family conversations about feelings. *Child Development, 63*, 336–349.

Brown, J. R., Donelan-McCall, N., & Dunn, J. (1996). Why talk about mental states? The significance of children's conversations with friends, siblings and mothers. *Child Development, 67*, 836–849.

Denham, S. A. (1986). Social cognition, prosocial behavior, and emotion in preschoolers: Contextual validation. *Child Development, 62*, 1352–1366.

Dunn, J. (1988). *The beginnings of social understanding.* Cambridge, MA: Harvard University Press.

Dunn, J. (1995). Children as psychologists: The later correlates of individual differences in understanding emotions and other minds. *Cognition and Emotion, 9*, 187–201.

Dunn, J. (1996). Children's relationships: Bridging the divide between social and cognitive development. *Journal of Child Psychology and Psychiatry, 37*, 507–518.

Dunn, J., Brown, J. R., & Maguire, M. (1995). The development of children's moral sensibility: Individual differences and emotion understanding. *Developmental Psychology, 31*, 649–659.

Dunn, J., Brown, J., Slomkowski, C., Tesla, C., & Youngblade, L. (1991). Young children's understanding of other people's feelings and beliefs: Individual differences and their antecedents. *Child Development, 62,* 1352–1366.

Dunn, J., Creps, C., & Brown, J. R. (1996). Children's family relationships between two and five: Developmental changes and individual differences. *Social Development, 5,* 230–250.

Dunn, J., & Dale, N. (1984). I a Daddy: 2-year-olds' collaboration in joint pretend with sibling and with mother. In I. Bretherton (Ed.), *Symbolic play: The development of social understanding* (pp. 131–158). San Diego, CA: Academic Press.

Dunn, J., Slomkowski, C. M., & Beardsall, L. (1994). Sibling relationships from the preschool period through middle childhood and early adolescence. *Developmental Psychology, 30,* 315–324.

Dunn, J., Slomkowski, C. M., Donelan-McCall, N., & Herrera, C. (1995). Conflict, understanding and relationships: Developments and differences in the preschool years. *Early Education and Development, 6,* 303–316.

Eisenberg, A. R. (1992). Conflicts between mothers and their young children. *Merrill-Palmer Quarterly, 38,* 21–43.

Feldman, C. F. (1992) The theory of theory of mind. *Human Development, 35,* 107–117.

Goodnow, J. J. (1990). The socialization of cognition: What's involved? In J. W. Stigler, R. A. Shweder, & G. Herdt (Eds.), *Cultural psychology* (pp. 259–286). Cambridge, England: Cambridge University Press.

Gordis, F. W., Rosen, A. B., & Grand, S. (1989, April). *Young children's understanding of simultaneous conflicting emotions.* Presentation at the biennial meetings of the Society for Research in Child Development, Kansas City, MO.

Gottman, J. M. (1983). How children become friends. *Monographs of the Society for Research in Child Development, 48*(3, Serial No. 201).

Gottman, J. M., & Parker, J. G. (1986). *Conversations of friends: Speculations on affective development.* Cambridge, England: Cambridge University Press.

Harris, P. L., & Kavanaugh, R. D. (1993). Young children's understanding of pretense. *Monographs of the Society for Research in Child Development, 48*(201).

Hartup, W. W. (1983). Peer relationships. In E. M. Hetherington (Ed.), *Handbook of child psychology, Vol. 4: Socialization, personality, and social development* (pp. 103–196). New York: Wiley.

Hartup, W. W. (1992). Conflict and friendship relations. In C. U. Shantz & W. W. Hartup (Ed.), *Conflict in child adolescent development* (pp. 176–215). Cambridge, England: Cambridge University Press.

Hartup, W. W. (1996). The company they keep: Friendships and their developmental significance. *Child Development, 67,* 1–13.

Hartup, W. W., Laursen, B., Stewart, M. I., & Eastensen, A. (1988). Conflict and the friendship relations of young children. *Child Development, 59,* 1590–1600.

Herrera, C. (1996). *Manual for coding of conflict incidents.* Unpublished manuscript, University of Michigan, Ann Arbor, MI.

Hughes, C., & Dunn, J. (1997). "Pretend you didn't know": Preschoolers' talk about mental states in pretend play. *Cognitive Development, 12,* 381–403.

Katz, L. F., Kramer, L., & Gottman, J. M. (1992). Conflict and emotions in marital, sibling, and peer relationships. In C. U. Shantz & W. W. Hartup (Eds.), *Conflict in child and adolescent development* (pp. 122–149). Cambridge, England: Cambridge University Press.

Kochanska, G. (1991). Socialization and temperament in the development of guilt and conscience. *Child Development, 62,* 1379–1392.

Lewis, C., Freeman, N. H., Kyriakidou, C., & Maridaki-Kossotaki, K. (1995, March). *Social influences on false belief access: Specific contagion or general apprenticeship?* Paper presented at the biennial meetings of the Society for Research in Child Development, Indianapolis, IN.

Leslie, A. (1987). Pretense and representation: The origins of "theory of mind." *Psychological Review, 94*, 412–426.

Lillard, A. S. (1993). Pretend play skills and the child's theory of mind. *Child Development, 64*, 348–371.

Perner, J. (1991). *Understanding the representational mind.* Cambridge, MA: MIT Press.

Perner, J., Ruffman, T., & Leekham, S. R. (1994). Theory of mind is contagious: You catch it from your sibs. *Child Development, 65*, 1228–1238.

Perry, D. G., Perry, L. C., & Kennedy, E. (1992). Conflict and the development of antisocial behavior. In C. U. Shantz & W. W. Hartup (Eds.), *Conflict in child and adolescent development* (pp. 301–329). Cambridge, England: Cambridge University Press.

Piaget, J. (1965). *The moral judgement of the child.* New York: Academic Press.

Roberts, W., & Strayer, J. (1987). Parents' responses to the emotional distress of their children: Relations with children's competence. *Developmental Psychology, 23*, 415–422.

Slomkowski, C., & Dunn, J. (1992). Arguments and relationships within the family: Differences in children's understanding disputes with mother and sibling. *Developmental Psychology, 28*, 919–924.

Slomkowski, C., & Dunn, J. (1996). Young children's understanding of other people's beliefs and feelings and their connected communication with friends. *Developmental Psychology, 32*, 442–447.

Stein, N., & Miller, C. (1993). The development of memory and reasoning skill in argumentative contexts: Evaluating, explaining, and generating evidence. In R. Glaser (Ed.), *Advances in instructional psychology* (Vol. 4, pp. 284–334). Hillsdale, NJ: Lawrence Erlbaum Associates.

Tesla, C., & Dunn, J. (1992). Getting along or getting your own way: The development of young children's use of argument in conflicts with mother and sibling. *Social Development, 1*, 107–121.

Vygotsky, L. (1978). *Mind in society: The development of higher psychological processes.* Cambridge, MA: Harvard University Press.

Wellman, H. M. (1990). *The child's theory of mind.* Cambridge, MA: MIT Press.

Youngblade, L. M., & Dunn, J. (1995). Individual differences in young children's pretend play with mother and sibling: Links to relationships and understanding of other people's feelings and beliefs. *Child Development, 66*, 1472–1492.

Chapter 13

Conflict and Averted Conflict in Preschoolers' Interactions With Siblings and Friends

Ganie B. DeHart
State University of New York at Geneseo

Children develop in the context of a network of relationships with adults and other children, both inside and outside the family, that expands and changes as they grow older. In the last two decades, tremendous progress has been made toward understanding how the different types of relationships in this network are themselves related. Hartup's (1979) map of childhood's social worlds continues to be elaborated and refined as researchers explore children's relationships with parents, siblings, and peers, charting the territorial overlaps, boundaries, and bridges between them. The mapping of children's various types of relationships with each other is very much an ongoing process; for example, we know a great deal about the terrain *within* sibling, peer, and friend relationships, but the connections *between* them have been much less clearly delineated.

In this chapter I examine the contrasts and linkages between children's sibling and peer relationships, concluding with a discussion of research my students and I are conducting on young children's conflicts and averted conflicts with their siblings and friends (DeHart, Konchalski, Keogh, & Miller, 1996; DeHart, Richardson, Petrelli, Laliberte, & Haseley, 1993). The unique pattern of cross-relationship similarities and differences between sibling and peer relationships makes them a particularly interesting setting for studying what young children carry from one relationship to another and the extent to which their social skills and interaction strategies are relationship-specific. The conflicts and averted conflicts that occur during children's interactions with siblings and friends can potentially reveal much about children's social skills and about the structure and quality of the relationships in which they occur.

SIMILARITIES AND DIFFERENCES BETWEEN SIBLING AND PEER RELATIONSHIPS

Predicting linkages between sibling and peer relationships requires an understanding of the similarities and differences between them—how they compare as contexts for interaction and development, and the extent to which they can serve similar functions. Children's friendships must also be differentiated from general peer relationships; these two types of relationships provide very different interactional contexts, and there is evidence that they are connected to sibling relationships in different ways (Mendelson, Aboud, & Lanthier, 1994; Stocker & Dunn, 1990).

Children's relationships with siblings, peers, and friends vary along three major dimensions—symmetry, closeness, and voluntariness (Laursen, Hartup, & Koplas, 1996). The dimension of symmetry measures the extent to which the partners in a relationship are on an equal footing. At one extreme are *asymmetrical* or *vertical* relationships, such as those between parents and children, which involve mainly *complementary* interactions. At the other extreme are *symmetrical* or *horizontal* relationships, such as those between same-aged peers, which involve predominantly *reciprocal* interactions (Hartup, 1989). Although sibling relationships are more symmetrical and reciprocal than parent–child relationships, they are also *less* symmetrical and more complementary than same-age peer relationships. The age difference between nontwin siblings produces inevitable differences in size, strength, power, knowledge, skills, and developmental status. Sibling relationships are thus a mixture of complementarity and reciprocity, occupying a unique position between adult–child relationships and peer relationships. Rather than being either truly vertical or truly horizontal, they may best be thought of as *diagonal* relationships, with steepness of slope depending on age gap and individual characteristics and gradually changing from nearly vertical in early childhood to nearly horizontal by the end of adolescence.

Through middle childhood, role asymmetry is evident in older siblings' tendency to initiate behaviors, manage, teach, and nurture, and younger siblings' tendency to imitate, be managed, learn, and accept nurturance. In contrast, peer interactions are more reciprocal, with both children initiating, imitating, teaching, and managing to about the same extent (Abramovitch, Corter, Pepler, & Stanhope, 1986; Brody, Stoneman, & MacKinnon, 1982; Whiting & Whiting, 1975). The content of children's interactions with siblings and peers is also affected by these differences in symmetry; for example, school-aged boys' play with friends often involves competitive physical activity, whereas their play with younger siblings is toy-centered (Stoneman, Brody, & MacKinnon, 1984). As sibling pairs grow older, their relationships become increasingly symmetrical (Buhrmester & Furman, 1990; Vandell, Minnett, & Santrock, 1987). Thus, in terms of symmetry, sibling relationships become more similar to peer relationships over time.

The dimension of closeness involves both psychological intimacy and the frequency and diversity of interactions between relationship partners (Laursen et al., 1996). Frequent, varied interactions form a basis for psychological closeness, although they do not guarantee that it will develop. In early childhood, siblings often spend more time with each other than with their parents or with children outside the family (Dunn, 1983). As a result, siblings are more familiar and predictable than peers, especially for young children—a difference that has many implications for the development and use of skills related to social understanding (Dunn & Munn, 1985). In early childhood, sibling relationships are more physically and psychologically intimate than peer relationships, but by adolescence intimacy is greater with friends than with siblings (Buhrmester & Furman, 1990). In part because of the closeness of their relationship, siblings often have particularly intense feelings toward each other, both positive and negative, resulting in interactions that are qualitatively different from those with peers (Dunn, 1983).

The dimension of voluntariness refers to the extent to which a relationship is chosen and structured by the partners. At one extreme are involuntary or *closed-field* relationships, which children do not choose and which are partially structured for them by law or custom (Berscheid, 1985). At the other extreme are voluntary or *open-field* relationships, which are freely chosen and in which a structure must be worked out by the partners. Although sibling relationships are clearly involuntary, peer relationships vary along this dimension; friendships are voluntary, but many peer relationships, such as those with classmates, are not (Maccoby, 1996). The duration of closed-field relationships is based on factors not controlled by the relationship partners, such as biology, law, institutional practice, and social custom; in contrast, the duration of open-field relationships depends to a large extent on how satisfying they are for the participants. Thus, sibling relationships are by definition more permanent than most peer relationships or friendships. At the same time, children are generally more concerned with maintaining a friendship than with maintaining a sibling relationship, inasmuch as friendships are based on choice and mutual liking, whereas sibling relationships are not. As a consequence, children report more reliable alliances *and* more conflict with siblings than with friends, and they show more prosocial behavior toward friends than toward siblings (Abramovitch et al., 1986; Furman & Buhrmester, 1985a).

To summarize, sibling relationships are less symmetrical and voluntary than peer or friend relationships, but similar to friendships in closeness, especially in early and middle childhood. General peer relationships are similar to friendships in symmetry, but not as close as friend or sibling relationships, and they vary in voluntariness. Friendships are the most voluntary of the three relationships and by adolescence the closest.

The complex pattern of differences and similarities among children's sibling, peer, and friend relationships suggests that they are not functionally equivalent for children. Instead, they are connected but distinct relationships with the potential for some overlapping functions. Interaction patterns based on the asymmetry of sibling relationships are not likely to transfer to more symmetrical relationships with peers. Behaviors that are acceptable in sibling relationships may be tolerated in some involuntary relationships with peers, but not in dealings with friends. Functions that require interpersonal closeness may be fulfilled by relationships with siblings or friends, but not by general peer relationships. Thus, the connections between sibling and peer relationships are likely to be different from those between sibling relationships and friendships.

LINKAGES BETWEEN SIBLING AND PEER RELATIONSHIPS

In the past 10 years, researchers have expressed heightened interest in linkages between relationships, both within families and between family and peer systems (Hinde & Stevenson-Hinde, 1988; Parke & Ladd, 1992). However, most of the attention has been focused on links between parent–child and peer relationships and between parent–child and sibling relationships. Less attention has been paid to links between sibling and peer relationships, even though sibling relationships are often assumed to provide a training ground for peer interaction or a bridge between parent–child and peer relationships (Hartup, 1979; McCoy, Brody, & Stoneman, 1994).

Past researchers have suggested several ways children's relationships with siblings, peers, and friends might be connected (Dunn, 1993). The simplest possibility is *behavioral continuity*, with similarity of behaviors or interaction strategies across the three relationships. Behavioral continuity could be produced either by transfer of behaviors learned in one relationship to another (Bank, Patterson, & Reid, 1996; McCoy et al., 1994), or by temperamental or personality characteristics that remain relatively constant across situations (Caspi & Elder, 1988).

A second possibility is *qualitative continuity*, in which quality is consistent across relationships but specific behaviors are not (Sroufe & Fleeson, 1988). Qualitative continuity could result from the transfer of social skills across relationships, from the operation of social cognitive factors, such as Bowlby's (1982) internal working models, or from the development of overall social competence in one relationship and its subsequent application in others.

It is also reasonable to hypothesize *discontinuity*, with highly relationship-specific behavior, little cross-relationship carryover, and the possibility of qualitative independence (Mendelson et al., 1994). Given the differences among sibling, peer, and friend relationships, many behavior patterns and interaction strategies that develop in sibling relationships may not readily transfer to relationships with peers.

A particular form of discontinuity is *compensation*, with quality varying inversely between relationships and little cross-relationship transfer of behaviors (Stocker & Dunn, 1990). Compensation can involve a positive relationship taking on the functions of a negative or missing relationship; for example, negative sibling relationships, or having no siblings, may push children to associate intensely with peers and to form close friendships. Conversely, warm, close sibling relationships may sometimes develop because other playmates are unavailable. However, inversion of quality between sibling and peer relationships does not necessarily imply compensatory effects. This type of discontinuity may also reflect interference between relationships; warm, close sibling relationships may make the formation of close peer relationships less likely, or the increasing importance of peers and the formation of close, lasting friendships in middle childhood and adolescence may push sibling relationships aside and negatively affect their quality.

Research on Sibling–Peer Linkages

The first evidence of connections between sibling and peer relationships came from studies comparing firstborns and laterborns or children with and without siblings on various measures of social competence and peer interaction. Miller and Maruyama (1976) found birth-order differences in others' perceptions of children's social competence, with laterborns rated as more popular by peers and more sociable and friendly by teachers than firstborns. Pepler, Corter, and Abramovitch (1982) found no differences in the day-care classroom and playground *behaviors* of preschoolers with and without older siblings, but some differences in other children's *reactions* to them. Specifically, more agonistic behaviors were directed to only children and more prosocial behaviors to children with older siblings. These findings suggest that having an older sibling can enhance a child's relationships with peers, but they provide no evidence for whether this enhancement involves transfer of specific behaviors or of more general social skills.

Studies focusing on direct carryover of specific behaviors from sibling to peer relationships have found limited evidence of continuity. In one home observation study (Abramovitch et al., 1986), 4- to 8-year-olds showed no carryover of prosocial, agonistic, or imitative behaviors between interactions with siblings and with peers. Another study of preschoolers (Berndt & Bulleit, 1985) found continuity between behavior at home with siblings and behavior in preschool with peers only for aggressiveness and time spent in unoccupied or onlooker behavior. However, children with siblings close to them in age also showed carryover of prosocial behavior and imitation, suggesting that behavior is more readily transferred to peer relationships from sibling relationships that are relatively symmetrical and therefore peer-like.

When behavioral continuity does occur, it often reflects a lack of social competence, as in aggressive or socially withdrawn behavior (Bank et al., 1996; Berndt & Bulleit, 1985). Social competence is assumed to produce flexibility and appropriate responses to different situations and interaction partners, whereas one mark of low social competence is inflexibility and persistence in inappropriate behavior across situations. Dunn (1993) notes that transfer of controlling behavior from sibling to peer relationships has been found in studies including secondborns, but not in those limited to firstborns. She suggests that controlling behavior toward siblings is the norm for firstborns, but if they are socially competent they will not carry it over to interactions with friends. For secondborns, however, controlling behavior toward siblings is atypical and may reflect a generally problematic interaction style that is likely to be generalized to other partners.

Research focusing on qualitative aspects of relationships and transfer of general social skills has uncovered more evidence of continuity between children's sibling relationships and their relationships with peers and friends. Vandell and Wilson (1987) observed that the quality of 6-month-olds' interactions with older siblings predicted the quality of their interactions at 9 months of age with unfamiliar peers; specifically, the more they initiated interaction and maintained coordinated interaction with their older siblings, the more they did so later with peers. Continuity between sibling and peer relationships has also been observed in the opposite direction; Kramer and Gottman (1992) found that the quality of 3- to 5-year-olds' play and conflict management with their best friends predicted the quality of later interactions with infant siblings.

Qualitative continuity has also been found between preschoolers' peer relationships and their relationships with siblings beyond infancy. In several studies, warmth and closeness in sibling relationships were positively correlated with cooperation and negatively correlated with conflict and disruptiveness in interactions with friends and other peers. Sibling conflict was negatively correlated with positive affect in friendships, and high sibling conflict was associated with being without friends or having no same-age friends (Graham-Bermann & Hartup, 1991; Gruys, Park, & Kelleher, 1992).

In one study of 4- to 6-year-olds (Dunn, 1993, this volume), children showed continuity across sibling and friend relationships in connected communication and conflict management style, but not in amount of positive or negative affect expressed.

In middle childhood, warmth in sibling relationships tends to be positively correlated with warmth in friendships and with teacher ratings of emotional control (Stocker, 1994; Stormshak, Bellanti, Bierman, et al., 1996). In contrast, high sibling conflict, especially when combined with low warmth, has been associated with poor best friendships and with teacher ratings of high aggression and low social competence (Graham-Bermann & Hartup, 1991; McCoy et al., 1994; Stormshak et al., 1996).

It is, of course, possible that both behavioral and qualitative continuity can be ascribed to stable characteristics of individuals, rather than influences between relationships. Indeed, there is some evidence that temperament contributes to continuity across relationships. Certain aspects of temperament are related to the quality of both sibling relationships and friendships; children rated by parents as having difficult temperaments report less warmth and more conflict in their sibling relationships and lower quality of best friendships than other children do (McCoy et al., 1994). Children's emotionality, as rated by their mothers, partially accounts for similarity in their rate of conflict with siblings and friends (DeHart, Laliberte, Strazza, & Keogh, 1995).

More complex connections among sibling, peer, and friend relationships have also been found. In a study of firstborn elementary schoolers, Stocker and Dunn (1990) found continuity in mothers' reports of positive aspects of children's sibling relationships and friendships (e.g., affection and nurturance), but not negative aspects (e.g., aggression, competition, and conflict). There was no connection between the quality of these children's sibling relationships and teacher reports of the quality of their general peer relationships. However, children observed to be competitive and controlling toward siblings were reported by their mothers to be high in peer leadership and to enjoy particularly close, positive friendships. As Dunn (1993) has pointed out, these results may actually reflect continuity in social competence, since control and competition toward younger siblings are appropriate behaviors for firstborns.

In a study of kindergartners, Mendelson et al. (1994) found that gender composition made a difference in how sibling relationships were connected to peer popularity and friendships. Positive feelings and identification with opposite-gender siblings were directly related to popularity with both opposite-gender and same-gender peers, but were unrelated to quality of same-gender friendships. Positive feelings and identification with *same-gender* siblings were directly related to same-gender popularity and unrelated to opposite-gender popularity. However, the quality of same-gender sibling relationships, indicated by extent of positive feelings and conflict, was *inversely* related to the quality of same-gender friendships. These findings suggest that positive sibling relationships foster skills that lead to popularity, especially with peers of the same gender as the sibling. But these skills may not lead directly to successful friendships, perhaps because a close same-gender sibling relationship at this age may minimize the need to form close friendships.

Two studies have uncovered evidence of compensatory effects between sibling and peer relationships. East and Rook (1992) found that socially isolated sixth graders who reported low social support from school friends also reported *higher* than average social support from their favorite siblings. In turn, high sibling social support was associated with lower anxiety and immaturity for socially isolated children, but not for aggressive or average children. Thus, a positive sibling relationship appeared to compensate in some ways for lack of close friendships. Stocker (1994) found that second graders who reported low warmth in both sibling relationships and friendships also reported more misbehavior than children who reported high warmth from both siblings and friends or low warmth from one and high warmth from the other. This result suggests that a satisfying relationship with *either* a sibling or a friend can make up for a lack of warmth in the other type of relationship—or possibly that the children who had unsatisfactory relationships with *both* siblings and friends were simply the least socially competent.

In summary, there is more evidence for qualitative continuity than for behavioral continuity in children's relationships with siblings, peers, and friends. Behaviors are for the most part *not* simply learned in sibling relationships and transferred to dealings with peers (or vice versa), but the level of broader social competence does seem to carry over, in quality and extent of coordinated interaction and conflict management. Some apparent discontinuity between relationships may actually reflect continuity in social competence. The extent and nature of continuity between sibling, peer, and friend relationships varies, depending on age, sibling age gap, gender composition of sibling and peer pairs, and degree of similarity between relationships. Compensatory connections between sibling, peer, and friend relationships seem to be the exception, but compensatory effects are sometimes seen, especially for socially isolated children.

SIBLING AND PEER CONFLICT

Children's conflicts are an interesting setting for examining contrasts and linkages between sibling and peer relationships because they are a significant context for the development of social understanding and social skills

(Dunn, 1988; Shantz, 1987; Shantz & Hartup, 1992). Although we know a fair amount about peer and sibling conflict, there has been surprisingly little research directly comparing the two types of conflict; there is more observational data comparing conflicts between friends and nonfriends. However, based on the similarities and differences among the relationships, some predictions can be made about sibling, peer, and friend conflicts.

The relative asymmetry of sibling relationships is expected to foster conflicts, especially those involving issues of dominance, and to result in relatively one-sided conflicts, resolved by force and insistence, with inequitable outcomes. On the other hand, the symmetry of peer and friend relationships is expected to facilitate give-and-take, producing longer conflicts, more negotiation, and more equitable outcomes (Katz, Kramer, & Gottman, 1992; Vespo, Pedersen, & Hay, 1995). The intimacy of sibling relationships also may foster conflicts and heighten their affective intensity, especially because siblings must share space, possessions, and parents on a daily basis (Shantz & Hobart, 1989). Finally, the involuntary nature of sibling relationships is expected to reduce the risks inherent in conflict and the motivation to preserve interaction, making siblings less motivated to avoid or mitigate conflict than peers or friends are.

Existing research evidence is equivocal as to whether there is a general difference in the amount of conflict between siblings, peers, and friends (Shantz & Hobart, 1989). Observational studies of 4- to 10-year-olds have found no difference between siblings' and peers' rates of agonistic behavior (Abramovitch et al., 1986; Hartup & Laursen, 1993; Stoneman et al., 1984), and preschoolers observed in both laboratory and home settings have shown rates of sibling conflict similar to those typically seen for peers (Dunn & Munn, 1985; Vespo et al., 1995). However, Vespo et al. found that siblings spent more time in conflict than peers did. Conflicts between preschool friends and nonfriends in open-field playground situations do not differ in frequency or length (Hartup, Laursen, Stewart, & Eastenson, 1988), but conflicts between school-aged friends in closed-field situations are more frequent and last longer than those between nonfriends (Hartup, French, Laursen, Johnston, & Ogawa, 1993). One questionnaire study found that parent ratings of preschoolers' sibling conflict levels were higher than teacher ratings of the same children's peer conflict levels (Graham-Bermann & Hartup, 1991). Questionnaire studies have found no consistent difference between sibling and peer conflict rates for young school-age children, but older children report more conflict with siblings than with peers or friends (Buhrmester & Furman, 1990; Furman & Buhrmester, 1985b; Graham-Bermann & Hartup, 1991; Hartup & Laursen, 1993). Adolescents' reports of naturally occurring conflicts put their incidence for siblings and friends higher than for other peers (Laursen & Collins, 1994).

Affect is generally more intense in sibling conflicts than in peer conflicts (Hartup & Laursen, 1993). Preschoolers' conflicts with friends are less intense than those with nonfriends, at least in open-field situations (Hartup et al., 1988), but conflicts between school-aged friends in closed-field situations are more intense than those between nonfriends (Hartup et al., 1993). Adolescents report the greatest negative affect in conflicts with family members and peers, with relatively little negative affect in conflicts with friends (Laursen & Collins, 1994).

In early childhood, object possession is the most common issue in both sibling and peer conflicts. By age five, issues of social control have become about as common (Shantz & Hobart, 1989); Hartup et al. (1988) found that about 60% of preschoolers' conflicts with both friends and nonfriends involved behavioral control. There is some evidence that preschoolers' conflict issues vary depending on interaction partner, with children more likely to start conflicts centered around object possession, facts, or name-calling with younger siblings than with older siblings or peers (Phinney, 1985). One common issue in preschool sibling conflicts that has no analog in peer conflicts is access to mother (Hartup & Laursen, 1993), and it is often assumed that rivalry is a latent issue in all sibling conflicts (Shantz & Hobart, 1989). Conflict issues for school-age siblings and peers are similar, but they become quite different in adolescence, with siblings continuing to argue about possessions and friends arguing about trust and loyalty (Hartup & Laursen, 1993; Vandell & Bailey, 1992).

Regardless of interaction partner, preschoolers tend to use rather unsophisticated conflict resolution strategies, with insistence the most common and negotiation rather uncommon (Shantz & Hobart, 1989). Preschoolers' conflicts with peers are more elaborate than those with siblings, and compromise and concession, though rare, are used more often with peers (Phinney, 1985). Parents and teachers report preschoolers are less likely to talk out problems and more likely to "fight it out" and rely on third-party intervention with siblings than with friends (Graham-Bermann & Hartup, 1991). Preschoolers use softer conflict resolution strategies, such as disengagement, with friends than with nonfriends, and conflicts with friends are more likely to end in compromise (Gottman, 1983; Hartup et al., 1988). School-age children tend to end sibling conflicts by withdrawing or ignoring each other, rather than by actively resolving them; with friends, they show more give-and-take (Vandell & Bailey, 1992). In adolescence, coercion, physical aggression, withdrawal, ignoring, and third-party intervention continue to be common sibling conflict resolution strategies, whereas friends are more likely to use compromise and less likely to use submission or disengagement (Hartup & Laursen, 1993; Vandell & Bailey, 1992). Peers use submission as a resolution strategy more than friends do, but they use compromise more and disengagement less than siblings do (Laursen & Collins, 1994).

Friends are more likely than siblings to report continued interaction and positive feelings after a conflict; tactics used in conflicts between friends, such as compromise, mitigate conflict's disruptive effects on interaction, whereas tactics used in sibling conflicts, such as submission, exacerbate them (Hartup & Laursen, 1993; Laursen & Collins, 1994). Sibling *relationships* are less vulnerable to negative effects of conflict than friendships are, perhaps because the involuntary nature of sibling relationships heightens tolerance of negative affect (Hartup & Laursen, 1993; Katz et al., 1992). Isolated conflicts seem to have little impact on sibling relationships or friendships, but they may damage relationships with other peers. Frequent, repeated conflict is more likely to have negative effects on all relationships (Laursen & Collins, 1994).

Although sibling and peer conflicts differ in a number of ways, conflict is involved in the linkages between sibling and peer relationships. As already mentioned, high sibling conflict is associated with low friendship quality (Graham-Bermann & Hartup, 1991; Gruys et al., 1992; McCoy et al., 1994). However, what carries over across relationships may not be propensity for conflict, but rather level of conflict management skills (Dunn, 1993). Kramer and Gottman (1992) found that frequency of preschoolers' conflict with friends was not associated with quality of sibling interactions, but frequency of *unmanaged* conflict was. Sibling relationships have been identified as an important context in which young children learn how to manage conflict (Dunn & Munn, 1985; Katz et al., 1992; Shantz & Hobart, 1989), but the specific conflict-related skills learned in sibling relationships may not transfer well to interactions with friends or other peers. As we have seen, though, broad skills related to social understanding and conflict management do transfer across sibling and peer relationships, despite the differences between them.

There are several gaps in the research base on preschoolers' sibling and peer conflict. The most important is the lack of observational studies examining the same children's conflicts with siblings and friends. What we know about similarities and differences between preschoolers' sibling and peer conflicts is based on results of separate studies. To complicate the comparisons, different research approaches have been used in studying preschoolers' sibling and peer conflicts; peer conflict has mostly been studied in laboratory and nursery school observations, and sibling conflict has mostly been studied with questionnaires and home observations, often with the mother present (Shantz & Hobart, 1989). Although differences in interaction settings contribute to the distinctions between sibling and peer relationships, there are some settings that are common to both, such as playing together at home. Our understanding of sibling and friend conflicts would be expanded by observing children with their siblings and friends in these common settings.

We also know relatively little about unilateral conflict, or unreciprocated opposition, between siblings and friends and how it compares to mutual opposition. There has been considerable disagreement about what constitutes a full-blown conflict, with some researchers including unilateral oppositions in their definition (e.g., Hartup et al., 1988; Laursen & Hartup, 1989) and others counting only episodes of mutual opposition (e.g., Maynard, 1985; Shantz, 1987). Laursen and Hartup (1989) compared episodes of unilateral and mutual opposition between preschool peers and found that they differed in intensity, resolution strategy, and probability of prior and continuing social interaction, suggesting that it is reasonable to treat them as separate phenomena. One way of differentiating between mutual and unilateral oppositions is to regard mutual oppositions as conflicts and unilateral oppositions as *averted* conflicts—situations in which a potential for conflict is created by one child's oppositional behavior, but the other child does not reciprocate. The term *averted* is not meant to imply that the interaction partners *intentionally* avoid a conflict; oppositional behavior could go unreciprocated for various reasons, including inattention and lack of interest. In any case, the differences between sibling and friend relationships suggest that friends might be less likely than siblings to reciprocate an oppositional behavior, in an attempt to minimize conflict and maintain interaction.

A STUDY OF SIBLING AND FRIEND CONFLICT AND AVERTED CONFLICT

As part of an ongoing longitudinal study of sibling and friend relationships in early and middle childhood, my students and I have examined preschoolers' conflicts and averted conflicts with siblings and friends. We have looked at differences in rate, nature, and context of conflicts and averted conflicts between siblings and friends in comparable closed-field situations, and we have begun to explore linkages between sibling and friend interactions and what the target children in the study carry between the two interaction contexts (DeHart et al., 1993; DeHart et al., 1996).

Thirty-two same-gender sibling pairs, 16 male and 16 female, participated in the study. Each pair included a target child who was approximately 4½ years old at the beginning of the study; half of the pairs included a sibling about 2 years older than the target, half a sibling about 2 years younger. Participants also included 32 same-gender friends of the target children. Each target child was videotaped at home playing for 15 minutes with the sibling on one day and for 15 minutes with the friend on another day. Both times the children played with experimenter-provided toys intended to provide opportunities for joint pretend play—on one visit, a toy farm; on the other, a toy village. Each of these sets had numerous pieces for the children to divide between them, with some particularly attractive pieces that created a potential for conflict.

After transcribing the observational sessions, we coded them for conflict, averted conflict, and social engagement. We defined *conflicts* as exchanges containing mutual opposition, either verbal or behavioral, and *averted conflicts* as exchanges containing unreciprocated oppositional behavior. *Social engagement* was coded at 10-second intervals, using categories based on Parten (1932)—associative play, cooperative play, parallel play, solitary play, onlooker, unoccupied, and indeterminate. These categories can be collapsed into three superordinate categories—engaged (associative and cooperative play), semiengaged (solitary/onlooker, unoccupied/onlooker), and unengaged (parallel play, combinations without onlooker).

Sibling-Friend Contrasts

As shown in Fig. 13.1, there were clear differences in extent of social engagement during sibling and friend sessions. Children were socially engaged a greater percentage of the time during sessions with their friends than during sessions with their siblings. Although sibling and friend sessions both represented closed-field situations, with no choice of interaction partner, children still were able to choose whether or not to interact with the partner who was available; during sibling sessions, they often chose not to interact. This suggests that the children's motivation to keep an interaction going was greater with their friends than with their siblings.

Both conflicts and averted conflicts occurred at roughly the same overall rate per minute for siblings and for friends (see Table 13.1). Our rates of conflict were higher than those reported in past studies, probably because of the closed-field setting (Hartup et al., 1993). When social engagement was taken into account, differences between siblings and friends became apparent. As we had expected, siblings had more conflicts per minute of social engagement than friends did; in fact, some sibling pairs became socially engaged only during conflicts. We were surprised to discover that siblings also had more *averted* conflicts per minute of social engagement than friends did; we had expected friends to have a higher rate of averted conflicts. Instead, siblings had a higher rate of oppositional behavior overall, whether reciprocated or unreciprocated. We compared the likelihood that an oppositional behavior would be reciprocated during sibling and friend sessions and found no difference; in both sibling and friend sessions, about half of all oppositional behaviors were reciprocated. Thus, it was *not* the case that one oppositional behavior was more likely to turn into a conflict between siblings than between friends. However, the *nature* of averted conflicts differed for siblings and friends. In many averted conflicts

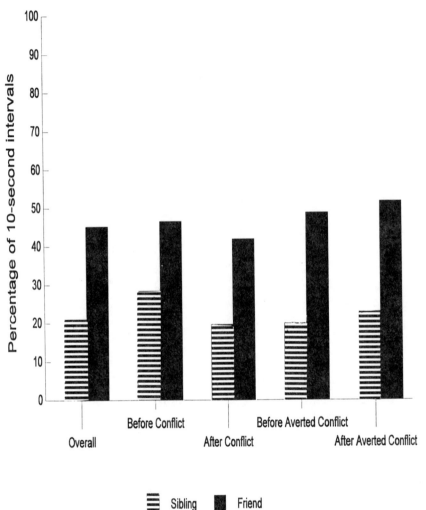

FIG. 13.1. Social engagement during sibling and friend play sessions.

between siblings, one child, often the younger sibling, did something ob-
noxious to get the attention of the other child but was ignored or responded to only briefly. Averted conflicts between friends were more likely
to involve a conciliatory or forgiving response to an oppositional behavior.

Siblings and friends consistently differed in likelihood of social engagement before and after conflicts and averted conflicts. Friends were much
more likely to have been socially engaged before a conflict or averted
conflict, and they were much more likely to remain engaged after it was
over (see Fig. 13.1). Oppositional behaviors between friends tended to

TABLE 13.1
Characteristics of Sibling and Friend Conflicts and Averted Conflicts

	Conflicts		Averted Conflicts	
	Sibling	Friend	Sibling	Friend
Rate per minute	.34	.40	.36	.38
Rate per minute of social engagement	2.22	1.03	2.92	.93
Proportion unprovoked	.50	.34	.42	.38
Proportion with aggression	.40	.26	.13	.18
Mean aggressive acts	1.32	.56	.25	.26
Mean affective intensity (5-point scale)	2.26	1.89	1.34	1.39

occur in the context of ongoing social interaction, as in the following averted conflict between a girl and her friend:

(Target child and friend dividing up pieces from village set.)
Friend: Oh, here's another biddy bed for me.
Target: Yeah, you got a biddy biddy bed.
Friend: There's two biddy beds for me, for the daddy and the mommy.
Target: No, that one is mine. I dropped it.
Friend: Whoops. Oh yeah. It's yours. *(Gives piece to target child.)*
(Target child and friend continue dividing up toys and talking.)

In contrast, sibling social interaction often was initiated with an oppositional behavior and ended when the conflict or averted conflict did. The difference in preconflict social engagement is also reflected in the fact that sibling conflicts were more likely to be unprovoked (50.4%) than conflicts between friends were (34.2%). That is, the opposition that started a sibling conflict was less likely to be a direct response to something a partner said or did. The following sibling conflict is an example of an unprovoked conflict without prior or subsequent social engagement:

(Target child and older brother playing with farm. Brother sets up corral and plays with animals in it; target child wanders around singing "Farmer in the Dell.")
Target: Dropping in! *(Drops animal into brother's corral.)*
Dropping in stinko! *(Drops another animal.)*
Brother: Stop!
Target: Dropping in a big lump of poop! *(Drops piece of silo into corral, laughs.)*
Brother: Don't! *(Takes silo piece, puts it behind his back.)*
(Target starts to drop roof piece into corral.)
Brother: Don't, Kyle! Don't drop any more in! You're not doing it the way I want you to! *(Grabs roof piece from target child.)*
(Target child turns away.)

TABLE 13.2
Conflict Termination Strategies and Averted Conflict Partner Responses

	Conflicts		Averted Conflicts	
	Sibling	Friend	Sibling	Friend
Termination Strategies/ Partner Responses				
Stand Firm	56.3%	49.7%		
Ignore			46.2%	34.1%
Surrender	10.2%	21.4%	42.0%	49.3%
Disengage	16.9%	15.4%	2.3%	4.0%
Distract	3.6%	2.0%	0.3%	1.4%
Negotiate	5.4%	6.5%	5.0%	8.8%
Third Party	2.3%	0.8%		
Indeterminate	5.3%	4.3%	4.1%	2.4%

As shown in Table 13.1, conflicts between siblings were more likely to include aggression than those between friends, the rate of aggressive acts per conflict was much higher for siblings than for friends, and sibling conflicts were more affectively intense than friend conflicts. In contrast, sibling and friend averted conflicts were about equally likely to include aggression, averaged the same number of aggressive acts, and had about the same affective intensity.

There were no significant differences between siblings and friends in conflict issues. Partner behavior was the most common issue (over 50%) in both conflicts and averted conflicts, whether siblings or friends were involved, with disputes over objects the next most common (over 25%). These rates are similar to those reported for preschool friends by Hartup et al. (1988). The consistency in issues across sibling and friend sessions may be partly due to the semistructured play sessions; the experimenter-provided toys and the task of setting them up fostered some types of conflicts and minimized others. For example, both sibling and friend conflicts frequently centered on where pieces belonged in the farm or village.

However, there were differences between siblings and friends in termination strategies for conflicts and in partner responses for averted conflicts, as shown in Table 13.2. Siblings were more likely than friends to appeal to a third party, usually the experimenter, and friends were more likely than siblings to end a conflict by surrendering, as in the following example:

(Target child and friend setting up farm.)
Friend: But there's no space.

> *Target*: Oh, no, no, no. There is. We gotta move this. *(Target moves piece of fence.)*
> *Friend*: Don't take the gate away. We need to keep the gate there.
> *(Target puts fence piece back.)*

In averted conflicts, siblings were more likely than friends to respond to a partner's oppositional or provocative behavior by ignoring it, as in the following example:

> *(Target child and younger brother playing with the village set. Younger brother looking for horses in pile of pieces, target child watching.)*
> *Target*:   Daniel, say yellow.
> *Brother*:   Lellow.
> *Target*:   Daniel says lellow. *(Throws piece at brother, narrowly missing him.)*
> *(Brother ignores target child, continues to look for horses.)*
> *Target*:   Lellow is yellow, right? *Yellow . . .*
> *Brother*:   *Hey*, another horse. Horse. Four horses. There four horses. Four
>   horsies.
> *(Picks up horse and walks off camera.)*

In most cases, as in this example, it was not clear whether the child was *intentionally* ignoring the sibling or was simply engrossed in an ongoing activity and not paying attention. Many of the oppositional or provocative moves that were ignored, however, were repeated or highly obtrusive, suggesting that some of the ignoring was intentional.

In contrast, friends were more likely than siblings to respond to an oppositional behavior by suggesting an alternative, which we coded as negotiation, as in the following averted conflict:

> *(Target child and friend setting up village.)*
> *Target*: A tree in the water. Let's put it right there. *(Puts tree on lake.)*
> *(Friend removes tree from lake.)*
> *Target*: Now when he sawed down the tree, it can go in the water down the
>   waterfall.
> *Friend*: Hey, maybe we can put an island around that. *(Puts block on lake and
>   tree on top of block.)*

For conflict outcomes, there were no overall differences between siblings and friends. Over 80% of both sibling and friend conflicts had a clear winner, and on the whole it was about equally likely to be the target child and the partner. However, target children with younger siblings won a much higher percentage of sibling conflicts than those with older siblings did—a straightforward reflection of the asymmetrical nature of sibling relationships.

Conflict-Averted Conflict Contrasts

The exchanges we coded as conflicts differed from those we coded as averted conflicts in several ways. With social engagement taken into consideration, averted conflicts occurred at a higher rate than conflicts for both siblings and friends. Compared to conflicts, averted conflicts were much less likely to include aggression, averaged a lower number of aggressive acts, and were lower in affective intensity. This may indicate that the children felt more strongly about the specific issues involved in conflicts than in averted conflicts or simply that acts of aggression were unlikely to go unanswered. Surrender was more likely to be used as a response in an averted conflict than in a conflict, and disengagement was more likely to be used in a conflict than in an averted conflict. Conflicts and averted conflicts were about equally likely to be unprovoked and to occur in a context of prior and continuing social interaction.

In the only previous study to compare episodes of unilateral and mutual opposition, Laursen and Hartup (1989) similarly found that those involving unilateral opposition were less intense. They also found that unilateral conflicts were more likely to be resolved by insistence, which probably includes our category of surrender. In contrast to our results, their unilateral conflicts were more likely to occur in a context of ongoing social interaction—a difference that may reflect the open-field setting in which their data were collected.

Sibling–Friend Linkages

We have some very preliminary evidence on linkages between sibling and friend conflicts and averted conflicts, based on correlations for dyadic interactions and for target child behavior across the sibling and peer sessions. Given the many differences we have identified between sibling and friend conflicts and averted conflicts, it is perhaps not surprising that we have so far found very little evidence of continuity across interaction partners.

At the dyad level, the only significant correlations between sibling and friend sessions were for number of turns per conflict ($r = .36$) and number of aggressive acts per conflict ($r = .39$). The target children showed significant correlations between sibling and peer sessions for aggressive acts per conflict ($r = .55$) and for the use of surrender in averted conflicts ($r = .65$). These findings are in accord with previous evidence that broad social competence, such as the ability to engage in connected interaction or the tendency to use aggression, shows continuity between sibling and friend relationships, but that specific behaviors show little cross-relationship continuity.

CONCLUSION

Sibling relationships and friendships provide substantially different inter-action contexts for young children and require them to use different social skills and strategies for managing conflict. Siblings tend to be less motivated to maintain interaction with each other than friends are, and their inter-actions contain more oppositions, both mutual and unreciprocated, than friends' interactions do. Oppositional behavior often serves as a means of socially engaging a sibling, whereas it arises in the course of ongoing interaction between friends. Conflicts between siblings are more affectively intense than those between friends and more likely to include aggression. Friends are more likely to use conflict resolution strategies that prolong interaction, such as negotiation and conciliation, while siblings are more likely to use strategies that disrupt interaction, such as ignoring the partner and appealing to a third party.

Many of the specific interaction strategies that are useful in sibling conflicts would be inappropriate in conflicts with friends; however, even young children manage to adjust to the demands of each relationship and to interact appropriately with both siblings and friends. It is important to note that interactions with siblings and friends do not require separate repertoires of social skills; instead, certain strategies, such as negotiation, are used more frequently with friends, and others, such as aggression, are used more frequently with siblings. The trick for children is recognizing the demands of a particular interaction setting and responding appropriately.

Because of the many differences between sibling and peer relationships, connections between them do not emerge primarily from transfer of re-lationship-specific social behaviors from one setting to another, but rather from the flexible application of more general social understanding across interaction contexts. Dunn (1988) has argued that sibling relationships provide a particularly favorable context for the development of social un-derstanding—the ability to understand and respond appropriately to an-other's thoughts and feelings. If this is the case, it makes sense that links between sibling relationships and other relationships would take the form of continuity of skill or flexibility in responding to others, not continuity of specific behaviors or interaction strategies. Indeed, children who develop the greatest social understanding in the context of their sibling relation-ships may actually show the *least* direct transfer of specific behaviors or interaction strategies from sibling relationships to peer relationships.

Mapping the links between sibling and peer relationships poses a chal-lenging task for researchers because behavioral flexibility is more difficult to trace than behavioral continuity. Making predictions about what form this flexibility might take is further complicated by the lack of a common theory of what constitutes a well-functioning sibling relationship and how that might change over the course of development. We have nothing comparable to attachment theory to generate predictions about children's functioning across sibling and friend relationships and, indeed, no generally agreed-upon way to measure quality in sibling relationships. Given the great diversity in qualitative and structural characteristics of sibling and peer relationships, it seems clear that no one pattern of linkage will hold true for all children's relationships with siblings and peers. Charting the terrain that connects sibling and peer relationships and exploring the various routes children take over that terrain is a task that will occupy researchers for years to come.

ACKNOWLEDGMENTS

This research was supported by a SUNY–Geneseo Presidential Summer Fellowship and by a grant from the National Institutes of Health (#1 R15 HD31656-01A1). I am grateful to the families who welcomed my research group and our equipment into their homes. Many undergraduate students assisted with the data collection, transcribing, coding, and analysis; I especially wish to thank Lydia Richardson, Jeanne Laliberte, Helene Strazza, Jennifer Keogh, Jennifer Konchalski, Susan Wozniak, Susan Habib, Kristin Parker, Gregory Fabiano, Aimee Bishop, and Anne-Marie Hoxie.

REFERENCES

Abramovitch, R., Corter, C., Pepler, D. J., & Stanhope, L. (1986). Sibling and peer interaction: A final follow-up and a comparison. *Child Development, 57,* 217–229.

Bank, L., Patterson, G. R., & Reid, J. B. (1996). Negative sibling interaction patterns as predictors of later adjustment problems in adolescent and young adult males. In G. H. Brody (Ed.), *Sibling relationships: Their causes and consequences* (pp. 197–229). Norwood, NJ: Ablex.

Berndt, T. J., & Bulleit, T. N. (1985). Effects of sibling relationships on preschoolers' behavior at home and at school. *Developmental Psychology, 21,* 761–767.

Berscheid, E. (1985). Interpersonal attraction. In G. Lindzey & E. Aronson (Eds.), *Handbook of social psychology: Vol. 2. Special fields and applications* (3rd ed., pp. 413–484). New York: Random House.

Bowlby, J. (1982). *Attachment and loss, Vol. I: Attachment.* New York: Basic Books.

Brody, G. H., Stoneman, Z., & MacKinnon, C. E. (1982). Role asymmetries in interactions among school-aged children, their younger siblings, and their friends. *Child Development, 53,* 1364–1370.

Buhrmester, D., & Furman, W. (1990). Perceptions of sibling relationships during middle childhood and adolescence. *Child Development, 61,* 1387–1398.

Caspi, A., & Elder, G. H., Jr. (1988). Emergent family patterns: The intergenerational construction of problem behaviors and relationships. In R. A. Hinde & J. Stevenson-Hinde

(Eds.), *Relationships within families: Mutual influences* (pp. 218–240). Oxford, England: Clarendon Press.

DeHart, G., Konchalski, J., Keogh, J., & Miller, K. (1996, August). *Averted conflicts in children's interactions with siblings and with friends.* Poster presented at the biennial meeting of the International Society for the Study of Behavioural Development, Quebec City.

DeHart, G., Laliberte, J., Strazza, H., & Keogh, J. (1995, March). *Continuity between preschoolers' sibling relationships and friendships: The roles of temperament and interaction strategies.* Paper presented at the biennial meeting of the Society for Research in Child Development, Indianapolis, IN.

DeHart, G., Richardson, L., Petrelli, S., Laliberte, J., & Haseley, J. (1993, March). *Preschoolers' conflicts with siblings and peers.* Poster presented at the biennial meeting of the Society for Research in Child Development, New Orleans, LA.

Dunn, J. (1983). Sibling relationships in early childhood. *Child Development, 54,* 787–811.

Dunn, J. (1988). *The beginnings of social understanding.* Cambridge, MA: Harvard University Press.

Dunn, J. (1993). *Young children's relationships: Beyond attachment.* Newbury Park, CA: Sage.

Dunn, J., & Munn, P. (1985). Becoming a family member: Family conflict and the development of social understanding. *Child Development, 56,* 480–492.

East, P. L., & Rook, K. S. (1992). Compensatory patterns of support among children's peer relationships: A test using school friends, nonschool friends, and siblings. *Developmental Psychology, 28,* 163–172.

Furman, W., & Buhrmester, D. (1985a). Children's perceptions of the personal relationships in their social networks. *Developmental Psychology, 21,* 1016–1024.

Furman, W., & Buhrmester, D. (1985b). Children's perceptions of the qualities of sibling relationships. *Child Development, 56,* 448–461.

Gottman, J. M. (1983). How children become friends. *Monographs of the Society for Research in Child Development, 483*(Serial No. 201).

Graham-Bermann, S., & Hartup, W. W. (1991, July). *Conflicts among children: Concordances between sibling and friendship relations in early and middle childhood.* Paper presented at the biennial meeting of the International Society for the Study of Behavioural Development, Minneapolis, MN.

Gruys, A., Park, K. A., & Kelleher, T. A. (1992, August). *Links between qualities of sibling and peer relationships in preschoolers.* Poster presented at the annual meeting of the American Psychological Association, Washington, DC.

Hartup, W. W. (1979). The social worlds of childhood. *American Psychologist, 34,* 944–950.

Hartup, W. W. (1989). Social relationships and their developmental significance. *American Psychologist, 44,* 120–126.

Hartup, W. W., French, D. C., Laursen, B., Johnston, M. K., & Ogawa, J. R. (1993). Conflict and friendship relations in middle childhood: Behavior in a closed-field situation. *Child Development, 64,* 445–454.

Hartup, W. W., & Laursen, B. (1993). Conflict and context in peer relations. In C. H. Hart (Ed.), *Children on playgrounds: Research perspectives and applications* (pp. 44–84). Albany: State University of New York Press.

Hartup, W. W., Laursen, B., Stewart, M. I., & Eastenson, A. (1988). Conflict and the friendship relations of young children. *Child Development, 59,* 1590–1600.

Hinde, R. A., & Stevenson-Hinde, J. (1988). *Relationships within families: Mutual influences.* Oxford, England: Clarendon Press.

Katz, L. F., Kramer, L., & Gottman, J. M. (1992). Conflict and emotions in marital, sibling, and peer relationships. In C. U. Shantz & W. W. Hartup (Eds.), *Conflict in child and adolescent development* (pp. 122–149). New York: Cambridge University Press.

Kramer, L., & Gottman, J. M. (1992). Becoming a sibling: "With a little help from my friends." *Developmental Psychology, 28,* 685–699.

Laursen, B., & Collins, W. A. (1994). Interpersonal conflict during adolescence. *Psychological Bulletin, 115*, 197–209.

Laursen, B., & Hartup, W. W. (1989). The dynamics of preschool children's conflicts. *Merrill-Palmer Quarterly, 35*, 281–297.

Laursen, B., Hartup, W. W., & Koplas, A. L. (1996). Towards understanding peer conflict. *Merrill-Palmer Quarterly, 42*, 76–102.

Maccoby, E. E. (1996). Peer conflict and intrafamily conflict: Are there conceptual bridges? *Merrill-Palmer Quarterly, 42*, 165–176.

Maynard, D. W. (1985). How children start arguments. *Language and Society, 14*, 1–29.

McCoy, J. K., Brody, G. H., & Stoneman, Z. (1994). A longitudinal analysis of sibling relationships as mediators of the link between family processes and youths' best friendships. *Family Relations, 43*, 400–408.

Mendelson, M. J., Aboud, F. E., & Lanthier, R. P. (1994). Kindergartners' relationships with siblings, peers, and friends. *Merrill-Palmer Quarterly, 40*, 416–427.

Miller, N., & Maruyama, G. (1976). Ordinal position and peer popularity. *Journal of Personality and Social Psychology, 33*, 123–131.

Parke, R. D., & Ladd, G. W. (Eds.). (1992). *Family-peer relationships: Modes of linkage*. Hillsdale, NJ: Lawrence Erlbaum Associates.

Parten, M. B. (1932). Social participation among preschool children. *Journal of Abnormal and Social Psychology, 27*, 243–269.

Pepler, D., Corter, C., & Abramovitch, R. (1982). Social relations among children: Comparison of sibling and peer interaction. In K. H. Rubin & H. S. Ross (Eds.), *Peer relationships and social skills in childhood* (pp. 209–227). New York: Springer-Verlag.

Phinney, J. S. (1985). The structure of 5-year-olds' verbal quarrels with peers and siblings. *The Journal of Genetic Psychology, 147*, 47–60.

Shantz, C. U. (1987). Conflicts between children. *Child Development, 58*, 283–305.

Shantz, C. U., & Hartup, W. W. (1992). *Conflict in child and adolescent development*. New York: Cambridge University Press.

Shantz, C. U., & Hobart, C. J. (1989). Social conflict and development: Peers and siblings. In T. J. Berndt & G. W. Ladd (Eds.), *Peer relationships in child development* (pp. 71–94). New York: Wiley.

Sroufe, L. A., & Fleeson, J. (1988). The coherence of family relationships. In R. A. Hinde & J. Stevenson-Hinde (Eds.), *Relationships within families: Mutual influences* (pp. 27–47). Oxford, England: Clarendon Press.

Stocker, C. M. (1994). Children's perceptions of relationships with siblings, friends, and mothers: Compensatory processes and links with adjustment. *Journal of Child Psychology and Psychiatry, 35*, 1447–1459.

Stocker, C., & Dunn, J. (1990). Sibling relationships in childhood: Links with friendships and peer relationships. *British Journal of Developmental Psychology, 8*, 227–244.

Stoneman, Z., Brody, G. H., & MacKinnon, C. (1984). Naturalistic observations of children's activities and roles while playing with their siblings and friends. *Child Development, 55*, 617–627.

Stormshak, E. A., Bellanti, C. J., Bierman, K. L., & Conduct Problems Prevention Research Group. (1996). The quality of sibling relationships and the development of social competence and behavioral control in aggressive children. *Developmental Psychology, 32*, 79–89.

Vandell, D. L., & Bailey, M. D. (1992). Conflicts between siblings. In C. U. Shantz & W. W. Hartup (Eds.), *Conflict in child and adolescent development* (pp. 242–269). New York: Cambridge University Press.

Vandell, D. L., Minnett, A. M., & Santrock, J. W. (1987). Age differences in sibling relationships during middle childhood. *Journal of Applied Developmental Psychology, 8*, 247–257.

Vandell, D. L., & Wilson, K. S. (1987). Infants' interactions with mother, sibling, and peer: Contrasts and relations between interaction systems. *Child Development, 58*, 176–186.

Vespo, J. E., Pedersen, J., & Hay, D. F. (1995). Young children's conflicts with peers and siblings: Gender effects. *Child Study Journal, 25*, 189–212.

Whiting, B. B., & Whiting, J. W. M. (1975). *Children of six cultures*. Cambridge, MA: Harvard University Press.

DEVELOPMENT AND RELATIONSHIPS: RETROSPECT AND PROSPECT

Chapter 14

Commentary: Integrating Relationship Knowledge

Ellen Berscheid
University of Minnesota

In 1869 at Promontory, Utah, railroad track begun in the east by the Eastern Union Pacific railway line was ceremoniously joined by a golden spike to railroad track begun in the west by the Western Pacific, creating the first transcontinental railway in the United States. By facilitating travel between the populated East and the still sparsely settled West, the driving of the golden spike marked the beginning of an era of development in the west and in many previously unpopulated areas in the country's midsection. The four chapters in this volume that are the subject of this brief commentary indicate that developmental psychologists, on the one hand, and we social psychologists, on the other, are beginning to mine the gold from which a spike eventually will be fashioned to join these two critically important but still relatively distant and unintegrated areas of the interpersonal relationship domain.

Like the American West in the mid-1800s, the young multidisciplinary science of relationships currently sprawls over great theoretical and empirical distances. It also is severely fragmented by discipline and by subdisciplines within discipline (see Berscheid, 1994), as the lack of integration of relationship research even within social and developmental psychology illustrates. Despite the facts that social and developmental psychologists have long shared a common interest in relationships, and that these subdisciplines of psychology are more theoretically and methodologically sympathetic than others engaged in the development of relationship science, discourse and collaboration between social and developmental scholars is not as frequent as one might expect.

Much of the communicative distance reflects the fact that although we share a common interest in interpersonal relationships, social and developmental psychologists tend to study different kinds of relationships. The relationships we social psychologists typically examine are those of late adolescents and young adults, principally their romantic premarital and early marital relationships, with little interest shown in young adult friendships and even less in parental and other family relationships. In contrast, developmentalists typically spade that portion of the relationship domain that is bounded, at the one end, by infancy and, at the other, by early adolescence; moreover, and in contrast to social psychologists, developmental psychologists have always addressed family relationships, and, now, thanks in important part to the influence of Willard Hartup's work, children's friendship relationships as well.

The life-course model of development presented by van Lieshout and his associates, which features the influence of the individual's relationships on his or her development throughout the life cycle, signals that developmental psychologists are constructing theoretical track that will run through that portion of the relationship domain populated by social psychologists and extend through other currently distant areas of relationship science as well. The breadth and complexity of their life-course model provides relationship scholars with a glimpse of the goal to which relationship science must aspire but, at the same time, their panoramic view of the task that confronts us is daunting. That task requires the collection and subsequent integration of frighteningly large amounts of empirical relationship data across the life span.

The present distance between the developmental and social regions of the relationship field does not augur well for our ability to integrate knowledge about people's relationships throughout the course of there lives. Given our common interest in relationship phenomena, albeit in different kinds of relationships and in relationship partners at different developmental stages, it often comes as a surprise to laypersons and to graduate students in psychology that relationship knowledge within these two subdisciplines is not well integrated, nor are each of these bodies of knowledge yet well integrated with those of the other contributing disciplines to relationship science. It is still possible, in fact, for a student to be trained in the study of relationships within each of these subdisciplines without making more than superficial contact with the work of relationship scholars in other disciplines or even of work in related areas within their own discipline.

Happily, however, that situation is changing at the University of Minnesota, as a consequence of our development of a free-standing doctoral minor in relationship research that brings together faculty and students in many different disciplines on the common ground of their interest in relationship phenomena. Many of us hope that such integrative programs will become common and ultimately will lead to the development of Departments of Relationship Science. In contrast to the training students now typically receive in Psychology and in other disciplines within the social and behavioral sciences, which focus on the *individual* as the basic unit of analysis, students in relationship science will be systematically trained in both theory and statistical and methodological techniques appropriate to the *dyadic* unit of analysis essential to relationship research, just as Robert Sears envisioned in his presidential address to the American Psychological Association in 1951. At present, however, the integration of relationship knowledge, the subsequent development of a superordinate body of knowledge applicable to all types of relationships, and the institution of Departments of Relationship Science that will further advance and disseminate such knowledge lie far in the future.

The monumental challenge that the task of integrating relationship knowledge represents was impressed on me not only by the life-course model presented by van Lieshout and his associates, but also by my own recent attempt, in collaboration with Harry Reis, to organize and integrate relationship research for the most recent edition of the *Handbook of Social Psychology* (Berscheid & Reis, 1998). Relationship research in social psychology, like relationship research in other disciplines, has exploded since the *Handbook* was last published (Lindzey & Aronson, 1985). Ten years ago, there were only faint signs that social psychologists were screwing up their courage to lay down their experimental scalpels and leave the pristine conditions of the laboratory for the jungle of naturalistically formed ongoing relationships (see Berscheid, 1985)—a jungle that our developmental colleagues had been exploring for years. In fact, the previous edition of the *Handbook* contained no chapter devoted to relationship theory and research. Today, however, so much relationship theory and research are available that despite the fact that we principally highlighted the work of social psychologists, as befits a social psychology handbook, and so discussed the work of scholars in allied fields only if it directly engaged current social psychological concerns, and even though space constraints required us to omit mention of an embarrassing number of meritorious studies, our "Attraction and Close Relationships" chapter quickly became book length.

I might note parenthetically that although, in the end, our magnum opus was much more than twice as long as had been requested, the editors not only did not ask us to excise a single word, but they actually requested that we lengthen the chapter by expanding on certain issues. We took their hitherto unheard-of editorial behavior as yet more testimony that relationship science is becoming recognized as critical to the advancement of the behavioral sciences in general and, in particular, to further progress in social psychology. Relationship science, it is becoming clear, is widely regarded as an important new frontier of the social and behavioral sciences. That's the good news.

The bad news is that, young though it is, relationship science already is too large for any one individual to easily absorb, let alone synthesize (a conclusion Robert Hinde [1997], who also recently attempted the task of integration, undoubtedly could corroborate). By the end of our marathon effort, Harry Reis and I not only were exhausted, but smoke was pouring from our ears as a result of brain overload from our attempt to consume and digest gargantuan mounds of far-flung and disconnected empirical findings and their associated theories. We concluded our review with the observation that the relationship frontier presently resembles the bustling California gold fields of the 1800s.

This extraordinary activity within the relationship field has come about because many scholars now view interpersonal relationships as their discipline's "mother-lode," the repository of an extraordinarily rich vein of knowledge that will provide new answers to the old questions their discipline traditionally has asked about human behavior. Joining the early pioneers in relationship science, many of whom are represented in this volume paying homage to Willard Hartup—who served as the wagonmaster who brought several important young researchers to the field and who has provided so much inspiration to the rest of us—many of the new immigrants are settling in the boomtowns that have popped up almost overnight (in social psychology, research on adult attachment style is one such teeming area [e.g., see Feeney & Noller, 1996; Shaver, Collins, & Clark, 1996] and research on social support is another [e.g., see Pierce, Sarason, & Sarason, in press; Stroebe & Strobe, 1996]). But other immigrants have carved out outposts in the wilderness, far from established lines of theory and methodological technique.

My faith that relationship scholars will be able to meet the challenge of integrating relationship knowledge was severely diminished by our attempt to survey this sprawling and dynamic field for social psychologists. The work represented in this volume, however, especially by the four preceding authors, has done a good deal to revive my optimism. Social and developmental psychologists appear to be independently constructing theoretical and empirical track that, I predict, will soon converge at our own "Promontory" in the relationship domain—peer relationships.

Newcomb and his colleagues, for example, are asking how dyadic friendships serve as a gateway to the remainder of the individual's peer world. It is precisely questions such as this that social psychologists are beginning to examine at last. "At last," because, as Parks and Eggert (1991) have observed, the study of personal relationships has been "peculiarly divorced from the study of the social contexts in which they are embedded" (p. 1). It is particularly curious that social psychologists have neglected the influence of social context given the emphasis that the founder of our discipline, Kurt Lewin, placed on the role the social environment plays in human behavior (see Berscheid & Reis, 1998, for a discussion).

Part of the reason that the immediate social context of a relationship is receiving more attention (e.g., see Milardo & Wellman, 1992) is that innovative ways of conceptualizing social networks have been developed, along with useful hypotheses about their influence on various relationship phenomena (see Berscheid, 1994; Berscheid & Reis, 1998). For example, one promising distinction relevant to questions addressed by Newcomb and his colleagues, as well as by Berndt in his impressive program of research on children's friendships, is between "psychological" networks, or relationships with persons the individual considers important, and "interactive" networks, or persons with whom the individual frequently interacts (Surra & Milardo, 1991). At least with young adults, there appears to be remarkably low overlap between the two networks. One wonders, then, to what extent the persons children name as "friends," or even "best friend," represents the identification of persons located primarily in one or the other of these two networks. One also wonders if tracing the influence of relationships on children's behavior would not benefit from knowing more about the nature of their psychological and interactive networks. The speculation by Newcomb and his associates that it may be "the entire friendship network as opposed to a child's single best friendship that is most important" begins to address such questions.

Whereas Newcomb and his developmental colleagues appear to be most interested in the effects of one specific current relationship on the individual's current behavior and on the individual's future relationships, social psychologists are focusing on how the constellation presented by an individual's entire relationship network is likely to influence the individual's behavior in a specific relationship. Their focus is an outgrowth of theoretical propositions advanced by the most influential theory presently guiding social psychological relationship research, Interdependence Theory (Thibaut & Kelley, 1959; Kelley & Thibaut, 1978), particularly its prediction that the goodness of the individual's alternatives to any specific relationship is the prime determinant of that relationship's stability. These different approaches to social context effects currently being pursued by social and developmental psychologists promise to eventually produce relationship knowledge that transcends type of relationship and partners' developmental stage.

Berndt's chronicle of the methodological difficulties he and his fellow developmentalists have experienced in identifying the residues of childhood friendship relationships on the individual will seem familiar to many social psychologists. For example, the problem of determining whether the similarity of the partners' behavior and characteristics is a cause or a consequence of their relationship is an old one in the social psychological literature. But I confess that many of the assumptions that Berndt and others who study children's friendships appear to be making were not as familiar. Reading their chapters, in fact, aroused a desire to have at my fingertips an "atlas" that would tell me and other social psychologists with whom children of various ages typically interact daily, for how long, what they do, and how their interaction patterns correspond both to their friendship choices and to other behaviors of interest to the investigator (e.g., studying). Berndt's citation of a study suggesting that adolescents spend about a quarter of their waking hours with "friends" was helpful but, again, one wonders whether those persons should be regarded as friends or merely interactants.

Like developmentalists' emphasis on friends, which suggests voluntary interaction, social psychologists also have traditionally emphasized voluntary relationships in contrast to the influence of involuntary relationships, where the individual is virtually compelled by environmental factors extrinsic to the relationship to interact frequently with certain others. The distinction between voluntary and involuntary relationships, and recognition that even involuntary interaction is likely to be influential and leave long-term effects, is becoming more recognized (e.g., see Berscheid & Lopes, 1997).

Other evidence that social and developmental psychologists are beginning to meet on the ground of peer relationships is provided by Furman's current work, which seeks to describe the role of friendship peer relationships in romantic relationships. His pursuit of this question could not be more timely for social psychologists, whom, as I've noted, have relatively ignored friendship relationships. The social psychological schism between friendship and romantic relationships is apparent in theory and research addressed to the phenomenon of romantic love. It is reflected, for example, in the enduringly popular "companionate love" versus "romantic love" distinction (Berscheid & Walster, 1974).

The distinction between companionate and romantic love has carried the implication that these two types of attraction—the former presumed to be characteristic of friendship and the latter to romantic relationships— not only are qualitatively different phenomena, but that the causal factors conducive to the development of companionate love (e.g., familiarity) and those facilitative of romantic love (e.g., sexual desire) are antagonistic to each other. In our recent investigation of the mental representation of romantic love and other related concepts, we found that, as hypothesized, sexual desire differentiates romantic love from other types of love (Berscheid & Meyers, 1996; Meyers & Berscheid, 1997). What we did not hypothesize, but what was overwhelmingly clear, is that among young adults today—where segregation by gender is much less frequent than it was just a few decades ago in schools, living quarters, and the work world—friend-ship also differentiates romantic love from other kinds of love (see also Hendrick & Hendrick, 1993). Our findings suggested to us that the ele-ments of companionate love (e.g., liking, trust, respect), which are strongly associated with friendship, and the element of sexual desire are both nec-essary and jointly sufficient for individuals to classify their feelings as ro-mantic love. If so—if today friendship is almost as essential to the experi-ence of romantic love as sexual desire is—it seems virtually certain that early friendships will have a direct influence on later romantic relation-ships, as Furman suspects.

I conclude, then, that, coming from their traditionally different direc-tions, social and developmental psychologists are beginning to approach each other in the arena of peer relationships. Not only are developmental psychologists becoming more interested in following the effects of chil-dren's relationships further down the life span, but, on our side of the relationship world, social psychologists have become much more aware that we need information about the influence an individual's early rela-tionships may have on their later relationships, especially their romantic relationships. Much of this awareness has resulted from the application of Bowlby's (e.g., 1988) concept of inner working models of relationships to adult relationships (e.g., Shaver & Hazan, 1993), and an interest in rela-tionship schemas generally (Berscheid, 1994).

Because we social psychologists have become more sensitive to the fact that we are always walking into the individual's relationship movie late, we have become more aware of our dependence upon developmental psy-chologists to film the first part of the relationship movie and to inform the work we are doing to film the second part. Unfortunately, if the two parts we've constructed so far were to be spliced together, Hollywood movie critics would say we had a "continuity problem." That problem will only be solved by more discourse between these two subdisciplines, more integration of what we do know about the peer relationships of late ado-lescents and young adults, and more collaborative efforts to collect yet more data. That the accomplishment of these aims to integrate two areas of relationship knowledge now seems not only possible but inevitable seems to me to be Willard Hartup's most valuable legacy to relationship science.

REFERENCES

Berscheid, E. (1985). Interpersonal attraction. In G. Lindzey & E. Aronson (Eds.), *The handbook of social psychology* (3rd ed., pp. 413–484). New York: Random House.

Berscheid, E. (1994). Interpersonal relationships. *Annual Review of Psychology, 45,* 79–129.

Berscheid, E., & Lopes, J. (1997). A temporal model of relationship satisfaction and stability. In R. J. Sternberg & M. Hojjat (Eds.), *Satisfaction in close relationships* (pp. 129–159). New York: Guilford.

Berscheid, E., & Meyers, S. A. (1996). A social categorical approach to a question about love. *Personal Relationships, 3,* 19–43.

Berscheid, E., & Reis, H. (1998). Attraction and close relationships. In D. T. Gilbert, S. T. Fiske, & G. Lindzey (Eds.), *The handbook of social psychology* (4th ed., pp. 193–281). New York: McGraw-Hill.

Berscheid, E., & Walster [Hatfield], E. (1974). A little bit about love. In T. L. Huston (Ed.), *Foundations of interpersonal attraction* (pp. 356–381). New York: Academic Press.

Bowlby, J. (1988). *A secure base.* New York: Basic Books.

Feeney, J. A., & Noller, P. (1996). *Adult attachment.* Thousand Oaks, CA: Sage.

Hendrick, S. S., & Hendrick, C. (1993). Lovers as friends. *Journal of Social and Personal Relationships, 10,* 459–466.

Hinde, R. (1997). *Relationships: A dialectical perspective.* East Sussex, England: Psychology Press.

Kelley, H. H., & Thibaut, J. W. (1978). *Interpersonal relations: A theory of interdependence.* New York: Wiley.

Lindzey, G., & Aronson, E. (Eds.). (1985). *The handbook of social psychology* (3rd ed.). New York: Random House.

Meyers, S. A., & Berscheid, E. (1997). The language of love: The difference a preposition makes. *Personality and Social Psychology Bulletin, 23,* 347–362.

Milardo, R. M., & Wellman, B. (1992). The personal is social. *Journal of Social and Personal Relationships, 9,* 339–342.

Parks, M. R., & Eggert, L. L. (1991). The role of social context in the dynamics of personal relationships. In W. H. Jones & D. Perlman (Eds.), *Advances in personal relationships, Vol. 2* (pp. 1–34). London: Jessica Kingsley.

Pierce, G. R., Sarason, B. R., & Sarason, I. G. (Eds.). (in press). *Handbook of social support and the family.* New York: Plenum.

Shaver, P. R., Collins, N., & Clark, C. L. (1996). Attachment styles and internal working models of self and relationship partners. In G. Fletcher & J. Fitness (Eds.), *Knowledge structures and interaction in close relationships: A social psychological approach* (pp. 25–61). Hillsdale, NJ: Lawrence Erlbaum Associates.

Shaver, P. R., & Hazan, C. (1993). Adult romantic attachment: Theory and evidence. In W. H. Jones & D. Perlman (Eds.), *Advances in personal relationships, Vol. 4* (pp. 29–70). London: Jessica Kingsley.

Stroebe, W., & Stroebe, M. (1996). The social psychology of social support. In A. Kruglanski & E. T. Higgins (Eds.), *Social psychology: Handbook of basic principles* (pp. 597–621). New York: Guilford.

Surra, C., & Milardo, R. (1991). The social psychological context of developing relationships: Interactive and psychological networks. In D. Perlman & W. Jones (Eds.), *Advances in personal relationships* (Vol. 3, pp. 1–36). London: Jessica Kingsley.

Thibaut, J. W., & Kelley, H. H. (1959). *The social psychology of groups.* New York: Wiley.

Chapter 15

Commentary: Development, Modalities, and Relationships

Carolyn U. Shantz
Wayne State University

In honoring the work of Willard Hartup, contributors to this volume have entertained the significance of relationships for development, particularly those of peers, friends, siblings, parent–child, and families. In this commentary, I examine a theme that provides both a larger context for these chapters, and a common thread among them.

MODALITIES OF HUMAN EXPERIENCE

In the fabric of everyday life, in the interactions with one another, two fundamental modalities of human experience have been proposed: communal relations and agency (power) relations. *Communion* refers to being a socially connected person, one who belongs to a larger social entity and who is motivated to be united with that entity and intimate. *Agency* typically refers to being an active person, one who is motivated to mastery and power that protect and enhance that assertiveness. These dimensions have been found to be orthogonal, independent dimensions of human experience. Their utility in capturing fundamental aspects of human existence is by considering them in relation to one another, that is, in combination (see Fig. 15.1a).

These dimensions of communion and agency, to use Bakan's (1966) terms, are not some arbitrary dimensions selected from many possible candidates. Rather, they have been proposed by an astonishing diversity

Panel a

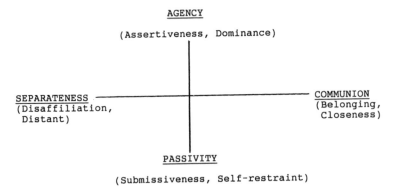

Panel b

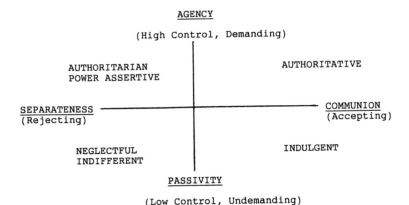

FIG. 15.1. Panel a: A structural representation of agency and communion (adapted from Wiggins, 1991); Panel b: Agency and communion structure applied to patterns of parenting (adapted from Maccoby & Martin, 1983, p. 39).

of scholars and have empirical grounding in studies of language, personality traits, and gender. Wiggins (1991) documented that "astonishing" array of work that "attests to the pivotal nature of the concepts of agency and communion in the social sciences and humanities" (p. 89).

Briefly, this array has been traced through the "world views" and personality theories of Adler, Angyal, Erikson, Sullivan, Bakan, and, more recently, by McAdams. Specific empirical data are offered—one example must suffice—that these two dimensions emerge when languages are compared for different forms of address (e.g., in French, *tu* and *vous*). Their pervasive use to frame social relations reflects, Roger Brown (Brown & Gilman, 1960) contends, the very structure of societies around solidarity–communion and power.

If we look closer to home, to topics of developmental psychology research, similar dimensions have emerged. Some examples follow: (a) Parenting. Early factor analyses of interviews and questionnaires repeatedly revealed two orthogonal dimensions: parental warmth–hostility and control–autonomy (e.g., Becker, 1964). As such, these dimensions can be put in the larger framework of the degree of communion (social acceptance), and agency (social control). Although these dimensions have been somewhat redefined over the years (Maccoby & Martin, 1983) by adding responsiveness to the warmth dimension and demandingness to the control dimension, the basic two dimensions are retained (see Fig. 15.1b). (b) Family systems. Emery (1992), working with empirical and clinical data, proposed that whatever the surface meanings of conflicts in families appear to be, their deep meanings invariably involve two primary dimensions: intimacy and power in family relationships. Again, the similarity to the communal and agentic dimensions are clear.

Even "closer to home," the chapters by Sroufe and by French reflect this theme. Sroufe cites what he sees as the significance of secure attachments:

> First, a history of emotional availability and responsiveness, which defines a secure attachment relationship, is a foundation for positive expectations concerning relationships with others, a basic sense of connectedness . . . [communion dimension]. Second, parental responsiveness leads to a complementary sense of effectance; that is, that the child can have an impact on the caregiver and, ultimately, the . . . mastery of the environment [agency dimension]. (p. 251)

The concept of attachment, as explicated by Ainsworth, reflects the tension embedded within (not between) each dimension. That is, on the communal theme, the conflict is being and remaining together versus separating, dissociating. On the agency dimension, it is passivity versus activity. Presumably intrapsychic conflict occurs for the infant as he or she orients both toward the secure base the mother represents and toward the fascinating world to be explored and mastered. So, too, many mothers may experience the tensions of "holding on" versus "letting go," to encourage dependency versus independency.

Sroufe focuses on peer competency, reflected in the communal dimension of forming friendships and participating in peer groups. He provides longitudinal data to support the belief that peer competency in childhood and adolescence is significantly related to a history of secure attachment in infancy and early peer relationships. Further assessments of concurrent parenting and concurrent peer relations will illuminate how the past and the present contribute to later—even lifelong—development of social competency.

Further, all social relationships, French underscores, are embedded in macrosystems of different subcultures and cultures. How have such cultural differences been conceptualized? By the very dimensions of communion and agency, reflected in French's samples of collectivist and individualistic societies. The definitions of collectivist societies (Triandis, 1994) suggest a cultural focus on the communal dimension: valuing the common good and concern for the consequences of one's actions for others; and, in combination with agency, valuing self-sacrifice and submissiveness to the group. Such a codimensional definition places collectivist societies, then, in the lower right cell of Fig. 15.1a.

Individualistic societies, in contrast, emphasize the agency dimension: valuing individual performance and assertiveness, and, in combination with the communal dimension, also encouraging separateness from others. These societies are situated in the upper left cell of Fig. 15.1a.

It is not the case that these two dimensions are the only dimensions of import. Indeed, as French points out, other additional dimensions may also describe societies, such as their complexity. Those who propose these two modalities of communion and agency view them as *most* basic to human experience, but not exclusive of other modalities.

SOCIAL CONFLICT AND THE MODALITIES

The chapters by Dunn and by DeHart address wholly or in part interpersonal conflict in social relationships. One central question is: How can we understand conflict in relation to the two modalities of experience just described? At first blush, it would seem that some simple equations are possible, particularly if one views conflict as inevitably antisocial, negative behavior. Conflict is, then, at the "negative pole" of communion, equated as it often is with hostility, disaffirmation, and separateness (which, in this dimensional scheme, also means that conflict is the opposite of togetherness and belongingness). I hope that, by reading the current research in peer, marital, and family conflict, most scholars have made a clear distinction between conflict and aggression or hostility. Conflict is often defined, as DeHart has done, as "mutual opposition" between two or more people. Thus, conflict includes petty bickering, quarreling, arguing, and debating; aggression or hostility may occur during a conflict episode or absolutely none may occur. Their absence or presence is irrelevant to defining operationally a state of conflict. Thus, in relation to the negative pole of communion, conflict cannot be equated with hostility.

Further, conflict can be situated anywhere along the communal dimension, as indicated by the distinction Deutsch (1973) made long ago: Conflict can have either a destructive, negative versus constructive, positive role in the lives of people. Destructive conflict occurs if participants frame conflict as "you versus me," do not stay focused on the major issue, use coercive strategies, and end dissatisfied or the relationship harmed. Positive and constructive conflicts occur when participants frame conflict as "our" problem, stay focused on the major issue, use constructive strategies, and feel satisfied at the outcome—even if the conflict is not resolved at that time. Given these proposals, conflict can be viewed as an interpersonal process that influences—enhances or inhibits—communion rather than being identified a priori with the negative pole of communion.

Likewise, conflict can serve as a process of agency. At the extreme assertive pole, being highly dominant, pressing one's needs and wishes can lead ultimately to being a bully, whereas at the other pole, extreme passivity in the face of opposition can lead to being easily controlled and victimized. Yet both poles encompass socially competent behaviors: At the agency end is the ability to assert positively at times one's own rights and needs or disapprove of what others say or do, and at the passivity pole knowing when to "let things pass" and not take constant issue (i.e., skill in selecting events to make an issue of). In summary, conflict is best conceived as a social process contributing to communion or separateness, to activity or passivity, but is not, in itself, situated anywhere in this codimensional scheme.

It bears noting that past writers have viewed high agency and communion poles as "socially good," because they are seen as "the essential ingredients of a well-ordered and harmonious society and of a psychologically fulfilled and well-integrated individual" (Wiggins, 1991, p. 105). Passivity and dissociation, then, are seen as "socially bad." This equation of poles as good or bad is unfortunate, I think. For example, separateness, rather than being viewed as inevitably negative, is essential for concentrated work, creativity, and privacy; so, too, passivity can reflect self-regulation, the ability to follow, or a willingness to not dominate, to "get along."

Up to this point conflict has been discussed as a very abstract social process. However, conflict is a complex social event, one that has many functions depending on the individuals involved, the issues, and motivations. For example, for individuals, conflict can serve a number of functions, such as a means to gain information, release anger, solve problems, or relieve boredom. For dyads, conflict can function to air and resolve differences between people, redefine relationships (such as friendships; Corsaro, 1985), or gain more autonomy vis-à-vis another. And for groups, conflict can serve to redefine boundaries within a family system (e.g., Emery, 1992) or unite children in forming alliances (e.g., "we girls" vs. "those boys"). Of course, conflicts vary in their orientation . . . (Is this for real? Is this serious opposition or not? [e.g., a joke, playful, just kidding]?).

They also vary in their frame: Is this about reality or are we pretending to be in conflict? By far, most of the research on conflict is about "in earnest," serious conflict in a real frame, and little is known about the other forms (e.g., Garvey & Shantz, 1992).

It is significant that over the years Dunn has selected and documented several social processes that contribute importantly to children's social–cognitive development: joint pretend play, conflict talk, observing others' interactions, and the affect of relationships. If one takes into account the substantial skills and affective salience of pretending and conflicting, it is not surprising that children engage in a good deal of both and learn important things about people and themselves in the process: creating and maintaining a pretend story with multiple actors, and when opposed, handling frustration by managing one's affect and justifying one's position. These are events occurring in real time with real meaning to the participants that make substantial demands for online reasoning, listening, planning, and self-regulation. An important finding by Dunn is children's sensitivities to the relationship within which they operate, showing higher quality conflict management with their friends than with their mothers or siblings. Why and how relationships have such an impact is a central and abiding question. Of note is that power and communal factors are often suggested: The equality of power among peers and the closeness of the relationship determine, in part, the freedom to talk, play, argue, and express feelings. So, too, as Hartup (1992) suggested, consideration needs to be given to whether relationships are voluntary or involuntary.

A more detailed examination of conflicts per se was provided by DeHart. A significant contribution of this study is her use of unilateral conflicts as times when "conflict is averted," that is, one child does not "rise to the bait" of being opposed. Opposition by another is a challenge, and it brings with it a certain demand to respond, much like, linguistically, a question demands an answer.

Whether nonresponse is considered a positive or negative phenomenon depends, likely, on several factors. For example, to not respond to opposition may be motivated by a wish to avoid conflict at any cost or extreme inhibition. Or it may be due to the child's view that the opposition is not worth the effort of arguing the point or be so unreasonable it is unworthy of response. In this sense, lack of response may show a social competence in picking one's fights over more important matters. It is notable that correlations between sibling and peer conflicts and averted conflicts were not significant for any measures, suggesting that the relationships themselves have an important impact on both the engagement in and avoidance of arguments. As such, DeHart concludes that to think of social behaviors such as these as matters of generalization or transfer from one type of relationship to another may be oversimplifications.

DeHart's focus on both conflict and averted conflict helps to underscore the importance of not becoming too narrow in our focus on one behavior. To understand conflict and its role in development, for example, one needs to understand nonconflictual interactions and relations. As Shantz and Hartup (1992) stated,

[A] major premise . . . is that the study of people as they engage one another in opposition or are engaged in internal disagreements is necessary for any clear understanding of social and cognitive development. It is this dynamic—the virtual "dance" of discord and accord, of disaffirmation and affirmation—that is critical to the comprehension of development. (p. 11)

It is hoped that this brief discussion of a simple structure of lifelong human experiences of uniting and dissociating, of ascending and not ascending is useful not only in "situating" the volume chapters, but will guide our future inquiries as well. So, too, have some social processes—communicating, conflicting, playing—been considered, which may contribute in different ways to these fundamental experiences of community and agency through the life span.

REFERENCES

Bakan, D. (1966). *The duality of human existence: Isolation and communion in Western man.* Boston: Beacon.
Becker, W. C. (1964). Consequences of different kinds of parental discipline. In M. L. Hoffman & L. W. Hoffman (Eds.), *Review of child development research* (Vol. 1, pp. 169–208). New York: Russell Sage Foundation.
Brown, R., & Gilman, A. (1960). The pronouns of power and solidarity. In T. A. Sebeok (Ed.), *Style in language.* Cambridge, MA: Technology Press.
Corsaro, W. A. (1985). *Friendship and peer culture in the early years.* Norwood, NJ: Ablex.
Deutsch, M. (1973). *The resolution of conflict: Constructive and destructive processes.* New Haven, CT: Yale University Press.
Emery, R. E. (1992). Family conflicts and their developmental implications: A conceptual analysis of meanings for the structure of relationships. In C. U. Shantz & W. W. Hartup (Eds.), *Conflict in child and adolescent development* (pp. 270–298). Cambridge, England: Cambridge University Press.
Garvey, C., & Shantz, C. U. (1992). Conflict talk: Approaches to adversative discourse. In C. U. Shantz & W. W. Hartup (Eds.), *Conflict in child and adolescent development* (pp. 93–121). Cambridge, England: Cambridge University Press.
Hartup, W. W. (1992). Conflict and friendship relations. In C. U. Shantz & W. W. Hartup (Eds.), *Conflict in child and adolescent development* (pp. 186–215). Cambridge, England: Cambridge University Press.
Maccoby, E. E., & Martin, J. A. (1983). Socialization in the context of the family: Parent-child interaction. In P. H. Mussen (Series Ed.) & E. M. Hetherington (Vol. Ed.), *Handbook of child psychology: Vol. 4. Socialization, personality, and social development* (4th ed., pp. 1–102). New York: Wiley.

Shantz, C. U., & Hartup, W. W. (1992). Conflict and development: An introduction. In C. U. Shantz & W. W. Hartup (Eds.), *Conflict in child and adolescent development* (pp. 1–11). Cambridge, England: Cambridge University Press.

Triandis, H. C. (1994). *Culture and social behavior.* New York: McGraw-Hill.

Wiggins, J. S. (1991). Agency and communion as conceptual coordinates for the understanding and measurement of interpersonal behavior. In W. M. Grove & D. Cicchetti (Eds.), *Thinking clearly about psychology: Vol. 2. Personality and psychopathology* (pp. 89–113). Minneapolis: University of Minnesota Press.

Chapter 16

Commentary: Aspects of Relationships in Child Development

Robert A. Hinde
St. John's College, Cambridge, England
and
Behaviour Laboratory, Madingley, Cambridge, England

This contribution contains some brief remarks on the chapters by Maccoby, Parke, and O'Neil, and Hetherington, and some comments on the present state of our knowledge about relationships.

Eleanor Maccoby refers to three labels applied to categories of relationships in the past—Exchange, Communal, and Coercive—and points out that none of them seems really to fit the parent–child relationship. It is too one-sided to be described as Communal, and both partners exercise coercion. Maccoby has tried to find interpretations of the parent–child relationship that would fit Exchange (or rather Equity) theory, but concludes they will not work with young children: for one thing, the parent seems to incur more costs than the child. An interdependence theorist might argue that this is a case of transformation of the matrix: by virtue of his or her nature or of cultural norms, or because he or she sees the parent–child relationship as a long-term investment, the parent may see the parenting role as self-reinforcing. Such a proposal, however, makes the interdependence model almost irrefutable.

As Maccoby says, perhaps purely Exchange, Communal, and Coercive relationships do exist, but most relationships contain elements of more than one, and in many cases of all three. In general, it is therefore perhaps preferable to apply the adjectives Exchange, Communal, and Coercive to interactions within relationships, rather than to the relationships themselves. This would involve some difficulty in that an *interaction* could be labeled as Exchange only because it involved expectation of future recompense in the course of the *relationship*. However, Maccoby might agree with it, because she cites Bugental and Goodnow's idea of domain-specific socialization processes. The domains involve attachment issues, power-based issues, and reciprocal exchanges, with partners switching from one domain to another. This is no different from saying that the interactions can be grouped into a number of categories. Maccoby points out that each domain may pave the way for particular relationships in later life. This, however, in my view is not "an evolutionary theme," if that implies that the three domains are to be regarded as evolved "modules"—that is a different issue, requiring further evidence.

Ross Parke and Robin O'Neil review an important study (and literature related to it) on parental influences on children's social behavior. It provides evidence that these influences are mediated in three ways—parental rearing practices, instruction, and management of the children's activities. The first part of the chapter focuses on evidence that each of the three modes of parental behavior does in fact influence children's social competence. The authors cite many interesting studies, some available only as conference papers or in other nonjournal sources. Later they assess the relative influence of aspects of the three modes of parent–child influence on four measures of social competence: peer-rated and teacher-rated social acceptance, and peer-rated and teacher-rated aggression. The effects are assessed separately for the four relationships: mother–daughter, mother–son, father–daughter, and father–son. Those independent variables that contributed accounted for a mean (across outcome measures) of 16%–29% of the variance. However, only two independent variables contributed to all four outcome measures in the mother–daughter and two in the mother–son analyses, and only one, the number of playmates acquired through the mothers' network of friends, contributed to both. In the father–daughter and father–son relationships only the father's enjoyment of contact with friends appeared to contribute.

Such data seem to emphasize two points. First, social competence is affected in different ways in the four types of relationships, and this suggests that it is far from a unitary dimension. There is nothing new in that, but it is worth emphasizing that social competence as a concept has its dangers. Second, as the authors emphasize, the parental strategies can operate in varying combinations, which may differ among the four types of parent–child relationships. This promises exciting insights when data analysis is completed.

Mavis Hetherington's chapter is a summary of some of the results from her studies of children from divorced families. The extent of the data is breathtaking, and only a few points can be made here. She notes that it is the balance between risk factors and social capital that influences both adaptive and maladaptive behavior. This is in harmony with an extension of the view that a relationship is more than the sum of its component interactions—one must take account not only of the relationship as a whole, but also the total situation.

Gender differences are conspicuous in these data, and one wonders if these are exacerbated by the stresses consequent upon parental estrangement. Turner (1991), studying the preschool behavior of 4-year-olds, found that gender differences were apparent only in those children previously assessed as insecurely attached, and not in the securely attached ones.

The concept of "social capital" Hetherington uses is, of course, a global one, and one must presume that, for instance, a close relationship with the mother has an effect different in kind from that with a sibling or a peer. Thus, the concept raises a host of questions about mechanism. What precisely is it about parental divorce that leads to such negative outcomes? Presumably the effects can be seen as mediated by changes in the self-system. Further insight into the processes involved might help us to ameliorate the effects of divorce.

Hetherington's data, involving several studies, contain much material of profound interest to issues other than those discussed in this volume, such as the factors making for marital stability.

During discussions at this meeting in honor of Bill Hartup, attention has been called to his habit of finishing his papers by pointing to deficiencies in the data available. The recent paper on "Friendships and Adaptation in the Life Course" (Hartup & Stevens, 1997) is no exception. Remarks like "Significant gaps appear in the data base"; "Conclusions are shaky because cross-sectional data have not been supplemented by longitudinal studies"; and "Qualitative dimensions need examination" occur throughout the last few pages. Perhaps the best way I can pay tribute to Bill is to conclude with my own list of needs for the study of relationships in general. We need a science, in the sense of an ordered body of knowledge, about human relationships (Hinde, 1997). The last 20 years have seen great strides forward, and in the study of children's relationships Hartup has been responsible for much of this. Now we can take stock and see where we are. I suggest that among our needs are the following:

1. If we are to have a real science, we need a firm basis of description and classification comparable to that provided for chemistry by the Periodic Table and for biology by the Theory of Evolution by Natural Selection. This must include aspects of both the component interactions and the relationships, and include properties of behavior, cognition, and affect in both their objective and subjective aspects. The subjective aspects are important because how the participants view a relationship may influence its future course. No scheme for describing relationships can be entirely satisfactory, in part because of the difficulty of including a diachronic per-

spective, but elsewhere a scheme for dividing into 12 categories the characteristics of interactions and relationships that seem to be important has been presented (Hinde, 1997). So far the bulk of the effort in developmental psychology has gone into the content of the interactions, with more limited exploration of the more subjective aspects, such as the children's views of their partners and of the relationships. As Hartup and Stevens (1997) remarked, "Studies (of friendship) center too much on having friends and the most superficial things about them."

2. We need to make clear distinctions between interactions and relationships. A relationship is more than the sum of its constituent interactions, because the interactions affect each other. We must remember that popularity, sociability, and the ability to form relationships are not the same thing.

3. Description must also involve both clear distinctions between successive levels of complexity (psychological–physiological processes, the self-system and individual behavior, interactions, relationships, groups and society, and also the sociocultural structure—see Hinde, 1997), and recognition of the diachronic dialectical relations between them. As Berscheid (this volume) has remarked, this involves crossing the boundaries between disciplines. The study of relationships must be integrated with greater understanding of the individual and of the social context.

4. We must ask how far we are culturally biased in the variables we choose to measure? Assertiveness may be a good thing in the United States of America, but that is not so everywhere—at least the optimum differs between cultures. Is emotion regulation to any degree always a good thing? Do we want a society of overphlegmatic individuals? Is it always better to have a large peer network? After all, as mentioned earlier, sociability is not the same as the ability to form relationships (Hinde, 1978).

5. We need further studies of the self-system, including the relations between emotion and cognition. Alan Sroufe (Sroufe, Egeland, & Carlson, this volume) alluded to this issue in chapter 11. In adult relationships considerable progress has been made (Fletcher & Fitness, 1996), but we are only just beginning to get insights into the developmental aspects of the self-system (e.g., Bowlby, 1969/1982; Bretherton, 1990; Stern, 1995). As a number of authors have emphasized, the self-system must be seen as including information about relationships, and Hartup and Stevens (1997) remarked that "Studies [of friendship] are inconclusive because we know too little about the complex manner in which relationships and their development interact with the development of the individual." However, the difficulties are considerable, in part because description has to be metaphorical, but we must recognize the metaphors for what they are and try to specify the limits of their usefulness. Concepts like "Internal Working Model," invaluable as they are, easily become unfalsifiable.

6. We need to integrate the description of relationships with studies of process. Of the diverse processes—interpersonal perception, attribution, exchange, and so on—involved in the dynamics of relationships, none is ubiquitously important, and their limitations must be specified in terms of the descriptive base.

7. We need to seek for better agreement about the variables we use in order to facilitate comparisons between studies. In the field of adult relationships the relations between the concepts of intimacy and closeness, and the relation of each to self-disclosure, has been a matter of considerable discussion (Berscheid, Snyder, & Omoto, 1989). The problems involved in using the same word for different entities has been referred to by Thorndike (1919) as the "jingle fallacy," and the use of different words for the same issue by Kelley (1927) as the "jangle fallacy." Block (1995) refers to such muddles as the "jingle jangle jungle." Problems with the concepts of "social competence" and "social capital" were mentioned earlier. Again, some of the concepts used in the study of relationships as unidimensional or dichotomous may turn out to be two-dimensional: this is already accepted for gender and may be the case for marital satisfaction (Fincham, Beach, & Kemp-Fincham, in press). These are difficult issues, because attempts to regularize the use of concepts can constrain creativity, but more discipline would be advantageous.

8. We need to balance studies involving group differences, regression analyses, and path analyses with ones that focus more on what happens to particular individuals. A survey of these issues is given by Cairns, Bergman, and Kagan (1998).

9. We need to seek to reconcile different explanations of the same phenomenon. As an example, models of the way in which information is stored in the self-system overlap. For instance, Kelly (1955) refers to constructs; Schenk (1982) to scripts, scenes, and memory organization packets; Fiske (1991) to relationship categories; Bowlby (1969/1982) to internal working models; Greene and Geddes (1988) to modular units; Baldwin (1995) to relational schemes; and Stern (1995) to schemata and representations. No doubt some of the differences between the concepts are important, but the commonalities are even more so and become lost in the diversity of terms.

As another example, consider the fact that individuals like to do things for those that they love. The lay view might be that of course one likes to do things for those whom one loves, but is not that circular? Early exchange theorists would say that one makes sacrifices in the hope of future gains, or to maintain the relationship to justify the costs already incurred (e.g., Blau, 1964). Interdependence theorists would see the rewarding nature of giving as involving a transformation of a Prisoner's Dilemma type matrix

(Kelley, 1979). Resource theorists would argue that in giving love one had more (Foa & Foa, 1974). Others would explain it by saying that forming a relationship involves including the other in the self (Aron & Aron, 1996). Or perhaps one likes oneself for putting effort into the relationship and liking oneself enhances one's liking for a partner who is perceived to like oneself. Or putting in effort might cause one to misperceive a partner as a worthy recipient of that effort (Newcomb, 1961). Or helping another might be ascribed to knowledge structures influenced by norms or social contracts (Lerner, 1974). Or is a relationship to be seen as a two-person group, with help to be given to the insider (Tajfel, 1978)?

Many of these issues are, of course, implied by the scholarship of Bill Hartup. In both developmental and social psychology (itself in many ways an unfortunate distinction) the study of relationships is a rapidly growing area, and we can hope for exciting progress in the coming years.

REFERENCES

Aron, A., & Aron, E. N. (1996). Self and self-expansion in relationships. In G. J. O. Fletcher & J. Fitness (Eds.), *Knowledge structures and interactions in close relationships* (pp. 325–344). Mahwah, NJ: Lawrence Erlbaum Associates.

Baldwin, M. W. (1995). Relational schemas and cognition in close relationships. *Journal of Social and Personal Relationships, 12,* 547–552.

Berscheid, E., Snyder, M., & Omoto, A. M. (1989). Issues in studying close relationships. In C. Hendrick (Ed.), *Close relationships* (pp. 63–91). Newbury Park, CA: Sage.

Blau, P. M. (1964). *Exchange and power in social life.* New York: Wiley.

Block, J. (1995). A contrarian view of the five-factor approach to personality description. *Psychological Bulletin, 117,* 187–215.

Bowlby, J. (1969). *Attachment and loss: Vol. 1. Attachment.* London: Hogarth. (2nd ed. 1982)

Bretherton, I. (1990). Communication patterns, internal working models, and the intergenerational transmission of attachment relationships. *Infant Mental Health Journal, 11,* 237–252.

Cairns, R. B., Bergman, L., & Kagan, J. (Eds.). (1998). *The individual in developmental research: Essays in honor of Marian Radke Yarrow.* Thousand Oaks, CA: Sage.

Fincham, F. D., Beach, S. R. H., & Kemp-Fincham, S. I. (in press). Marital quality: A new theoretical perspective. In R. J. Sternberg & M. Hojjat (Eds.), *Satisfaction in close relationships.* New York: Guilford.

Fletcher, G. J. O., & Fitness, J. (1996). *Knowledge structures and interaction in close relationships.* Mahwah, NJ: Lawrence Erlbaum Associates.

Foa, U. G., & Foa, E. B. (1974). *Societal structures of the mind.* Springfield, IL: Thomas.

Greene, J. O., & Geddes, D. (1988). Representation and processing in the self-system: An action-oriented approach to self and self-relevant phenomena. *Communication Monographs, 55,* 287–314.

Hartup, W. W., & Stevens, N. (1997). Friendship and adaptation in the life-course. *Psychological Bulletin, 121,* 355–370.

Hinde, R. A. (1978). Interpersonal relationships—In quest of a science. *Psychological Medicine, 8,* 373–386.

Hinde, R. A. (1997). *Relationships: A dialectical perspective.* Hove, England: Psychology Press.

Kelley, H. H. (1979). *Personal relationships.* Hillsdale, NJ: Lawrence Erlbaum Associates.

Kelley, T. L. (1927). *Interpretation of educational measurements.* Yonkers-on-Hudson: World Book Company.

Kelly, G. A. (1955). *The psychology of personal constructs.* New York: Norton.

Lerner, M. (1974). Social psychology of justice and interpersonal attraction. In T. L. Huston (Ed.), *Foundations of interpersonal attraction* (pp. 331–355). New York: Academic Press.

Newcomb, T. M. (1961). *The acquaintance process.* New York: Holt, Rinehart & Winston.

Schenk, R. C. (1982). *Dynamic memory.* Cambridge, England: Cambridge University Press.

Stern, D. (1995). *The motherhood constellation.* New York: Basic Books.

Tajfel, H. (1978). *Differentiation between social groups.* London: Academic Press.

Thorndike, E. L. (1919). *An introduction to the theory of mental, and social measurements* (2nd ed.). New York: Teachers College.

Turner, P. J. (1991). Relations between attachment, gender, and behaviour with peers in pre-school. *Child Development, 62,* 1475–1488.

Chapter 17

An Annotated Hartup: Developmental History in a Personal Context

Brett Laursen
Florida Atlantic University

> *Everyone who comes into the world has need of friends.*
> —Attributed to Samuel Johnson in James Boswell (1785),
> *Journal of a Tour to the Hebrides with Samuel Johnson*

Willard Wert Hartup's professional career spans more than four decades of rapid growth in developmental psychology. As witness to and participant in many of the critical intellectual crossroads confronting this generation of child psychologists, his bibliography is a case study of past and current trends in the field. Nowhere is this better illustrated than in research on children's close relationships. Hartup nurtured and guided the nascent study of peer relationships; his name is synonymous with the notion that friendship is a developmental boon.

This select bibliography is a chronicle of Hartup's intellectual and professional career. It is not a list of greatest hits or best sellers, although every effort was made to capture the highlights. The works are drawn from each phase of his career, with particular attention to publications that represent his unique and instrumental contributions to the field of developmental psychology. For every book, article, or chapter listed, there may be five or ten on a similar topic; one must be selective when faced with a vitae in excess of 150 publications. This annotation is but an entry point and, given its idiosyncratic nature, interested readers are encouraged to explore the Hartup *oeuvre* on their own.

The bibliography is divided into five sections. Organized around distinct phases of Hartup's career, these sections also capture emerging trends in the study of close relationships as developmental contexts. The Iowa years encompass 1955 to 1963. This was a formative period: Hartup absorbed prevailing behaviorist tenets, honed his experimental skills, and finally settled on peer relationships as a research domain. The early Minnesota years encompass 1964 to 1970. As programs in developmental psychology embraced experimentation with a renewed fervor, Hartup conducted several classic studies that established him as a leader in the new field of peer relationships. The Director of the Institute of Child Development years encompass 1971 to 1982. This was a golden era: Public support for the study of child development climbed to unprecedented levels and exceptionally talented students flocked to the area. Hartup's research on peers set a standard for scholarship, and he made the first of many administrative marks on developmental psychology. The Editor of *Child Development* years encompass 1983 to 1989. This was a time of consolidation for developmental psychology, as the rapid scientific and organizational gains from the previous decade were integrated into paradigms and structures designed to maintain earlier successes. The scope of Hartup's work continued to expand, however, as he sought to place peers within the broader developmental context of close relationships. Two endowed chairs mark the period of 1990 to 1997. As developmental psychology girded for a new era, Hartup remained focused on the future, identifying challenges confronting the next generation of scholars.

THE IOWA YEARS: 1955 TO 1963

> *I'm like the Romans, "happy to come, happy to depart."*
> —Attributed to Samuel Johnson in James Boswell (1785)
> *Journal of a Tour to the Hebrides with Samuel Johnson*

The Hartup mold was cast at Harvard University and at the University of Iowa Child Welfare Research Station. These years are notable for the ascendance of experimentation within psychology, which reinvigorated programs of child development. As a graduate student at Harvard University, Hartup participated in the epic Patterns of Child Rearing Project directed by Robert Sears, Pauline Sears, Eleanor Maccoby, and Harry Levin. Yet Hartup's thesis was his own, designed to experimentally examine the effects of nurturance withdrawal on children.

Shortly after completing his dissertation in 1955, Hartup served a short stint as a Visiting Professor at the University of Rhode Island. There he was recruited by Boyd McCandless, Director of the Child Welfare Research

Station, to take a faculty position at the University of Iowa where McCandless was to establish the country's first program in experimental child psychology. McCandless and Hartup knew one another from their days at Ohio State University, where the latter received his M.A. in psychology in 1951, so the actual job interview was conducted by Ruth Updegraff (over dinner during the floor show at the Biltmore Hotel in Providence). Hartup's first assignment was to the laboratory nursery school, working with Updegraff, and it was Updegraff who convinced him to be Program Chair for the National Association of Nursery Education (now the National Association for the Education of Young Children), a defining moment for the new Assistant Professor.

The Research Station (later disbanded) played a pivotal role in the history of developmental psychology, attracting prominent behaviorists such as Charles Spiker and defining the parameters of experimental child psychology by the rigorous application of orthodox Hull-Spence learning theory. Claiming to have always been a behaviorist, Hartup was infused with a positivism at Iowa that circumscribed his scholarship and reputation. Promoted to Associate Professor in 1960, Hartup describes this as the period in which he "painted his nudes," mastering classical research techniques prior to settling on his own form of expression. By the close of the Iowa years, Hartup had selected his medium: peer relationships.

Hartup, W. W. (1958). Nurturance and nurturance-withdrawal in relation to the dependency behavior of preschool children. *Child Development*, 29, 191–201.

This paper was based on Hartup's Ed.D. thesis submitted to the Laboratory of Human Development at the Harvard University Graduate School of Education. Hartup was Levin's first graduate student and the project represented a new course of inquiry for both scholars. The central thesis (derived from Freud's psychoanalytic theory and Mowrer's learning theory) held that the withdrawal of adult nurturance elicited more dependent behavior in young children than nurturance alone. Participants included 34 children enrolled at the Harvard University Preschool. An example of what Urie Bronfenbrenner later referred to as an analog study (i.e., contrived conditions obliquely analogous to real life), children interacted with an adult in a laboratory setting for 10 minutes; the adult was either consistently nurturant for the entire period or was nurturant for 5 minutes and nonresponsive for 5 minutes. Girls and highly dependent boys in the nurturant–withdrawn condition performed more efficiently on a learning task than those in the consistently nurturant condition. Hartup concluded that withdrawal of nurturance frustrates dependence and deprives the child of social reinforcers; the negative emotion resulting from this frustration prompts improved learning as the child attempts to win back nurturance.

Hartup, W. W., & Keller, E. D. (1960). Nurturance in preschool children and its relation to dependency. *Child Development, 31,* 681–689.

One of the first naturalistic observations conducted by Hartup, this study involved 41 children attending the nursery school at the Child Welfare Research Station. Adopting methods inspired by the Patterns of Child Rearing Project, Hartup observed each child for 55 3-minute outdoor free play periods. Instances of nurturance and dependence directed by target children toward peers and adults were noted. Nurturant behavior, a relatively infrequent occurrence on playgrounds, was positively associated with some dependency behaviors, such as seeking help and physical affection, but negatively associated with other dependency behaviors, such as maintaining physical proximity. Beyond the significance of the results, the study confirmed Hartup's aptitude for naturalistic observation during an era devoted to experimental manipulation.

Hartup, W. W. (1963). Dependence and independence. In H. W. Stevenson (Ed.), *Child psychology: The 62nd yearbook of the National Society for the Study of Education* (pp. 333–363). Chicago: University of Chicago Press.

The first in a long line of consummate reviews, this paper established the Hartup genre: A nonpartisan review of conceptual issues followed by a detailed, atheoretical depiction of research methodologies and empirical findings. In this instance the topic was the development of dependence and independence (although little was known at the time about the latter), dependency behaviors, and dependency drives. Hindsight affords the opportunity to identify prescience: "It is not known how long such molar constructs as dependence and independence will continue to be useful to scientists in their attempts to control and predict behavior" (p. 359). Despite being well-received in its time, the chapter represented Hartup's swan song in this area of scholarship, as his interests soon shifted to peer relationships.

Hartup, W. W. (1964). Friendship status and the effectiveness of peers as reinforcing agents. *Journal of Experimental Child Psychology, 1,* 154–162.

Although published during Hartup's first year at the University of Minnesota, the investigation was conceived and conducted entirely at the University of Iowa. This was a critical juncture for the author and the field of social development, because it represented Hartup's first foray into friendship. Anecdotes offered by his spouse, Rosemary Hartup, about their children, and by his graduate students about preschool classmates, prompted

Hartup to examine peer relationships. Despite its significance as a study that helped to define a field of inquiry, the method and results stand primarily as an historical curiosity, a monument to the short-lived but popular paradigm of marble dropping. Adapting a technique pioneered by Harold Stevenson, 36 preschool children participated in an experimental task in which each child was given 6 minutes to drop 500 marbles—one at a time—into holes in a tabletop. The design reflected Hartup's particular brand of behaviorism: Children were paired with either a liked peer or a disliked peer (assessed via picture sociometrics), who gave the marble dropper continuous attention and periodic verbal approval for successful marble drops. Surprisingly, rates of marble dropping were better maintained by reinforcement from disliked peers than from liked peers. Studies of this ilk were typical of early experimental child psychology and, although marble dropping is important in its own right as one of the first standard experimental procedures in social development, Hartup and Stevenson later agreed that the practice afforded few findings of lasting consequence.

THE EARLY MINNESOTA YEARS: 1964 TO 1970

It is by studying little things that we attain the great art of having as little misery and as much happiness as possible.
—Attributed to Samuel Johnson in James Boswell (1791)
The Life of Samuel Johnson

Professional incentives and the appeal of big city lights lured Hartup to the Twin Cities of Minneapolis and Saint Paul as an Associate Professor at the University of Minnesota's Institute of Child Development. Fortuitous circumstances surrounded the move. Prior to assuming a position at the University of Minnesota, soon-to-be Director Stevenson spent a semester at the University of Iowa in 1959, affording the two an opportunity to get acquainted. Stevenson, charged with reorganizing the Institute of Child Development, promptly hired Shirley Moore, a recent University of Iowa graduate and former head teacher at the Child Welfare Research Station's preschool laboratories, where she worked closely with Hartup. A semester at the Institute of Child Development in 1961 as a Lecturer attracted Hartup to the open intellectual climate at the University of Minnesota that stood in contrast to his perception of doctrinal constraint at the University of Iowa. About this time, William Charlesworth, David Palermo, Anne Pick, Herbert Pick, Britt Ruebush, and John Wright came to Minnesota. Invitations were extended to Hartup and John Hill in 1964; John Flavell, John Masters, Alan Sroufe, and Albert Yonas joined the faculty shortly thereafter. The stage was set for a dynamic enterprise.

From a research perspective, these were productive years. Hartup rode
the wave of experimental psychology that engulfed the study of human
development and that became a signature of research at Minnesota. While
acknowledging the influence of Albert Bandura's work, Hartup claims to
have been primarily following his nose during this period. Hartup's nose
led him to empirically establish the relevance of peer relationships, identifying the unique social reinforcers provided by friends and delineating
correlates of peer behavior as a function of sociometric status. This research
on sociometric status and peer assessment was so influential that it is
popularly (but inaccurately) described as his first inquiry into peer relationships.

Promoted to Professor of Child Psychology in 1964, Hartup served as
Associate Director of the Institute of Child Development from 1966 to
1971. Milestones along the way include service as Program Chair for the
Society for Research in Child Development's biennial meeting in Minneapolis, and Division 7 (Developmental) representative to the American Psychological Association's Council of Representatives. An appointment to
the U.S. National Institute of Child Health and Human Development's
Growth and Development Research and Training Committee marked Hartup's first experience on a federal government advisory panel.

**Hartup, W. W., & Coates, B. (1967). Imitation of a peer as a function of
reinforcement from the peer group and rewardingness of the model. *Child
Development, 38*, 1003–1016.**

This widely cited paper combined naturalistic observations and experimental manipulation to examine whether the effects of a peer model
depend upon previous experience in the peer group. Free-play observations
of 56 nursery school participants established each child's history of generalized social reinforcers from peers. Subjects were divided into two
groups: those receiving frequent reinforcement from peers and those receiving infrequent reinforcement from peers. Prior to attempting a novel
puzzle task with "trinkets" as a reward, subjects were exposed to an altruistic
model, a nonaltruistic model, or no model. The results indicated that
observation of an altruistic model increased altruistic behavior, but that
children with a history of frequent peer reinforcement tended to imitate
rewarding peer models whereas those with a history of infrequent peer
reinforcement tended to imitate nonrewarding models. In a departure
from his usual style of dustbowl empiricism, "the broad coverage of diverse
theories of human behavior is a distinctive feature of the article. Hartup
strongly linked his research on children's behavior to the major currents
of psychological thought at the time" (Berndt, personal communication,
January 1996).

Hartup, W. W., Glazer, J. A., & Charlesworth, R. (1967). Peer reinforcement and sociometric status. *Child Development, 38,* **1017–1024.**

This influential study claims humble origins. "The behaviors studied, the methodology, and the analyses were pretty simple and straight forward compared to the complexities of design and analysis found in today's literature. Never in our wildest dreams did we think our little research projects would get so much attention" (Charlesworth, personal communication, April 1996). Devising a technique later adopted by other laboratories, naturalistic observations of 32 preschool children measured the frequency of positive and negative peer reinforcement. Picture sociometric interviews determined peer group status. "The results documented what preschool teachers already knew: that young children give each other varying amounts of a variety of social reinforcements and these have an effect on how peers feel about each other" (Charlesworth, personal communication, April 1996). More specifically, positive reinforcement was correlated with acceptance but not rejection; negative reinforcement was correlated with rejection but not acceptance. Children received more positive reinforcement from liked peers than disliked peers; rates of negative reinforcement did not differ across groups. This use of picture sociometrics anticipated the growth of research on peer acceptance and rejection: "It is a cornerstone of the literature on sociometric status" (Furman, personal communication, November 1996). The study had reputational salience for its author: During an age when psychology was dominated by behaviorists, Hartup was identified as the behaviorist in the new field of peer relationships.

Hartup, W. W., & Smothergill, N. L. (Eds.) (1967). *The young child: Vol. 1. Reviews of research.* **Washington, DC: National Association for the Education of Young Children.**

This volume illustrates Hartup's commitment to build bridges between developmental psychology and early childhood education, culminating years of work dedicated to the dissemination of research. "In the early 1960s, Hartup took on the task of recruiting authors for a series of research reviews written specifically for practitioners who worked with young children. Beginning in 1962, the reviews appeared as a regular feature in the *Journal of the National Association of Nursery Education.* Many of the authors he recruited were young scholars in the early years of their careers who were not as well known at that time as they are today" (Moore, personal communication, April 1996). Ultimately, an edited text was culled from his tenure as Research Editor of the *Journal of the National Association of Nursery Education* (later renamed *Young Children*). It (and one that followed) was a best seller in the academic book world, especially popular among teacher educators. And the review series that spawned the book remained a prominent feature on the early childhood education landscape: "Subscriptions to *Young Children* escalated from 1,500 in 1962, when the first *Reviews of Research* were published, to 94,000 in 1996" (Moore, personal communication, April 1996).

Hartup, W. W. (1970). Peer interaction and social organization. In P. H. Mussen (Ed.), *Carmichael's manual of child psychology* (pp. 361–456). New York: Wiley.

Although the preceding Murchison and Carmichael volumes of the *Manual of Child Psychology* had chapters on social development that included sections on peers, this was to be the first complete chapter in the series devoted exclusively to the topic. The task was daunting: Where to begin? A year passed researching the subject, the typewriter remained still, and Hartup fretted a looming deadline. Enter Moore, with a large basket of lollipops in hand. The author could have one lollipop for every three pages of manuscript completed. Three months later, the job was finished and so was the basket of candy. ("I never really liked lollipops," Hartup was overheard to grump.) The result was monumental, "a manifesto for the significance of peer relationships in social development. For a field which in the 1970s operated from quite adultcentric assumptions about what influences children's social development, it was a revolutionary message for many developmentalists" (Shantz, personal communication, January 1996). The major topics of review remain important today (e.g., peer influences, peer group status, and interactions with agemates), but the chapter also forcasts growth in several areas of study. Friendship, for instance, received just two pages of discussion. "One wonders if, in the process of reviewing this research in the late 1960s, Hartup first saw the potential of friendship as a significant relationship for development. None of the articles on friendship reviewed in the 1970 chapter were by him, and yet almost 25 years later his Presidential Address to the Society for Research in Child Development reflected his extensive work" (Shantz, personal communication, January 1996).

THE DIRECTOR OF THE INSTITUTE OF CHILD DEVELOPMENT: 1971 TO 1982

> *It was not the wine that made your head ache, but the sense I put into it.*
> —Attributed to Samuel Johnson in James Boswell (1791)
> *The Life of Samuel Johnson*

A confluence of prosperity, demographics, scientific promise, and social concern marked the first half of this decade as a period of unprecedented opportunity. Universities were completing a rapid expansion designed to accommodate a burgeoning student population. Programs in developmental psychology grew even faster in response to the prevailing political and cultural emphasis on children and families. The recognition accorded to experimental child psychology prompted new sources of public and private funds for research. Former Director Stevenson bequeathed a bountiful legacy to incoming Director Hartup that included a building expansion, a training grant from the U.S. National Institute of Mental Health (which continues to this day), and the *Minnesota Symposia on Child Psychology*. Hartup and his colleagues positioned the Institute of Child Development to take advantage of the strengths nurtured by Stevenson. Accomplished faculty recruited during this period included W. Andrew Collins, Megan Gunnar, Daniel Keating, Michael Maratsos, Marion Perlmutter, Philip Salapatek, Sandra Scarr, and June Louin Tapp. The University of Minnesota Child Care Center was established, as was the Center for Early Education and Development. The Hartup years may well be remembered as a time when the Institute of Child Development's international reputation flourished as a center for scientific training and research. Looking back, Hartup labels service as Director of the Institute of Child Development the most important professional activity of his career.

Talented graduate students, never in short supply at the Institute of Child Development, flocked to the University of Minnesota, enticed by gifted faculty and an infusion of research support. Reflecting this trend, a colorful cast collaborated with Hartup on innovative studies of friendship. Of the former Institute of Child Development students contributing to this volume of the *Minnesota Symposia on Child Psychology*, the majority were trained during these years; together with other alumnae they exert considerable influence over the contemporary study of peer relationships.

During this time, Hartup wrote several influential conceptual papers, underscoring his reputation as a spokesman for developmental psychology. Abandoning the long-held adult-centered notion (popularized by behaviorists) that the child was a passive participant in the socialization process, scholars increasingly embraced a view of development that emphasized reciprocal influences, depicting the child as actively shaping the social world. Jean Piaget was the most visible advocate of this activist perspective, but Hartup recalls being especially influenced by the work of Harriet Rheingold and her students. Hartup catalyzed the research community in his own way, suggesting that if the child was a competent and effectual organism, then playmates and friends represented a critical and distinct arena of social influence. In response to his *Manual of Child Psychology* chapter, research on peer relationships grew exponentially. During this period, concerns about ecological validity swept aside many established experimental research practices and Hartup's scholarship reflected this struggle with a renewed emphasis on conceptual clarity and practical applications. His research perspective broadened to encompass aggression, competition and cooperation, and social skills. Forecasting a trend that would dominate the next decade, Hartup examined individual differences to identify features that distinguished adaptive from maladaptive peer relationships.

Hartup's leadership shaped the field's nascent professional organizations. During his first sabbatical leave at the University of Nijmegen, he helped to organize the inaugural meetings of the International Society for the Study of Behavioural Development, serving later on the Executive Committee and as the third President. Hartup was also elected President of the American Psychological Association's Division 7 (Developmental). He served as Chair of the Society for Research in Child Development's Publications Committee and as a member of the U.S. National Institute of Child Health and Human Development's National Advisory Council. This period is further distinguished by appointment as a Fellow to the Center for Advanced Study in the Behavioral Sciences.

Monks, F. J., Hartup, W. W., & de Wit, J. (Eds.) (1972). *Determinants of behavioral development.* **New York: Academic Press.**

This text, although not widely circulated, illustrated Hartup's participation in the move to create a formal organization dedicated to the international community of developmental psychologists. "It contains the proceedings of the inaugural symposium of the International Society for the Study of Behavioural Development, held in 1970 at the University of Nijmegen, The Netherlands, during Hartup's first sabbatical in Europe. The list of participants included many scholars who shaped the International Society for the Study of Behavioural Development during the next quarter of a century. Hartup was a central figure in this process, contributing to the enormous expansion and internationalization of the field and the Society in the years that followed" (van Lieshout, personal communication, March 1996). Thus, the volume should be considered an historic document that marks the birth of a professional organization, opening channels of communication between developmental psychologists in Europe and North America that were soon extended to scholars on other continents.

Hartup, W. W. (1974). Aggression in childhood: Developmental perspectives. *American Psychologist, 29,* **336–341.**

Still a Hartup favorite, the article is noteworthy for its original empirical data and its conceptual distinctions. Drawing from ideas promoted by

Norma Feshbach and Seymour Feshbach, Hartup delineated distinctions between instrumental aggression and hostile aggression. Hostile aggression describes person oriented harm-doing, whereas instrumental aggression encompasses object oriented harm-doing. The former was hypothesized to be linked to frustration producing stimuli threatening the subject's ego and to inferences that the agent of frustration behaved intentionally. The latter was hypothesized to be linked to goal blocking. Naturalistic observations of 102 nursery school and grade school children were conducted over a 10-week period. Time and event sampling procedures detailed aggressive events. In absolute terms, older children and girls were less aggressive than younger children and boys; age differences resulted from variations in instrumental aggression and gender differences resulted from variations in hostile aggression. In relative terms, the ratio of hostile aggression to instrumental aggression was greater for older children than for younger children. The function of different types of aggression also differed according to age: Goal blocking, for instance, produced more instrumental aggression among younger children than older children. The paper ended on a prophetic note, "wondering whether there is a systematic relation between social cognition and aggression, thereby anticipating the later increase of interest in social cognition research with children" (Cillessen, personal communication, April 1996).

Graziano, W., French, D., Brownell, C. A., & Hartup, W. W. (1976). Peer interaction in same- and mixed-age triads in relation to chronological age and incentive condition. *Child Development, 47,* 707–714.

Most accounts hold this to be an especially entertaining project, although Hartup claims to have been excluded from the hilarity. The school was awash with rumors of kidnapping ("as a result, at least some of the children were less than eager to come with us") by researchers (mustachioed and otherwise) whose nonnormative behavior was actually limited to hitting golf balls at a driving range near the school during lunch and learning to use a router and belt sander to construct wooden blocks (French, personal communication, January 1996). A total of 231 first- and third-grade children participated in an experimental study of small group processes within same-age and mixed-age triads under conditions of individual or group rewards. "Hartup encouraged us to come up with a task or setting that could be easily manipulated experimentally and that would yield clear and interpretable dependent measures of group process and function. We ultimately adapted Maccoby's block-building task in which children's job was to build a tower as tall as possible, as a group, in a limited time" (Brownell, personal communication, May 1996). The results indicated that older peers neither helped nor hindered achievement:

Mixed-age groups performed as well as same-age groups. In mixed-age groups, however, productivity in conditions of individual rewards varied according to the presence of other children of the same age. Regardless of age, group rewards produced greater productivity than individual rewards. The study was widely emulated and tower building replaced marble dropping as the experimental method of choice. Hartup used the task, on and off, for the remainder of the decade.

Furman, W., Rahe, D. F., & Hartup, W. W. (1979). Rehabilitation of socially withdrawn preschool children through mixed-age and same-age socialization. *Child Development, 50,* 915–922.

This paper was derived from Wyndol Furman's Ph.D. thesis, which Hartup supervised. It stands as one of the few intervention studies in Hartup's career. A total of 262 preschool children were each observed during free play for 9 minutes. Isolated children were identified on the basis of these observations. Locating social isolates was extremely time consuming: "It took 18 months to find 24 subjects as we had stringent criteria and there were typically only one or at most two such children per class" (Furman, personal communication, November 1996). Isolates were divided into three experimental groups: (1) those assigned to treatment sessions with a same-age partner; (2) those assigned to treatment sessions with a younger partner; and (3) those assigned to no treatment control groups. Treatments consisted of 10 dyadic play sessions, each 20 minutes in length. During these sessions children played with toys designed to encourage social interaction. Following treatments, freeplay observations resumed in all classes. Rates of peer interaction, especially positive reinforcement, increased for isolates in the intervention group but not in the control group. Within intervention groups, isolates with younger partners showed greater improvement than those with same-age partners. The implications were profound: Effective intervention with isolated children need consist of little more than opportunities to practice social interaction skills with peers.

Newcomb, A. F., Brady, J. E., & Hartup, W. W. (1979). Friendship and incentive condition as determinants of children's task-oriented social behavior. *Child Development, 50,* 878–881.

Block building by grade school children returned in this examination of relationships and reward structures. A total of 176 children in the first and third grades completed sociometric ratings of friendship, supplemented by teacher reports of social interaction. Half of the children were paired with mutual friends and the other half were paired with nonfriends in a 15-minute dyadic task. During block-building phases one and three, children worked under a promotive goal structure, wherein partners were rewarded on the basis of dyadic performance. Reward conditions for participants varied during the second phase: Half worked under a system with rewards provided according to individual contributions and the other half worked under conditions in which only the individual making the greatest contribution was rewarded. Friends differed from nonfriends in task interactions, with patterns unaffected by reward conditions. Social contact and positive affect were greater among friends than nonfriends, and interactions between friends were more apt to entail references to equity, reciprocity, and mutuality than were those with nonfriends. This study, coinciding with the growing popularity of cooperative learning, suggested that who children are paired with in educational tasks may be more important than how their performance is rewarded.

Hartup, W. W. (1979). The social worlds of childhood. *American Psychologist,* **34, 944–950.**

Not previously known for controversial positions, Hartup decided to take a public stand on a long-running dispute. In this paper, published in a special issue of the *American Psychologist* devoted to developmental psychology, Hartup argued that children inhabit two (rather than one) social systems: "The evidence, then, suggests that children live in distinctive, albeit coordinate, social worlds. Children may not conceive of separate normative worlds until early adolescence, because child associates are not used extensively as normative models before that time. But the family system and the peer system elicit distinctive socioemotional activity many years before these normative distinctions are made" (p. 947). Family relationships, it is argued, promote specific competencies and provide a secure base for exploring the wider social world, which brings the child into contact with agemates who extend and develop these competencies. Articulating what was previously implied, Hartup argued that the study of friendships ought not be subordinated to the study of parent–child relationships. Given a recent opportunity to equivocate, Hartup remained firm in his conviction that children inhabit two social worlds connected by structural and affective continuities.

THE EDITOR OF *CHILD DEVELOPMENT:* 1983 TO 1989

> *You are entering upon a transaction which requires much prudence. You must endeavor to oppose without exasperating; to practice temporary hostility without producing enemies for life.*
> —Attributed to Samuel Johnson in James Boswell (1791)
> *The Life of Samuel Johnson*

Free of administrative duties as Director, Hartup could not refuse an invitation to be the Editor of *Child Development*. Demanding and time consuming editorial responsibilities were coupled with a heavy travel schedule arising from leaves and visiting appointments at Cambridge University, South China Normal University, the University of Pavia, and Duke University, and advisory appointments to the Foundation for Child Development, the W. T. Grant Foundation, the National Research Council, the MacArthur Foundation, and the International Union of Psychological Sciences. As a publication of record, *Child Development* maintained its standards with Hartup at the helm. Although the total number of submissions declined during this period, the number of published pages and the rejection rates remained constant, in part because of an increase in special issues and special sections devoted to cutting edge topics. Nothing during Hartup's tenure as Editor, however, attracted as much attention as the redesign of the cover. Hartup desired a change but, being a traditionalist, he retained the little stick figures and simply substituted lime green for forest green in the background. Soon afterward the University of Chicago Press revamped the covers of all Society for Research in Child Development publications, a decision purportedly unrelated to Hartup's recent alterations. Gone were the stick figures, replaced by Hartup's choice of an emerald green that had an alarming tendency to fade to blue. Hartup still likes the color, but his tenure concluded with an Editor's note tactfully acknowledging dissenting views, including an appraisal from a correspondent who likened the color to "the product of a horse urinating in an ink well."

Perhaps it is not surprising that this period is best known for literature summaries and conceptual arguments, despite the fact that his empirical research continued at a prodigious rate. Influenced by Carolyn Shantz, Hartup extended his work on peer relationships into the realm of interpersonal conflict. But this research was dwarfed by a seemingly ubiquitous series of books, chapters, and invited articles. As is often the case, this phase of Hartup's career was indicative of changes in the field as a whole. The expansion of developmental psychology during the preceding decades made it difficult for scholars to keep abreast of current research trends, giving rise to a burgeoning traffic in integrative literature reviews. An explosion of empirical research was followed by an explosion of narrative summaries. Edited volumes and special issues became indispensable, so senior scholars were recruited to ruminate publicly.

Hartup's scholarship widened as a result of this reflection. No longer content to be confined by the boundaries of the peer social world, Hartup sought to place friendships in a wider social context. He began to consider the influence of parents alongside that of peers. As Editor, Hartup reaped the intellectual benefits of scholarly discussions with authors from around the globe. His conceptualizations also profited from prodding by Robert

Hinde and Ellen Berscheid, as well as from insights offered by Institute of Child Development colleagues Collins and Sroufe. Eventually, Hartup's behaviorism incorporated concepts from exchange and equity theories, and it acknowledged neoanalytic and ethological perspectives on attachment.

Hartup, W. W. (1983). Peer relations. In E. M. Hetherington (Vol. Ed.), P. H. Mussen (Series Ed.), *Handbook of child psychology: Vol. 4. Socialization, personality, and social development* (pp. 103–196). New York: Wiley.

One of the few to be offered a second chance, Hartup revised and updated his previous *Manual of Child Psychology* chapter to capture new research on peer relationships. His credo was familiar: "In most cultures, the significance of peer relations as a socialization context is rivaled only by the family" (p. 103). Acknowledging difficulties disentangling the contributions of the peer system from those of other social networks, Hartup nevertheless identified features of peer relationships that are particularly salient to socialization: "The unique elements in child–child relations would appear to be the developmental equivalence of the participants and the egalitarian nature of their interaction" (p. 104). Aside from the historical overview, the chapter was completely recast; Hartup claimed it harder to write than the first, both because there was more to say and because it had to be said differently. This time relationships were featured prominently, reflecting a surge in research on friendship and peer reputation. Like its predecessor, the chapter was enormously influential, anticipating the growth of research in areas such as peer networks and contextual diversity. It rained citations for a decade. The work had utilitarian value too. At well over 200 manuscript pages, Hartup was fond of giving this formidable paper to aspiring students (including the author of this chapter) with the injunction that it be read carefully prior to any discussion of research proposals.

Hartup, W. W. (1986). On relationships and development. In W. W. Hartup & Z. Rubin (Eds.), *Relationships and development* (pp. 1–26). Hillsdale, NJ: Lawrence Erlbaum Associates.

Re-entering the academic book market, Hartup signaled that his scholarship would expand beyond peers to the developmental significance of close relationships. Indeed, the book touched many of the same issues (and included some of the same scholars) as the present volume of the *Minnesota Symposia on Child Psychology*. The text, sponsored by the Social Science Research Council, grew out of Hartup's participation in the Committee on Social and Affective Development, chaired by Martin Hoffman. In his introductory essay, Hartup constructs a framework that specifies the conditions necessary for a developmental perspective on the study of relationships. Close relationships are presumed to shape individual development because (a) they provide the context for most socialization, (b) they constitute important resources, and (c) they serve as models for future relationships. His expansive perspective found room for many voices; attachment, interdependence, even personality—themes given greater prominence in later writings—are invoked as potentially useful tools for understanding parent–child and peer relationships. Hartup does not shy away from "the conclusion that relationships bear a causal relation to individual differences" (p. 13) and that "the weight of the evidence indicates that experience in well-functioning relationships is associated with good functioning in individuals and that important continuities in relationships exist across time and generation" (p. 23).

Hartup, W. W., Laursen, B., Stewart, M. I., & Eastenson, A. (1988). Conflict and the friendship relations of young children. *Child Development, 59,* 1590–1600.

In this study, Hartup offered a new twist to the old practice of naturalistic observation. Paper–pencil and videotape records were eschewed in favor of observers dictating narrative accounts of the activities of focal children into audio tape recorders. In this manner, 53 preschool children were each observed for 36 minutes during free play. Friendship status was determined by picture sociometrics and by the observed amount of time children spent together. Instances of interpersonal conflict were identified and 12 behavioral components of each conflict were classified; in this manner, the study operationalized Shantz's framework for understanding peer conflict. The results revealed that, in contrast to nonfriends, conflict between mutual friends had less negative affect and coercion, and more equal outcomes and continued social interaction. In most instances, the conflicts of unilateral associates (i.e., nonreciprocated friends) were similar to those of nonfriends, although they resembled friends in that they tended to be followed by continued social interaction. When a critical reviewer denounced the procedures as reminiscent of Gump, Hartup responded with a history lesson: Gump's classic work was timeless, he intoned, and any method good enough for Gump was certainly good enough for Hartup. This investigation provided one of the clearest examples to date of Hartup's evolving conceptual orientation, describing differences between relationships in terms of their exchange properties.

Hartup, W. W. (1989). Social relationships and their developmental significance. *American Psychologist, 44,* 120–126.

Hartup was again featured in the once-a-decade developmental psychology special issue of the *American Psychologist.* Earlier papers reflected his growing interest in the developmental significance of close relationships, but this article epitomized the transition. "Many investigators believe that the quality of relationships affects the child in more or less enduring ways. This argument has been made for centuries; for example, 'as the twig is bent, so grows the tree.' And it remains controversial" (p. 120). This premise turned out not to be especially controversial, but Hartup did raise eyebrows with his discussion of the relative developmental significance of parent and peer relationships. Distinctions between relationships were identified. Vertical (i.e., parent–child) relationships emerge first; their significance is best captured by early attachments with primary caregivers. Horizontal (i.e., peer) relationships appear somewhat later; their significance is best captured by friendships with agemates. After reviewing the properties of each, Hartup concluded that peer relationships constitute a developmental advantage, in contrast to parent–child relationships which are a developmental necessity. "Although children who have many friends may be better off generally than children without them, one can guess that good socialization outcomes probably do not require these relationships in the same way they require a stable relationship with a caretaker" (p. 125). This was a provocative stand, even if few outside of the close-knit peer relationship world appreciated the gravity of the suggestion that optimal adaptation need not include friendship. Yet Hartup downplayed the argument, focusing instead on the conclusion that "the construction of well-functioning relationships may be the most significant achievement in the child's socialization" (p. 125).

THE ENDOWED CHAIRS: 1990 TO 1997

> *A generous and elevated mind is distinguished by nothing more certainly than an eminent degree of curiosity.*
> —Attributed to Samuel Johnson in James Boswell (1791)
> *The Life of Samuel Johnson*

This period of well-deserved accolades began with the 1990 appointment as Rodney S. Wallace Professor for the Advancement of Teaching and Learning, followed by the 1993 appointment as a University of Minnesota Regent's Professor, the first Institute of Child Development faculty member accorded either honor. Hartup was elected President of the Society for Research in Child Development, a fitting recognition from the research community that he recalls with fondness. The American Psychological Association awarded him the G. Stanley Hall Award for Distinguished Contributions to Developmental Psychology. When the International Society for the Study of Behavioural Development met in Minneapolis, Hartup was the Conference

Organizer. Free moments away from the Institute of Child Development were spent at the University of Nijmegen, working in the laboratory of one of his former graduate students, Cornelis van Lieshout.

The books, chapters, and invited articles increased to an average of three per year, yet Hartup managed to maintain a steady output of empirical research on friendship. It is a period that is not easily categorized; it is difficult to identify historic trends from a contemporary vantage. In many ways, Hartup returned to his roots. Taking advantage of his prominence, Hartup challenged scholars to consider peers in a different light, encouraged research on the normative significance of friendship, and outlined new directions for the study of interpersonal conflict. Perhaps nothing was more provocative, however, than his assertion that qualitative characteristics of friendships may be of greater developmental significance than the mere presence or absence of these relationships. Expect a surge of research on this topic in the years to come.

Cillessen, A. H. N., van IJzendoorn, H. W., van Lieshout, C. F. M., & Hartup, W. W. (1992). Heterogeneity among peer-rejected boys: Subtypes and stabilities. *Child Development, 63*, 893–905.

This paper is the fruit of collaborative work on the Nijmegen longitudinal study of peer relationships. Many leaves and sabbaticals were spent in The Netherlands laboring on this project; indeed, Hartup spent so much time in Holland that some referred to it as his second office. Sociometric and classroom assessments of peer relationships were collected from 146 Dutch boys. Structured play sessions and interviews were conducted with a group of rejected children. Cluster analyses of rejected boys revealed four subtypes: aggressive rejected, shy rejected, antisocial moderate, and prosocial moderate. Follow-up sociometric assessments one year later indicated that aggressive rejected boys were twice as likely to remain rejected as were boys in other rejected subgroups, suggesting that rejection based on aggression is more stable than rejection based on other attributes. Some said Hartup had mellowed: Despite lively discussions concerning the execution of the study and the analysis of the data, his colleagues still referred to him as that "nice guy from Minnesota" (Cillessen, personal communication, April 1996; van Lieshout, personal communication, March 1996). Beyond reflecting his comportment, the paper exemplified Hartup's increased focus on individual differences in adaptive processes.

Shantz, C. U., & Hartup, W. W. (Eds.) (1992). *Conflict in child and adolescent development*. New York: Cambridge University Press.

"Why anyone writes or edits a book is not known to science—with any specificity. In this case, a simple conviction started the process: 'The time is right for a book on conflict,' Hartup said in his phone call proposing the project, 'and I think the field would profit from it.' And yet we had some doubts. We did not know each other well, and we came from very different theoretical backgrounds. Each of us was, in essence, on the brink of eloping with a stranger" (Shantz, personal communication, January 1996). This said, there can be little doubt that the timing of the union was perfect. The editors had recently piqued the interest of many developmental scholars with separate articles on interpersonal conflict among peers. "Because the field had so long been dominated by the study of aggression, we wondered whether contributors would be able to create significant and useful messages about conflict per se. The black hole of published books yawned before us, making us chary to commit ourselves and others to days of our lives working on a book which, amongst all the others, might be lost, ignored" (Shantz, personal communication, January 1996). To ensure that the book was not overlooked, a prominent roster of contributors was recruited. Their aim: To address processes of development and characteristics of close relationships linked to conflict, as well as to identify the negative and positive contributions of conflict to social competence and adaptation. The book appeared to be on target. Should research on interpersonal conflict continue to expand at the present rate, much of the impetus for this trend will be traced to this volume.

Bukowski, W. M., Newcomb, A. F., & Hartup, W. W. (Eds.) (1996). *The company they keep: Friendship in childhood and adolescence.* **New York: Cambridge University Press.**

Encouraged by the success of the conflict book, Hartup was, for the second time in a decade, on the phone urging a colleague to edit a book. This time the subject was friendship; unbelievably, Hartup had yet to publish a text on this topic. A congenial group gathered in the October cold in Montreal for a prepublication workshop. The plan was that each speaker would present a 10-minute overview of her or his chapter, followed by questions from the group. That no one was able to limit their remarks to this brief span of time can surely be attributed to the great enthusiasm each felt for the project. Topics in the volume ranged from friendship processes to the measurement of friendship to friendship sequelae. Hartup denied what his coeditors explicitly confirmed: Many of the contributors were his intellectual progeny or a product of this lineage, not by design but because of the profound and pervasive influence Hartup exerted over the developmental study of friendship. It is a foregone conclusion that this book will define scholarship on friendship for years to come.

Hartup, W. W. (1996). The company they keep: Friendships and their developmental significance. *Child Development, 67,* **1–13.**

Hartup's 1995 Presidential address was delivered to members of the Society for Research in Child Development assembled in Indianapolis,

Indiana. The meeting provided current and former students and colleagues with occasions to extol his career. Levity does not, however, characterize this article. The introductory anecdote (a troubling story of a boy, abetted by a friend, who murders his mother) made it clear that this was not business as usual. Hartup took to the presidential bully pulpit, encouraging peer researchers to avoid the assumption that friendships are linked to developmental competence in the absence of compelling evidence. The style is gentle—bonbons are delivered all around—but a careful reading makes it clear that Hartup was dissatisfied with contemporary conventions that assumed the significance of friendship stems from being liked or disliked. "The review, like all of Hartup's work, is distinctive for its extensive coverage (from 1932 to the present) and for the many thoughtful, integrative conclusions. Hartup consistently tackles big questions: Why are friends similar to one another? Does it matter whether a child has a best friend? How are aspects of friendships connected with family relationships, success in school, and other influences on development?" (Berndt, personal communication, January 1996). Hartup's conclusions captured the contributions of his past research and set the stage for the future: "First, having friends is a normatively significant condition during childhood and adolescence. Second, friendships carry both developmental advantages and disadvantages so that a romanticized view of these relationships distort them and what they may contribute to developmental outcome. Third, the identity of the child's friends and friendship quality may be more closely tied to individual differences than merely whether or not the child has friends" (p. 2).

CONCLUSION

> *If a man may indulge in honest pride, in having it known to the world that he has been thought worthy of particular attention by a person of the first eminence in the age in which he lived, whose company has been universally courted, I am justified in availing myself of the usual privilege of a Dedication, when I mention that there has been a long and uninterrupted friendship between us.*
>
> —James Boswell (1791)
> *The Life of Samuel Johnson*

The last period described in this chapter should not be considered the final one. Hartup remained an active scholar after his teaching and administrative responsibilities lessened upon retirement in 1997. A suggested title for the next period: The Emeritus Years. Readers are encouraged to keep an addendum to mark his progress. Yet ultimately it is neither the publications nor the positions that make Willard W. Hartup special, but rather his service to the field, his commitment to collaborators and co-workers, and his dedication to those who look to him as a mentor and a model. Those of us who know him as a friend and as a colleague expect to continue in relationships that proffer a warm and supportive context for development.

ACKNOWLEDGMENTS

Support for the preparation of this manuscript was provided by the U.S. National Institute of Child Health and Human Development (R29 HD33006). Thanks are extended to Tom Berndt, Celia Brownell, Rosalind Charlesworth, Toon Cillessen, Doran French, Wyndol Furman, Cornelis van Lieshout, Shirley Moore, and Carolyn Shantz for providing summaries and recollections. Bill Hartup cheerfully assisted with a review of his bibliography, but responsibility for the final selection and annotation of material rests with the author of this chapter.

Author Index

Subject Index